University of California, Berkeley

THE CAMPUS GUIDE

University of California, Berkeley

An Architectural Tour and Photographs by
Harvey Helfand

Princeton Architectural Press
NEW YORK | 2002

To Mary Ann Hiserman (1947–1996), a close friend and colleague, whose accomplishments in the independent-living and disability-rights movements and barrier-free environmental design have been an inspiration and benefit to so many on campus and in the community.

This book has been made possible through the generous support of the Graham Foundation for Advanced Studies in the Fine Arts.

This guide is published independently by Princeton Architectural Press. The University of California, Berkeley does not endorse or sponsor the guide, its publisher, or officers.

Princeton Architectural Press
37 East 7th Street
New York, NY 10003

For a free catalog of other books published by Princeton Architectural Press, call 1.800.722.6657 or visit www.papress.com
All rights reserved

Series editor: Jan Cigliano
Series concept: Dennis Looney
Design: Sara Stemen
Layout: Mary-Neal Meador
Copy editor: Heather Ewing
Maps: Jane Garvie
Special thanks to Nettie Aljian, Ann Alter, Amanda Atkins, Nicola Bednarek, Janet Behning, Megan Carey, Penny Chu, Tom Hutten, Clare Jacobson, Mark Lamster, Nancy Eklund Later, Linda Lee, Anne Nitschke, Evan Schoninger, Lottchen Shivers, Jennifer Thompson, and Deb Wood of Princeton Architectural Press
—Kevin C. Lippert, *publisher*

ISBN 1-56898-293-3

05 04 03 02 01   5 4 3 2 1 First Edition

Library of Congress Cataloguing-in-Publication Data is available from the publisher

Printed and bound in China

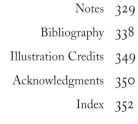

How to use this book

This guide is intended for visitors, alumni, students, faculty, staff, and others who wish to have an insider's look at the most interesting historic buildings and natural features on the University of California, Berkeley campus. From John Galen Howard's Beaux-Arts ensemble with its landmark Campanile, to Bernard Maybeck's Faculty Club and Charles Moore's Haas School of Business, the *Campus Guide* tells of the persons and traditions that give meaning to each place.

Following a historical Introduction, the book is divided into ten Walks covering the major areas of the campus and the surrounding community. Each Walk, or chapter, describes the history of the area, illustrated with an annotated map that locates each structure on the Walk, followed by entries on each place. The entries are accompanied by photographs and historical and architectural information about each site's defining characteristics.

Campus buildings: Monday–Friday 9am to 5pm for nonresidential buildings, with evening and weekend hours for some buildings.

Grounds open: daily access, year-round.

Walking tours: Monday–Friday 10am starting at the Visitor Center at 101 University Hall; Saturday 10am and Sunday 1pm starting at the Campanile. Admission: free. Special group tours can also be reserved for a fee.

Electric cart tours: Monday–Friday with reservations for up to five passengers. Fee: $25.00.

Sather Tower (The Campanile): Monday–Friday 10am to 4pm; Saturday and Sunday 10am to 5pm. There are 38 stairs from the top elevator floor to the observation platform. Carillon concerts are daily at 7:50am, noon, and 6pm, with longer concerts on Sunday at 2pm. Admission: $2 for 18 years and over; $1.50 for 12–17 years; $1 for 3–11 years; discounts available for Berkeley alumni, seniors, UC retirees and their guests; free, children under 2 years, registered students, and faculty and staff members; reduced fees for large school groups.

Cal Student Store open: Monday–Friday 9am to 6pm; Saturday 10am to 6pm; Sunday noon to 5pm.

For information including museums, exhibits, visual and performing arts:
www.berkeley.edu

For information about the City of Berkeley:
Berkeley Convention & Visitors Bureau
2015 Center Street
Berkeley, CA 94704-1204
1.800.847.4823
www.berkeleycvb.com

Further information from:
Visitor Services, University of California, Berkeley
101 University Hall
2200 University Avenue
Berkeley, CA 94720
510.642.5215 and 510.642.INFO
www.berkeley.edu/visitors

Hearst Gymnasium, main pool, and sculpture

From the creation of the University of California as a federal land-grant university in 1868, this architectural tour spans three centuries in its description of the buildings and landscape settings that physically embody the academic and cultural values of the Berkeley campus.

At its heart is John Galen Howard's historic Beaux-Arts ensemble of buildings, oriented to the Golden Gate and adorned with Greek and Roman classical symbols, but rendered uniquely Californian with its mission influences and granite hewn from the Sierra Nevada range. The outcome of the International Competition for the Phoebe Hearst Architectural Plan at the close of the nineteenth century, it is set with cross-axial esplanades and glades between the two forks of Strawberry Creek that give the campus its extraordinary natural beauty, vegetated with oaks, redwoods, buckeye, ginkgoes, and eucalyptus. Howard's grouping is intact, complemented by the works of Bernard Maybeck, Julia Morgan, and others, though compromised by subsequent twentieth-century developments that now give the campus its overall eclectic character derived from Art Deco, modern, postmodern, and other architectural styles.

These built and natural places are, in a sense, time capsules of our collective institutional heritage. Not merely of granite or concrete, of bronze or marble, of greenery or pavement, each has associations with generations of students, faculty, and staff, and with traditions that define the California Spirit.

For visitors this guide will serve as an introduction to this architectural heritage. For alumni returning to their alma mater, it is hoped that it will rekindle fond memories and inform about campus renewal. For present-day students, faculty, and staff, it may enhance appreciation of that which is experienced on a daily basis.

The places also reflect our continuing tradition of both public and private support. From Sather, Hearst, Doe, Boalt, Bowles, and Morrison, to Haas, Valley, Soda, and Goldman, the legacy of private giving is evident. Funding from the state has also been substantial, making possible numerous facilities, from Wheeler, Gilman, and Wellman Halls to Wurster Hall, Life Sciences Addition, and the Gardner Stacks. Student support and other sources have added to these resources enabling construction of such facilities as the Student Center and Recreational Sports Facility. Class gifts, in the form of courtyards, glades, gateways, sculpture, and other landmarks, also enrich the campus environment and remind us of the special affection students and alumni have for their university.

Much as President Benjamin Ide Wheeler identified the needs of the university on the threshold of the twentieth century, a new vision for the campus is at the forefront of the twenty-first. It is remarkable that priorities common to both eras include planning for increased student enrollment, the pursuit of both public and private support, improvements to buildings and equipment, and enhancement of the library collections.

But whereas the educational needs of one hundred years ago emphasized mining engineering, agriculture, forestry, professional schools, literature, art, and architecture, today's needs correspond to new directions that will reshape the campus to meet the needs of society in the new century. These include interdisciplinary research in such areas as the health sciences, genomic research, bio-engineering, neuroscience, material science, information technology, the humanities, and the arts. Coincident with these directions are the upgrading of the campus infrastructure and a seismic retrofit program that is renewing major structures, including the Howard landmark Hearst Memorial Mining Building. And just as the university a century ago formulated a new vision with the Hearst Architectural Plan, we now look forward with a New Century Plan as a prelude to the preparation of a new campus long-range development plan.

Former campus planner Harvey Helfand, Class of '66, gives us a lively and loving tour that evokes the unique aesthetic and cultural qualities of the campus. We are indeed fortunate to be the stewards of such a beautiful place. It is a fitting home for the exceptional community of scholars that makes Berkeley the premier public university in the United States.

Robert M. Berdahl
Chancellor
University of California, Berkeley

Introduction to the University of California, Berkeley

The physical drama of the University of California, Berkeley campus comes from the interplay between its natural and built forms. With the scenic East Bay hills and Strawberry Canyon as a backdrop, the long sweep of meadow directed toward the Golden Gate forms a contoured stage for this "City of Learning," rooted in one of the country's best preserved Beaux-Arts architectural ensembles, which architect John Galen Howard created in the early twentieth century. Built upon earthen plinths, this "great group of beautiful white buildings embowered in greenery"[1] steps up the slope, flanking the valley formed by the two forks of Strawberry Creek that cradle the campus between their western confluence and the steep rise of foothills to the east. Though incomplete, the group formed a predominant and unified classical composition until nearly mid-century, when its coherence began to be diminished by modernist structures rapidly developed after World War II.

Sather Tower, University of California, Berkeley campus, and San Francisco Bay

Among these large-scale buildings of the past half-century, the intact classical elements—clustered about the soaring Campanile and gracefully set within their natural setting—still form the architectural and symbolic heart of one of the world's greatest teaching and research universities.

The first of the university's ten-campus system, the campus extends into the hills and peripheral community, occupying approximately 1,200 acres within the cities of Berkeley and Oakland, in addition to over 200 acres in Albany, Richmond and other outlying areas. The 178-acre, academically concentrated central campus is defined by Hearst Avenue, Gayley Road–Piedmont Avenue, Bancroft Way, and Oxford–Fulton Street. Approximately 1,350 distinguished faculty members include seven Nobel Laureates (seventeen from 1939 to 2000), sixteen National Medal of Science recipients, 124 National Academy of Sciences, and 85 National Academy of Engineering members, in addition to more Guggenheim Fellowships and National Science Foundation Young Investigators than any other American university. The fourteen colleges and schools offer more than 300 degree programs per year to a culturally and ethnically diverse student body of some 21,000 undergraduates and 9,000 graduates, with one of the highest-ranked doctoral programs in the nation. One of the premiere research institutions, Berkeley has over 150 programs conducted by forty-five departmental and interdisciplinary organized research units, twenty-four renowned campus libraries containing over eight million book volumes, and collections and museums of scientific distinction.

Oakland Beginnings and the College of California

It was the verdant creeks that formed a pleasing contrast to the surrounding grain fields when in the spring of 1855 the trustees of the College of California—precursor of the University of California—first visited the land five miles north of Oakland that would later become the Berkeley campus. They were taken, trustee Samuel Hopkins Willey observed, with "the very striking landscape scenery, the mild air, and especially the dignified old oak trees, and the fine line of evergreen shrubbery which encircled the grounds."[2] Its prominent position opposite the Golden Gate also impressed them, affording a panoramic view of the bay from Oakland to the Marin hills.

Reverend Willey was among several New England Protestants who had come West to provide spiritual and educational guidance to gold-smitten Californians. Chartered on April 13, 1855, the College of California developed from the Contra Costa Academy, a small Oakland preparatory school established two years earlier in a former *fandango* house at the corner of Fifth Street and Broadway by Reverend Henry Durant, a Yale-educated Congregational minister and teacher. Moved to a larger site to the north bordered by Twelfth, Franklin, Fourteenth, and Harrison Streets, the college

College of California, Oakland, 1863

opened with ten freshmen in 1860.[3] Durant—who would later become the first president of the University of California—served as professor of Greek languages and literature, while Willey was appointed vice-president and acting president in 1862.

    The new college, a small oak-studded complex of mostly two-story buildings with pyramidal-roofed cupolas and towers, was founded on high academic standards influenced by leading East Coast colleges, especially Yale and Harvard. In addition to its core courses of Greek, Latin, English, mathematics, natural science, and history, it offered instruction in the modern languages of French, German, and Spanish—a progressive curriculum for the time. Though non-denominational, it was imbued with Christian principles, which motivated the trustees to search for a larger and more suitable permanent site away from the distractions of Oakland, where a proper college community might develop.

Berkeley Site

That search was begun in earnest by Connecticut Congregational preacher and Yale graduate Horace Bushnell, who tirelessly combed the Bay Area from July through December 1856 for possible sites, evaluating each for water, transportation, land prices, proximity to cities, climate and other conditions. He enthusiastically recommended a Napa Valley property, but when it was taken off the market the trustees resumed their interest in the 140 acres of land opposite the Golden Gate—which they had previously dismissed because of doubts about its water supply.

Landowner and retired sea captain Orin Simmons, whose ranch along the banks of Strawberry Creek included the present sites of the Hearst Greek Theatre and California Memorial Stadium, soon appeased their concerns. Simmons explained to his friend Durant that damming the creeks and opening up springs could easily provide water for the college. Convinced of its merits and with binding agreements for its purchase, on March 1, 1858, the trustees adopted the site as the permanent home of the College of California. Two years later Willey, Durant, and other trustees gathered at the northern part of the property at the outcropping later named Founders' Rock to dedicate and consecrate the new college grounds (see Walk 2).

Once the camping grounds of the Ohlone people, the land was part of nearly 45,000 acres granted in 1820 to Sergeant Luis Maria Peralta in gratitude for his long service to the King of Spain. Named Rancho San Antonio, it was later inherited by Peralta's four sons, with the northwestern portion—which included the present cites of Albany and Berkeley and a part of Oakland—given to Jose Domingo Peralta, who eventually sold nearly all of his 19,000 acres.

To develop their college the trustees sought donations but found few takers during the Civil War years, while facing competition from other fund-raising enterprises in California. An alternative scheme, the College Homestead Association, was formed in 1864. One- to five-acre lots in what would be the new college town would be sold from a subdivision of 160 acres of land purchased by the college, a platted grid that encompassed the area now called Southside. The college land, assembled from the former tracts of five early Berkeley pioneers, now extended east and south of Strawberry Creek. With the adjoining gridiron of lots and roads laid out, the trustees turned their attention to preparing a plan for the college.

Olmsted Plan of 1866

That same year landscape architect Frederick Law Olmsted (1822–1903) was commissioned to plan the 200-acre grounds of Mountain View Cemetery in Oakland. Experienced as supervisor of Central Park and administrator for the United States Sanitary Commission, the Boston resident had come to California near the end of 1863 to manage the large Mariposa Estate gold mine in the Mother Lode. Through his management of the estate, Olmsted became friendly with trustee and lawyer Frederick Billings and was asked to survey and prepare a plan for the new campus. But when he inspected the grounds in the spring of 1865, he was challenged, as he had been at Mountain View, by the arid California landscape. "It is an accursed country," he reported to his associate Calvert Vaux, "with no trees & no turf and it's a hard job to make sure of any beauty."[4]

Conceived as a "Campus park," Olmsted's plan was influenced by the picturesque 400-acre suburban Llewellyn Park in West Orange, New

Jersey, planned by architect Alexander Jackson Davis with landscape gardener Eugene Baumann and begun in 1853. Olmsted created an informal grouping of areas surrounding a formal center, defined by vegetation and a network of winding roads. Though much smaller in scale, it recalled the contrasting relationship of the informal Ramble to the formal Mall in his 1858 plan for Central Park in New York. He sited two college buildings on a small terrace at the head of an allée, a central axis aligned with the Golden Gate. This extended westward to a central curvilinear drive and an informal "public grounds." Bordered by Strawberry Creek on the south, the informal areas included reserve sites for future academic expansion flanking the central building site, and "grounds for residences" to the east and west, as well as to the south between the creek and the College Homestead subdivision. Extending southward from the campus along what is now Piedmont Avenue, Olmsted linked the campus grounds to a winding parkway with overhanging trees and a prestigious residential subdivision called the "Berkeley Property" (see Walk 8).

Olmsted completed his final plan for the college after his return to New York in 1866. But in the depression that followed the Civil War, the College Homestead lots did not sell, and the prospects of constructing the first campus building dimmed. His plan would be abandoned, except for the later completion in general of the Piedmont parkway neighborhood. But four important elements rooted in his plan for the college grounds—a central axis, orientation to the Golden Gate, picturesque creek landscaping, and the concept of the "Campus park"—influenced subsequent plans and are in evidence to the present day.

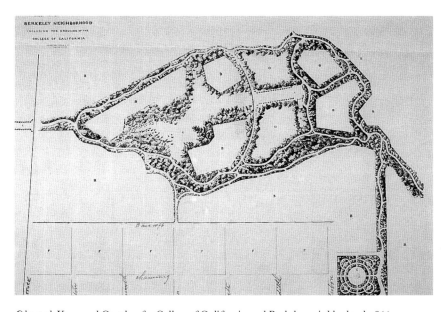

Olmsted, Vaux and Co. plan for College of California and Berkeley neighborhood, 1866

Creation of the University of California in 1868

Also in 1866 the State of California established an Agricultural, Mining and Mechanical Arts College in response to the federal Morrill Land Grant Act of 1862. That act, authored by Vermont Congressman Justin S. Morrill and signed by President Abraham Lincoln on July 2, 1862, allowed for the creation of sixty-eight "Land Grant Colleges" in the United States. Each college or university would receive endowment support from the invested proceeds of public land sales, with the stipulation that at least one institution per state would emphasize agriculture and mechanical arts and include the training of military tactics in its curriculum.

The new state institution was first proposed to be sited about a mile north of the College of California site, but at commencement exercises in 1867, Governor Frederick F. Low suggested that the resources of the state might be combined with the land assets of the financially-poor college to create the new institution. The trustees reluctantly agreed and on October 9, 1867, voted to donate their site to the state and to disincorporate, with the condition that their college would become a College of Letters within the new university.

Passed by the assembly and senate, *An Act to create and organize the University of California*—now called the Organic Act of the University of California—was signed by Governor Henry H. Haight on March 23, 1868, the date now celebrated as the university's Charter Day. The act designated Colleges of Arts—including Agriculture, Mechanic Arts, Mines, and Civil Engineering—a College of Letters, and Colleges of Medicine, Law, and other professions. It established the Regents of the University of California as the controlling board of directors, authorizing them to adopt a plan "as shall set aside separate buildings for separate uses and yet group all such buildings upon a general plan, so that a larger and central building hereafter erected may bring the whole into harmony as parts of one design." In addition, they were to "take immediate measures for the permanent improvement and planting of the grounds of the University."[5]

Wright and Sanders Plan of 1868

Four months later the newly created Regents resolved to construct as soon as possible "an edifice of sufficient capacity to accommodate Students." The building would be for the immediate use of "the Colleges of Agriculture, Mechanic Arts, Mines, Engineering and Letters; and at the future time to be made a part of a larger whole, when the wants of the University may require it."[6] To initiate this building program, they held a competition for a new plan and in October 1868 selected San Francisco architects John Wright and George H. Sanders (variably spelled Saunders in the literature). The previous year the well-known firm designed the first building for the California Institution of the Deaf and Dumb, and Blind, about a half mile south of the university grounds, on the present site of the Clark Kerr Campus.

Wright and Sanders plan for the University of California, 1868

Responding to a larger program than the small college of Olmsted's plan, Wright and Sanders proposed a formal symmetrical arrangement of five principal buildings, oriented to the west, as Olmsted had done, but situated further south alongside Strawberry Creek. The plan featured a large central building for the College of Letters and Library opening onto a terraced west plaza and surrounded by four smaller college buildings—all suggested in a Gothic–Romanesque Revival style that was characteristic of the firm's work. Uphill to the east, they sited buildings for the Colleges of Medicine and Law, as well as faculty residences and a small "Magnetic Observatory" building.[7] The following July the Regents enthusiastically adopted the plan and voted to construct a College of Agriculture building as soon as possible, as well as two smaller structures. But two months later, dissatisfied with the amount of their fee, the architects withdrew their campus and building plans.

Kenitzer and Farquharson Plan of 1869
Rather than turn to the competition runner-up, in August 1869 the Regents contracted with David Farquharson and Henry Kenitzer for a new plan, as well as working drawings, specifications, and construction supervision. The San Francisco architects were well known by Regent William C. Ralston, for whom they had designed the Bank of California, completed in 1867. Adopted by the Regents in September, their plan featured six "spacious and elegant buildings" in a staggered arrangement that maintained Olmsted's Golden Gate axis—shifted southward and aligned with a main central building opening to a plaza and glade as Wright and Sanders had proposed. Instead of a symmetrical arrangement, however, this central Hall of California was flanked on the north by the Colleges of Mines, Civil Engineering, and Mechanic Arts, and on the southwest, alongside the creek, by the Colleges of Letters and Agriculture. Smaller structures included faculty

Kenitzer and Farquharson plan for University of California, 1869

and student residences and two observatories. When Kenitzer and Farquharson dissolved their partnership about 1870, Farquharson continued under contract and was credited with the work.[8] That included the university's first building, the mansard-roofed College of Agriculture, later named South Hall, completed in 1873 according to the adopted plan. Farquharson also designed the second building that same year, the College of Letters (North Hall), but the plan was altered to site the building directly north of South Hall, where Doe Annex now stands. Eight one-story wooden student cottages were also built in 1874, six sited north of the present site of Edwards Stadium and Evans Baseball Diamond and two in the vicinity of where the Faculty Club now stands.

Hall Plan of 1874

With South and North Halls under construction, in March 1873 the Regents addressed "the matter of laying out the grounds, planting trees, Shrubbery etc.,"[9] as mandated in the Organic Act. The following September they contracted with William Hammond Hall, engineer and superintendent of Golden Gate Park in San Francisco, "for the preparation of plans for the improvement of so much of the University grounds, as may be needed immediately."[10] Hall corresponded with Olmsted about the Berkeley site although he lacked the benefit of seeing Olmsted's final campus plan, which had apparently become lost. He was influenced by Olmsted's picturesque small-college scheme, but his own plan responded to the greater needs of the state university. He sited several buildings informally along the natural contours, connected with a winding loop road, with terraces primarily at

North and South Halls, as Olmsted had proposed for two buildings at the head of a central dell. He also established experimental agricultural and horticultural grounds in the northwest part of the campus, and a botanical garden and conservatory in the central valley, uses which influenced future development decisions.[11]

Late Nineteenth-Century Development

Despite these plans, as the campus approached the close of the nineteenth century it presented a somewhat random pattern of disparate development, which lacked the coherence and order required of a major university. By 1895 enrollment at Berkeley had grown to more than 1,300 students—about seven times that when the campus opened in 1873—accommodated in seven principal buildings.[12] Farquharson's Second Empire–style North and South Halls formed a triangular center of student life with the Victorian-Gothic, brick and stone Bacon Art and Library Building (John A. Remer, 1881) at the apex overlooking the Golden Gate. To the east, stood the Dutch-Gothic brick Chemistry Building (Clinton Day, 1891) and the stone and brick mansard-roofed Mining and Mechanic Arts Building (Alfred A. Bennett, 1879). On a bluff to the north was the classically pedimented brick Mechanical and Electrical Engineering Building (William Curlett, 1893). And tucked alongside the creek to the west, wooden octagonal Harmon Gymnasium (1879) also functioned as the main assembly hall. As Hall had suggested, the central swale contained the Botanical Garden (established 1890) with its glass and steel Victorian Conservatory (Lord & Burnham, 1891) perched at the base of Observatory Hill, which was topped by the

University of California campus view from Dana Street entrance, 1897

small domed Students' Observatory (Clinton Day, 1886). Near the juncture of the two forks of the creek was the oval Cinder Track (1882), protected from the wind by the Eucalyptus Grove (planted 1877), while agricultural experiment gardens and Farquharson's row of one-story student cottages (1874) stood near the Center Street entrance. Tying all this together was Hall's informal loop road and an unplanned network of crisscrossing wooden, gravel, asphalt, and concrete walkways.

The City of Berkeley, incorporated in 1878, was also on the rise, expanding from a population of about 5,000 in 1890 to 13,000 by 1900, compared to the approximately 450 people who were scattered from the shoreline village of Ocean View to the farmlands that surrounded the campus grounds in 1873.

The International Competition for the Phoebe Hearst Architectural Plan, 1897–1899

Into this changing landscape, an extraordinary woman, Phoebe Apperson Hearst (1842–1919), entered to enable the realization of a new vision for the growing university. Her contributions during the following two decades, along with those of four other remarkable university figures—President Benjamin Ide Wheeler, Regent Jacob B. Reinstein, and architects Bernard Maybeck and John Galen Howard—would build a new "City of Learning" of international renown.

It was from the mines of California and Nevada that her husband, U. S. Senator George Hearst, made the immense fortune that he left to his wife upon his death in 1891. In 1895, two years before her appointment as a University Regent, the widow met with President Martin Kellogg to propose construction of a building for the College of Mining in memory of her late husband. For assistance, Kellogg turned to the only architect on the faculty, Drawing and Descriptive Geometry Instructor Bernard Maybeck, establishing what would become a continuing tradition of involving architectural faculty in the planning and design of the campus. Maybeck's sketch for a building, presented against a backdrop of drapery and potted plants in Kellogg's North Hall office,[13] was admired by Mrs. Hearst, who then raised the question of where to locate the structure on the campus grounds.

This issue elicited Maybeck's recommendation that a new physical plan should first be prepared, leading Mrs. Hearst to write to Regent Reinstein in October 1896 of her strong support for "a comprehensive and permanent plan for the buildings and grounds" of the university. Adding that she intended to fund the construction of two buildings—the Hearst Memorial Mining Building and Hearst Hall, a reception and women's social hall—she offered to fund an international competition for the plan without any cost restriction. "I have only one wish in this matter," she emphasized, "that the plans adopted should be worthy of the great University . . . [and]

PROPOSED PLAN FOR STATE UNIVERSITY BUILDINGS AT BERKELEY.

(From a colored perspective by B. R. Maybeck, instructor in architectural drawing at the University, intended to illustrate Regent Reinstein's ideas. The proposition as made to the entire board met with unanimous approval, and it is probable that an effort will be made in the near future to put it into execution.)

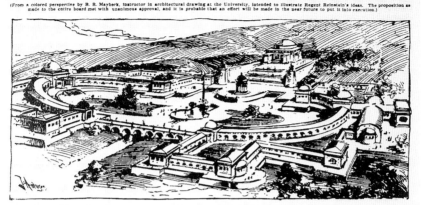

"Proposed Plan for State University Buildings at Berkeley," from a drawing by Bernard Maybeck, April 30, 1896

harmonize with, and even enhance, the beauty of the site . . . [and] redound to the glory of the State whose culture and civilization are to be nursed and developed at its University." To manage the competition, she recommended a special committee of trustees consisting of Governor James H. Budd representing the state, Professor William Carey Jones the university, and Reinstein the Board of Regents. Finally, she asked that Maybeck be granted a leave of absence, in order that he might coordinate the undertaking at her expense.[14]

Born in New York, Maybeck (1864–1957) had attended the École des Beaux-Arts in Paris, where many Americans, beginning with Richard Morris Hunt in the mid-nineteenth century, received their training in the ateliers of French architects. The influence of its principles—classicism, monumentality, historic and allegorical ornamentation, axial compositions, symmetry, and hierarchy—would be seen in the program and entries of the competition.

In the following months Reinstein and Maybeck toured the major cities of the East Coast and Europe to consult with "leading architects, artists and landscape gardeners" and make arrangements for conducting a two-stage *International Competition for the Phebe Hearst Architectural Plan of the University of California.* (Following the competition, Mrs. Hearst's name was commonly spelled Phoebe.) A prospectus published in August 1897 described the project as the creation of a comprehensive university of at least twenty-eight buildings. The existing campus buildings were to be ignored and the grounds extending into the hills considered "a blank space, to be filled with a single beautiful and harmonious picture, as a painter fills in his canvas." Art was to take precedence over business: "The architect will simply design; others must provide the cost."[15]

The following December a detailed program, developed by the Berkeley faculty and the trustees of the plan and written primarily by Professor Julien Gaudet of the École in Paris with Maybeck, was distributed in 8,000 copies printed in English, French, and German. A topographic map was included, and plaster models and photographs of the Berkeley site were placed in architectural societies, where they could be studied by architects, who had from January through June of 1898 to prepare their schemes. In addition to the 245 acres of land then owned by the university, competitors were allowed to extend their plans to approximately sixty additional adjacent acres, including the Hillegass Tract south of the creek and a strip of property north of the campus boundary.[16]

A distinguished international jury assembled by Maybeck included architects Jean Louis Pascal of France (jury president), Richard Norman Shaw of England,[17] Paul Wallott of Germany, Walter Cook of New York, and Regent Reinstein. The jury met in the Royal Museum of Fine Arts in Antwerp, Belgium, in September and October 1898 to judge 105 anonymous preliminary entries, nearly all of them large-scale, axial concepts imbued with the principles of the École. From these, eleven finalists—six American, three French, one Dutch, and one Swiss—were invited to California to visit the site and enter the final competition. The final judging, scheduled around gracious receptions planned by Regent Hearst, was conducted at the Ferry Building in San Francisco in September 1899. Four principles guided the jurors in the final competition: representation of a university in the architectural concept; convenient grouping of the academic areas without overcrowding and with room for future expansion; clarity of purpose of the fifteen departments of instruction; and adaptation of the architectural form to the site while preserving its natural qualities.

After one week of judging, the $10,000 first prize was awarded to Paris architect Henri Jean Émile Bénard, whose magnificent renderings evoked both public praise for their artistic beauty and criticism for the extravagance they depicted. The four runners-up were all East Coast American firms: second place, Howells, Stokes and Hornbostel, New York; third, Despradelle and Codman, Boston; fourth, Howard and Cauldwell, New York; and fifth, Lord, Hewlett and Hull, New York.

Emile Bénard and the 1900 Hearst Plan

As a student at the École, Bénard was awarded the prestigious Premier Grand Prix de Rome in 1867, and after studying four years in Italy, he practiced in his native Le Havre and Paris. He was one of two finalists who did not come to Berkeley prior to the second stage of judging, visiting instead some two months after his award was announced. During a six-week stay he reluctantly agreed to make revisions to his scheme, in order to reduce the size and modify the siting of some buildings, reduce the amount of earth moving required for buildings and terraces, and better preserve the natural features of Strawberry Creek. He was also asked to include a President's House (University House), which was designed in 1900 by San Francisco architect Albert Pissis, who had advised the university on the competition program. It would be the only building sited in accordance with his plan.

Bénard's revised plan, called the New Project, was completed in Paris. The architectural composition, designed in a Franco-Roman style, was oriented along a central east-west axis aligned with University Avenue. It was entered by a court leading to a large open Library Square, defined by a group of academic buildings forming a north-south cross-axis and bordered by the creeks and natural areas. Eastward from this group the main axis became a formal central botanical garden, with groups balanced across the garden forming additional north-south cross-axes. These extended to the south, where the relatively level Hillegass Tract was used—as in many of the competition entries—for an athletic stadium and fields. The foothill included a natural amphitheater, from which a road and pathway ascended the hill, which was surmounted by an observatory and terraced in areas for possible residences, a hospital, and student dormitories.

In his submission Bénard made an effort to assure the Regents that his scheme was flexible and subject to further revision, and he included three new perspective drawings to illustrate his "*le grand plan d'ensemble*."[18] Although the Regents adopted his revised plan in December 1900, Bénard had worn out his welcome with the university during his visit the previous year, proving himself to be lacking in diplomacy and unsuited for the role of supervising architect.[19] But Bénard's plan—which bore some similarities to

Bird's eye view, revised Hearst Plan (New Project), 1900, Emile Bénard

the fourth place scheme of architect John Galen Howard—established a point of departure for the Hearst Plan that would be developed by Howard and guide campus development for the next thirty years.

Supervising Architect John Galen Howard and the 1908 and 1914 Hearst Plans

Born near Boston, John Galen Howard (1864–1931) studied architecture at the Massachusetts Institute of Technology and apprenticed in the Boston office of the great Romanesque Revival architect Henry Hobson Richardson and Richardson's successors, John Shepley, Charles Rutan, and Charles Coolidge. He was familiar with California, where he worked for about a year in Los Angeles and traveled to sketch its missions and adobe houses, which would later influence the regional style he would develop for the University of California. After the first of his many trips to Europe—where Italy most inspired him—Howard took a position with the leading firm of McKim, Mead and White. He first worked for the firm in Boston and then in New York, where he contributed to the design of Madison Square Garden. With support from Charles McKim, Howard returned to Europe and in 1891 entered the École, where for three years he attended the atelier of architect Victor Laloux. He later opened his own New York office, teaming up with engineer Samuel Milbank Cauldwell in 1894. The firm's commissions, mostly in the New York area, included townhouses and homes, public buildings, and hotels, including the Renaissance and the Essex. The firm finished second to Carrère and Hastings in the competition for the prestigious New York Public Library, two years prior to placing fourth for the Hearst Plan.[20]

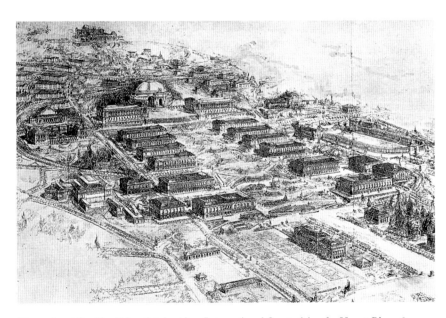

Howard and Cauldwell fourth prize plan, International Competition for Hearst Plan, 1899

When the Regents adopted Bénard's plan they also established an advisory board of four prominent East Coast architects. It included Howard, along with his former employer and sponsor Charles McKim, Désiré Despradelle of the third runner-up for the Hearst Plan, and John Carrère of the firm that was awarded the New York Public Library over Howard and Cauldwell. With the plan in place, Phoebe Hearst now turned her attention back to the building that would be a memorial to her late husband. Impressed with Howard—and possibly influenced by Maybeck, as well as several Bay Area architects and artists who favored Howard's fourth-place scheme over Bénard's—she commissioned him to design and supervise construction of the Mining Building. Howard began design studies in his New York office, but in surveying the site in the spring of 1901 he discovered inaccuracies in Bénard's siting of the building and realized that the plan would require revision to better relate it to the topography. The following December, after staking-out many of the buildings of both Bénard's and his plan, he proposed shifting the axis of the plan to reduce the amount of cut-and-fill and to correspond to the "natural line of drainage" of the grounds. "It is extremely interesting to note," Howard observed, "that the axis thus placed is parallel with that of the principal buildings at present on the grounds."[21] The alignment with the Golden Gate, first proposed by Olmsted in 1865 and established by Farquharson's South and North Halls in 1873, was reaffirmed for the new plan. Persuaded by Howard's command of the situation, the Regents that same month appointed him supervising architect, "[i]n order that all future building operations and changes of the campus may be in harmony with each other and with the site, and in accord with the dictates of the best taste."[22] Howard soon wrapped up his East Coast projects—which then included the Electric Tower for the 1901 Pan-American Exposition in Buffalo—and moved to Berkeley, where he would integrate his Mining Building with a reworked Hearst Plan.

The new century optimism that surrounded the Hearst Plan competition and coincided with Howard's appointment was given additional energy and spirit with the inauguration of Benjamin Ide Wheeler (1854–1927) as the eighth president of the university in 1899. A professor of comparative philology and Greek at Cornell University, Wheeler brought with him a love of classical antiquity that gave him an appreciation of the Greek and Roman references that Howard would employ in his Beaux-Arts ensemble. Wheeler's skills in communicating the university's needs and in raising both private and public funds provided critical support for the building program. For Howard, the twenty years of Wheeler's presidency—concurrent with the support of Phoebe Hearst, who contributed part of Howard's salary—would be his most productive and effective period as supervising architect.

Howard's planning approach was to preserve the fundamental ideas of the Bénard Plan but to treat it only as a preliminary scheme to be adapted to existing conditions. His own plan would also retain some aspects from the Howard and Cauldwell competition plan. Like Bénard's, that plan was organized about a central east-west axis, but the buildings flanking the axis were more symmetrically and regularly placed, similarly designed, and fitted to the sloping contours. At the base of the foothill was a monumental domed auditorium as a focal point at the head of the axis, in the genre of Thomas Jefferson's plan for the University of Virginia. Ascending the hillside behind the dome were dormitory buildings arranged in a radial pattern, with a smaller domed observatory at the ridgeline. Like Bénard, Howard sited the athletic complex on the broader plateau of the Hillegass Tract. While the jurors acknowledged the plan for its "general reasonableness," they found the long rows of buildings monotonous, the layout of dormitories lacking, and the group as a whole short of conveying their idea of a university.[23]

Working with the reoriented axis, Howard modified the Bénard Plan while improving his own original concept. He envisioned the grounds as naturally forming four parts, which he likened to "the House with its Forecourt or Garden to the west, its secluded Retreat and Promenade to the east, and its Playground and Field for Sports to the south." The most important part—the "House" extending along the main axis—was suited for "the construction of a great monumental group of buildings." In the heart of this group Howard placed the library, which Bénard had sited with its associated humanities buildings at the northwest corner of the campus. As "the intellectual center of the University," it was sited west of North Hall, a centralized position with the humanities grouped adjacently to the east and west and affording convenient access by all departments. Placed midway between two cross-axes—one formed by the introduction of the tower and esplanade, the other by Sather Road—and on a prominent rise above the central garden, the library could also be expanded in the future to the south (where Wheeler Hall now stands). Balancing the library on the north side of the axis on Observatory Hill, Howard proposed a major museum with related departments for art, natural history, and ethnology.[24]

East of the museum he placed an engineering group around the existing Mechanical and Electrical Engineering Building to form a cross-axial balance with the tower and group of buildings around the esplanade. This group exemplified Howard's practical approach—made easier because of the matching axes—of recognizing the established pattern of academic departments and planning around the old buildings, which would be removed and replaced over periods of time. It also showed more flexibility on his part and the influence of Bénard's plan in establishing the cross-axial balance with asymmetrical compositions.

Further east the Mining Building, first of the main ensemble to begin construction in 1902, was placed close to Bénard's designation, as was a building for physics and chemistry, sited across the Mining Circle "as a pendant to Mining." At the head of the axis, Howard retained his domed auditorium, but in his first adopted plan of 1908 included the option of using the site for an open concourse. The Hearst Greek Theatre, the first Howard structure completed in 1903, was nestled in the foothill. On the hillside above, he initially retained his group of dormitories, but placed along the contours rather than radially, with the central axis continuing up to an observatory. But in his 1908 plan, he moved the dormitories to the western end of the campus to form a peripheral demarcation of "the frontier between the University and the town."[25]

West of the museum he established the Agriculture Group (the present complex of Wellman, Hilgard, and Giannini Halls), balanced across an oval glade by a Natural Science Group (which later took the form of George Kelham's monolithic Valley Life Sciences Building). The wooded creeks and the Eucalyptus Grove were sensitively preserved and helped define the Crescent drive leading from the University Avenue and Center Street entrances.

By the time Howard's first plan was officially adopted in 1908, the nucleus of the ensemble was taking shape. Along with the Greek Theatre, California Hall and the Mining Building were complete, and the first phase of the Library was under construction, with Boalt (Durant) Hall and Sather Gate and Bridge about to start. Also complete were his brick Power House (Old Art Gallery) and Senior Hall, the rustic log cabin near Faculty Glade for the student society of the Order of the Golden Bear. The first of his several temporary buildings, including the shingled Architecture Building (North Gate Hall) that housed his school near the Euclid entrance, were in place, as was California Field, a temporary football stadium on the Hillegass Tract.

The most significant change to the plan in the 1914 revision was the deletion of the dormitories along the western periphery, reflecting a Regents' policy not to build housing on campus. The large auditorium at the head of the axis was reaffirmed without reference to an alternate concourse, and in the foothill to the north of the Greek Theatre a second smaller amphitheatre was added. The Agriculture Group was better defined, and an unidentified building placed about where Mulford Hall now stands near the Crescent. Howard also reconfigured the group south of the Mining Circle for chemistry, physics, and mathematics and modified the area south of the present Valley Life Sciences Building for an alumni hall and student union. The Mining Circle itself was reduced in size, while the central garden to the west was enhanced with a large sunken oval at the cross-axis of Sather Esplanade. Permanent stadiums for football and track were proposed south of the creek on the Hillegass Tract.

Most development either completed or started between the two plans—the first phase of Doe, Boalt, Sather Gate, and Sather Tower—reflected President Wheeler's success in obtaining donations. Funding by

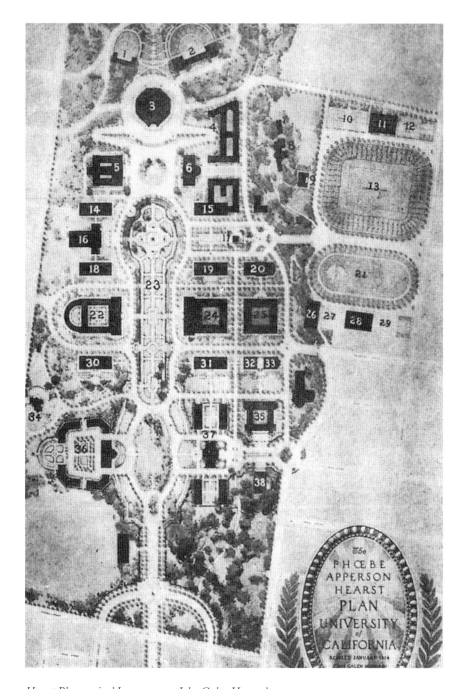

Hearst Plan, revised January 1914, John Galen Howard

state bonds for Agriculture (Wellman) Hall was the notable exception, and the next period of development would also rely on public funding. Howard's revised plan, issued in January 1914, was useful in an alumni campaign to convince voters to support a $1.8 million University Building Bond issue the following November. New facilities were needed to alleviate the outmoded and overcrowded conditions in the numerous older facilities.

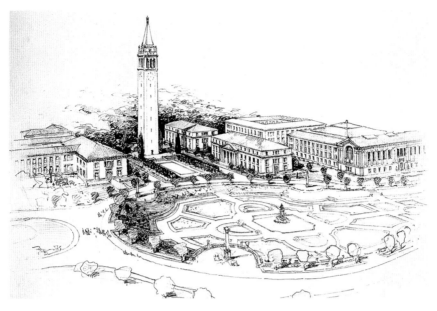

Sather Tower and central axis study, 1914, John Galen Howard

Enrollment had increased to about 7,000 students from 2,500 at the turn of the century, making the university the second largest in the nation, without a respective increase in classrooms and other space. Passage of the bond measure enabled construction of four additional Howard structures, including the completion of Doe, Wheeler Hall for classrooms and the Humanities, Gilman Hall for Chemistry, and Hilgard Hall, the second increment of the Agriculture Group.

By the time of Wheeler's retirement in 1919, eleven permanent structures of the Hearst Plan had been built. Five more would be completed by Howard in the early 1920s—the student union Stephens Hall, LeConte Hall for Physics, Haviland Hall for Education, Hesse Hall for Engineering, and California Memorial Stadium. But following Wheeler's departure and with the death of Phoebe Hearst the same year, Howard lost considerable support. His own authoritarian style and history of difficult contract negotiations with the Regents also contributed to the situation. Things came to a head in 1922 when the site for the stadium was selected against his recommendations and he was bypassed in favor of Bernard Maybeck for a grand memorial to Phoebe Hearst (of which only Hearst Gymnasium would be built). When President Campbell took office the following year, Howard offered his resignation as supervising architect, then retracted it when Campbell offered support. But problems persisted, and in November 1924 Howard's contract with the Regents was abruptly cancelled.[26]

The magnitude of Howard's legacy is evident in his twenty-two remaining campus structures, most of them historically acclaimed and composing the partially finished Beaux-Arts ensemble that distinguishes the campus. It is also measured by the success of the School of Architecture he established in 1903 (and where he continued to teach until his death in 1931), which has produced many of the Bay Area's leading architects.

Supervising Architect George W. Kelham (1927–1936) and the 1933 Plan Study by Warren C. Perry

Although George Kelham (1871–1936) was reported to immediately succeed Howard as supervising architect, he was not officially appointed to the Berkeley position until 1927. Two years earlier he assumed similar responsibilities for the new Los Angeles campus (UCLA), where he prepared a campus plan and designed several major buildings. Like Howard, Kelham was born in Massachusetts, but studied at Harvard University before attending the École in Paris in 1896 and beginning his career in New York two years later. Working for the firm of Trowbridge and Livingston, he was sent to San Francisco to supervise construction of their Palace Hotel, which replaced an earlier hotel destroyed in the 1906 earthquake and fire. Upon its completion in 1909, Kelham remained on the west coast and opened his own office, soon becoming one of the more successful designers of large commercial buildings, as the city was being rebuilt from the rubble and ashes. Many of his downtown and Civic Center buildings remain today as prominent landmarks, among them the Beaux-Arts former San Francisco Public Library (1916), Gothic-ornamented Russ Building (1927), and Moderne-style Shell Building (1929).

Kelham respected Howard's work, supporting him against criticism by some members of the San Francisco Chapter of the American Institute of Architects in 1913 concerning Howard's handling of architectural commissions for the San Francisco Civic Center. And in an article he wrote about the Berkeley campus for *The Architect* in 1917, he praised Howard's transformation of the Bénard Plan into a "final scheme of great beauty and practical working value."[27]

During his supervisory period, Kelham designed nine permanent campus buildings and one addition. All but two of these—Crocker Radiation Laboratory, razed in the 1960s, and Harmon Gymnasium, partially demolished and reconstructed as Haas Pavilion in the 1990s—are still standing. (His original wing of Davis Hall is planned for removal in the near future.) Only the Valley Life Sciences Building (which consumed the site of a planned group of five smaller buildings) and an addition to Hesse Hall fully conformed to Howard's plan. Others, such as Bowles Hall, which established housing in the foothill, and Moses Hall, which formed a Tudor-style complex with Stephens Hall, were generally compatible with Howard's intentions. Although Kelham received some criticism for the massiveness of Life Sciences and his eclectic styles, many of his buildings have withstood the test of time with some measure of aesthetic admiration.

But with the Regents wanting greater control over the "final scheme" than they had with Howard, Kelham was given fewer planning responsibilities and did not prepare a new campus plan during his tenure. Instead, President Robert Gordon Sproul established a new advisory Committee on Campus Development and Building Location in 1931. Sproul desired that important siting decisions be given "the thought and study of men who are not only familiar with architectural standards but with the life and needs of the University."[28] Warren C. Perry (1884–1980), Howard's successor as Director of the School of Architecture, headed the committee.[29] Perry was one of Howard's first students and draftsmen, graduating from the university in 1907, after which he attended the École in Paris from 1908 to 1911. He began teaching in the school soon after, continuing until his retirement as dean in 1950. The committee determined the southwest sites for Kelham's Harmon Gymnasium and adjacent baseball field and Perry's Edwards Stadium, and influenced the future siting of Sproul Hall.

In 1933, at a time of building inactivity, Perry prepared a restudy of the central portion of the campus, with a rendered plan reflecting the committee's desire "to develop (occasionally to recover) the great features" of Howard's Hearst Plan. Emphasizing the "Academic Area" between the two forks of the creek, the study reaffirmed the general pattern of building groups established by Howard around the central axis. But it recommended shifting the axis by about sixteen feet to the south between Life Sciences and the Mining Circle, in order to compensate for crowding created by the siting of Kelham's McLaughlin Hall in the Engineering Group two years earlier. The proposed shift—never executed—would have contracted the central sunken garden but created more space to better develop buildings on the north side of the axis in the spirit of the original plan. It also allowed for a "North Central" Group of four buildings on Observatory Hall, similar to Howard's plan, for a museum or future Humanities expansion, so that "a decided architectural linking with the Library across the axis is reasonable and effective from the design standpoint." The study proposed retaining the natural features of the campus while creating new formal courts, with pedestrian areas protected from automobile intrusion. While the study accommodated additional growth in the Engineering, Natural Science, and Humanities Groups, it sensitively retained the scale and density envisioned by Howard but could not possibly foresee the growth that would come in the following two decades.[30]

Supervising Architect Arthur Brown, Jr. and the 1944 General Plan
Following the death of George Kelham in 1936, the Regents were at first slow to appoint a new supervising architect, reasoning that Kelham's junior partner Harry Thomsen was handling work left in progress and that the building program was otherwise dormant. But as planning advanced for

*Aerial view of the University of California, Berkeley campus, 1938, showing John Galen
Howard's Beaux-Arts ensemble prior to post-World War II growth.*

building a new dormitory (Stern Hall) and Administration Building
(Sproul Hall), President Sproul urged the Regents to appoint a replacement,
and in May 1938 architect Arthur Brown, Jr., (1874–1957) was selected from
nine candidates.

    Born in Oakland, Brown graduated from the university's College
of Civil Engineering in 1896 and from the École in Paris in 1901, where he
was one of the most distinguished American students—attending, like John
Galen Howard before him, the atelier of Victor Laloux. His partnership
with fellow university graduate John Bakewell, Jr., (1872–1963) from 1905 to
1927 produced a number of outstanding buildings, including Berkeley City
Hall (1908) and San Francisco City Hall (1915), probably the greatest Beaux-
Arts structure in the United States. Also in the San Francisco Civic Center,
Brown associated with Albert Lansburgh in the design of the War Memorial
Opera House and Veterans Auditorium (1932). His work on the Berkeley
campus had included the Class of 1910 Bridge (1911) in Faculty Glade, with
Bakewell, and the neoclassical Cowell Memorial Hospital (1929–1930),
which housed the University Health Service for more than sixty years.
Brown was no stranger to Howard, who was also associated with the devel-
opment of the Civic Center and hired Brown as an acting professor in the
School of Architecture in 1919.

    Working with only vague policies about enrollment, building size
and character, acquisition, parking, student housing, and recreation, Brown
produced a series of "Key Plan" studies, which were based on several planning assumptions: that the 1900 Bénard Plan had been abandoned; the 1914
Howard Plan had been modified; the permanent buildings of the past thirty-

five years must be regarded as the plan nucleus; the campus buildings and landscaping should be treated as a comprehensive architectural group; and buildings would be limited to a four-story height without student elevators.

Brown retained Howard's east-west central axis, but he shortened it, siting a new building for mathematics and department libraries east of its intersection with the north-south axis of Sather Esplanade (on the present site of Evans Hall). Abandoning the Mining Circle, he planned a minor north-south axis between the Mining Building and the creek. On either side of the old central axis the engineering and physical sciences groups were expanded with some similarities to Kelham's scheme and Perry's study. Planning for postwar growth, Brown designated the corners of the campus for Forestry, Agriculture, and Home Economics in the northwest, and Jurisprudence, Anthropology, and the Arts in the southeast.

As Perry had suggested, Brown also continued Howard's plan to balance Doe Memorial Library across the axis, proposing buildings for future library expansion and architecture on Observatory Hill, while placing a building to the east of Doe for Doe Annex, one of the priorities identified during the war. These proposals to keep the axis open and site the Annex caused controversy between Brown and Architecture Professor William C. Hays, Howard's former junior partner and now chairman of President Sproul's Committee on Campus Development and Building Location.

Hays' committee and an administrative committee on library problems recommended that the axis be abandoned, seeing the open space north of Doe as an area of "wasteful and unsightly neglect" that should be used

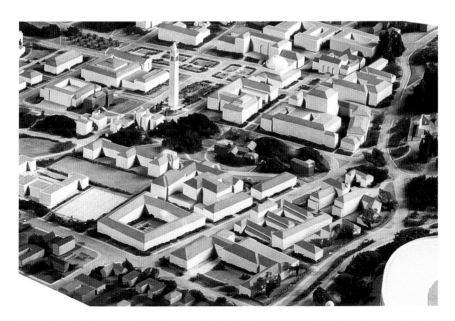

Model of plan for the University of California, Berkeley campus, 1948, showing Arthur Brown's 1944 General Plan, including shortened central axis and low-rise buildings.

as the Annex site. Influenced by the then-innovative Union Square with its underground parking garage in San Francisco (Timothy Pflueger, 1942), the group proposed underground book stacks with landscaping above, thus foreseeing an idea that would actually be realized in the Gardner Stacks some fifty years later. But in addition, they recommended construction of a new main library in the central axis, as well as a new building north of the axis on Observatory Hill to balance Doe. The new development, they envisioned, might then form "a handsome Humanities Court (a possible War Memorial?)," a concept also remarkably similar to the future Memorial Glade.[31] However, Brown maintained that his Annex site would meet projected program requirements, suggesting that the central axis and Observatory Hill might be reconsidered for future expansion. President Sproul and the Regents agreed, approving the "old North Hall site" in 1944, leading a discontent Hays to resign as committee chairman. The central axis—already compromised by Brown's proposed mathematics building— was momentarily spared from further in-fill, but the process fired the first volleys at the Hearst Plan, signaling an emerging reluctance to preserve its essential features in the face of oncoming postwar growth.

Brown's own neoclassical tile-roofed buildings during this period— Sproul Hall, Donner Laboratory, Minor Hall, and Doe Annex—were generally compatible in style, materials, and scale with Howard's ensemble. But the campus was at a turning point, its low-rise Beaux-Arts building composition about to be strained beyond its limits. Brown's desire to preserve some of the old principles while accommodating expansion seemed impossible within the confines of the 178-acre central campus, and his final General Plan K-18, adopted by the Regents in 1944, was characterized by sprawling low-rise buildings with limited public open space.

Brown's approach, in conflict with Hays as well as the university's architectural staff, was viewed as no longer effective for meeting modern needs. At the same time he was at odds over contract issues with the university, further reducing his support from the administration. Now into his seventies and without the large office staff he once had, he did not receive a renewal of his contract and resigned as supervising architect in 1948.

In addition to his own buildings, Brown's plan influenced the siting of Engineering's Cory Hall, Mathematics' Evans Hall, the Chemistry and Physics groups, the Humanities' Dwinelle Hall in the campus center, and the groups in the northwest and southeast corners. It also revealed the need for more comprehensive planning to deal with postwar development pressures.

The Office of Architects and Engineers' 1951 Campus Plan Study and Postwar Development

Following Brown's departure, the university's Office of Architects and Engineers (A & E) assumed supervisory responsibility for campus planning and development. Established in 1944, the office, under the direction of chief architect Robert J. Evans, produced a Campus Plan Study in 1951 as part of a physical planning report that would lay much of the groundwork for the next official plan in 1956. Opposing Brown's Beaux-Arts views, the study cautioned against "blindly following policies and concepts of monumentality unsuited to contemporary requirements." That approach, it stated, "would straight-jacket a live and vital University into inflexible buildings ... placed about on the campus in such a manner as to deprive it of its open spaces, its natural beauty and its true monumentality."[32]

The A & E study assumed an enrollment of 20,000 at Berkeley and emphasized balancing open space and building mass by developing parts of the campus more densely. A building coverage not to exceed twenty to thirty percent was proposed as a way to govern the height of buildings, rather than the uniform walk-up height established by Brown. The study also specified the principles of grouping related functions and maintaining a ten-minute class change interval, while using peripheral sites for more independent programs. And in a dictum of modernism, it stated that new buildings "should be designed honestly with the materials available, to respond to the organic requirements of the occupants and to create maximum practical internal flexibility."

Building upon the recommendations of a 1948 Alumni Association planning study directed by city planner L. Deming Tilton, the A & E study proposed a new Student Center and the acquisition of about forty-five acres of land, mostly in Southside, for the construction of high-rise residence halls. In 1952—the same year that the chief administrative responsibilities for the campus were transferred from the president to Berkeley's first chancellor, Clark Kerr—the Regents adopted the study in principle, established the policy of providing university-owned housing for twenty-five percent of the student body, and approved the land acquisition program.

The large building program following the war evolved from a 1941 state public works employment program that released $1.1 million to the university for the preparation of plans for contemplated development. By 1951 the Berkeley program amounted to approximately $27 million in construction projects. The first buildings of this postwar boom extended Brown's transitional theme of stripped neoclassical designs that maintained a dignified compatibility with Howard's monuments. Chemistry's Lewis Hall (E. Geoffrey Bangs, 1946–48), Forestry's Mulford Hall (Miller & Warnecke, 1947–48), Brown's Doe Annex (1948–49), Physics' LeConte Hall addition (Miller & Warnecke, 1949–50), and even sprawling Dwinelle Hall (Weihe, Frick & Kruse, 1950–52) for the Humanities were in this mode. The Law Building (Warren C. Perry, 1950–51) formed a bridge to the Modern, while others, such as Engineering's Cory Hall (Corlett & Anderson, 1948–50), Public Health's Warren Hall (Masten & Hurd, 1953–55), and Stanley Hall

(Michael Goodman, 1950–52), the virus lab at the head of the axis, introduced flat-roofed and often anonymous forms. The influx of large modernist buildings was right around the corner.

William Wilson Wurster and the 1956 Long Range Development Plan

To transform the A & E study into a new Long Range Development Plan, in 1955 the Regents appointed a high-level Committee on Campus Planning to perform the duties of supervising architect. The triumvirate included Regent Donald H. McLaughlin as chairman, Chancellor Clark Kerr, and William Wurster, who was both Campus Consulting Architect and dean of the College of Architecture. Wurster (1895–1973) succeeded the retiring Warren Perry as dean in 1950 to reform the Beaux-Arts program to be competitive with the modern thinking of eastern schools. Born in Stockton, he studied under Howard, Hays, and Perry, graduating from the university in 1919. He brought experience from Harvard, Yale, and M.I.T., where he was dean of the School of Architecture and Planning.

In his simultaneous roles, Wurster exerted a great deal of influence in the development of planning principles, siting of buildings, architect selection, and building design. Faced with the pressures of postwar growth, Wurster—reflecting the Harvard and Bauhaus influence of Walter Gropius—promoted the construction of some high-rise buildings in order to preserve open space and "restore the campus to its old sculptural form."[33]

The new plan was necessary to guide campus growth in response to the postwar enrollment surge with more realistic projected needs than could be estimated by Brown. Enrollment had risen from a wartime low of about 11,000 in 1944–45 to an unprecedented high of over 25,000 in 1948–49, influenced by returned veterans studying under the GI Bill, with a leveling-off to about 19,000 when the plan was published in 1956.

A projected enrollment of 25,000 formed the basis for the plan, which established several principles refined from the A & E study. It reaffirmed use of the central campus for academic needs, clustered by related disciplines and with a ten-minute class exchange time centered about Doe Library. Buildings were to be constructed "to the maximum size that the building sites permit" with a more specific limit of over-all density of buildings to land area of twenty-five percent. The natural, landscape, and historic features of the campus were to be preserved, with pedestrian areas separated from automobiles, which would be accommodated in underground or structure parking to preserve open space. And it incorporated the land acquisition program for functions requiring proximity to the central campus, especially the high-rise residence halls and recreational facilities in the Southside.

The plan retained Brown's proposed shortening of the central axis but with an undergraduate library sited to the west of the Mining Circle. The remainder of the axis—since occupied with temporary Navy barracks

Long Range Development Plan, University of California, Berkeley 1956, model, showing tall buildings to accommodate post-war student growth.

known as the T-buildings—was to remain open, but as an informal glade rather than an axial Beaux-Arts composition. Despite the new land coverage rules, much of the initial development following completion of the plan was kept to a reasonable scale. This included Music's Morrison and Hertz Halls (Gardner Dailey, 1956–58) and the first phase of the Student Center (Hardison and DeMars, 1959–61), while Astronomy's boxy Campbell Hall (Warnecke & Warnecke, 1957–59) struggled to look compatible with its tiled hipped roof. The peripheral properties sprouted high-rises, with University Hall (Welton Becket & Associates, 1957–59) on Oxford Street and the first two units of the Residence Halls (Warnecke & Warnecke, 1958–60) in Southside. The six-story Earth Sciences Building (now McCone Hall; Warnecke & Warnecke, 1959–61) foretold of the larger buildings to come on the central campus.

The 1962 Long Range Development Plan and the Boom of the 1960s

To reflect changes in conditions and needs, a revised Long Range Development Plan was prepared in 1962 under the direction of an expanded Campus Planning Committee headed successively by Chancellors Glenn T. Seaborg and Edward W. Strong. In addition to Wurster in his two roles, the committee included Consulting Landscape Architect Thomas D. Church, Campus Architect Louis A. DeMonte of the Office of Architects and Engineers and four other university officials. The new plan reiterated the main principles established in 1956, but summarized interim development and expanded the scope in three main areas. It related to the state-adopted "Master Plan for

Higher Education in California" of 1960, which established the roles of the public junior colleges, state college system, and the University of California, and the subsequent "University Growth Plan" prepared by now-President Clark Kerr to guide academic development of the university. Enrollment levels in particular were established with a maximum at Berkeley of 27,500 projected for the mid-1960s. The plan also included the use of Strawberry Canyon and the hill area, as well as outlying campus properties not previously considered. And it incorporated several landscaping proposals prepared by Church for the central campus.

Development that followed the plan fulfilled the dictates of density and ground coverage but revealed a lack of unified architectural or urban design vision for the campus. Exceptions, most notably the Student Center by Hardison and DeMars, relied on the strength of individual architects in the absence of a strong supervising architect. The Hearst Plan was abandoned, but the new pattern of development did not provide a cohesive architectural scheme. Rather, it produced an assemblage of individually sited buildings rapidly emplaced to satisfy growing research needs and an expanded enrollment.

Now the high-rises sprouted like mushrooms, changing the scale of the campus. Mathematics' Evans Hall (Gardner Dailey, 1968–71) most tangibly signified the assault on Howard's plan, clogging the central axis on the site west of the Mining Circle that Brown first suggested for a smaller building. Adding insult to injury, the ten-story behemoth dwarfed Howard's Mining Building, casting a tall shadow on the richly modeled facade of that historical landmark, as well as on the grassy slopes of the Circle. Regent and former committee chairman McLaughlin saw the impact too late, realizing that Evans "finally grew under pressure into a huge building that will be painfully intrusive."[34]

To the west, the flag of surrender could be seen, allowing further incremental encroachment into the axis, with the construction of Moffitt Undergraduate Library (John Carl Warnecke and Associates, 1967–1970), an important change from the 1956 Plan that also interrupted the cross-axial relationship between California and Haviland Halls. Some twenty years later, the Life Sciences Addition (MBT Associates, 1986–1988) would also intrude into the axis while upsetting the long-established balance between the Agriculture Group and Valley Life Sciences Building.

In the southeast part of the campus the new home of the College of Environmental Design, nine-story Wurster Hall (DeMars, Esherick and Olsen, 1962–64) took its dominant position in the arts area. Further west the siting of eight-story Barrows Hall (Aleck L. Wilson & Associates, 1962–64) behind Brown's Sproul Hall—for Business Administration, Political Science, Economics and Sociology—became a matter of contention with members of the faculty and design professions. Thomas Church objected to its impact in blocking views of the Bay and cutting off the view of the Campanile from

Telegraph Avenue. Student Center architect Vernon DeMars foresaw its looming appearance when viewed from the terrace of the Student Union. Other members of the Environmental Design faculty opposed it but could not convince Dean and Consulting Architect Wurster, who felt the site was appropriate for the high-rise in order to conserve open space.[35] McLaughlin was again regretful, proclaiming Barrows as the "worst thing that happened architecturally on the campus . . . just inexcusable."[36] But he was also unsuccessful in trying to lower the building and roof it with red tiles.

In all, seventeen major buildings went up on the central campus during the 1960s. Several more were developed on the peripheral sites—Engineering's Etcheverry Hall (Skidmore, Ownings & Merrill, 1962–64), the University (Berkeley) Art Museum (Mario J. Ciampi, 1967–70), the Unit 3 Residence Halls (John Carl Warnecke and Associates, 1961–64), in addition to several parking structures. The upper hill was also developed with two buildings by Anshen and Allen, Lawrence Hall of Science (1965–68) and the (Silver) Space Sciences Laboratory (1964–66).

By the end of the period, the built space on campus had approximately doubled since the end of World War II. Much of it related to the expanded emphasis in research—often federally funded during the Cold War years—that was an outgrowth of the breakthrough atomic age discoveries of Ernest O. Lawrence, Glenn T. Seaborg, J. Robert Oppenheimer, and other leading scientists before and during the war. Coincidental with the social revolution and unrest of the times, the campus was transformed to a dense environment with its newer massive structures seeming to symbolize the bureaucratic authority and anonymity of the establishment that was being opposed.

Late Twentieth-Century Regulation, Infill, and Restoration

In contrast to the development that transformed the campus during the two decades following the war, the 1970s were slowed by limited resources and characterized as the "Steady State" by Chancellor Albert H. Bowker. His concern shifted to the older facilities, reporting to the Regents in 1973 "that our physical plant, which is presently undermaintained, will become progressively more and more obsolete."[37] To bring state legislators and prospective donors face-to-face with unsafe and outmoded facilities, he conducted a graphic "crummy and seedy tour" through the labs, classrooms, and back rooms of such antiques as Kelham's Life Sciences Building.[38]

At the same time, new priorities were established by local, state, or national requirements for energy conservation, access for people with physical disabilities, correction of seismic and other life-safety deficiencies, environmental impacts, and historic preservation. They were also shaped by community activism. The exigencies of space needs had led to some insensitive actions, such as the interior gutting of Howard's California Hall in the late 1960s. But campus and community opposition to the proposed removal of two other Howard buildings—Senior Hall in 1973 and the Naval Architecture Building in 1976—resulted in more caring design and planning decisions.

A major influence on the process was Environmental Design Dean Richard Bender, who—as Dean Warren Perry had done nearly a half-century earlier—provided direction in the absence of long-range planning. In the wake of the transformation of the campus during the growth years, a series of urban design studies and historic resource surveys were prepared by a college group headed by the Dean to guide future development within a broader context of architectural and historical continuity. The effort affected building design and led to the designation in 1979 of a number of buildings, structures, and natural and landscaped features for inclusion in the National Register of Historic Places and listing as state landmarks, as are described in the following Walks. (A plaque identifying the historic core of campus as a California Registered Historic Landmark is located at the head of Campanile Way.)

By the end of the 1970s the built-up campus had grown to about 30,000 students. New construction during the decade was limited to Optometry's sleek addition to Brown's Minor Hall (Mackinlay, Winnacker, McNeil, 1977–78) and the Bechtel Engineering Center (George Matsumoto, 1978–80) that was imaginatively re-sited to save Howard's Naval Architecture Building.

Planning begun at the same time to alleviate a severe student housing shortage led to the university's acquisition and reuse of the fifty-acre former home of the California Schools for the Deaf and Blind. Spearheaded by campus physical-planning coordinator Dorothy A. Walker, the site's twenty-five buildings were restored (several architects, 1982–84) to create the Clark Kerr Campus for over 800 students in the first major housing facility since the high-rise dormitories of the 1960s.

In addition to renewing the deteriorated facilities that Chancellor Bowker first identified, the following decade saw a concerted effort to meet cutting-edge technological advances, such as in recombinant DNA research in the biological sciences and in computer sciences. Recalling the spirited fund-raising efforts of President Wheeler some eight decades earlier, a $470 million "Keeping the Promise" capital campaign—the largest in campus history—was undertaken by Chancellor Ira Michael Heyman to upgrade the changing teaching and research environment.

During the 1980s and early 1990s the final pieces that generally related to the 1962 Plan were dropped into place. Koshland Hall and its companion Genetics and Plant Biology Teaching Building (Hellmuth, Obata and Kassabaum, 1986–90), part of the biological sciences complex, filled in the Hearst Avenue frontage and clarified the dense northwest corner of campus. Foothill Student Housing (William Turnbull Associates and The Ratcliff Architects, 1989–91) recalled the Bay Tradition heritage, taking the place of a high-rise complex that was proposed at Hearst and La Loma and extending behind Stern Hall to accommodate about 800 students. Chemistry's Tan Hall (Stone, Marraccini and Patterson, 1992–96) finally completed the definition of the esplanade that extends southward from the Mining Circle.

Other buildings not in accordance with the old plan were added incrementally. To alleviate outgrown Harmon Gymnasium, the Recreational Sports Facility (ELS/Elbasani & Logan, 1982–84) was constructed along the Bancroft edge. And, completing part of the biological sciences program, the Life Sciences Addition (MBT Associates, 1986–88) was inserted between the Valley Life Sciences Building and the Eucalyptus Grove.

The 1990 Long Range Development Plan

To provide guidance until 2005, the Regents adopted a new Long Range Development Plan in 1990, prepared by the university's Physical and Environmental Planning office and San Francisco consultants ROMA Design Group, with the advice of a faculty-based committee.

The plan was formulated on academic planning premises and projected a reduction in Fall headcount enrollment from its 1988 level of about 31,360 to an estimated 30,000 by the end of the planning period in 2005. On the already dense central campus, the plan reaffirmed the clustering of related programs in designated academic precincts, confirmed the preservation of historic and natural resources, and proposed concentrating future development in selective urbanized areas to maintain open space and the traditional park-like setting within an auto-free zone.

An ambitious program to meet continued student housing needs— influenced by the removal of thousands of private housing units from the market during the 1980s—was also proposed with new residential sites identified especially in the Southside and potentially along the South Shattuck corridor. These sites contributed to the plan's theme of the "University in the City," recognizing the academic, natural, historic and cultural resources that the campus provides for the community and the extension of the campus beyond its centralized park-like environment.

The rehabilitation and expansion of the main library facilities and reestablishment of part of the axis as a glade were centralized features of the plan. Construction of the underground Gardner Stacks (Esherick Homsey Dodge and Davis, 1992–94) and Memorial Glade (Richard Haag and Royston Hanamoto Alley & Abey, landscape architects, 1997–98) recaptured an element of Howard's plan, while reemphasizing the grandeur and symbolism of Doe Memorial Library as "the intellectual center of the University." Another major change was the removal of old Cowell Memorial Hospital and an adjacent former fraternity house to construct the cloistered Haas School of Business (Moore Ruble Yudell with VBN Corporation, 1992–95) along the Piedmont-Gayley edge. Construction on the campus periphery included Computer Sciences' Soda Hall (Edward Larabee Barnes Associates with Anshen and Allen, 1992–94) in Northside and the University Health

Services' replacement for Cowell, the Tang Center (Anshen and Allen, 1991–92) in Southside. The latter project, along with Chemistry's Tan Hall and plans for a future East Asian Center, reflected the effectiveness of Chancellor Chang-Lin Tien in raising funds from Asian sources.

Additions to existing structures also completed according to the plan included expansion of Dwinelle Hall (Simon Martin-Vegue Winkelstein Moris, 1996–98), the Law Building (The Ratcliff Architects, 1995–96), and Minor Hall (Fong & Chan, 1991–92).

Planning for the Twenty-First Century

Just as the campus experienced a "tidal wave" of enrollment following World War II, it is responding to a second projected "wave" in the first decade of the new century, resulting from the needs of children of the baby boomer generation and the increased state population. A New Century Plan has been undertaken as a comprehensive strategic framework for preparation of a new Long Range Development Plan. The needs associated with increased enrollment are being integrally planned with the retrofit or replacement of seismically poor buildings, upgrading of aging labs, class-rooms and infrastructure, and accommodation of new programs

At the forefront of planning is the university's $500 million Health Sciences Initiative, an interdisciplinary program involving biology, physics, chemistry, and bioengineering that will include the proposed replacement of two outmoded postwar buildings. A second opportunity to develop the head of the axis east of the Mining Circle will be created by a new molecular-engineering complex (Zimmer Gunsul Frasca) planned to replace Michael Goodman's molecular and cell biology and virus lab, Stanley Hall (1950–52). Along the west edge of campus Public Health's Warren Hall (Masten & Hurd, 1953–55) will make way for a new center of biomedical and health sciences.

Other academic program improvements are either under way or planned. Replacement of the north wing of Davis Hall (George W. Kelham, 1929–31) by a new microfabrication Engineering facility will be part of the statewide California Institutes for Science and Innovation. In Northside, construction of a building at Le Roy and Hearst (Architectural Resources Group, 2001–02) will provide additional classrooms and offices for the Goldman School of Public Policy. A new Music Library (Scogin Elam and Bray) is planned to the south of Morrison Hall. And a multi-use building (Heller Manus, 2001–02) on the Oxford Tract across from the northwest corner of campus will accommodate programs displaced from buildings undergoing seismic renovations.

Aided by funds from the Federal Emergency Management Agency, several major buildings developed during the growth years of the 1960s have required seismic retrofits in an extensive renewal program. These include Barrows (Aleck L. Wilson & Associates, 1962–64; Hansen/ Murakami/Eshima, 2000–01), Barker (Wurster, Bernardi & Emmons, 1962–64; Anshen and Allen, 2001–02), Wurster (DeMars, Esherick and Olsen, 1962–64; Esherick Homsey Dodge and Davis, 2000–02), Latimer and Hildebrand (Anshen and Allen, 1960–66, 2000–01), and McCone (Warnecke & Warnecke, 1959–61; Gordon H. Chong and Associates, 1997–99) Halls on the central campus, and Silver Space Sciences Laboratory (Anshen and Allen, 1964–66; Fisher Friedman Associates, 2000–01) on the hill.

A remarkable program of seismic restoration of several historic campus landmarks has also been accomplished, the most recent being the turn-of-the-century rehabilitation of Howard's Hearst Memorial Mining Building (NBBJ, 1998–2001). It was preceded by Farquharson's South Hall (Esherick Homsey Dodge and Davis, 1986–88), Pissis's University House (Brocchini Associates, 1990), and three other Howard monuments renovated by Hansen/Murakami/Eshima, Wheeler (1988–89) and California (1991) Halls and Doe Memorial Library (1996–97). Howard's LeConte Hall and California Memorial Stadium are also scheduled for retrofits.

Also under way is the provision of new housing for approximately 870 students that will be integrated with planning for the Southside and fulfill some of the needs identified in the 1990 Plan. Included are apartments for 120 students at the southeast corner of College and Durant (Michael Pyatok Associates, 2001–02), peripheral suites and apartments at Residence Halls Units 1 and 2, and apartments at Channing and Bowditch. The latter two projects are planned to follow completion of a central dining and office facility (Cannon Dworsky Associates, 2001–02) at Channing and Bowditch.

The campus plan "is not a dead fetich, a rigid and unchangeable form," John Galen Howard prophesized in 1903, "it is a living organism, a loving hand-maiden, capable of responding today, tomorrow, through all generations, to the quick needs of the University."[39] Howard likely never visualized the magnitude of growth that has led to the alteration of his "City of Learning." But his "great group of beautiful white buildings embowered in greenery"[40] is a lasting reminder that stewardship of those valued architectural, natural and cultural features that distinguish Berkeley must accompany the changes that sustain its academic greatness.

Central Campus Classical Core

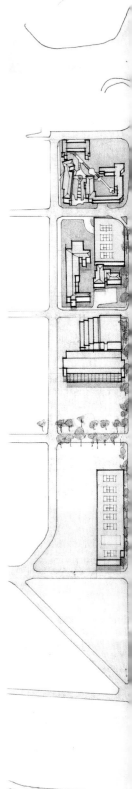

Sculpture by Jo Mora, Class of 1920 Bench

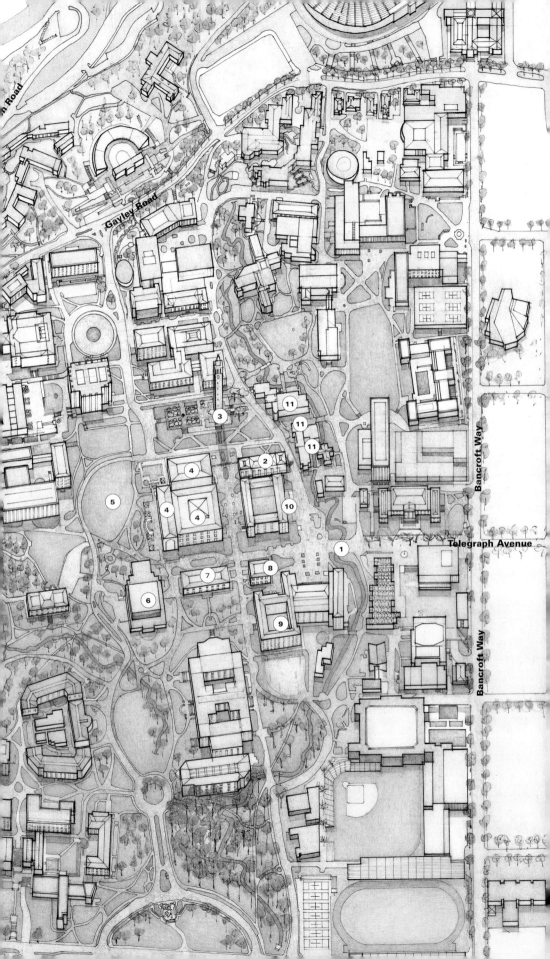

Gayley Road

Bancroft Way

Bancroft Way

Telegraph Avenue

3

11

11

11

2

4

5

4

4

10

1

7

8

6

9

The Heart of John Galen Howard's "City of Learning"

Entered through the bronze archway of Sather Gate, this Walk encompasses the compact center of John Galen Howard's incomplete Beaux-Arts ensemble that comprised the Hearst Architectural Plan. It is the only part of the campus where his vision of classical granite-sheathed buildings topped with red mission-tile roofs and copper skylights and cresting can be appreciated as an uninterrupted composition. The intact group of California, Durant and Wheeler Halls, Doe Memorial Library, and Sather Tower makes this possible. The other elements of Howard's ensemble—Hearst Memorial Mining Building, the Agriculture Group, Gilman, LeConte, Haviland and Hesse Halls—are more dispersed around the campus and separated either by vegetation or large-scale buildings of the modern period.

The domain of two academic precincts—Library and Administration, and Humanities and Social Sciences—this Walk maintains the importance Howard emphasized in establishing the library with related humanities buildings at the campus center. It contains two of the nation's great libraries, the main library complex that now includes Doe with its Gardner Stacks linked to Moffitt Undergraduate Library, and the Bancroft Library housed in adjacent Doe Annex.

Within this dignified classical core can be seen Howard's remarkable ability to maintain the unity of his architectural theme while still achieving diversity in the styles of his individual buildings. The Greco-Roman Doe Memorial Library, California and Durant Halls, the Venetian Campanile, and the French-Baroque Wheeler Hall are each unique yet harmoniously related to Howard's governing vocabulary of forms and materials. Built from 1903 through 1917, all were faced with the same white Raymond granite quarried from the Sierra foothills, a material replaced by concrete and stucco in Howard's subsequent classical buildings.

Picturesque Memorial Glade, the foreground to Doe Memorial Library, has replaced the formal central-axis garden that Howard envisioned between his Beaux-Arts library and a proposed museum to the north, though the series of open spaces extending from the west Crescent to the Mining Circle has been interrupted. A minor east-west axis, Campanile Way is intact, extending from the Campanile through the center of the ensemble. At its intersection with Sather Road, the grouping of Howard's buildings is most clear, with the Library, California, Durant, and Wheeler Halls forming the corners of the crossroads, and the tower standing as its eastern terminus.

The Victorian-era origins of the university are also present on this Walk in historic South Hall, the first building constructed at Berkeley. So is the heritage of student government and organizations, which occupied Howard's creek-side Stephens Hall, the former student union building, and its Tudor-style companion, George Kelham's Moses Hall, for some forty years until completion of the California Student Center in the 1960s.

Men's Octet performing, Sather Gate

1. Sather Gate and Bridge   *John Galen Howard, 1908–1911*

Designed as the Telegraph Avenue entrance to campus, Sather Gate is both a symbolic passageway to the "City of Learning" and a portal to its architectural heritage. Just north of the bridge and the south fork of Strawberry Creek—the original southern campus boundary—stands Howard's historic Beaux-Arts ensemble, of which the gate is a key element.

When the first classes were held on campus in the fall of 1873, a wooden footbridge made this crossing under a canopy of arching oaks. Flanked by a picket fence, it led from the terminus of the horse-drawn streetcar line that made the trip from Oakland in about one hour. In 1885 the old bridge was replaced by "Huggins' Bridge," named for its designer, recent university graduate Charles L. Huggins, who would become City Engineer for the growing Berkeley community. By then the horses had been replaced by a steam dummy, which would soon yield to the electric cars of the Oakland and Berkeley Rapid Transit Company.

Huggins' Bridge would serve as the main southern entrance until the construction of the new concrete wagon-and-foot bridge, with its monumental entrance gate funded in 1908 by Jane Krom Sather, one of the major benefactors of the rising university. The wealthy widow of Peder Sather, a pioneer San Francisco banker and trustee of the College of California, she arranged—with the guidance of President Wheeler—for her estate to pass on to the university. In addition to establishing two professorships in classical literature and history, she made possible the tower and esplanade that bear her name, completed about four years after Sather Gate, which is named for her husband.

When Howard was informed that the gate and bridge would be funded, he could find only a perspective sketch and an old set of study drawings that survived the destruction of his San Francisco office in the fire that followed the 1906 earthquake. The sketch was probably one done in 1905 in a French Baroque style that he supplemented with additional studies of classical and Baroque themes in December 1908.[1] His final design bears some resemblance to this early study: four concrete-backed granite piers surmounted with illuminated glass globes and spaced to form three ornamental bronze gateways. Flanking the gate are granite classical balustrades, which also form the sides of the concrete bridge that arches over Strawberry Creek. These terminate with monumental granite urns mounted on pedestals that "anchor" the bridge at its four corners.

Sather Gate detail; panels sculpted by Melvin Earl Cummings

The wide central gateway is a segmental arch that bears the name of the gate and an oval laurel wreath containing the five-pointed university star with emanating rays of light, a symbol of the discovery and dissemination of knowledge. Beneath the star is the university motto, added to the design by President Wheeler, *Fiat Lux* ("Let There Be Light"). The two smaller flat arches open to what originally were pedestrian sidewalks on either side of the bridge roadway. Mounted on both sides of the twelve-foot-high piers are eight panels of white Italian marble with bas-relief allegorical nude figures symbolizing eight scholarly pursuits of the university. The four female figures represent Agriculture, Art, Architecture, and Electricity, and the four male figures, Law, Letters, Medicine, and Mining.

These three-foot-high panels became the objects of a bizarre series of events with all the undertones of a Greek tragedy. Along with the four decorative urns, they were designed by sculptor Melvin Earl Cummings (1876–1936), modeling instructor in the Department of Architecture, and also known for the Sloat Memorial in Monterey, California, and figures at Golden Gate Park and the California Palace of the Legion of Honor in San Francisco. Cummings studied under Douglas Tilden at the Mark Hopkins Art Institute in San Francisco and, under the sponsorship of Phoebe Apperson Hearst, at the École des Beaux-Arts in Paris. He came highly recommended by Howard for whom he designed work for other campus structures, including the bronze bust of Athena over the entrance of Doe Memorial Library, the chairs of honor in the Hearst Greek Theatre (see Walk 6), and the memorial plaques in Hearst Memorial Mining Building (see Walk 2).

At first President Wheeler wanted the Sather Gate panels to be granite, but Howard's persistence for using marble was typical of his attention to details and the quality of construction; as he wrote in 1909: "[T]his material lends itself to the subtleties of delicate modeling of the human figure, especially when at a small scale, much better than granite. The danger, too, of a fleck or flaw in the granite just where it might give a leer to an eye or a smooch to a nostril or a lip, makes me question the granite for the panels, which depend for their effect on the flawless beauty of modeling and material."[2]

But Wheeler kept close to the creative process. After visiting Cummings' San Francisco studio to approve the models, he was not hesitant to criticize "the discomfort which Agriculture must feel leaning her bare arm upon the chilly scythe,"[3] or request that the artist "take the book out of the hand of the figure of Law."[4] Cummings was his own severe critic, devoting a great deal of time in modeling the panels and destroying several until he reached perfection. Regent John A. Britton also stopped by the studio and reported to the president that he thought the work was "a very great stride in the advancement of art, so far as it has been exhibited in our western States." But he also anticipated that the nude figures might be highly criticized "in view of the fact that they are to form a part of the structures of the University," adding that, "we should be bold enough, in our appreciation of art, to accept any criticism that may be offered."[5]

Britton proved to be the prophet. Shortly after the panels were installed in December 1909, well-positioned leaves were found pasted onto the male figures, which then adorned the south side of the piers above the gate inscription, "Erected by Jane K. Sather." When Mrs. Sather, confined to her Oakland home with illness, was informed of the incident and shown photographs, she insisted that the panels be removed, informing President Wheeler of her "philosophic objection to the use of the nude in decoration of the Sather Gate."[6] Her reaction, though often considered prudish, seems to have been rooted more in her belief that objects of high culture would be best removed from public view, rather than be subjected to desecration by individuals she felt might be too uncultivated to appreciate them.[7]

Howard made an impassioned plea to keep the panels in place, arguing that "it would be a great mistake to take too seriously the idiotic levity of some irresponsible artist in leaves and paste."[8] He cautioned that their removal would likely cause damage to the piers and suggested that, if they had to go, the figures might instead be erased by cutting back and then replaced with new ones. But, he added, such a drastic measure would cause an unfortunate injustice to Cummings. The determined artist presented an estimate to Howard in March 1910 for replacing the panels with new ones featuring draped figures, but to no avail. In April Howard was ordered to remove the panels "at the earliest possible moment" and replace them with ones of plain granite. They were removed the following month, the university reporting that they were "inconsistent with the architectural tone of the rest of the structure." In August, Howard was informed that Mrs. Sather desired new panels sculpted for the gate, not by Cummings, but "a sculptor of talent—no matter whether American or European."[9] Although Howard and his staff considered several other sculptors, the matter was apparently forgotten after Mrs. Sather's death in December 1911.

The drama had come to an end—or had it? A serendipitous conclusion was in order. When the eight marble panels were removed in May 1910, they were placed in campus storage, moving from building to building during a seven-decade intermission. It was when items stored under the bleachers of Edwards Stadium were transferred to a university warehouse in Richmond in early 1977, that the saga resumed. There, two of the panels with female figures were discovered by the curator of the Lowie (now Hearst) Museum of Anthropology. News of the discovery reached the Amador Marble Company in Oakland, where the other six panels—possibly acquired from a scavenger some twenty years earlier—were found in the yard lost among headstones. After being recovered by the university, the reunited panels were exhibited at the museum and in December 1979— seventy years after their original short-lived installation—reinstalled on Sather Gate. But this time the males were strategically placed on the north, beyond the view of the inscription on the other side.

Cummings, who likely imagined his panels would never see the light of day again, also faced opposition to the design of his four granite urns. They were to be encircled with friezes of allegorical figures representing the four seasons of life: Childhood, Youth, Maturity, and Age. But indecision on the part of the university as to whether to use marble or granite delayed progress by some nine months. Cummings modeled the urns, each with up to fifteen figures, but despite the fact that the figures were draped, Mrs. Sather would have none of them following the controversy of the panels. Garlands of roses, the vine, the oak, and the laurel were then proposed, but only the latter was finally used to decorate the four urns.

Since Sather Gate was completed in 1911, its paved oval forecourt has been a natural gathering point for student campaigns, leafleting, and various other activities. From the 1930s through the 1950s, it also became the setting for political rallies and speakers—establishing freedom of speech and assembly principles, prior to the conversion of Telegraph Avenue into Sproul Plaza in 1961 (see Walk 4). Since then the gate has acquired an additional significance as the northern terminus of that major plaza.

Sather Gate and Bridge are listed on the National Register of Historic Places, are included in the Berkeley campus designation as a California Registered Historical Landmark, are listed on the State Historic Resources Inventory, and are a City of Berkeley Landmark.

2. South Hall

David Farquharson, 1870–1873;
John Galen Howard, addition, 1913;
Kolbeck, Cardwell and Christopherson, alterations, 1968–1970;
Esherick, Homsey, Dodge and Davis, seismic alterations and restoration, 1986–1988;
Gonzales Associates, alterations, 1996–1997

South Hall embodies the founding spirit of the university. Now the home of the School of Information Management and Systems, it is the first campus building and the only surviving major work of architect David Farquharson, who sited it according to his 1869 campus plan.

Construction began on the building—first named the College of Agriculture—in April 1870 but was suspended the following January when the Regents found themselves short of funds. The nearly complete basement was covered until June 1872, when work resumed following an appropriation of funds from the State Legislature and a change in contract rates, which had contributed to the initial budget problem. The following October the long-postponed cornerstone ceremony was held with the help of the

South Hall

Masonic Order and the Fourth Army Band of the Presidio. Approximately 1,000 people looked on as Governor Newton Booth received the granite stone from the contractor and requested that it be examined by Farquharson, who found it "square and true, sound and solid, and of strength and beauty fit to become the 'headstone' of the corner." Placed inside the stone were samples of grains, various documents, a fragment of the cornerstone of San Francisco City Hall, and a piece of oak from the U.S. Frigate *Constitution*.[10]

The building was completed in November 1873, two months following Farquharson's second building, the College of Letters (North Hall), a wooden structure of similar style begun earlier that year and completed under controversial circumstances without the supervision of the architect. That building initially housed the humanities, social sciences, mathematics, and engineering, as well as the President's and Recorder's offices and student activities. Occupying South Hall were laboratories for agriculture and the physical and natural sciences, the library, and the office of the Secretary of the Regents.

Characteristic of the Second Empire style, the four-story brick building is distinguished by its slate mansard roof that is topped with ornamental cast-iron cresting and penetrated by dormers with decorative hoods and oeil-de-boeuf or bull's-eye windows at the attic. Numerous ornamented brick chimneys and former laboratory flues accentuate the facades and rooftop. The half-basement forms a rusticated base of Folsom granite for the horizontally divided first and second stories above. These are fenestrated with cast-iron hoods of segmental arches on the first floor and round arches on the second. The slightly projecting north and south end wings have cast-iron bas-relief panels at the second story that display California grains and fruits—a link to the building's agricultural roots—while just beneath the cornice brackets, satyr's heads hold iron downspouts in place. The cast-iron pilasters that define the building's corners and the entrance bays are not merely decorative, but were used by Farquharson, who was aware of the earthquake risk in the Bay Area, to secure iron reinforcing bars through the brick masonry walls.

The interior was finished in varnished white cedar, with walnut and laurel used for furnishings in the laboratories and lecture rooms. Carved plant motifs on the newel post of the central open stairway are another reference to the building's origins. Two second-floor "grand lecture rooms," now used as a classroom and computer lab, originally had cove ceilings and skylights and were equipped with tiered seating and curved laboratory benches. One of these was the classroom of Joseph LeConte, legendary professor of geology, natural history, and botany, who taught in the building from its opening until his death in 1901.

The historic value of South Hall was not fully appreciated until late in the twentieth century. In the Hearst Plan, it was to be replaced, like North Hall, with a classical building just to the east. In 1913 a one-story concrete annex was added to the north side of the building by Howard to provide a workshop for the Department of Physics. It was first opposed by the Regents' Committee on Grounds and Buildings, who were concerned that, with the construction of the Campanile, "the campus ought not be marred" by the addition." The annex was later reused for student honorary societies and a placement center, and now houses the Center for the Study of Higher Education, although it has been designated for removal since 1944.

South Hall was emptied in 1964, when the School of Business Administration and the departments of economics, political science, and sociology moved to Barrows Hall. It remained in a deteriorating state for the next three years, its future uncertain as both the university and the old building approached their centennial anniversaries. The alumni magazine sounded a subtle alarm: "For the moment, South Hall remains, a unique, beautiful, doddering old firetrap. But with every passing day of the university's hundredth year it becomes more vulnerable to the expedient side of progress."

With the support of Chancellor Roger Heyns, a commitment was made to save the building, the first in a series of campus renovations of historic buildings. The east entry porch was provided with a bifurcated stairway (a west porch and stairway were removed) during initial rehabilitation in the late 1960s (Kolbeck, Cardwell and Christopherson). Passage of a state bond issue in 1986 enabled a more complete restoration for seismic strengthening (Esherick, Homsey, Dodge and Davis), which used an innovative method of reinforcing the brick masonry walls with steel and a polyester resin and sand grout. In 1997 architect Irving Gonzales reconstructed and replicated the porch and stairway with steel and the use of glass-fiber-reinforced-concrete to replace deteriorated concrete finials and other decorative elements. The entrance, which had been previously modernized, was rebuilt in a manner sympathetic to the original style. The new ornamental castings were done by Michael H. Casey, who discreetly added a small sculpted bear on the restored facade, as he did on the Granada Building at the corner of Telegraph and Bancroft.

South Hall is listed on the National Register of Historic Places, is included in the Berkeley campus designation as a California Registered Historical Landmark, is listed on the State Historic Resources Inventory, and is a City of Berkeley Landmark.

3. Sather Tower (The Campanile) and Sather Esplanade

Sather Tower (The Campanile)   *John Galen Howard, 1913–1914*

Sather Esplanade

   John Galen Howard, with John W. Gregg and MacRorie-McLaren, landscaping, 1915–1916

Sather Tower

"I am anxious," donor Jane Krom Sather wrote to President Wheeler in February 1911, "to arrange for the erection on the university campus at Berkeley of a Campanile, to be known as the 'Jane K. Sather Campanile.'"[11] John Galen Howard was also anxious. Inspired by the campanile of San Marco in Venice, he had been making design studies for a tower since at least February 1903, and in 1911 he explored concepts with Romanesque and French Baroque influences, and options for using the tower as habitable space. These included student or faculty housing—ideas Howard did not champion because he desired as few windows as possible, so that the tower would not appear like an apartment building. Other novel suggestions were made to Howard: a housing co-op in the base of the tower with open loggias to take the place of the old North Hall steps; a stairwell configured to permit "vertical experiments" by the physics department; and the university flag or a wind gauge and weather vane affixed to the spire. Ultimately, the Regents agreed with Howard's aesthetic concerns and authorized him to plan the interior with "one room to the floor."

Howard located the tower to establish a minor east-west axis and a transverse north-south one to intersect the sunken garden of the central axis. Its site was hallowed ground, the location of the wooden flagpole, which for years marked the center of campus life in the area between Bacon, North, and South Halls. (The original flagpole, removed for construction of the Campanile, was sent to St. Mary's College in Moraga. It was later replaced by the steel flagpole that stands west of California Hall, a gift of the Class of 1927.) It was here that President Wheeler delivered his famous first address at the university on the morning he assumed office, October 3, 1899. Standing on a blue-canopied platform before a gathering of students and the cadet regiment, he aroused the spirit of those around him: "This University shall be a family's glorious old mother, by whose hearth you shall love to sit down. Love her. It does a man good to love noble things, to attach his life to noble allegiances. . . . Cheer for her; it will do your lungs good. . . . Love her; it will do your heart and life good."[12]

Howard's tower would also be a noble thing. "I want the Campanile to rise with a slender, simple stem," he envisioned, "bursting into bloom at the summit, like a great white lily."[13] Ascending from a thirty-four-foot-square base to a height of just over 303 feet at the top of its bronze lantern, the tower is eight feet narrower and twenty feet shorter than its counterpart at San Marco. Howard accentuated its slenderness with narrow pilasters at the corners and slit windows centered on each facade. And to maintain the desired perspective, he tapered the tower inward by three and one-half feet to the base of the belvedere, changing at that point to a vertical shaft up to the entablature and the fleur-de-lis balustrade that forms the base of the steeply-pitched pyramid spire. The great bronze finial flames that crown four corner obelisks symbolize, along with the illuminated

Sather Tower under construction, 1914

lantern, the aspiration for enlighten-ment. The Campanile itself amplifies this symbolism. Standing on ground some 250 feet above sea level, it is vis-ible for miles, an enduring icon of the university and "a lodestone for stu-dent pride and affection."

The tower is formed from a structural steel frame with reinforced concrete walls, floors and roof and is faced with blocks of Raymond granite. The pyramid at the peak is surfaced in white Alaska marble, a material cho-sen by Howard for economical rea-sons, instead of an earlier preference for lead or lead-coated copper. The steel frame extends ten feet into the ground, where it is anchored to a steel-beam grid embedded in an eight-foot-thick reinforced-concrete slab that is forty-eight feet square. This foun-dation rests upon a hardpan base eighteen feet below grade. Steel cross-bracing was used on every other level of the tower to accommodate window placement, but primarily to allow structural elasticity in earthquake or wind loads. Howard's consulting engineer, the dean of the College of Civil Engineering, Charles Derleth, Jr.,[14] used the fable of the stiff oak and the slender willow to describe the structure: "The oak is broken by the storm, but the willow, though less in strength, being greater in yielding qualities, rides the tempest." When the first steel column was swung into place in November 1913, newspapers across the country covered the dra-matic moment with an account of "an acrobatic mechanic clinging to its top," and predicted the Campanile would become one of the world's most famous towers. The following spring, to celebrate completion of the 500-ton framework, Derleth and President Wheeler were hoisted in a skip up to the open belvedere where they were guests of honor at a ceremonial banquet for the steelworkers.

But Derleth's "slender willow" would require future attention. In 1927 cracks in the Campanile's granite skin were first noticed. By 1951 they affected nearly one-quarter of the 2,800 stones and resulted in occasional falling chips—at first baffling investigators and leading to rampant spec-ulation as to the causes. But in 1955 it was determined that the tower exhib-ited characteristics found in other tall steel-frame structures faced in stone, in which loads expected to be carried by the steel frame were instead transferred to the rigid stone facing. Rusted anchors were found as a secondary cause, explaining why marble chunks had also fallen from the pyramid spire. Interim measures were taken to guard against the falling hazards: the spire was given a steel-mesh corset, and a wooden barrier fence was erected at the base of the tower. As a more permanent precaution, the granite-curbed planting bed at the base of the tower and the bronze and concrete canopy (Walter T. Steilberg) were constructed in 1958 to shelter the entrance and the Class of 1920 Bench that was relocated from the west facade. (The canopy features a curious anomaly on its soffit, where the university motto is inscribed in reverse—the result of a misunderstanding between architect and contractor.) Repairs supervised by architect-engineer Jack Kositsky in 1976 involved a steeplejack team that scaled and recaulked the tower's mortar joints to prevent further erosion from moisture.

Today more than 70,000 annual visitors ascend more comfortably than the president and dean did in 1914—by elevator to a seventh-floor landing, which connects by steps to the belvedere. A winding 316-step stairway also rises within the tower. The four floors above the first-floor lobby that were once considered for human habitation are occupied by other species—or rather, their remains. Closed to the public, the U-shaped spaces contain an estimated fifty tons of dinosaur and other animal bones, many pulled from the La Brea Tar Pits in Los Angeles. Dating back 200 million years this valuable research collection has been stored here by the department of paleontology since 1915.

The belvedere—a classically ornamented belfry—has triple-arched openings on all four sides that frame panoramic vistas of the Bay Area. The twenty-two-foot-high arches, which rise over classical balustrades, are supported by paired Corinthian columns with paired pilasters at the corners and are surfaced with carved rosettes. It is the home of the carillon, an unusual bell instrument that hails originally from the lowlands of Belgium and Holland. Within a glass-enclosed playing cabin, the carillonneur plays baton-like manual keys and foot pedals connected by wires to the clappers, which are pulled against the inner rims of the sixty-one bells suspended beneath the coffer-decorated ceiling.

Jane Sather's inspiration for funding the Campanile stemmed from her girlhood memories of the chimes of Grace Church in New York, and

Detail, belfry arches, Sather Tower

Bells, Sather Tower

before she died in 1911 she requested that bells, rather than bars or tubes, be used for the tower's chime. In 1915 twelve "Sather Bells" were cast from ingot copper and pure block tin by the world-renowned bell-founder, John Taylor and Sons in Loughborough, England. The work was supervised by a campanologist from the British Museum who reported the bells to be "in perfect tone and harmony" following the use of a new mechanized method of thinning the metal near the crown of each bell to achieve precise tuning. Near the beginning of 1917, just months before the United States entry into World War I, the bells were loaded onto an American ship bound for San Francisco, where they arrived in April, having "safely threaded their way through the submarines." Stored until an expert could arrive from the English foundry, they were delivered to the university in October for installation, and were greeted by crowds of students gathered on Sather Esplanade to watch them emerge from their packing crates. Weighing from 349 to 4,118 pounds, each bell carries the university seal and the donor's name, while the largest bell features an inscription composed by Greek Professor Isaac Flagg:

> We ring, we chime, we toll,
> Lend ye the silent part,
> Some Answer in the heart,
> Some Echo in the soul.

The Sather Bells were arranged in a circle, rigidly suspended from the belfry ceiling. A thirteenth bell, along with its clockwork, was installed in 1926 to strike the hours. Named for Regent William Ashburner, it was transferred from Bacon Hall, where it had tolled since 1899, after that building's belfry was removed as an earthquake precaution. The bells were rung for the first time on November 3, 1917, during a football game against visiting Washington on nearby California Field.

One of the celebrated tower personalities was Margaret E. Murdock, who played the bells beginning in 1923 for sixty years. She became part of campus lore, first in 1933, when, to alert the campus of a fire she noticed in the demolished rubble of Old Harmon Gymnasium, she gave an unscheduled rendition of "Scotland's Burning, Look Out, Fire, Fire." Ten years later during World War II, she received a discreet complaint from Vice-President and Provost Monroe E. Deutsch questioning why the Fascist hymn "Giovenezza," the national song of a United States enemy, had been played for several days. The apologetic Murdock responded that in complete innocence she found the piece "in the subversive source of the Cooperative Store in Stephens Union.... In fact I was very pleased to add to the chimes collection and must have played the 'hymn' with special gusto because it sounds so like a gay folk tune." She closed diplomatically, "There is no danger of repetition."[15] The west steps at the base of the Campanile are dedicated to Murdock.

In 1979 the original chime of twelve bells was transformed into a full carillon—a keyboard instrument of 23 or more bells—with the addition of thirty-six bronze bells cast in 1978 by Pierre Paccard of Annecy, France. The Class of 1928 presented it to the university as a fiftieth anniversary gift. The additional bells, ranging in weight from 28 to 3,000 pounds, were accompanied by funds for a new clavier, or keyboard, as well as a carillonist's office and exhibit room.

Five years later, the carillon was expanded again to sixty-one bells, with the addition of thirteen bells also cast by Pierre Paccard, ranging in weight from a twenty-pound treble to the bourdon, or lowest, the "Great Bear Bell," at five and one-half tons. This massive bell—over five feet high and seven and one-half feet in diameter—is adorned with bas-relief bears and the names of fifteen significant university-associated individuals. The next three largest bells—the "Clipper Ship Bell," the "Gold Rush Bell," and the "Explorer Bell"—carry the names of individuals linked to their respective themes. These latest bells were donated by alumni Jerry Chambers (Class of 1928) and his wife, Evelyn Hemmings Chambers (Class of 1932). Funds were also provided to endow the University Carillonist's position and for additional practice rooms and keyboards, a campanology library, and a Carillon Festival, a week-long event showcasing the best carillonists from around the world.

Since the original bells were installed, concerts have been played on a regular schedule with special performances on traditional occasions. The ominous "They're Hanging Danny Deever in the Morning," is played on the last day of class before exams, while during football season rousing renditions of "We're Sons of California," "All Hail, Blue and Gold," "The Golden Bear," or other school songs can sometimes be heard.

The high visibility of the Campanile has made it the object of occasional displays—official and otherwise—which have altered its appearance over the years. Large university service banners were hung on its west face during both World Wars to honor students, alumni, and faculty serving in the Armed Forces. Other assorted acts have included a fraternity-crafted Mickey Mouse clock-face, mysterious appearances of an Easter bunny and Halloween pumpkin affixed to the lantern spike, an animal-rights demonstration, and a botched Stanford scheme to hang a large red block "S" during Big Game Week.

Sather Esplanade

The formal setting for the Campanile—Sather Esplanade—was envisioned by Howard to be "the great open-air rendezvous of the students, taking the place of the upper class bench when North Hall is destroyed." Howard presented two alternatives in 1915, one a more elaborate and expensive scheme with sculpted fountains and urns at the northern end. Built upon earth removed from the excavation for Wheeler Hall, the esplanade serves as a podium for the tower and forms the cross-axis that was intended to link the Campanile with the central-axis garden to the north.

The esplanade consists of raised lawn-beds with a formal arrangement of six rows of pollarded London plane trees (*Platanus X acerifolia*) separated by walkways of brick laid in a herringbone pattern. Classical

Study for Sather Esplanade, Scheme "A," 1915, John Galen Howard

Sather Esplanade

balustrades and hedges border this terrace, with openings for broad brick and granite stairways that descend to the adjacent grounds. (The bronze handrails, designed by Noll and Tam, Architects with ironworker Michael Bondi, were installed in 2000.) Howard consulted with Landscape Gardening and Floriculture Professor John W. Gregg on the use of the knobby-branched trees, similar to those used at the San Francisco Civic Center, which was planned by an advisory board headed initially by Howard. Horticulturist John McLaren also used the trees on the grounds of the 1915 San Francisco Panama-Pacific International Exposition, from which they were moved to the campus and planted on the esplanade by McLaren's firm in 1916. They are also used prominently elsewhere on campus, especially at Sproul Plaza, along Sather Road and Campanile Way, as well as Mulford Hall and the Agriculture Group.

Several distinctive monuments rooted in the history and traditions of the university adorn the esplanade and its surroundings. Set into the brick pavement in front of the Campanile is a large granite tablet with bronze lettering memorializing Howard, who died in 1931. It was designed by architecture professor Stafford L. Jory and Warren C. Perry, who succeeded Howard as director of the School of Architecture. Both were also former students and employees of Howard. It was funded, along with the establishment of a permanent scholarship, by the Architectural Alumni Association. In addition to recognizing Howard's teaching and founding of the school, the tablet lists his permanent campus structures, an impressive testimonial that concludes with the phrase, "His Greatest Monuments You

See About You." This wording, suggested by President Robert Gordon Sproul, was no doubt influenced by Howard's own remarks at the dedication of the Greek Theatre in 1903: "An architect feels that when he has said his say in terms of his own art, he has a right to be excused from verbal utterance. He may well paraphrase the epitaph of Sir Christopher Wren, upon whose tomb we read, '*Si monumentum requiris, circumspice*,' 'If you would see his monument, look around.' So I might say, 'Would you have speech, hear this architecture.'" With Mrs. Howard present, the monument was dedicated in May 1932 with a special playing of the Campanile chimes, followed by an exhibition of Howard's work in the Ark (North Gate Hall), where he taught for three decades.

In the center of the plane tree grove stands the Mitchell Monument, a granite cannon-ball-like sphere and pedestal with a bronze drinking

Mitchell Monument

fountain. It was designed by Howard and memorializes John Mitchell, the handlebar-mustachioed armorer for the University Cadets from 1895 to 1904, and a Congressional Medal of Honor winner in the Indian Wars. For most of that period, Mitchell's armory was in the basement of nearby North Hall. The monument also serves to recall the origins of military instruction on campus, established under the provisions of the Morrill Land Grant Act of 1862. The cadets, who at the time numbered about 1,000—about two-thirds of the undergraduate male students— dedicated the monument in 1905 at approximately the same location where it now stands on the esplanade.

Beneath the canopy at the tower's entrance is a marble bench provided by the Class of 1920 "to Commemorate the Heroism of the Sons of this University who died in the Great War." Designed by class member Lional H. Pries, it was originally placed in 1920 against the west facade of the Campanile oriented toward the Golden Gate, but was moved in 1958 to its present location to escape the tower's falling chips, as described above. The pair of mourning bears, surmounting the sides of the bench, were sculpted in native travertine marble by San Francisco artist Joseph Jacinto ("Jo") Mora (1876–1947), a prolific and renowned artist of Western subjects. Among Mora's most revered works are the Cervantes Memorial in San Francisco's Golden Gate Park, the Bret Harte Memorial of the Bohemian Club in San Francisco, and the Serra

Sarcophagus at San Carlos Mission in Carmel. He also created the lobby decorations in Julia Morgan's Los Angeles Examiner Building and the stone sculptures at the Bernard Maybeck–designed Los Angeles home of Earle C. Anthony (the donor of Anthony Hall).

On the south side of the Campanile, the large bronze bust of President Abraham Lincoln is the work of John Gutzon de la Mothe Borglum (1867–1941), best known for his epic presidential portraits on Mount Rushmore, South Dakota. It was cast from an original marble head done by Borglum for the Capitol building in

Washington, D.C. Presented to the university in 1909 by alumnus Eugene Meyer, Jr., (Class of 1896) for placement inside Doe Memorial Library (then under construction), it was ultimately placed on its pedestal (donated by Ralph W. Kinney of San Francisco) at the Campanile and dedicated by President David P. Barrows in 1921. Its presence is a reminder of Lincoln's role in signing the Morrill Land Grant Act of 1862, which led to the establishment of colleges devoted to the teaching of agriculture and the mechanical arts, and to the creation of the University of California. In this context, Lincoln is well situated, facing Moses Hall, the site of the university's first two agriculture buildings and, with a westward glance, South Hall, former home of the College of Agriculture.

Bust of Abraham Lincoln by Gutzon Borglum

Opposite Lincoln is a neoclassical bench, given in 1994 by the Class of 1955, as "Beneficiary to Benefactor," along with a $400,000 endowment for a faculty chair. To the south of this bench on the lower terrace the white marble pedestal with a bronze sundial was placed on axis with the Campanile in 1915. Donated by the Class of 1877, it was later renovated by the Engineering Class of 1996. It was designed by Clinton Day (1846–1916, Class of 1868, LL.D. 1910),

Class of 1877 sundial

architect of eight nineteenth-century campus buildings and the son of civil engineer Sherman Day, one of the founders of the College of California. Only the preserved cupola of the Chemistry Building (1891) standing between Gilman and Hildebrand Halls and the relic of Leuschner Observatory (1886) on Observatory Hill remain of Day's campus buildings. One of his commercial buildings, the Golden Sheaf Bakery (1905), survives in downtown Berkeley at 2071 Addison Street.

Between the esplanade and Doe Annex is the C-shaped Jubilee Bench, donated by the Class of 1897 on the occasion of its twenty-fifth anniversary "in gratitude and loyalty to our Alma Mater." The marble bench was installed in 1922 on approximately the site of the "Senior C," a large wooden monument that was built by the Class of 1898 as a place for senior men to congregate, an activity that soon proved to be uncomfortable and, therefore, unpopular. When the wooden "C" was stolen one night in 1899, the students sent a letter of gratitude to the suspected raiders, the Stanford student body. In 1908, the tradition was revived with the creation of the first Senior Men's Bench outside North Hall. Subsequent benches for the senior men were located on Campanile Way, across from Wheeler Hall, and in front of Moses (then Eshleman) Hall. The donor class suggested that the marble Jubilee Bench serve as the first element of a "Jubilee Court," where other class silver anniversary gifts might be located.

Sather Tower is listed on the National Register of Historic Places and the State Historic Resources Inventory, and is a City of Berkeley Landmark. Sather Tower and Esplanade are included in the Berkeley campus designation as a California Registered Historical Landmark.

Class of 1897 Jubilee Bench

Doe Memorial Library

4. Doe Memorial Library, Doe Annex, and Gardner Stacks

Doe Memorial Library

> *John Galen Howard, 1907–1911 and 1914–1917;*
>
> *Walter Ratcliff, Jr., Morrison Library interior alterations, 1927–1928;*
>
> *Office of Architects & Engineers, interior alterations, 1953;*
>
> *Kolbeck, Cardwell and Christopherson, interior alterations, 1964;*
>
> *Theodore C. Bernardi of Wurster, Bernardi & Emmons, East Reading Room restoration, 1975;*
>
> *Esherick Homsey Dodge and Davis, Information Center interior alterations, 1992–1994;*
>
> *Hansen/Murakami/Eshima, seismic alterations, 1996–1997*

Doe Annex

> *Arthur Brown, Jr., 1948–1949; Skidmore, Owings & Merrill, interior alterations, 1973*

Gardner Stacks *Esherick Homsey Dodge and Davis, 1992–1994*

The main library has grown in increments spanning most of the twentieth century, from the initial phase of Doe Memorial Library to the present complex of interconnected buildings. Through it all, the original gable-roofed north wing of Doe remains both the physical and intellectual heart of the campus and the library's identifying landmark.

Here is the Greco-Roman centerpiece of Howard's classical ensemble. Sited on an elevated bluff and projecting slightly into the great central axis, the 225-foot long wing assumes a position of prominence, the

Parthenon on the Acropolis of the Athens of the West. Howard, who visited a number of European and East Coast libraries, designed Doe around a central book stack, "the heart of the organism, from which radiates the life-blood of books to all readers." To do this he configured the building in two contiguous blocks: the north entry wing containing the reading rooms, and a nearly square south block comprised of the central stack surrounded by seminar rooms and other functions on the east, south, and west.

Construction was made possible by an unexpected gift from the estate of San Francisco businessman Charles Franklin Doe, but became uncertain when the earthquake and fire of 1906 caused a devaluation of proceeds from the estate. The disaster also nearly caused the loss of the library plans in Howard's San Francisco office, had it not been for Henry A. Boese, one of his draftsmen, who broke through police lines on the morning of the great fire and climbed six floors of the condemned Montgomery Street building to rescue drawings of the library, as well as those of the Hearst Plan and other valuable documents.

After postponing the project, the Regents instructed Howard to reduce costs and prepare plans for constructing the library in two phases, the first being a partial but fully operational facility, which would be completed in a second phase when future funds were available. The change in the scope of work caused a dispute over fees between the Regents and Howard, who had nearly completed bid packages for the entire building just prior to the earthquake. Compounding the situation was Howard's frustration with having to work on the design with three Regents' committees in addition to a faculty library committee, causing him to complain that "I sometimes think that it is impossible ever to come to a conclusion in study."[16]

Despite these obstacles, construction of the first phase began in 1907, but the following year was interrupted for several weeks because of a delay in shipping the steel framing from the East Coast. Dependency on the East for steel had increased following the earthquake, when Eastern manufacturers began to underbid local firms to control the market. To keep the job going, stone masons were employed preparing the blocks of Raymond granite, which, despite not being the lowest-bid stone for the project, was used to insure a match with the other buildings of the Hearst Plan. Overcoming these setbacks, on Thanksgiving morning of 1908 the university held a ceremony to lay the cornerstone of the building at the northeast corner of the north wing, and the Greco-Roman monument began to take form.

For the great north facade, what Howard called "the blossom of the library," the architect situated the smaller first-floor reading rooms to form a plinth, upon which a monumental Corinthian colonnade defines the main reading room on the second floor. But the rhythm of the giant-order columns is broken, the facade symmetrically divided in the center to announce the main entrance. On either side of this break, the large colonnade

Columns, Doe Memorial Library

terminates in paired columns at each end, so that the reading room is expressed in two east and west sections. Above the entry two smaller Ionic columns—symbolizing Athena's authority over Ionic states—support a lintel and entablature bearing the inscription "The University Library."

At the east and west gabled ends are the giant Roman-arched windows, interrupting the broken-bed pediment, and flanked on either side with paired Corinthian pilasters. The classical decoration provides a rhythm that unifies the facade and is enriched with allegorical carvings. In the great Corinthian capitals, books are propped open by small, fanged serpents—considered sacred to Athena, goddess of wisdom and knowledge—who coil amidst half-opened acanthus leaves. To ornament the corners of the copper roof cornice, Howard intended to use owl-and-globe figures but settled on foliated forms instead, after President Wheeler objected that the wise birds would be beneath the dignity of the

West facade, Doe Memorial Library

Copper roof ornamentation, Doe Memorial Library

building. When the south block was completed in the second phase, lamps of knowledge were designed into its decorative frieze.

Athena herself (occasionally referred to as the Roman Minerva) appears in bronze in the panel above the north bronze entry doors, and received much attention from President Wheeler before she was cast. The

work of sculptor Melvin Earl Cummings (who at the same time created the panels and urns on Sather Gate and Bridge) was also scrutinized by a faculty expert, who advised on Athena's helmet until he found the clay model to be "archeologically satisfactory." So extensive was the review that Howard eventually intervened on Cummings' behalf, pleading: "As Mr. Cummings has been engaged on this work for many months now, he is anxious to get it out of hand, especially as it requires almost as much attention as a baby.

Athena sculpture by Melvin Earl Cummings, Doe Memorial Library

He cannot leave town for more than a few hours until the head is cast, because of the necessity of keeping it constantly moist."[17]

The main entrance opens to a glazed vestibule that contains an elaborate classical bronze plaque honoring Charles Franklin Doe, who willed the library "to the use of all the recurring generations of the young." Inside is a lobby corridor which originally served the two first-floor reading rooms: to the west, the periodicals room, later to become the reserve book room and now the Morrison Library; and to the east, the Bancroft Library, later the Map Room and presently the library information center. This corridor, now the Bernice Layne Brown Gallery (dedicated in 1989 to honor the wife of former California Governor Edmund G. "Pat" Brown), with its white marble floor and wall panels, was influenced by a similar passage in the Palazzo Farnese in Rome.[18]

At the south end of the lobby, a bifurcated stairway ascends from a marble bench-alcove to the former Catalogue and Delivery Room on the second floor, a space presently used as a study and computer area. This room is relatively intact today with its arched entryways and Corinthian pilasters in Caen stone and doors covered in imported pigskin. Absent are the hanging globe chandeliers and the elegant delivery desk of carved Istrian marble and ornamental bronze that originally graced the room.

From this anteroom, monumental bronze doors lead to what History of Art Professor Loren W. Partridge has called "the greatest architectural space on the Berkeley campus and one of the greatest of the

Main Reading Room, Doe Memorial Library

Beaux-Arts period."[19] Here is the 210-foot long main reading room, filling the full length of the north wing and rising forty-five feet to its coffered elliptical barrel-vault ceiling. Designed for 400 readers (said to be second in size at the time only to the New York Public Library), the room features three large skylights, which combine with the bank of high north windows and the tall Roman-arched end windows to fill the voluminous space with a diffused ambient light. President Wheeler had to be convinced that one large reading room would serve the university well, instead of dividing the space into separate rooms for men and women. Influenced by his Greek scholarship, the president also had to be persuaded that the east and west windows should be large Roman arches to relate to the scale of the space, rather than be formed by Greek columns and entablatures.[20]

  The room was decorated by J. Henry P. Atkins, of the San Francisco design firm Vickery, Atkins and Torrey, working with architect Henry Gutterson, then on Howard's staff. When Howard had contractual difficulties with the Regents, Atkins' firm was put in charge of supervising all the interiors, including the custom oak furniture, shelving, and marble work in Doe, as well as in nearby Boalt (Durant) Hall, which was under construction at the same time. This decision did not rest well with Howard, and when work did not meet his standards he saw it as "another instance of too many cooks spoiling the broth. I don't like to harp on an old, thread-bare subject, but this sort of mix-up is the inevitable result of bringing in two or three different parties to accomplish what should rightly be solely in the architect's hands to manage."[21]

With the exception of the main reading room, the building was planned on a fifteen-foot cubic module. The central core book stack was designed to be ultimately 105 feet square in plan and capped with a skylight to transmit light through nine tiers of floors inlaid with one-inch thick, sand-blasted glass panels. In the first construction phase, only five tiers on the northern half of this planned floor area were built, providing an initial capacity of 300,000 volumes in steel shelving. As the books were being moved into the stacks, complaints came in that attendants were prone to bumping their heads on the low crossbeams. Howard, probably realizing that little could be done about the problem, replied sarcastically: "I think that if the stack attendants will use ordinary precautions they will have no difficulty. Attendants of unusual saltatory tendencies might be given special employment in the Reading Room where the head room is higher."[22]

The remaining portion of the south block, containing seminar rooms encircling the stacks on three sides, was built only to a one-story height in the first phase, and for several years stood with column stubs extending through a temporary roof. The first phase provided only about sixty percent of the final plan, with expectations that it might be another ten to twenty years before the remaining space could be built. But the great north wing was complete. In August 1910, as the finishing touches were applied to the painting and marble work, an ebullient Victor H. Henderson, Secretary of the Regents, reported to Howard (then in Europe) that "the noble proportions and beautiful detail of the rooms stand out most strikingly. And particularly beautiful are the great bronze doors and the bronze work of the main entrance. Athena has taken her place over the door-way."[23]

The second phase, made possible by a 1914 building bond measure, completed the skylight-topped central core to house the stacks, and added four tiers of shelving to the northern half of the space. (The nine tiers of the southern half were equipped with shelving by another bond measure in 1926, increasing the storage capacity to one million volumes, but leaving a central light well between the two stack sections, which was filled in with additional shelving in 1953.) The south block around the stacks was completed with two additional stories and an attic level to house library offices on the west, additional seminar rooms, and a second large reading room on the east, needed to augment the already overcrowded main reading room.

This new reading and periodical room, converted in 1953 to the loan room and presently used for the Government & Social Science Information Service, is the most significant part of the 1914–1917 addition. The second floor space was designed in the style of an Italian Renaissance palace, featuring a carved polychromatic plaster ceiling, twelve chandeliers, and a surrounding frieze decorated with marks of historic publishers and the names of fifteen notable writers and thinkers. Above the pillared north entrance of marble and bronze is the Latin inscription, *BENE LEGERE*

East Reading Room, Doe Memorial Library

SAECLA VINCERE, or "To read well is to vanquish the centuries." Fitting Howard's module, the room is 135 feet long and 45 feet wide, and rises two stories high. The high windows originally bathed the room with east light for the 216 readers, but now admit a more diffused illumination from the lightwell created by the construction of Doe Annex in 1949.

That reduction of daylight, combined with the limited effect of the original chandeliers, resulted in the need for more illumination for card-catalogue users. In 1960 a modern hung ceiling with paneled fixtures was installed, concealing the carved plaster and obscuring the integrity of the grand Beaux-Arts space. Had it not been for a requirement by the State Fire Marshal some fifteen years later that a sprinkler system be installed, the ceiling might still be a lost artifact. But it was rediscovered, and the university redeemed itself by bringing in architect Theodore C. Bernardi, a graduate of Howard's School of Architecture in 1924. Bernardi ingeniously integrated sprinkler heads and custom-designed mercury-vapor lamps into the old ceiling in place of some carefully removed carved rosettes.

The south wall of this room displays the monumental American Revolution battlefield scene, *Washington Rallying the Troops at Monmouth*, painted in 1854 by the artist Emanuel Leutze, of the Dusseldorf School. Created during the same period as Leutze's more famous 1851 scene, *Washington Crossing the Delaware*, now in the Metropolitan Museum of Art, the painting was intended for the nation's capitol, but was eventually acquired by Mrs. Mark Hopkins, who donated it to the university in 1882. First exhibited in Bacon Hall, it was moved to Doe upon its opening in 1911, but was later removed and placed in storage in the basement of Hearst Gymnasium, where it remained, rolled up, until it was discovered after an inquiry in 1964. The painting was restored and exhibited in the University Art Museum (now the University of California, Berkeley Art Museum) for twenty years, until being moved back to Doe and installed in its current location in 1993.

Ten years after the completion of Doe, architect Walter Ratcliff, Jr., formerly of Howard's office, was asked to redesign the old reserve book room at the west end of the first floor, as a special reading room to house the book collection of the late San Francisco attorney Alexander F. Morrison. The 15,000 volumes, along with funds for the renovation, were donated by his wife, May T. Morrison (Class of 1878) who requested that the room be used for recreational reading—similar in concept to the Farnsworth Library at Harvard. Working with Vickery, Atkins and Torrey, who decorated Doe originally, Ratcliff created an attractive retreat featuring a carved plaster ceiling with brass chandeliers, golden oak wall wainscoting, and cork herringbone flooring. The elegant space is appointed with easy chairs and sofas, oak tables, floor lamps, Persian carpets, and, in the Poetry Corner that honors English Professor Josephine Miles, a Fortuny tapestry. The room is also used for noon-time poetry readings and special events.

Across the gallery lobby, the former Bancroft Library and Map Room was renovated as the library information center in 1992–1994 by Esherick Homsey Dodge and Davis in conjunction with their design of the Gardner Stacks. The room, which houses an information desk, catalog terminals and study tables, is finished with wood-paneled wainscoting, custom chandeliers, and a glossy terrazzo tile floor. It also serves as a colonnaded passageway to the circulation desk and underground stacks.

Seismic renovations within Doe in 1996–1997 by Oakland architects Hansen/Murakami/Eshima included demolition of the nine unstable stack tiers and strengthening of the four-story stack core for future reuse of the space, as well as new shear walls, foundations, and a concealed roof truss system in the north wing.

Doe Memorial Library is listed on the National Register of Historic Places, is included in the Berkeley campus designation as a California Registered Historical Landmark, is listed on the State Historic Resources Inventory, and is a City of Berkeley Landmark. It is open during the academic calendar year Monday through Thursday from 9am to 10pm, Friday and Saturday from 9am to 5pm, and Sunday from 1pm to 10pm. Hours vary during summer and other periods. Phone 510–643–4331. The Morrison Library is open during the academic calendar year Monday through Friday from 9am to 5pm. Phone 510–642–3671.

Doe Annex

Constructed as part of the postwar building program, Doe Annex is occupied primarily by the distinguished Bancroft Library, established at the university in 1905 from the collection of California bookseller and historian Hubert Howe Bancroft. Initially housed in the attic of California Hall, the collection was located in Doe Memorial Library prior to moving to the Annex. It is one of the nation's largest libraries of manuscripts, rare books, and special collections, mostly related to the history of the western United States and Latin America, and has special collections dating back some 4,000 years, which include hieroglyphic carvings, papyri, and medieval manuscripts.

Supervising Architect Arthur Brown, Jr., faced the difficult challenge of harmoniously linking a large structure to one of Howard's monuments. In addition, he had to present a compatible relationship to the Campanile and the overall ensemble of the Hearst Plan. Given the size of the Annex, it could only result in compromise. Howard intended for the east facade of Doe to be seen and for light to enter the two-story windows of the East Reading Room. He planned a humanities structure to the east of North Hall, which would then be removed, leaving open space between the two buildings. With North Hall no longer present—the wooden upper floors were razed in 1917 after Wheeler Hall was built, and the concrete basement removed in 1931—Brown faced fewer restrictions.

His design for the five-story, reinforced-concrete structure utilized Beaux-Arts principles, with a symmetrical and hierarchical treatment of the stripped neoclassical facade. From a narrow plinth, the first two floors have a regular window pattern, with taller windows on the first floor, which houses the Edward Heller Reading Room. Rustication reinforces the corners

Doe Annex

of the facade, which on the east features a recessed central entry, simply framed with a modest cornice. The blank wall panels within this entry porch were intended to have inscriptions, which were never executed. A continuous, projecting cornice separates the lower stories from the attic, which has smaller, more closely spaced windows. Capped with a simple cornice and compatible red-tile hipped roof, the Annex returns slightly at its western corners to form recessed entrances leading to the common corridor that links to Doe. The option of using expensive granite was no longer feasible, leaving Brown to use a terracotta facing (which he also used on Sproul Hall) to try to match the texture and color of Doe and the other early Howard buildings. (The building was resurfaced with another facing material in 1985.)

A marble bust of Hubert Howe Bancroft in the lobby is the work of sculptor Johannes Sophus Gelert (1852–1923) and was presented to the university by Bancroft's sons in 1908. Adjacent to the lobby at the entrance to the reading room is the Bancroft Gallery, which has changing exhibitions of materials from the library's collections.

The Bancroft Library is open during the academic year Monday through Thursday from 9am to 6pm, Friday from 9am to 5pm, and Saturday from 1pm to 5pm. Hours vary during summer and other periods. Phone 510–642–3781.

Gardner Stacks

The decision to build underground stacks to the north of Doe Memorial Library was reached following a seismic safety study of the libraries by

Gardner Stacks

San Francisco architects Kaplan, McLaughlin and Diaz in 1981. The new facility, named in honor of David Pierpont Gardner, sixteenth president of the university, replaced the unstable Doe stacks as part of a phased construction program coordinated with seismic renovations of Doe and Moffitt Undergraduate Library. Excavation for the four-level stack structure resulted in a rectangular canyon approximately fifty feet deep, 125 feet wide, and 475 feet long, extending from Moffitt on the west to beyond Doe Annex on the east.

Esherick Homsey Dodge and Davis organized the building in two contiguous sections for seismic and fire safety requirements. Beneath skylit cupolas at the east end are the circulation desk and an atrium stairway that descends to three underground stack levels. These extend to the west where two full levels and a partial mezzanine are illuminated by four skylights that rise to the formal entry terrace of Doe. The two sections are linked by a continuous open circulation spine that connects to Moffitt at the bottom two levels.

Though subterranean, the west section is effectively open and illuminated by the light wells, while the light-colored wood paneling, white walls, soffits and ceilings contribute to the warmth of the space. The east section has private study rooms adjacent to the four-story atrium. The concrete spiral stairway and skylight structure within this space are Brutalist in treatment, a rather incongruous contrast to the articulation of the rest of the facility and especially to Howard's elegant Doe, the mother building. It is well that they are hidden from Athena's view.

A team of thirty students transferred the collection of one and one-half million volumes from the old Doe stacks, at a rate of about 45,000 volumes per day, into the underground addition, which can accommodate about two million volumes. Providing the core collection for the humanities and social sciences, the facility seats about 400 readers. The interconnected library complex is one of the largest academic facilities in the world.

5.   Memorial Glade

Richard Haag, landscape architect, preliminary design; and
Royston Hanamoto Alley & Abey, landscape architects, 1997–1998

Memorial Glade is the topping on the underground layers of the Gardner Stacks. Although the stacks extend beneath only part of the greensward, the structure was inseparably planned with the glade to recapture a portion of the central axis that had been clogged with wooden temporary buildings (T-Buildings) for some fifty years.

The glade was made possible by the War Classes of 1945, 1946, and 1947, who contributed over $1 million to construct it in honor of students, faculty, and staff who served in World War II and to establish an endowment for the Berkeley Roundtable on the International Economy. The gift reflected the philosophy of the classes, according to 1945 alumnus Dick Heggie: "The two projects mirror each other: one looks back to war, and the other forward to peace."[24]

The six remaining T-Buildings, which were among eighteen U.S. Navy surplus buildings acquired by the campus in 1947 to ease postwar space needs, housed classes and services for students spanning six decades. Their removal along with assorted trees—some remaining from the botanical garden that occupied the area from the 1890s to the 1920s— had an immediate and profound impact. It liberated the classical north facade of Doe as Howard had intended it to be seen some eighty years earlier. But instead of being shaped by Beaux-Arts formality, the regained open space became picturesque in form, adapting to the surrounding

Memorial Glade

architectural constraints created in the modern period by the construction of Evans Hall to the east, Moffitt Undergraduate Library to the west, and McCone Hall to the north.

The reconfiguration of the area was planned in general by Skidmore Owings & Merrill architect Philip J. Enquist, in coordination with the design of the Gardner Stacks and the ROMA Design Group's work on the 1990 Long Range Development Plan. It included realignment of University Drive to the north side of the axis, as a curving road within a park. Continuation of the drive in a reverse arc to the Mining Circle was proposed to re-establish a linkage between the open spaces, while accommodating new development at the base of Evans (a site that has since been reevaluated).

Seattle-based landscape architect Richard Haag (Class of 1950) saw in the Enquist plan "an archetypal landscape deeply etched into the collective human memory—the landscape of prospect and refuge." His glade design—completed by Royston Hanamoto Alley and Abey—combined "earthform, tree pattern, and shade . . . in a sequence of spaces (a family of glades) evocative of activities from major planned events to impromptu poetry readings or quiet reflections."[25] It has three elements: the large oval lawn with the terraced library forming a monumental backdrop, a small grove of trident maples (*Acer buergerianum*) along the edge berm, and, across the main east-west pathway, a circular memorial reflecting pool surrounded by coast redwoods (*Sequoia sempervirens*). Thresholds mark the area on the three principal pedestrian walkways in the form of eight-foot-diameter bronze bas-relief medallions bearing an inscription and the university seal.

The grove was first intended to be composed of katsura trees, but because of their size and susceptibility to fungus, trident maples, which produce fall color, were substituted. One-hundred-and-sixty trees were to stand in regimented rows to evoke the image of a military cemetery or a California orchard. But the quick adoption of the new lawn by sun worshippers and Frisbee and volleyball players drew an outcry concerning the number of proposed new trees. Protests included the reduction of open lawn area and concerns that the trees would block the view of Doe. In deference to popular sentiment, the number of trees was reduced to approximately ninety, more closely and randomly spaced. Other mixed woods were included and two small "pocket glades" created along the east berm.

The shallow Memorial Pool, surfaced in reflective polished black granite, is dedicated to members of the war classes and Berkeley students, faculty, and staff who lost their lives in World War II. When the encompassing redwood grove matures, it will create "a cathedral-like place for memory and meditation," as one class member envisioned, "a reminder that a lot of Cal people were involved in an historic effort that made it possible for us to live the way we do today."[26]

6. Moffitt Undergraduate Library

John Carl Warnecke and Associates, 1967–1970;
Esherick, Homsey, Dodge and Davis, alterations, 1992–1993;
Swatt Architects, alterations, 1999–2000

Constructed to serve the growing population of undergraduate students, whose needs differed from the research functions of Doe, Moffitt Undergraduate Library followed a national trend begun with the opening of

Moffitt Undergraduate Library

Lamont Library at Harvard University in 1949. Berkeley's library would honor James Kennedy Moffitt (1865–1955), Regent for thirty-seven years and 1886 graduate who was active in student affairs and president of the California Alumni Association.

As the university approached its centennial celebration in 1968, the new library was linked to the beautification of the campus. Ironically, the siting of Moffitt—like Evans Hall to the east—would intrude upon Howard's central axis, and, in addition, interrupt the cross-axial relationship between Haviland and California Halls.

It was initially planned to be sited approximately 140 feet west of its present location, but was changed to be closer to Doe and to better integrate with its natural setting. The central location provided convenient student access and required the relocation of University Drive to a curving route along the north side of the axis. When redwood trees near Strawberry Creek were endangered by this realignment, the road was redesigned following a campus protest (see Wickson Natural Area, Walk 3).

Funded by a state bond issue, the $4 million modernist concrete-frame library was designed to accommodate a collection of 150,000 volumes and provide study and reading space for 1,800 undergraduates. John Carl Warnecke and Associates organized the library in two sections, a five-story pavilion of reading rooms linked to a smaller three-story east wing of classrooms and offices. The building was suppressed at the lower levels to reduce its presence in the planted surroundings, with the main entrance on the south side at mid-level. The open reading rooms, supported by waffle slabs and a post-and-beam system, extend into the landscape with a sunken west courtyard at ground level and surrounding cantilevered terraces or balconies at the top three floors. The deep overhangs and horizontally proportioned balcony rails provide a lightness suggestive of a Japanese garden pavilion.

Seismic strengthening by Esherick, Homsey, Dodge and Davis in 1993 modified the openness of the pavilion by adding four windowed shear walls on the north and south facades. Subsequent interior alterations by Swatt Architects included the Free Speech Movement (FSM) Café, which gave new life to the west terrace for outdoor dining. Funded from a three-part $3.5 million gift from alumnus Stephen M. Silberstein in recognition of the FSM and in memory of its leader, Mario Savio, the cafe was dedicated in February 2000, some thirty-six years after the eventful demonstration that rocked Sproul Plaza (see Walk 4). The gift also included funding for the Mario Savio/FSM Endowment and the FSM Archives at the Bancroft Library.

The FSM Café in Moffitt Undergraduate Library is generally open Monday through Thursday from 7am to 2am, Saturday from 7am to 5pm, and Sunday from 1pm to 2am.

California Hall

7. California Hall

John Galen Howard, 1903–1905;
Germano Milono with Walter T. Steilberg, alterations, 1968–1970;
Hansen/Murakami/Eshima, seismic alterations, 1991

The first of Howard's buildings to be occupied, California Hall originally served a dual purpose, as both a major classroom building and the busy headquarters of President Wheeler's administration. The three-story steel-frame structure is clad in Raymond granite laid in alternating large and small courses that contribute horizontal proportion and scale to the 200-foot long facade. Set atop a plinth, the symmetrically composed elevations each feature a centrally placed hooded doorway flanked by regularly spaced wood casement windows. These have a hier-archical treatment, those on the first floor with bracketed granite hoods, and the smaller second floor windows simply framed with slightly projecting sills. A frieze of rosette medallions beneath the cornice creates a horizontal rhythm around the facade. The main entry was designed to be the ornamented and inscribed west doorway, but was shifted to the less elaborate east doorway, as the campus became oriented to Sather Gate.

Classical ornamentation, California Hall

In its original configuration, California Hall contained a large lecture hall, classrooms, and academic offices on the first floor and the administrative offices on the second. In the basement were housed palaeontological collections and storage of files and publications, as well as mechanical equipment. Howard designed the interior to be flexible, using metal-stud and plaster partitions between rooms arranged on a fifteen- by twenty-five-foot module, which was reflected in the exterior window spacing.

The tiered lecture hall accommodated about 500 students and occupied the north end of the first floor. As one of the few early large assembly areas, it was used regularly for classes in history, English, and botany, as well as for faculty meetings, but was notorious for its acoustical shortcomings. Various experts were consulted and remedies tried, such as stringing wires from the paneled plaster ceiling and installing tarpaulins to the walls. A Harvard professor even recommended fitting the room with unsightly swaths of hair-felt and cheesecloth, causing Howard to object to President Wheeler that "we who have to do with buildings for the University, are betwixt the devil and the deep sea. Counsels of perfection in one direction lead us into the jaws of disaster in another."[27] The north entrance to the building originally opened behind the podium of this room, to enable lectures to be held in the evening when the rest of the building was closed.

While the student domain of the first floor was rather utilitarian in appearance with exposed structure and old-ivory tinted walls, the second floor was a dignified environment for the administrators. Here Howard designed a Roman atrium, a wide lobby-corridor lined on both sides by Tuscan colonnades supporting a carved plaster frieze and glass ceiling that transmitted filtered daylight from the attic skylight above. Opening off this central chamber were wood-paneled peripheral offices for the President and his staff, deans, and Regents' officers, as well as a faculty room and other administrative functions. Wood-frame windows facing the corridor allowed the offices to benefit from the skylight and also provided openings for business to be conducted "as in the main office of a bank." Solid oak or mahogany furnishings were used as well as cork carpet, which was praised for being "soft to the foot and soundless."[28]

The attic space was used almost immediately for housing some 50,000 volumes and 100,000 manuscripts of the newly acquired Bancroft Library. However, it had inadequate ventilation, heating, and lighting, and was not improved until 1911, when it was occupied by the drawing department. Its use necessitated replacement of the glass ceiling of the second-floor atrium with heavier glass "sidewalk lights" which could double as the attic floor.

With mechanical systems often ineffective around the turn of the century, ventilation problems were not confined to the building's attic.

Howard was swamped with early complaints, such as: "President Wheeler and Mrs. Cheney won't keep their windows shut, declaring that they cannot get enough air to breathe simply through the ventilating system."[29] When Howard advised that occupants must keep the casement windows closed to permit the mechanical system to work properly, things only worsened: "Last Friday we tried closing the windows in the big lecture room . . . and leaving the ventilation to the ventilating plant. Within fifteen minutes two men had fainted and had to be carried out."[30]

Following President Wheeler, California Hall was home to Presidents David Prescott Barrows, William Wallace Campbell, and Robert Gordon Sproul, who moved to the newly-built Administration Building (Sproul Hall) in 1941 (see Walk 4). In the late 1960s—in what was not a great bureaucratic moment—the grand atrium-lobby and other original interior spaces were gutted and modernized as offices for the Chancellor and Graduate Division. Since 1970 Chancellors Roger W. Heyns, Albert H. Bowker, Ira Michael Heyman, Chang-Lin Tien, and Robert M. Berdahl have occupied the building.

In 1910 Howard added the brick herringbone-pattern sidewalks and the paved road terminating in the elongated cul-de-sac between California Hall and Doe Memorial Library, which was then under construction but influencing greater attention to the grounds in its vicinity. The sloping grass strip in the middle of the turn-around was soon claimed by men of the sophomore class who would take pleasure in hazing intruding freshmen, intimidating them with such ditties as: "If in the sun ye fain would yawn; Rest ye not on Sophomore Lawn." In response, the freshmen would raid the lawn at night, burning their class numerals into the grass. In time hazing was prohibited and the name and legacy of Sophomore Lawn faded from memory. Since the return of the administration to California Hall, the lawn has occasionally been used for political protests and demonstrations. Facing the building across the lawn are the small carved marble cherubs that flank the Miller Clock, installed in 1928 in memory of Albert Miller, Regent of the university from 1887 to 1900.

California Hall is listed on the National Register of Historic Places, is included in the Berkeley campus designation as a California Registered Historical Landmark, is listed on the State Historic Resources Inventory, and is a City of Berkeley Landmark.

Durant Hall

8. **Durant Hall** *John Galen Howard, 1909–1911*

Built to house the School of Jurisprudence, Durant Hall is the northern half of an uncompleted building-couplet planned as a balance to California Hall across Campanile Way. It was the first permanent home for the school, which developed from a course in Roman Law taught in 1882 by Latin instructor William Carey Jones, who later become the school's first dean.

Originally named Boalt Hall, the building commemorated Judge John Henry Boalt, an early authority of mining, corporate, and patent law in California, who took an interest in the university prior to its move from Oakland to Berkeley in 1873. His widow, Elizabeth Josselyn Boalt, funded two-thirds of the construction with a gift of $100,000, along with the establishment of two professorships. The remaining third was met by subscriptions of $50,000 from seventy-five members of the state bench and bar to fund the Lawyers Memorial Hall, the main reading room of the law library.

The three-level steel-frame and concrete structure is the same width (seventy feet) as California Hall and nearly square in plan, designed to connect by colonnade and bridge to its future companion building of similar size to the south. President Wheeler at first contemplated that Boalt would contain only recitation rooms and offices, with the future southern half used for the library and a large lecture room. Later plans by Howard designated the second building for the department of philosophy; it was envisioned as an identical twin to Boalt, except for a projecting bay on its south facade. A classical pediment would have formed the entrance to the pair at their central link.

The granite facade is divided into a half-basement level that forms a plinth for the first and second floors. The east and west facades of this upper section each have a central inset of three bays flanked by two corner bays. These center bays, which are defined by Tuscan pilasters, are differentiated by single windows with decorative friezes and curved pediments on the first floor, and paired windows divided by Doric columns above. The wood double-hung windows reflected a change in policy by the Regents in 1906 to no longer use French, or casement, windows as was done in California Hall. The north and south end facades each feature a central flat hood supported by double-curved consoles with volutes at the recessed entrances. Paired oak-framed entry doors, which open to a split-level landing between the basement and first floors, are glazed and ornamented with metal rosettes and surmounted by oak-framed transoms. Consistent with Howard's adjacent buildings, Durant is crowned with a classical entablature and a hipped red mission-tile roof that culminates in a copper-framed skylight.

Howard was asked to give the interior "the atmosphere and flavor of a club-house—a real intellectual and spiritual home for the law students."[31] Space for student organizations was provided in the half-basement, while the first floor housed classrooms accessed from a wide central lobby-corridor, trimmed in oak and white Italian marble and with a plaster vaulted ceiling. For this space, as well on the second floor, Howard designed special "lamp of learning" light fixtures engraved on the bottom with the university seal. Extra-wide oak-framed doors admit additional light to the corridor through diffused glazing.

Corridor with "lamps of learning," Durant Hall

A marble stairway with a cast-iron balustrade ascends to the second floor stair hall, which opens to two small meeting rooms and, through an inscribed doorway, The Lawyers Memorial Hall, one of Howard's significant interiors. This reading room is illuminated by a central skylight, which springs from a cove ceiling above a denticulated cornice, supported by

Lawyers Memorial Hall, Durant Hall

Chinese lion sculpture, Durant Hall

Doric columns and pilasters of Siena marble. Four custom chandeliers hang beneath the skylight, while additional "lamps of learning" accentuate adjacent spaces and the stairway lobby that leads to the hall. The original mahogany reading tables were furnished by J. Henry P. Atkins, of the San Francisco design firm Vickery, Atkins and Torrey, who also contributed to the interior of Doe Memorial Library. The south side of the hall contains two levels of book stacks, adjacent to faculty offices.

The law library was designed to accommodate about 100 readers and 17,000 volumes, but by the late 1930s these numbers had more than tripled, causing severe overcrowding and underscoring the need for a larger school. When the new Law Building (see Walk 5) was built in the southeast corner of campus in 1951, the Boalt name was transferred to its west wing. The old building was then renamed for the first president of the university, Henry Durant (1870–1872), a name originally applied to Minor Hall in 1949.

The building presently houses the Department of East Asian Languages and, in the Memorial Hall, the East Asian Library, a comprehensive research collection of materials in Chinese, Japanese, Korean, Manchu, Mongolian, and Tibetan. In relation to this use, a pair of stone Buddhistic Lions, or Dogs of Fo, were installed at the south entrance, as they would be placed as traditional guardians at the gate of a Buddhist temple, the lion with a ball of silk brocade facing the lioness with her cub. The pair were moved in the 1980s from the Old Art Gallery (see Walk 5), where they were originally placed in 1934, purchased from a San Francisco importer by art patron Albert Bender, who also raised funds to furnish the gallery.

Durant Hall is listed on the National Register of Historic Places, is included in the Berkeley campus designation as a California Registered Historical Landmark, is listed on the State Historic Resources Inventory, and is a City of Berkeley Landmark. The East Asian Library is open during the academic calendar year Monday through Thursday from 9am to 7pm, Friday from 9am to 5pm, and Saturday and Sunday from 1pm to 5pm. Phone 510–642–2556.

9. Dwinelle Hall

Weihe, Frick & Kruse, with Eckbo Royston & Williams, landscape architects, 1950–1952;
Simon Martin-Vegue Winkelstein Moris, addition and alterations, 1996–1998

Containing classrooms, auditoriums and offices for the humanities, Dwinelle Hall was one of several buildings constructed to meet the needs of the expanding enrollment following World War II. It was sited to provide convenient access for students and faculty, reflecting the shift of the

Dwinelle Hall

campus center southward towards Sather Gate. The $3.5 million building was named in honor of Regent John Whipple Dwinelle, who as a member of the state legislature introduced the bill to establish the university in 1868.

Consisting of a three-story south classroom block with over eighty-five classrooms and three large lecture halls, and a four-story north office block of about 300 faculty offices, the building challenged students with over a mile of rambling corridors. Quickly dubbed "a modern maze," it became the subject of tales about students, who, as author William Rodarmor described, would "enter Dwinelle in their freshman year and emerge, blinking in the sunshine, just in time for graduation."[32] Rumors abounded that Dwinelle was either designed as two hastily combined separate buildings or the product of two unacquainted architects. But Ernest E. Weihe, Edward L. Frick, and Lawrence A. Kruse all worked for classical architects John Bakewell, Jr., and Arthur Brown, Jr., before forming their partnership during World War II.

Weihe and Frick both studied at the École des Beaux-Arts in Paris (Kruse was Harvard trained), and this influence can be seen in the main east facade of Dwinelle, with its stripped neoclassical style and symmetrical side wings that engage Dwinelle Plaza. These wings actually splay in plan to form a subtle transition: the north wing and its adjacent office block align with Howard's central axis and classical core of buildings, while the south wing parallels Arthur Brown's Sproul Hall (1941) and the city grid to the south. The style and red-tile hipped roof give the building a quiet compatibility with Howard's granite ensemble, a quality described as "a California flavor" by the architects. Granite though was no longer a viable facing option, and the reinforced-concrete building was finished in cement plaster. Landscaping of the building by Eckbo Royston & Williams included Dwinelle Plaza, as well as the paved forecourt to Wheeler Hall, bench alcoves along Sather Road, and repaving of Sather Bridge.

The north block of Dwinelle housed the office of the first Berkeley Chancellor, Clark Kerr, and succeeding Chancellors Glenn T. Seaborg, Edward W. Strong, Martin Meyerson, and Roger W. Heyns, who moved to California Hall in 1970. (In 1993, the interior courtyard of the north office block was named in honor of Ishi, the last known member of the Yahi tribe of California Native Americans, whom anthropology professor Alfred Kroeber brought to the university's Museum of Anthropology in San Francisco in 1911 to enable the study of Yahi language and culture.) The 1998 addition to Dwinelle by Simon Martin-Vegue Winkelstein Moris expanded the building by about twenty percent without increasing its footprint. The $10 million state-funded project added two compatible stories to the north block for offices and graduate instruction and research, and converted the south block attic for additional offices.

Wheeler Hall

10. Wheeler Hall

John Galen Howard, 1915–1917; DeMars and Wells, auditorium alterations, 1973;
Hansen/Murakami/Eshima, seismic alterations, 1988–1989

In June 1915 when the Regents named their new classroom and humanities building "Benjamin Ide Wheeler Hall," they broke with the tradition of not honoring living individuals. It was a special tribute to the president, then in his sixteenth remarkable year as the university's administrative head. "Here in this stately hall," Wheeler said at the cornerstone ceremony the following Charter Day, "each generation will transmit to its successors the lessons of the past. . . . Go now to thy place, old stone. Take up thy long burden of the years."[33]

This stately hall, the fourth of Howard's central cluster of classical buildings, was designed with a south-facing main entrance that recognized the shift in campus orientation from the west. Its site directly south of Doe was originally planned for a Library Annex, while the humanities were to be housed in two buildings to the east of North and South Halls. It fulfilled an acute need for classrooms, a large auditorium, and faculty offices, resulting from the surge in campus enrollment and the removal of old North Hall, which had been a worrisome fire hazard since the groundbreaking of Doe to its west in 1907.

Funded by the state bond measure of 1914, the neoclassical building is composed of four stories and a basement in a nearly square

Apollo sculpture, Wheeler Hall

plan. Peripheral classrooms and offices are arranged around a central core, originally planned as an interior court but occupied on the first three stories by the much-needed auditorium. The French Baroque facade is organized hierarchically and is formidably expressed on the principal south elevation. The first story, with seven arched doorways leading to the auditorium lobby and one at each end leading to the corridors, is composed as a rusticated base. Rising above, six Ionic columns extend to the height of the middle two floors in the center of the facade, while the pilastered stairwell bays at each end feature an arched window, topped with the sculpted head of Apollo, representing the light of truth. At the attic level, the rhythm of the colonnade below is echoed with allegorical elements, as described by Howard, in six "urn-shaped lamps, which, with their flames, symbolize the light of learning. The lamps are decorated with heads of rams, symbolizing procreant power, and garlands, symbolizing the flowers of wisdom."

This rich facade, gleaming white in the sunlight, is one of the most impressive views of Howard's classical ensemble, just inside Sather Gate with Durant and California Halls and Doe Library to the north and the Campanile ascending to the east. The Raymond granite, clad over the building's steel frame, matches that of Howard's neighboring structures, although its use became doubtful when a strike was called by granite cutters in 1915, causing the Regents to consider concrete with a plaster finish as an alternative. The availability of steel, which had to be shipped from the East Coast, also caused concern when the Panama Canal was blockaded during World War I. The Regents authorized the final order to be sent by rail, after a previous shipment by water had to be diverted through the Straits of Magellan.

The auditorium lobby features groin vaults and is illuminated by fanlight windows within the entry arches. The original 1,000-seat auditorium featured a central skylight and carved wooden ceiling with deep octagonal coffers and decorative rosettes. But on a January night in 1969, it was destroyed by a fire suspected but never proven to be arson. In addition to being the main lecture hall, it had been used for student meetings and memorable dramatic performances, including student actor Gregory Peck's first starring role in a 1939 production of Eugene O'Neill's *Anna Christie*. One professor who lectured there expressed what many felt at its loss: "It was almost a sacred hall to me—and it actually took me two days to get over the sadness of its wilful destruction."[34] Despite its aesthetic and senti-

Lobby, Wheeler Hall

mental appeal, the auditorium had some practical shortcomings. Howard designed it primarily for lectures, and its limited stage facilities made it a difficult place to perform. And, as with Howard's large lecture room in California Hall, the acoustics were problematic, as were the sightlines. The redesign of the space by architects Vernon DeMars and John Wells in 1973 reduced the seating to about 800 but improved ventilation, lighting, and conditions for performances.

The dedication of Wheeler on Commencement Day in May 1917 was a ceremonial milestone in campus traditions, as it simultaneously marked the end of North Hall, which was soon to be demolished (except for its concrete basement, which would continue in use until 1931). Wheeler would accommodate over three times the number of students and four times the number of faculty as the old wooden building, which had also served as a student center and gathering place. An alumni pilgrimage was made from Faculty Glade to the old building, where farewell exercises were held, followed by a procession to transfer "the lares and penates of student tradition to Wheeler Hall." While the adequate reestablishment of a student center would not be realized until the opening of Stephens Hall in 1923, the sunny steps of Wheeler became a popular spot, supplanting those of North Hall. Tradition found men students claiming the western portion, while women gathered at the eastern end and under the original Wheeler Oak, a shady spot reserved for them at the request of President Wheeler. "Meet you at North Hall steps," was gradually replaced by "Meet you at the oak." A

plaque in the pavement near the present oak (planted in 1951) commemorates the original tree, which dated from 1824 but was lost to disease in 1934.

Wheeler Hall is listed on the National Register of Historic Places, is
included in the Berkeley campus designation as a California Registered
Historical Landmark, is listed on the State Historic Resources Inventory, and
is a City of Berkeley Landmark.

11. Stephens Hall, Moses Hall, and The Class of 1925 Courtyard

Stephens Hall

> *John Galen Howard, 1923; George W. Kelham, alterations, 1936; Germano Milono, interior alterations, 1964*

Moses Hall   *George W. Kelham, 1931; Germano Milono, interior alterations, 1965–1967*

The Class of 1925 Courtyard

> *George W. Kelham, 1931; Joanna Kaufman, campus landscape architect, landscaping, 1982*

Among the priorities described by President Wheeler in his first report to
the Governor of California in November 1900 was an "Alumni hall which
shall form the center of the daily social life of the students, alumni, and
teachers." Wheeler envisioned a facility modeled after Houston Hall (1895)
at the University of Pennsylvania, the first student union in the nation and

Stephens Hall

one based on the competition-winning design of then students William C. Hays and M. B. Medary, Jr., who were named assistant architects for the project. (Coincidentally, Hays later became the junior partner of John Galen Howard and a professor of architecture at Berkeley; he designed Giannini Hall and contributed to the design of Doe Memorial Library and other Berkeley campus buildings.) Like that building, Berkeley's hall would resemble a student club, equipped with lounges, billiard rooms, dining facilities, shops, and offices for the Associated Students, organizations, and college publications. It was also seen as a place where students and faculty could meet and returning alumni could visit.

Since 1873, some of these activities had shared the concrete basement of North Hall with the armory of the university cadets. After the upper three floors of the building were removed in 1917, the basement continued to be used, while funding was sought for a real student union, "a common gathering-place for student life where the spirit of democracy may flourish wholesomely." Added impetus was created with the unexpected death in 1919 of History Professor Henry Morse Stephens, cherished deeply by students, faculty and alumni. Stephens, who was born in Scotland, was educated in England, earning his degree at Oxford University, where he later lectured, as well as at Cambridge University. When he moved to Cornell University in 1894, he became a close friend and faculty colleague of Wheeler, who later recruited him to join the Berkeley faculty in 1902. During his tenure, Stephens was instrumental in the establishment of the Bancroft Library and was a strong supporter of student self-government and honorary organizations. Shortly after Stephens' death, Wheeler, in the last commencement address of his presidency, characterized his old friend as "one who was gifted beyond all ordinary measure in stirring young men and women to realize the power that was in them and to fulfil it." Those young men and women, students and alumni as well as faculty members, were also stirred to create the Stephens Memorial Union. Their subscriptions of approximately $225,000 combined with $175,000 appropriated from Associated Students' funds to make the long-identified need a reality.

Howard explored different options for the union on sites south of where Valley Life Sciences Building is now located. The site finally selected did not conform with his 1914 Plan, which maintained an open axis from the Campanile to athletic facilities proposed south of Strawberry Creek. However, the decision to instead place the football stadium at the mouth of Strawberry Canyon changed this relationship and probably influenced the siting of the union.

Howard's choice of the Tudor or Collegiate Gothic style for the building may have recalled Stephens' associations with Oxford and Cambridge. The concrete building is characterized by its octagonal turrets, oriel windows, and grouped chimneys. The parapets were originally

Vaulted passageway, Stephens Hall

perforated with decorative quatrefoils and other motifs but were rebuilt as solid walls during structural alterations by George Kelham in 1936. It is the only one of Howard's permanent campus buildings that departs from a classical or Beaux-Arts theme. But he adapted the style effectively, using informal massing to step down from the upper entrance to the winding creek and Faculty Glade. He organized the union into two wings linked by the vaulted entrance passageway that extends through the building. This round-arched entryway has three ribbed vaults and also serves as a portal to the glade via the south stairway and the Class of 1923 Bridge that spans the creek.

The larger five-level west wing originally contained the Student Cooperative Store on the basement and mezzanine floors, an area now occupied by the Ethnic Studies Library and the International and Area Studies Teaching Program. The store opened onto both the courtyard to the west and the bridge to the east, where the "Ink Well," an octagonal kiosk, dispensed an endless supply of fountain-pen ink for thirty years. The floor above, now used for academic programs and centers, contained the men's clubrooms and "Tap Room." The cloistered terrace that overlooks the creek and glade from this level was then a popular gathering place for students. The floor above with the smaller terrace contained the women's clubrooms and now houses the Academic Senate office and research centers. The smaller east wing originally contained offices for athletic tickets, publications, the Associated Students, and the Alumni Association and is now occupied by various programs and research centers.

Occupying the central tower on the floor above is the Stephens Memorial Room, one of Howard's notable interiors, originally furnished in style and intended for special occasions, but now used as a Phi Beta Kappa and Graduate Lounge. Modeled after an Oxford commons room, this two-story space is illuminated at each end by bay windows that are aligned with the north-south axis of the Campanile—a brilliant way for Howard to form a transition from the Beaux-Arts ensemble to the informal creek-side union. The monumental room has a walk-in fireplace with a black marble hearth and surround, an inscribed gift of the Class of 1921. It is equipped with original wrought-iron dragonhead andirons and candelabras. Above the fireplace is an oil portrait of Stephens framed in an oak surround that is integrated with oak wainscoting lining the east and west sides of the room. Carved Corinthian pilasters and rosettes decorate this paneling, which also functions as built-in cabinetry.

Oak detail, Stephens Memorial Room, Stephens Hall

Opposite the fireplace is an exquisitely carved oak entablature supported by large Corinthian pilasters, which flank carved doors that originally opened to the adjacent paneled student-council meeting room. Wood beams with polychromatic motifs span the room, which features a pair of brass chandeliers.

Stephens Memorial Union opened in February 1923 and was formally dedicated the following month on the afternoon of a university open house attended by Governor Friend W. Richardson and a delegation of 600 from the State Legislature. It served as the student union until completion of King Student Union in 1962 and the following year was renamed Henry Morse Stephens Hall.

Stephens Hall is listed on the State Historic Resources Inventory.

Moses Hall

Moses Hall—originally Eshleman Hall—was built as a companion to Stephens Hall, primarily to house the student publication offices that were scattered in various locations. These included the newspaper *The Daily Californian*, the annual yearbook *The Blue and Gold*, the humor magazine *Pelican*, the literary magazine *Occident*, the *California Engineer*, and the Associated Students' News Bureau. These activities energized the building with the journalistic fervor of newsroom editors, reporters, advertising managers, and sales staff. In accompaniment were the practice tones and activities of the Associated Students' Band, Glee Club, Treble Clef, Little Theatre, and Debating, which also occupied the building. As the 1943 edition of *The Blue and Gold* quipped: "Eshleman's inmates stay up all night to rehearse and meet dead lines, make big deals all day and even attend an occasional class."

Moses Hall

Funded by the Associated Students and the state, the building was initially named as a memorial to alumnus John Morton Eshleman (1876–1916), former student body president (1901–1902) and Regent (1915–1916) who served the state as a legislator, chairman of the railroad commission, and Lieutenant Governor (1915–1916). In 1963, prior to completion of the new Eshleman Hall, the student office building in the Student Center, the building was renamed in honor of Bernard Moses, professor of history and political science, who was considered the father of the social

Class of 1925 Courtyard

sciences at the University of California. The renaming reflected the use of the building at that time for the Bureau of Public Administration, now the Institute of Governmental Studies (IGS), and the Institute of Industrial Relations. IGS and other institutes and programs as well as the Department of Philosophy occupy the building today.

George Kelham fit his building between the bank of Strawberry Creek and South Drive, creating a two-building student center with Stephens across a central courtyard. This courtyard—variably called "Stephens Union Court" or "Eshleman Court"—became the social cross-roads of campus, a "market place of hawkers" of student magazines, dance bids, and theatre tickets, as well a place for election balloting and special auctions. It was formally named the Class of 1925 Courtyard in 1984, following landscape improvements funded by the same class that donated the steps some sixty years earlier.

Moses is approximately L-shaped in plan, with a three-story east wing linked at a central entry tower to a stepped-down west wing. To harmonize with Stephens, Kelham used a compatible Tudor or Collegiate Gothic style, but with different detailing. He topped the entry tower and its octagonal turret with crenellated parapets, and introduced a hint of the Moderne with geometric diamond-and-square motifs cast into the parapets of the wings. Unlike Howard's round arch on Stephens, Kelham used a slightly pointed Tudor archway at his entry. And whereas Stephens was treated in a cement plaster finish, Kelham left the rough texture of the

horizontal form-boards exposed. This was typical of all his campus buildings, which also featured finely executed cast-in-place details. Examples of
this work can be seen above the entry arch, where the university seal is
flanked by two shields bearing images of printing presses, representing the
building's original users. The moldings of the arch and the window above
are of similar quality.

Although most of the interior of Moses has been reconfigured,
some notable spaces retain the character of the original design. Tudor
arches are repeated throughout the second-floor entry and third-floor stairway loggia, which is illuminated by skylights and has solid concrete railings
pierced with decorative quatrefoils. A small auditorium at the northeast corner of the third floor has been altered for a graduate student lounge and
office cubicles, but its wooden floor and stage remain intact. The exterior
north facade of the building reflects this use by its lack of fenestration at the
stage wall.

The finest space—one of Kelham's notable campus interiors—is the
former Eshleman Memorial Publications Library, located at the southeast
corner of the third floor. It is now the Howison Philosophy Library and consists of a main reading room with open mezzanine stacks on one side. The
reading room emulates the Stephens Memorial Room with its two-story
height and tall end bay windows, which form oriels on the exterior similar
to those on Stephens. Like the Stephens Room, it features a large fireplace,
but of white marble with an oak surround that has pilasters with foliated
capitals. Arched beams that rest on carved foliated corbels support the sloping ceiling, from which three large bronze chandeliers are suspended.
Columns with foliated plaster friezes carry the load from the corbels on the
mezzanine side of the room. The open mezzanine stack, accessed by small
stairways at either end, resembles, at a smaller scale, the Morrison Library
in Doe Memorial Library.

The Howison Philosophy Library in Moses Hall is open during the
academic calendar year Monday through Friday from 9am to 6pm. Phone
510–642–6516.

Howison Philosophy Library, Moses Hall; former Eshleman Memorial Publications Library

Central Campus Northeast and Northside

Sculpture by Edmund Schultz Beckum, near McLaughlin Hall

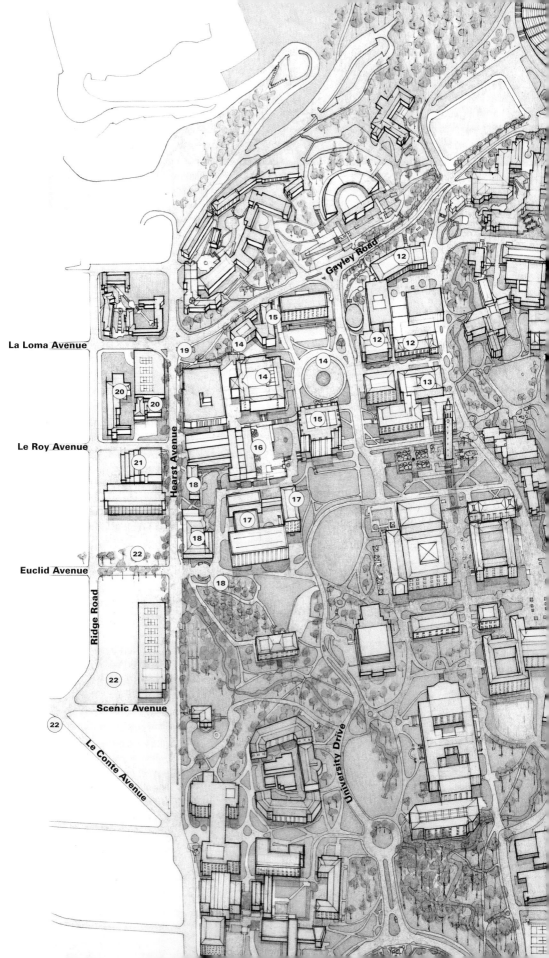

La Loma Avenue

Le Roy Avenue

Euclid Avenue

Scenic Avenue

Ridge Road

Hearst Avenue

Gayley Road

University Drive

Le Conte Avenue

12
12
12
12
13
14
14
14
15
15
15
16
17
17
18
18
18
18
19
20
20
21
22
22
22
22

Mining, Atomic Science, and "The Ark"

Home to two academic precincts—Mathematics and Physical Sciences, and Engineering and Earth Sciences—this diverse Walk is imbued with the history of world-awakening scientific discovery, the beneficence of Phoebe Apperson Hearst, and the legacy of John Galen Howard.

It was here that the atomic age emerged, where Ernest O. Lawrence invented the first cyclotron in LeConte Hall in 1929. In neighboring Gilman Hall in 1941, scientists Glenn T. Seaborg and Edwin M. McMillan discovered the world's first synthetic element, called plutonium-238. And, also in LeConte, a team of theoretical physicists led by J. Robert Oppenheimer developed the workings of the atomic bomb in 1942. While standing between these two similar classical—and otherwise modest—buildings, it is impossible not to contemplate their place in scientific history and world events.

The area is rooted in the nineteenth century, when the first buildings dedicated to chemistry and engineering established the pattern of designated academic areas that influenced future development. It is now a complex of eclectic architectural styles—Beaux-Arts, neoclassical, modern, and postmodern—that exemplify the periods of growth and change spanning the twentieth century.

Anshen and Allen's three-building plaza complex of Chemistry's Latimer (1960–63) and Hildebrand (1963–66) Halls and the oval lecture pavilion Pimentel Hall (1963–64) replaced the old cluster of physics and chemistry buildings, where early scientific history was made. A trophy from

Old Chemistry Building, 1905

that period, the wooden cupola from Clinton Day's Chemistry Building (1891), is the only survivor, installed on the plaza between Gilman and Hildebrand. The beloved L-shaped brick building that it topped was Dutch-Gothic in style, with stepped gables, ogee roofs, and decorative brick buttresses, corbels and cornices. Appended to Day's building was Howard's concrete Chemistry Auditorium (1913). Also removed was the Old Radiation Laboratory (Frederick G. Hesse, 1885; addition, Howard, 1911), a wood-frame building that began as the Mechanic Arts Laboratory (1885–1907), then became the Civil Engineering Testing Laboratory (1907–1931), until it was remodeled to house the thirty-seven-inch cyclotron and the pioneering research of Lawrence. Another Howard building razed was the Chemistry Annex (1915), a three-story wooden laboratory building that relied only on windows to ventilate its teaching labs of noxious gases and was fondly known as "The Rat House" by its graduate-student occupants. Removed from the site of Pimentel was the Crocker Radiation Laboratory (George W. Kelham, 1937), which housed Lawrence's sixty-inch cyclotron, and Howard's concrete Freshman Chemical Laboratory (1915).

Across the esplanade, Campbell Hall (Warnecke & Warnecke, 1957–59) was the first of the modern boxes topped with a "McLaughlin Hat." The name derived from the influence of Regent Donald H. McLaughlin, chairman of the Committee on Campus Planning, who promoted the use of red-tile roofs to avoid flat-top boxes and to relate to the older campus buildings. McLaughlin's idea was not lacking in merit, but the fitting of the "hat" to the simple box seemed to "caricature the neo-classical monuments," as architectural critic Allan Temko saw it.[1] The capped-box trend would continue with Birge Hall (also Warnecke & Warnecke) to the west of LeConte, and Barker Hall (Wurster, Bernardi & Emmons) in the northwest part of campus, both completed in 1964. But McLaughlin's concern for the architectural appearance of Campbell was understandable, given its prominent site on the south side of the Mining Circle and its presence in defining the north-south esplanade between the Chemistry and Physics groups. To clear the site, one of the earliest campus buildings was removed, the four-story stone and brick Mining and Mechanic Arts Building (Alfred A. Bennett, 1879, later named the Civil Engineering Building and the Anthropological Museum), which occupied the north end of the esplanade.

To the north of the Chemistry complex, the Hearst Memorial Mining Building, the first building initiated in Howard's Beaux-Arts ensemble, stands as the focal point of the area and one of the historic treasures of the university. The building and its forecourt Mining Circle are remnants of his Hearst Plan, whose great central axis was unfortunately blocked by Gardner Dailey's Brutalist high-rise, Evans Hall, in the late 1960s. Stanley Hall (Michael Goodman, 1950–52) was an inadequate substitute for the domed auditorium that Howard visualized at the head of the axis. But its site to the east of the Circle will be given a second chance with the planned replacement of Stanley by a new molecular engineering complex (Zimmer Gunsul Frasca).

The north edge of the central campus contains two additional Howard buildings of an entirely different nature and with a rich history tied to the education of many Bay Area architects, some of whom later taught or designed buildings on campus. Shingled North Gate Hall (originally the Architecture Building or "The Ark") was initially completed in 1906 to house Howard's department of architecture as well as his office as supervising architect for the execution of the Hearst Plan. Its neighbor, the Naval Architecture Building (originally the Drawing Building) went up eight years later, like North Gate Hall, as a temporary structure to relieve space shortages.

It was a convenient location for Howard, who—like architects Bernard Maybeck and Almeric Coxhead—lived in Northside (called "Northgate" in the past), an area that attracted other artists and intellectuals as well. It was also home to poet and naturalist Charles Keeler, who advocated the philosophy of the American Arts and Crafts Movement through the use of natural materials and construction in harmony with the Berkeley Hills. His principles for residential design were influenced by the rustic homes of Maybeck and espoused by the Hillside Club, which was founded in 1898 and published Keeler's book *The Simple Home* in 1904. By the early 1920s Northside was transformed from a late-Victorian community to one filled out with homes influenced by Keeler's philosophy. Brown-shingle and clinker-brick houses, designed by leading Bay Area architects, gave the neighborhood its unique character and contributed to the style known as the First Bay Tradition.[2]

But during the hot and dry afternoon of September 17, 1923, the neighborhood was devastated by a wildfire that was fanned by high winds and swept down from Wildcat Canyon. Within just a few hours nearly 600 buildings were destroyed, among them homes designed by Howard, Maybeck, Julia Morgan, Ernest Coxhead, and John Hudson Thomas. Stopping just short of the campus, the fire spared only a handful of buildings from this period. They include two featured on this Walk, Howard's shingled Cloyne Court (1904) at 2600 Ridge Road, and Ernest Coxhead's English Tudor fraternity house (now the Goldman School of Public Policy, initially built in 1893) at 2607 Hearst.

Also saved was Ernest Coxhead's "Allenoke Manor," across the street from Cloyne Court at 1777 Le Roy. The clinker-brick estate, built in 1903, was once the home of Carol and Robert Sibley, who was a mechanical engineering professor, as well as director of the California Alumni Association and one of the founders of the East Bay Regional Park System. Nearby is a Flemish clinker-brick home designed in 1896 by Albert C. Schweinfurth, a leader in the First Bay Tradition (see also 2401 Bancroft Way, Walk 4). The house, originally named "Weltevreden" and located at 1755

Le Roy, is now known as "Tellefsen Hall," a residence for members of the University of California Marching Band, occupants since the mid-1960s. Another survivor, at 1772 Le Roy, is a stucco studio designed by Maybeck for photographer Oscar Maurer and built in 1907.

Maybeck's use of stucco and a tile roof for the Maurer Studio was ahead of its time and influenced the rebuilding of the neighborhood following the firestorm. With the rapid growth of the university larger stucco-sided apartment buildings were introduced in the neighborhood, as was the cluster of schools of the Graduate Theological Union west of Euclid Avenue on "Holy Hill."

Along Hearst the scale of the neighborhood was also changed by the university, which acquired property during the 1950s and 1960s. Six-story Etcheverry Hall (Skidmore, Owings & Merrill), a neo-Brutalist concrete and concrete block structure, began the expansion of the College of Engineering into Northside in 1964. It was followed by two multi-level tennis court-topped concrete parking structures (Anshen and Allen) later that decade. Computer Sciences' Soda Hall (Edward Larrabee Barnes with Anshen and Allen) filled in the site between Etcheverry and Le Roy in the early 1990s.

12. Gilman Hall, Lewis Hall, and Tan Hall

Gilman Hall *John Galen Howard, 1916–1917; Anshen and Allen, interior alterations, 1963*
Lewis Hall *E. Geoffrey Bangs, 1946–1948*
Tan Hall *Stone, Marraccini and Patterson, 1992–1996*

Gilman Hall

As the "large new fire-proof chemical laboratory," under Dean Gilbert N. Lewis, Gilman Hall was envisioned to house chemical research that would support the industrial development of a resource-rich West. "With California's enormous supply of mountain water power and of cheap fuel," the university proclaimed, "with vast stores of raw materials of infinite variety, and with the ocean at hand for export, there are illimitable possibilities in the development of chemical manufactures." World War I also heightened the awareness of American manufacturers to the importance of applying scientific research to industry, as Germany had done employing leading chemists prior to the war. Funded by the 1914 state bond measure, the building was named for Daniel Coit Gilman, the university's second president (1872–1875), under whose initiative the College of Chemistry was established by the state legislature in 1872.

John Galen Howard planned the building as the first increment— the west wing—of a large Beaux-Arts complex in a figure-eight plan with two interior courtyards. For this reason, the east facade of Gilman, meant to face an interior court, was designed with little architectural ornamentation and to be finished in concrete. The more public north, west, and south facades were to be granite, in keeping with the standard of all the permanent buildings of the Hearst Plan. But with the bond funds stretched for four buildings, the Regents were forced to compromise, choosing to use concrete for Gilman, in lieu of the more expensive granite. The Regents struggled with this decision, which marked a break in the standard of quality for the execution of the plan. Howard argued that the extra cost of granite was justified because Gilman would be part of one of the main campus buildings facing the central axis on the north. The site was also near the College Avenue entrance to the campus, then considered a major permanent gateway. And, Howard predicted, the building was "intended to be the finest laboratory of its kind in this country and perhaps the world, and as such will be widely known."[3] But confronted with a trade-off between using better material and providing all of the space requested by Dean Lewis, the Regents instructed Howard to design the building in concrete with a cement finish.

Gilman was sited, in general conformance with Howard's 1914 revised Hearst Plan, between two Clinton Day buildings, wooden East Hall (1898) to the west where LeConte Hall is now located, and, to the east, the brick Chemistry Building (1891), to which Howard had appended an auditorium in 1913. It was anticipated that the ultimate build-out of Gilman would advance eastward when the old Chemistry Building became obsolete. Between the two older buildings and beneath the footprint of Gilman was the circular "Chem Pond," scene of many a student hazing and dunking in earlier times.

Gilman is a classical three-story building with a red mission-tile roof. Its north and south gabled end wings flank a central facade of nine bays, defined by a row of engaged Ionic columns rising from a plinth formed by the rusticated basement. The central entrance is framed by classical molding and surmounted with a hood supported by consoles. This facade later formed the eastern half of a paired composition, when LeConte was completed in 1923 with a similar, but not identical, facing elevation.

Howard's view that Gilman "will be widely known" was prophetic. In a region of the campus rich with the making of American scientific history, the building stands on hallowed ground. In addition to work that advanced the fields of chemical thermodynamics and molecular structure, research performed in the building led to two Nobel Prizes. William F. Giauque received the award in 1949 for his studies of extreme low temperature. But more momentous was a breakthrough discovery of the atomic age in a small third-floor research laboratory. Glenn T. Seaborg, one of the principal scientists involved, later recalled the historic event in a 1985 *New York Times* article:

> On the stormy night of Feb. 23, 1941, Art Wahl performed the oxidation that gave us proof that what we had made was chemically different from all other known elements. It was the first realization of the alchemist's dream of large-scale transmutation, the first synthetic element seen by man.
>
> That experiment, and the first identification of the element with the atomic number 94, took place in room 307 of Gilman Hall. This form of the element was known as plutonium-238.

The discovery, for which Seaborg and co-discoverer Edwin M. McMillan shared the Nobel Chemistry Prize in 1951, made possible the development of atomic explosives and nuclear energy reactors.

Room 307, Gilman Hall, is a National Historic Landmark. Gilman Hall is a National Historic Chemical Landmark, is listed on the State Historic Resources Inventory, and is a City of Berkeley Landmark.

Lewis Hall

Lewis Hall was the first project of the university's postwar state-funded building program, the largest construction boom at that point in university

Lewis Hall

history. It was named for Gilbert Newton Lewis, professor of chemistry and dean of the College of Chemistry (1912–1941), known also for his research involving electron theory, chemical thermodynamics, and isotopes separation.

To create a site for Lewis and enable the continued use of Clinton Day's Old Chemistry Building, Gayley Road was rebuilt, shifted from its junction with College Avenue some two hundred feet eastward to its present alignment with Piedmont Avenue. The building was then tucked between the embankment below Gayley on the east and Old Chemistry and its annex on the west. It provided the College of Chemistry with twenty-two additional research and teaching laboratories, offices, and a 350-seat lecture hall.

San Francisco architect E. Geoffrey Bangs, a graduate of Howard's School of Architecture, worked as a designer draftsman in Howard's office when Gilman, Hilgard, and Wheeler Halls and the second phase of Doe Memorial Library were being designed. Familiar with the classcial vocabulary of the campus, Bangs treated Lewis in a stripped neoclassical style, similar to other campus buildings during the 1940s by Beaux-Arts trained Arthur Brown, Jr.

A cement-plastered concrete and steel-framed building, Lewis is composed of a four-story laboratory wing running parallel to Gayley and a lower south lecture-hall wing angled to align with other buildings in the Physics and Chemistry area. It is ornamented with simulated quoins and striated rustication, an arched east entrance, classical balustrades, and a simplified cornice with dentils beneath its red-tile hipped roof.

Tan Hall

Tan Hall has provided the first new space for the College of Chemistry since the completion of Hildebrand Hall in 1966. In the intervening thirty years, new directions in biophysical, synthetic, and laser chemistry, and growth in chemical engineering—with related increases in faculty, postdoctoral research and undergraduate and graduate enrollments—contributed to the building's need.

The third unit of a long-range chemistry program following Latimer and Hildebrand Halls, Tan Hall filled in the long-vacant northwest corner of the group, on a site that had been a surface parking lot for nearly thirty years. It completed the definition of the minor north-south esplanade between the Chemistry and Physics groups and was designed as a counterbalance to Campbell Hall across the esplanade, as Gilman relates to Le Conte at the south end of the esplanade. Though campus design guidelines for Tan Hall recommended matching its height to Campbell and aligning its west facade with Gilman, the building exceeded these parameters at the margins to provide the space required by the chemical engineering and chemistry programs. To keep it within reasonable limits, San Francisco

Tan Hall

architects Stone, Marraccini and Patterson placed two levels underground, extending beneath the esplanade and to the northwest, to house special labs, offices and mechanical equipment. From the chemistry plaza, the building rises seven stories, containing a lecture hall and computing center on the plaza level, five lab floors, and a bay-view conference room and chemical storage facilities on the top floor. It increased college space by twenty percent.

The modular pre-cast concrete window bays and red-tile hipped roof of Tan Hall relate to its older companion, Campbell. But unlike boxy Campbell, it rises from a base that expresses the wider structural bays of its concrete columns, and has setback corners that help reduce the apparent size of the building. Ventilation shafts are set at forty-five-degree chamfers within these setbacks. The sixth floor is treated with a touch of postmodernism, with its rustication and brackets beneath the slightly projecting roof soffit. The enclosure of the smaller seventh floor, with its recessed terrace within the hipped roof, also effectively reduces the mass of the building. In addition to its basement connections, the building is linked by bridges to both Latimer and Gilman.

Along with state and campus funds, Tan Hall was financed mostly by private donors, including those honoring Chinese industrialist and philanthropist Tan Kah Kee, for whom the building was named. Dedication of the building coincided with a celebration of the 125th anniversary of the college, which was first housed in South Hall in 1873.

13. LeConte Hall

John Galen Howard, 1923–1924;
Miller & Warnecke, addition, 1949–1950;
John Carl Warnecke and Associates, alterations, 1964

LeConte Hall was constructed to provide a larger home for the physics department, which had outgrown historic South Hall while trying to meet the enrollment increases that followed World War I. The state-funded building was the fourth largest physics facility in the nation and one of the largest in the world when it was completed in 1924, and its provision of forty rooms for individual research was exceptional.

It was dedicated "to the memory of the two great men who first kindled the torch of science on the Pacific slope": John LeConte, the first professor of physics and third president of the university (1876–1881), and his brother Joseph LeConte, professor of geology, natural history, and botany. Inseparable from the early development and traditions of the university, the two brothers are also honored by the LeConte Oak in the Grinnell Natural Area (see Walk 3) and two commemorative chairs in the Hearst Greek Theatre (see Walk 6).

John Galen Howard sited LeConte as a companion building across the esplanade from Gilman Hall, in general accord with his 1914 revised Hearst Plan, although he originally designated the site for Mathematics, while Physics was to be sited as a north terminus to the esplanade, across from the Mining Building. To clear the site, East Hall (Clinton Day, 1898), a three-story, U-shaped wooden building that housed the Department of

LeConte Hall

Zoology, was moved in three sections to the south side of Faculty Glade on a portion of the future site of Morrison Hall.

A reinforced concrete building with stucco facing, LeConte has four stories above a partial basement. The fourth-floor attic skylight originally illuminated a two-story tiered lecture hall, which was later removed. The fourth floor also housed the School of Optometry, which was then a division of the Physics Department. The first three floors contained research rooms, labs, offices, classrooms, and included a library and reading rooms on the second and third floors.

LeConte's east facade virtually mirrors the west facade of Gilman, with gabled end wings on either side of a nine-bay central wing featuring an engaged Ionic colonnade. LeConte differs with its two main entrances, instead of the one central entrance of Gilman, and in its decorative classical detailing. As with Gilman, Howard designed the rear (west) facade of LeConte with fewer details—pilasters take the place of the fluted Ionic columns—in anticipation of a future westward expansion, which later took the form of Birge Hall (Warnecke & Warnecke, 1962–64). With the building's completion, the Physics and Chemistry groups took their places on opposite sides of the esplanade, which soon became known as "The Court of the Lewises," in recognition of the offices of Physics Chairman E. Percival Lewis in LeConte and Chemistry Dean Gilbert N. Lewis in Gilman.

Like Gilman, LeConte would become forever associated with the makers of American scientific history and the emergence of the atomic age. Among the notable scholars recruited to conduct research in the building were Ernest O. Lawrence and J. Robert Oppenheimer. It was in the basement of LeConte in 1929 that Lawrence built his first cyclotron, which he then tested in his third-floor laboratory. The invention enabled research of subatomic particles and led to the development of the Radiation Laboratory (now the Lawrence Berkeley National Laboratory) and to the Nobel Prize in Physics for Lawrence. Twelve years later, a team of theoretical physicists, under Oppenheimer and including Edward Teller, met during the summer of 1942 in two fourth-floor attic rooms, where under wartime security measures they worked out the theory of the atomic bomb.

LeConte Hall addition

Following World War II, LeConte was no longer adequate to accommodate the large increase in graduate students and the expansion in nuclear physics and related fields of study. Miller & Warnecke's addition alleviated the overcrowding, nearly doubling the space for Physics. Their offset wing to the northwest of Howard's building followed Arthur Brown's 1944 General Plan. The four-story concrete and steel-frame wing was faced with terracotta on the base and plaster above to form a symmetrical stripped-classical backdrop to Sather Esplanade.

14. Hearst Memorial Mining Building, Lawson Adit, and Mining Circle

Hearst Memorial Mining Building
> *John Galen Howard, 1902–1907;*
> *Michael Goodman, alterations, 1948;*
> *NBBJ, with Rutherford & Chekene Consulting Engineers, rehabilitation and*
> *addition, 1998–2002*

Lawson Adit *College of Mining, 1916–ca. 1938*
Mining Circle *John Galen Howard, 1914*

It may always be a matter of debate as to whether Hearst Memorial Mining Building or Doe Memorial Library is John Galen Howard's masterpiece. The Library is his cut diamond; the Mining Building his gold nugget, polished on its public face but still rough and craggy like the mother lode it evokes—in Howard's words, "a kind, bluff brother amid a bevy of lovely sisters."

Phoebe Hearst's generous budget for the memorial to her late husband permitted Howard and Samuel B. Christy, dean of the College of Mining, to tour mining schools in the United States and Europe during the summer of 1901. Most of what they saw was utilitarian in nature—nothing that would compare to what Howard desired for Berkeley, "to build a building which shall fitly house the spirit of the place and express its character." To that end, he would be assisted at the drafting table by Julia Morgan, who joined Howard's staff shortly after returning from the École des Beaux-Arts in Paris.

In a fitting display of the natural elements, the cornerstone ceremony on the afternoon of November 18, 1902, was greeted with a steady downpour. On the muddy construction site a crowd of nearly 2,000 gathered under umbrellas to hear the remarks of President Wheeler, Phoebe Hearst, William Randolph Hearst, and Howard and to witness the setting of the three-ton stone. Jack London, reporting for the Hearst-run *San Francisco Examiner*, captured the moment: "Heads were bare more often than not and every one seemed to feel the sacredness and solemnity of the occasion. The cornerstone . . . was laid with a spirit very much like that with which the cornerstones of the old cathedrals must have been laid. The spirit of the new University, instinct with life, was in the air."

The building, facing onto the central east-west axis, would establish the theme for its "lovely sisters" to come thereafter: facades of Raymond granite from the Sierra Nevada foothills and roofs of red mission tile with copper-framed skylights to create a blend of Beaux-Arts classicism and California vernacular. Howard, who as a young architect sketched the California missions, drew upon this influence in the Mining Building.

The style is strongly emphasized on the central projecting portion of the south entrance facade with its three twenty-eight-foot-high arched windows facing onto the landscaped pool of the Mining Circle. Within each arch is an entablature supported by a pair of Tuscan columns, which, in

Hearst Memorial Mining Building

Memorial Vestibule, Hearst Memorial Mining Building

the central arch, frame oak entry doors carved with the faces of cherubs. Greek fretwork lines the inner surface of the granite arches, which are accentuated with braided moldings on the facade, while large granite wreaths anchor the composition at each side. This fine stone detailing is contrasted with the six heavy timber brackets that support the tiled eave. These, in turn, are supported by granite corbels of sculpted heroic figures by artist Robert Ingersoll Aitken. Aitken studied under sculptor Douglas Tilden and later succeeded him as head of the Department of Sculpture at the Mark Hopkins Institute in San Francisco. Among the artist's many works were, in San Francisco, figures at Golden Gate Park, City Hall, and the bronze *Victory* atop the Admiral Dewey monument in Union Square. Howard praised Aitken's Mining Building sculptures as "the symbolic intent of our work . . . most appealingly summed up. Upon the west he has wrought the primal elements; upon the east the eternal forces; and in the center, fresh, mysterious, pure,— emerging from the vague of chaos the ideal arts, the final flower of life."

Sculpture by Robert Aitken, Hearst Memorial Mining Building

Behind the arches rises one of Howard's great interiors, the Memorial Vestibule, a three-story lobby-museum space with slender iron columns supporting open perimeter galleries at the second and third floors. Above, iron arches support three dome skylights that admit diffused illumination over pendentives of herringbone-pattern Guastavino tile. This work is a fine example of the unique Catalan vaulting of lightweight fireproof tiles created by Rafael Guastavino and used in many distinctive structures by American architects from the late nineteenth to mid-twentieth centuries.

Howard's design of the vestibule recalls the reading room (1862–1868) of the Bibliothèque Nationale in Paris, where architect Henri Labrouste used nine vaulted terracotta domes of similar form supported by slender iron columns. Howard contrasted the lightness of the industrial-like iron framework against the buff-colored brick facing of the surrounding walls and open archways. But this earthy aesthetic was nearly changed about one year before the building's completion when William Randolph Hearst expressed his regrets that the space "was not finished from floor to ceiling in marble rather than in brick."[4] Though Howard was taken aback by the late criticism, he was not opposed to the change in material, responding that it was "not too late to finish the Memorial Vestibule in marble throughout,—a proposition to which I would accede with enthusiasm."[5] However, although white marble was used on the double flights of stairways, the brick floor and walls were left unchanged, probably because of increased costs and labor problems brought about by the 1906 San Francisco earthquake and fire.

The main floor and galleries of the vestibule were used for special displays. Two bronze tablets memorializing George Hearst, one featuring a dedicatory inscription written by President Wheeler and the other a bas-relief bust of the Senator, were installed on the stairway walls two years after the building was completed. They were designed by modeling instructor Melvin Earl Cummings and—as with Cummings' other campus sculptures—were closely scrutinized by President Wheeler. Within the grand space the Museum of Mining and Metallurgy exhibited a collection of models of mines, machinery, and furnaces, as well as ore samples and manufactured metal products, displayed on pedestals and in glass cases and cabinets. Completing the more public facilities of the south wing, the lower extensions to the east and west of the vestibule contained offices, a library, and lecture halls.

To the north of the memorial wing, the building branched into three wings devoted to the raw rudiments of mining technology, where, in Howard's words, "everything is work-a-day, substantial and convenient, but totally devoid of ornament, as a building of this character should be." A great mining laboratory, nearly fifty feet wide by 120 feet long, formed the central wing on axis with the building's main entrance. Here a skylit four-story atrium was equipped with a traveling crane to facilitate the movement of equipment, and galleries on either side provided observation points for students to study mining operation demonstrations. Separated from this laboratory on either side by three-story open light wells, the east and west wings housed metallurgical and research labs, with drafting rooms above. The central portion of the north side of the building contained a three-story crushing tower, which was flanked on the east by a shop for smelting copper and lead, and on the west by a gold and silver mill.

The atrium laboratory—its original use for heavy-machinery experiments abandoned—and the adjacent light wells were converted into compartmentalized facilities for Engineering and Paleontology programs by architect Michael Goodman in 1948. But these original spaces have been reclaimed in the $68 million rehabilitation by NBBJ begun in 1998. In a dual triumph of historic preservation and innovative structural engineering, the building—which stands just 800 feet west of the Hayward Fault—has been seismically strengthened and restored for use by the Department of Materials Science and Mineral Engineering, the descendant program of the College of Mining. But instead of smelters and rock crushers, students occupying the Mining Building in the early twenty-first century will be using electronic microscopes and the latest computer technology. Sub-atomic analysis in clean laboratories will replace the meltdown of ore in raging furnaces. New materials will be researched, "the key to breakthroughs in electronics, medicine, aerospace and other industries," Chancellor Chang-Lin Tien pointed out in 1997. "It is at the forefront of California's future, just as mining was at the turn of the century."[6]

Funded from state bond revenues and gifts, the restoration included construction of new footings and a base isolation system to permit a horizontal displacement around the building of up to twenty-eight inches in a major earthquake. Pioneered by Civil Engineering Professor James Kelly, the system includes twenty-four fluid dampers and 134 high-damping rubber base isolators, which support a grid of concrete beams under the structure. Three-story additions at the northwest and northeast corners replaced space lost by the reclamation of the atrium and light wells. Designed to complement, but not mimic Howard's building, these additions are granite based with panels of aluminum and glass, and retain the original exterior granite walls in the new interior spaces. The restoration also strengthened the roof parapets and the twenty distinctive chimneys that recall the original use of the building, and installed new mission roof tile. Interior preservation included reinforcement of the Guastavino tile vaults in the Memorial Vestibule, and reclamation of a large lecture hall that had been unused since 1978 because of seismic safety concerns.

These changes would likely please John Galen Howard. At the dedication ceremony of the Mining Building on August 23, 1907, he described, somewhat prophetically, his attempt to make the floor plan as elastic as possible, "so that its main structure shall be ... a mere shell, whose interior portions may be torn out, adjusted, rebuilt if necessary, without affecting the strength or aspect of the whole." His concept has proven sound nearly a century later.

The Hearst Memorial Mining Building is included in the Berkeley campus designation as a California Registered Historical Landmark, is listed on the National Register of Historic Places and the State Historic Resources Inventory, and is a City of Berkeley Landmark.

Lawson Adit

In 1916, some nine years after the opening of the Mining Building, the dean of the College of Mining, Andrew C. Lawson, conceived the idea of boring into the hill east of the building to create an underground laboratory for the training of mining engineers. One of the most unusual features of the campus, the tunnel was created with the help of gifts from the mining industry, including 1,000 pounds of dynamite from the Hercules Powder Company and the latest type of ore-car from a San Francisco iron works. By October, students under Professor of Mining Frank H. Probert had driven the "Lawson Adit" 150 feet into the hillside, with expectations of continuing to about 2,000 feet. In addition to giving the students "sound, practical training in drilling, drifting, blasting, timbering, and mine surveying,"[7] it

Mining students with Dean Andrew C. Lawson (far right) and Professor Frank H. Probert (center, third from right) at Lawson Adit, 1917

was hoped that the effort might also develop a source of water for the campus. Rails from the adit were extended into a workshop at the northeast corner of the Mining Building, enabling ore-cars to enter through double doors to facilitate instruction within the building.

By the late 1930s the tunnel was extended horizontally to about 750 feet, passing through the Hayward Fault and under the site then proposed for Stern Hall (see Walk 6), aiding geological studies for that dormitory. Thirty years later, it was maintained only to a distance of about 260 feet, but deep enough for underground observations of the fault line, and today it continues to provide geologists and seismologists a unique opportunity to study signs of fault activity. The closed entrance to the adit has been equipped with a new gate and concrete frame in conjunction with the restoration of the Mining Building.

The Lawson Adit is listed on the State Historic Resources Inventory.

Mining Circle

The Mining Circle, along with its circular drive and the granite and brick approaches and planting at the Mining Building, was constructed in 1914 with additional financial assistance from Phoebe Hearst. It was the first formal landscape feature of Howard's Hearst Plan to be completed and has taken on renewed importance with the rehabilitation of the Mining Building. An important element of that plan, the Mining Circle was meant to be the eastern landscaped terminus in the series of open spaces beginning with the west crescent that would form the great central garden axis.

The Circle today is similar to that depicted in Howard's 1914 Plan, though the vegetation on the east side of the pool has grown larger than

Howard envisioned. But with the construction of Evans Hall, which blocked the west vista, and the creation of an esplanade (instead of a facing building) to the south, the orientation of the Circle shifted ninety degrees to a north-south alignment extending from the Mining Building to the creek vegetation at Faculty Glade. Both of these changes were established in the 1944 Plan of Arthur Brown, Jr., who also suggested replacing the Circle with a linear planted strip. The Circle was not removed, though in the 1962 Long Range Development Plan Consulting Landscape Architect Thomas Church proposed moving it forty feet north of the central axis to align with Evans on the west and Stanley Hall (Michael A.

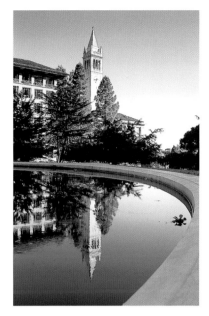

Mining Circle Pond with Campanile

Goodman, 1950–52) on the east, to create more space for University Drive on the south. This idea and a proposal to construct a parking garage beneath the Circle were never implemented.

15. Evans Hall and Donner Laboratory

Evans Hall

> *Gardner A. Dailey and Yuill-Thornton, Warner and Levikow,*
> *with Thomas D. Church, landscape architect, 1968–1971*

Donner Laboratory

> *Arthur Brown, Jr., 1941–1942; Reynolds & Chamberlain, addition, 1953–1955*

Bearing the reputation expressed by many as the most despised building on campus, Evans Hall was the last in the series of high-rise blockbusters of the postwar years. Its most dubious distinction, aside from its architectural treatment and impact on the Mining Building, was its blockage of the central axis. Architect Gardner Dailey never saw Evans completed. Following his death in 1968, his associates Yuill-Thornton, Warner and Levikow took over as executive architects.

Initially state-funded, Evans was on the boards in Dailey's office for three years as a smaller building, when two sizeable federal grants were awarded to the campus in 1966. It was designed originally as a nine-story building to house classrooms, a branch library, and teaching labs for the departments of Mathematics and Statistics, but the boost in funds increased

Evans Hall

these functions and added a computing center. The reconfigured project added two basement levels and a tenth floor and increased the total bulk of the building by fifty percent. The added height made the building even more prominent on its elevated site (about 300 feet above sea level) increasing its visibility from across the Bay. Its impact was slightly lessened in 2000, when it was painted a darker tone following repair of the bare concrete.

Named for Griffith Conrad Evans, emeritus professor and former chairman of the mathematics department, the reinforced-concrete block identifies with the Brutalist trend of the period. Four protruding bays on the east and west facades, and three on the shorter north and south sides, are cradled by pairs of columns, which are expressed along the building's periphery. The ground floor, at the Mining Circle level, stands taller to accommodate the library and features an open loggia around the base of the building.

This use of a colonnaded loggia or breezeway was incorporated by Dailey in his other campus buildings as well—Morrison and Hertz, Kroeber, and Tolman Halls—perhaps a reflection of the indoor-outdoor philosophy that characterized the regionalist tradition of residential design, in which he was often distinguished. In that sense, Evans seems to exemplify the difficult transition that Dailey and other prominent Bay Area residential architects—such as William Wurster (Barker and Simon Halls), Michael Goodman (Stanley Hall), and Joseph Esherick (Wurster Hall)—had to make in designing large institutional buildings.

Donner Laboratory

Built for medical physics research, the original south wing of Donner Laboratory is a stripped neoclassical building located to the northeast of the Mining Circle. One of three campus buildings designed by Supervising Architect Arthur Brown, Jr. around the beginning of World War II (along with Minor and Sproul Halls), it is a three-story rectangular concrete structure with simulated quoins and rustication at the ground floor, and a cornice molding beneath a mission tile roof. The slightly projecting entry block has a framed opening to a recessed doorway.

Funded by the Donner Foundation (previously called the International Cancer Research Foundation), the lab was established in memory of Joseph William Donner, a cancer victim and son of foundation president William H. Donner. Under the direction of John H. Lawrence, it grew from early cyclotron research into the first research and teaching center in the world devoted to the use of atomic energy in biology and medicine. Pioneering accomplishments in the facility included the use of radioisotopes and experiments with heavy particles in disease treatment. During World War II, the lab was also pressed into service to conduct research in high-altitude flying, using volunteer Naval and Army ROTC students in decompression-chamber simulation tests. The modern four-story concrete

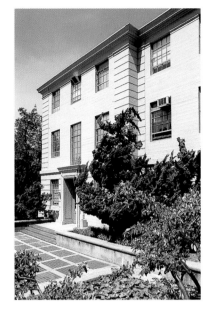

Donner Laboratory

north wing by Reynolds & Chamberlain was added to Donner to meet new space and equipment requirements in the 1950s.

16. Bechtel Engineering Center

George Matsumoto, with Royston Hanamoto Alley & Abey, landscape architects, 1978–1980

George Matsumoto's terraced Bechtel Engineering Center, named for donor and 1923 graduate Stephen D. Bechtel, was the first major campus building constructed partially underground in order to preserve open space. The site at the south end of Davis Hall was approved by the Regents after an original proposal in 1976 to construct the center on the site of John Galen Howard's Naval Architecture Building was strongly opposed by historic preservation advocates (see Naval Architecture Building).

The second effort proved to be the charmer, for not only was the old shingle-style building preserved, but the new design unselfishly improved the landscape and pedestrian circulation within a larger campus context. Matsumoto was given an unfinished quadrangle surrounded by prominent buildings. On the south loomed Gardner Dailey's ten-story Brutalist block, Evans Hall, facing the arched neo-Brutalist concrete facade of Davis (Skidmore, Owings & Merrill, 1966–69) across the quadrangle. On the east stood Howard's landmark Beaux-Arts Mining Building, and to the west the neoclassical entrance facade of George Kelham's McLaughlin Hall. Within this disparate urbanized framework, Matsumoto inserted a

Bechtel Engineering Center

sunken building with rooftop landscaping to provide a centralized place for the Engineering community, while also knitting together the surroundings with greenery and connecting walkways.

The building contains two interior levels and a rooftop split-level terrace. The south ground-level entrance leads to the Kiely Atrium, an open circular light-well in which the suspended metal-rod sculpture *Standing Waves* (Jerome Kirk, 1980) represents the mathematical construct of a sine wave.[8] The atrium serves as an elevator lobby and access to conference rooms, a student lounge, and the Kresge Engineering Library. The underground library was established to consolidate several College of Engineering resources and contains over 200,000 volumes in various engineering specialties. The inviting multi-level, ramped space is trimmed in oak and illuminated by a domed skylight that penetrates the mounded roof-lawn above. The middle level, accessed from a higher south entrance, contains offices and the 280-seat Sibley Auditorium, used for lectures and meetings of the Berkeley Academic Senate.

The rooftop Trefethen Terrace (named for 1930 alumnus Eugene E. Trefethen, Jr.) was designed in two levels. The west terrace, above the auditorium wing of the building, includes the elevator tower, a vertical element linked by a trellis to a small wood-sided food pavilion. The east terrace is formed by the upper roof of the library stacks and contains a trellised niche and outdoor roofed and glazed study carrels. The balconied terrace adjoins the podium walkway of Davis to provide pedestrian circulation to the north side of campus. Along with the turfed areas, the terrace of the suppressed building provides the desired open space that was envisioned in the 1962 Long Range Development Plan.

McLaughlin Hall   *George W. Kelham, 1931*
Hesse Hall

> *John Galen Howard, 1924;*
> *George W. Kelham, addition, 1931;*
> *Corlett & Anderson, addition, 1947;*
> *Van Bourg/Nakamura & Associates, O'Brien Hall addition, 1959, and*
> *Courtyard Building addition, 1961–1962*

George Kelham's state-funded McLaughlin Hall—originally named the Engineering Building—was sited as the west wing of a U-shaped Engineering Group aligned with the north-south axis of the Campanile, similar in general concept to John Galen Howard's Hearst Plan and reaffirmed in Warren Perry's 1933 Plan Study. Completion of the complex required the removal of the old Mechanics Building to the east, but by the time that building was razed in 1965 (for construction of the south wing of Davis Hall) this axial configuration had been abandoned.

McLaughlin now forms the south side of a contiguous but eclectic group that includes O'Brien Hall on the east, Hesse Hall on the north, and McCone Hall on the west. The four-story reinforced-concrete and steel-frame building also forms a partial northern edge to Memorial Glade. It houses offices, classrooms, and institute and library facilities of the College of Engineering.

The rectangular building has a peripheral red mission-tile hipped roof, except at the southeast corner tower, which projects slightly from the facade and contains a classical entrance portico on the east supported by two monumental fluted columns. Characteristic of Kelham's work, the concrete facade is textured by horizontal formwork and has Moderne influences in its cast decorative details. These include foliated capitals of the portico columns and corner pilasters and medallions beneath the tower pediments. The tall bays of the building appear to relate to high interior spaces, but actually include an intermediate spandrel between the second and third floors.

The building was renamed in 1966 to honor Donald H. McLaughlin, dean of the College of Mining and College of Engineering (1941–1943)

McLaughlin Hall

and Regent of the university (1951–1966), who also served as chairman of the Committee on Campus Planning during preparation of the 1956 Long Range Development Plan.

On the raised lawn to the north of the brick entry plaza are two reclining bronze Russian black bears, created by Beaux-Arts sculptor Edmund Schultz Beckum about 1915. Originally commissioned by the Rossia Insurance Company of Petrograd, Russia, they were installed at the entrance to the company's U. S. headquarters in Hartford, Connecticut. When the building was scheduled to be demolished, the bears were acquired by alumnus A. John Macchi (Class of 1936), president of Macchi Engineers in Hartford, who donated them to the university in 1987. Beckum sculpted the bears using the *repoussé* process of hammering the bronze. The bears form a distinctive foreground to the view of the Campanile to the south.

Hesse Hall

Hesse Hall includes the only fragment of an engineering group planned by John Galen Howard as a cross-axial balance to the Campanile and its neighboring buildings. Hesse was to form part of a building meant to align with two humanities buildings planned to replace North and South Halls. But this intended relationship is now obscured, since the two humanities buildings were never built and the eventual build-out of the Hesse-O'Brien-McLaughlin-McCone group modified the original plan.

The original part of Hesse, built as a heat and power laboratory, was a rectangular concrete building with classical detailing, including

rusticated flat-arch window and door surrounds and quoins, and a dentilated cornice. It was expanded to the west by George Kelham in 1931 (still in keeping with Howard's plan) and a three-story addition by Corlett & Anderson in 1947. Hesse was named for Frederick G. Hesse, head of the College of Mechanics (1875–1904) and professor of industrial mechanics, whose hydraulic engineering work contributed to the early development of hydroelectric power plants in California.

A modernist three-story addition by Van Bourg/Nakamura in 1959 was named O'Brien Hall in 1968, in honor of College of Engineering Dean

Hesse Hall

Morrough P. O'Brien (1943–1959), known for his leadership in civil engineering hydraulics. The building, which contains Environmental Water Resources laboratories and the Water Resources Center Archives, forms the east side of the building group and includes a glass-enclosed link to McLaughlin.

18. North Gate Hall, Naval Architecture Building, Class of 1954 Gate, and Observatory Hill

North Gate Hall
> *John Galen Howard, 1905–1906, and additions, 1908 and 1912;*
> *Walter T. Steilberg with Warren C. Perry, addition, 1935–1936;*
> *Howard Moise, addition and alterations, 1952;*
> *Stoller Knoerr Architects, alterations and restoration, 1993*

Naval Architecture Building   *John Galen Howard, 1913–1914; east end demolished, 1929*

Class of 1954 Gate
> *Reid & Tarics Associates, with Royston Hanamoto Alley & Abey,*
> *landscape architects, 1990*

Observatory Hill

Now home to the Graduate School of Journalism, North Gate Hall, the small brown-shingled building at the Euclid Avenue entrance to campus, was the revered studio of architecture students for nearly sixty years. It began as a small temporary building and evolved organically from being considered an expendable firetrap to a cherished historic structure worthy of preservation. It forms a link to generations of Bay Area architects and to the legacy of Supervising Architect John Galen Howard, the first chairman of the Department of Architecture.

Early students aspiring to be architects—among them John Bakewell, Jr. (Class of 1893), Arthur Brown, Jr. (Class of 1896), and Julia Morgan (Class of 1894)—studied under Frank Soulé in the civil engineering department and Herman Kower in the drawing department.[9] Instruction in architecture developed from Bernard Maybeck, who was recruited by Soulé in 1894 to teach instrumental drawing and descriptive geometry and used his home for conducting an informal course in architecture. Amidst the excitement surrounding the Hearst Architectural Plan, President Wheeler identified the need for a formal curriculum in his inaugural address on October 25, 1899. "Among all the arts," the president proclaimed, "that of architecture will, by common consent, be allowed to represent California's greatest present lack. When the University shall have once begun to teach this art by good example, it may also and must undertake to teach by good doctrine as well." Two years later, Howard was appointed to supervise the

North Gate Hall, with original "Ark" wing on left

plan and in 1903 establish the new department. Without adequate campus facilities, the department began as an atelier attached to Howard's downtown Berkeley office (see Walk 10), where his small group of students included future architects Henry H. Gutterson, John Hudson Thomas, and Warren C. Perry, who in 1927 would succeed Howard as head of the school.

In May 1905 President Wheeler agreed that it would be wiser to spend a few thousand dollars "in the erection of a shanty north of the Mechanics Building" for both architecture instruction and Howard's office, instead of continuing to pay the downtown rental.[10] The original "shanty," named the Architecture Building, was a two-story, wood-framed building, clad in redwood shingles that harmonized with the Northside residential community. The small hipped-roof building, characterized by dormers, small balconies, exposed interior framing, and a trellis, faced west and contained a drafting room, Howard's office, and a library with a nucleus of nearly 500 volumes donated by Phoebe Hearst.

"This first unit of the building," Warren C. Perry later explained, "a charming little rectangular block about 30 x 60 feet, with banks of square-paned casement windows, and a great shapely cypress tree outside, was promptly dubbed 'The Ark,' a title suggested not only by its form, but serving ever since as a campus abbreviation for 'architecture.'" [11]At the helm of the Ark was Howard, or "Father Noah," as he came to be known. This tradition stemmed from a remarkable esprit de corps that developed in the busy workshop, as recalled by Henry Gutterson: "Work went on day and night in the best Beaux-Arts tradition with *Esquisse-esquisse* [sketch projects], *Charette* [projects on deadline], *Rendu* [final renderings] in quickening tempo and with rapidly increasing success."[12] The heritage of the École des Beaux-Arts in Paris was also evident in the role of design instructors who maintained professional practices, and the life of the students, who wore imported French linen smocks and received critiques at their drafting tables and judgment of their work "on the wall."

To relieve overcrowding the Ark was expanded in 1908 by two drafting rooms stepping uphill along Hearst Avenue to form an L-shaped building. This wing was designed with a high bank of windows breaking through the cornice line to capture north light for the studios. Four years later, the east wing was constructed to create a C-shaped plan. This added drafting rooms on the north, an exhibition hall at the east end, and a 200-seat lecture hall with a projecting bay on the south. Howard was assisted on these additions by William C. Hays, who had joined his office in 1904 and the architecture faculty in 1906. As Warren Perry described it, the building had now become a "rambling brown structure" of character that fit "like an old shoe."

Within the next five years Howard designed two more temporary buildings near the Ark, the Drawing Building (Naval Architecture Building) in 1914 and Home Economics Building in 1917, creating a small cluster of shingled buildings along the north edge of campus. Concern for the safety of these temporaries and other campus buildings was heightened by the firestorm that devastated north Berkeley in 1923. Fearing the Ark would be lost, students removed its valuable books, and went to Howard's Northside house to wet it down and remove its furnishings.

To safeguard the growing architectural library, a freestanding concrete and concrete block building was added in 1936 by architect Walter Steilberg, a graduate of the school who also worked in the offices of Howard and Julia Morgan. Also a structural designer, Steilberg was innovative in the use of reinforced concrete and used concrete arches

North Gate Hall courtyard

within the reading room, light-weight pumice concrete for the roof slab, and concrete-tile exterior walls that were an early form of concrete-block construction.[13] The rectangular building formed the south side of the court-yard and was linked to the shingled building by an open trellis extended from one built with Howard's 1912 addition.

In 1940, when the Regents allocated funds toward development of the courtyard, Perry gladly reported to President Sproul that "the word has spread throughout the Ark and there is great rejoicing thereat on the part of both students and faculty."[14] The southwest corner of the complex was com-pleted in 1952 by architect and professor Howard Moise, along with interior alterations to the original Ark to accommodate the office of William W. Wurster, the new head of the school.

When Architecture moved to newly built Wurster Hall in 1964 as part of the College of Environmental Design, the Ark was assigned to the College of Engineering and renamed North Gate Hall, and in 1981 was reas-signed to the Graduate School of Journalism. But President Wheeler's "shanty" was now showing its age, and in 1993 was restored by Berkeley architects Claude Stoller (once a faculty lecturer in the Ark) and Mark Knoerr, who studied old documents of the structure. When it was found that the north wall was rotted beyond repair, a replica of the facade was created, con-cealing new steel framing within wood construction, and reproducing the wood shingles and the look of the original windows. The courtyard trellis, removed at an earlier time, was recreated, and the building's interior was renovated for Journalism. The former design studios became newsrooms, their T-squares and ruling pens replaced by laptops and television monitors.

The intimacy of the old Ark enables journalism students and faculty to interact in a workshop atmosphere, in a spirit not unlike that described by Perry in 1920: "We are a close-knit group in the midst of this far-flung University, a little family of itself, loyal indeed to the larger community that gives us life, but bound together by the ties that, we think, only a school of artists understand."

North Gate Hall is listed on the National Register of Historic Places, is included in the Berkeley campus designation as a California Registered Historical Landmark, is listed on the State Historic Resources Inventory, and is a City of Berkeley Landmark.

Naval Architecture Building

The sudden growth in enrollment that occurred in the second decade of the twentieth century resulted in a shortage of classroom and laboratory facili-ties, reported to the Regents in 1913 as "an almost insuperable difficulty." To help alleviate the situation, John Galen Howard was asked to provide a temporary Drawing Building on the north side of the grounds, to the east of his Ark (North Gate Hall). The new structure enabled the transfer of drawing instruction from East Hall (then located on the site of LeConte Hall), in order

Naval Architecture Building

to free space in that building for six additional classrooms. It would become a workhorse of a building, adapting to a succession of occupants (and name changes) and, like its neighbor to the west, persevering through years of planned demolition and attaining an historic status never originally imagined.

Howard designed a long, rectangular building that stepped up the hill in two sections, completing first a two-story west section, followed by three stories to the east. Continuing the vernacular style of the Bay Area Tradition used in the Ark, he created a gabled, wood-frame, shingled building with high north-facing windows along Hearst Avenue to illuminate the drawing studios. Two Craftsman-style gabled entrances were centered on the south facades of each section, with a pedimented doorway provided from a second-floor balcony on the west end. Together, the two buildings formed a compatible transition to the adjacent brown-shingled neighborhood.

In 1923 the building was renamed the Art Building, to recognize the newly established Department of Art that evolved from the drawing curriculum. But the general area was earmarked for Engineering, and in 1929 the east end of the building was lopped off just short of its gabled entrance to make room for George Kelham's Engineering Materials Laboratory (the north wing of Davis Hall, 1929–31), which nearly touched the remaining portion of the shingled building.

When the Department of Art moved in 1930, the building was added to the growing Engineering complex and renamed the Engineering Design Building. That designation would continue until 1951, when it was changed to the City and Regional Planning Building, home to the new department headed by T. J. Kent and aptly placed adjacent to Architecture.

When these two departments moved to Wurster Hall in 1964, the building was returned to the College of Engineering, becoming the Naval Architecture Building in 1965.

In July 1976, despite extensive opposition, the Regents approved the design of the Engineering Center Building, a three-story concrete structure to be built on the site of the Naval Architecture Building. But opposition to the demolition of the old building from preservationists, the community, and students influenced them to rescind their previous approvals for the site and design and approve construction of the Bechtel Engineering Center south of Davis Hall instead. Given new life and historic status, Howard's "temporary" building dusted off its shingles and has remained in use, presently housing Engineering offices, the Naval Architecture and Offshore Engineering program, and the UC Transportation Center. Although most of the drawing studios have been partitioned, the eastern-most room is intact and provides a glimpse of the original function that utilized natural light admitted by the high north-facing windows.

The Naval Architecture Building is listed on the National Register of Historic Places and the State Historic Resources Inventory, and is a City of Berkeley Landmark.

Class of 1954 Gate

Class of 1954 Gate

A counter-balance to Sather Gate, the Class of 1954 Gate is a northern anchor for the cross-campus walkway that passes through the traditional academic center of campus and links Euclid and Telegraph Avenues. Part of a thirty-fifth anniversary gift to the university, the gate was funded by the campus and a $350,000 contribution by the class, which also endowed a $400,000 Chair for undergraduate teaching. It is the product of a two-stage alumni design competition in 1987—the first conducted internationally since the Hearst Architectural Plan in 1897—that resulted in 113 entries and five finalists. The winning design by architects Gary Demele (Class of 1974) and Robert Olwell, of San Francisco–based Reid & Tarics Associates was selected in the spring of 1988.

The project presented the opportunity to not only create a symbolic pedestrian gateway, but to resolve visual, physical and circulation problems in the area, which functioned as a minor Northside entrance since the late nineteenth century. Except for a suggestion in a 1933 plan study by Warren C. Perry, a formal gateway had never been proposed.

Completed in 1990, the gate is set within a brick-bordered circle of concrete-aggregate pavement and consists of a pair of twenty-four-foot-high concrete pylons surmounted by bronze lanterns. The striations and pre-cast moldings of the pylons give the gate a neoclassical connection to the traditional campus, while the craftsman-like articulation of the lanterns relates well to the Bay Region style of North Gate Hall. Semicircular concrete seat-walls and peripheral concrete traffic bollards define the plaza. Budget restrictions modified the original design, which proposed granite facing for the pylons, radial brick pavement, and flanking Japanese cherry trees. The inscribed medallion in the center of the plaza covers a time capsule containing class-related memorabilia.

Observatory Hill

Maintained in a semi-natural state, Observatory Hill draws its name from the Students' Observatory constructed at the top of the hill in 1886. A clapboard-sided wood-frame building designed by architect Clinton Day, it featured an octagonal domed observatory which the 1887 *Blue and Gold* yearbook likened to "a roc's egg, silvered for Easter . . . above the pretty grove of young firs." It housed a twenty-inch reflecting telescope and other equipment used for instruction in astronomy, a course then required for all senior engineering students. Incremental alterations and expansion of the facility led to a "bungalow court" of seven small wood-shingle structures by 1926, containing classrooms, offices and several telescopes and astronomical transits. This grew to nine structures by 1951, when the facility was renamed the Leuschner Observatory, in honor of Armin Otto Leuschner, director of the observatory (1898–1938) and chairman of the Department of Astronomy (1900–1938). In 1972, thirteen years after the department moved to Campbell Hall, the buildings were demolished, with the exception of the

Leuschner Observatory relic

relic that still stands on the hill today, spared because it supported old wisteria vines. A nearby plaque commemorates the observatory.

Once a hillside of cypress and pine groves, much of the area was envisioned by John Galen Howard as the site for a museum, a classical counterpoint to his Doe Memorial Library across the central axis garden. Arthur Brown, Jr., maintained a similar concept in his 1944 General Plan, but in 1956 the idea was abandoned, and the campus Long Range Development Plan pledged to maintain the hill as a mostly open natural landscape amenity. A Northside student center was planned for the site in the 1960s but never built.

In 1966 the hill was proposed as an ecological study area, recognized for its chaparral habitat, plant and bird life, and native bee population, but it did not attain the status of the Wickson, Grinnell, and Goodspeed Natural Areas that were established on the campus three years later. Subsequent plans called for the "preservation and enhancement" of the natural hill, and led to the conversion of a parking lot near the Class of 1954 Gate to a landscaped meadow. The pathway that descends the west side of the hill to Haviland Hall dates from the late nineteenth century and offers a glimpse of the type of oak-dotted natural landscape that characterized the grounds prior to development of the campus.

19. Founders' Rock

On a clear spring day in 1860, twelve men—nine of them trustees of the College of California—gathered at the large "outcropping ledge" that today marks the northeast corner of the central campus. They had traveled the four miles from Oakland by horse-drawn carriages that sixteenth day of April to dedicate the grounds they had selected for the permanent site of their college two years earlier.

After exploring the sloping terrain between the two creek ravines, they chose this vantage point for their commemoration. The eucalyptus grove that now shades the area did not exist then, nor was there a building in sight. The entire grounds lay before them, a grain field with "grand old oaks" standing along the creeks and dotting the hills, the view sweeping toward the bay and out through the Golden Gate. "Ships were coming in and going out," one participant observed. "Asia seemed near—the islands of the sea looking this way." Following optimistic speeches, a prayer was offered to consecrate the new campus, and the group returned to Oakland, "well satisfied that the site was well chosen."

Six years later, the trustees had settled on the street names of their College Homestead community (see Walk 9), but remained tentative on a name for the town. Landscape architect Frederick Law Olmsted offered a long list of suggestions, ranging from geographical connotations to

Peralta—which was nearly adopted—for the holder of the vast Spanish land grant that once encompassed the college site. In May 1866 during a return visit to the rock by some of the trustees, Frederick Billings, inspired by the view of the Golden Gate, recited the following lines now associated with the city and university:

> Westward the course of empire takes its way;
> The four first acts already past,
> A fifth shall close the drama with the day;
> Time's noblest offspring is the last.[15]

They formed the last stanza of a poem in an essay by George Berkeley, written in *On the Prospect of Planting Arts and Learning in America.*

Founders' Rock

Berkeley, an eighteenth-century philosopher and Bishop of Cloyne, Ireland, had aspired to establish a university for British subjects in Bermuda. His vision of America as the westward hope for humanity—though nearly 150 years earlier—captured the imagination of the trustees, who on May 24 voted unanimously to name the town after the bishop.

Other notable gatherings at "Founders' Rock" would follow. Thirty years later, the Class of 1896 placed a plaque on the rock memorializing the dedication of the site in 1860. In April 1910, tribute was paid to recognize the event's fiftieth anniversary, the principal speaker being Samuel H. Willey, one of the trustees present at that original gathering. And in April 1960, the centennial of the site dedication was observed by Governor Edmund G. Brown, President Clark Kerr, Regents' Chairman Donald H. McLaughlin, and Lee Griswald and Richard Monges, two alumni who were present at the fixing of the plaque fifty years earlier.

Founders' Rock is listed on the National Register of Historic Places, is included in the Berkeley campus designation as a California Registered Historical Landmark, is listed on the State Historic Resources Inventory, and is a City of Berkeley Landmark.

20. Goldman School of Public Policy (2607 Hearst Avenue) and Cloyne Court (2600 Ridge Road)

Goldman School of Public Policy (2607 Hearst Avenue)
> *Ernest Coxhead, 1893;*
> *Bakewell and Brown, east addition, 1909;*
> *Architectural Resources Group, alterations, 1999*

Cloyne Court (2600 Ridge Road) *John Galen Howard, 1904*

Home to the Goldman School of Public Policy, the English Tudor-style building near the corner of Hearst and Le Roy Avenues is an important example of the First Bay Tradition and the work of Ernest Coxhead. The British-born architect used a variety of materials for the wood-frame struc-ture—wood shingles, stucco, half-timbers, and brick—to create a village-like house in 1893 for Beta Theta Pi, one of the earliest fraternities established at Berkeley. The fraternity occupied the house until 1966, when it moved to a larger Northside building. Acquired by the university, the house was first reused for a liberal arts undergraduate program before being assigned to the school in 1969. The school was named in 1997 for the alumni donors who also established the Richard and Rhoda Goldman Fund, a major Bay Area philanthropy.

The three-story building is comprised of four interconnected wings with steeply pitched gable and hipped roofs. The distinct architectural finish

Goldman School of Public Policy (2607 Hearst Avenue)

of each wing provides the impression of an assemblage of individual European homes, which though contrasting, together form a harmonious composition. The separate elements corresponded at one time to the interior functions of the fraternity that included a den and study rooms in the south wing, living room adjacent, dining room and bedrooms in the tall stuccoed section, and kitchen and bedrooms in the north wing. The variegated forms suggested a sense of differing time periods, as well as the medieval qualities often expressed in the English Arts and Crafts Movement. The simple residential treatment and rustic elements also exemplified the First Bay Tradition, with its emphasis on natural living, regional design, and compatibility with the landscape.

Coxhead arrived in America in 1885 and first worked in Los Angeles before settling in San Francisco four years later. He was among several young architects, including Bernard Maybeck and Albert C. Schweinfurth, who came to the Bay Area in the late nineteenth century and created new design alternatives to the ornamental Victorian period. The three architects were close colleagues, and comparisons of Coxhead's fraternity house with Maybeck's Faculty Club (see Walk 5) and Schweinfurth's former church at 2401 Bancroft Way (see Walk 4) illustrates their differing individual styles within the Bay Tradition Movement.

Expansion of the internationally recognized school was begun in 2001 with the construction of a second building (Architectural Resources Group) west of the house to provide additional classrooms, offices, seminar rooms, and research facilities.

2607 Hearst Avenue is listed on the State Historic Resources Inventory and is a City of Berkeley Landmark.

Cloyne Court (2600 Ridge Road)

Cloyne Court (2600 Ridge Road)

Built in 1904 as "a high class modern apartment house" and hotel, Cloyne Court catered especially to faculty and graduate students, as well as others residing in the university community. Named for the Irish home of Bishop George Berkeley, namesake of the city, it was developed by the University Land and Improvement Company, which had several university-affiliated backers, including Regent and benefactress Phoebe Apperson Hearst, donor Jane K. Sather, members of the faculty, and the building's architect, John Galen Howard. The home-like accommodations received distinguished visitors and provided initial housing for new professors and others associated with the university in the early twentieth century, among them Regent James K. Moffitt, the Howard family, and Howard's junior partner William C. Hays. Occupancy swelled in 1906 when residents extended their hospitality to refugees of the San Francisco earthquake and fire.

Though relatively large—about 200 feet along its Ridge Road facade—Cloyne Court was set back from the street and blended with the wood and clinker-brick residential Northside neighborhood. It was one of Howard's early shingled buildings and reflects his use of Beaux-Arts principles as well as the natural characteristics of the First Bay Tradition. A symmetrical three-story U-shaped wood-framed building with a hipped roof, it forms a courtyard—once a lush garden—on the south. The courtyard facades of the east and west wings are accentuated by polygonal staircase towers with pyramidal roofs, while the south facade of the central wing has projecting sunroom bays, balconies, and trellises. A small first floor space, originally a music room, that extends into the courtyard opposite the main entrance, was added to the building in 1911. The north facade has a central recessed entry with a bracketed shed roof that is surmounted by a shallow balcony. Additional balconies are centered within the bays of the facade on either side of the entrance.

In 1946, to help meet the increased demand for affordable housing for World War II veterans, the hotel was purchased by the University Students' Cooperative Association (USCA) and modified for use as a dormitory for approximately 150 male students. In the 1960s it was purchased by the university and leased back to the USCA until 2005. Now a co-ed facility, Cloyne Court is one of twenty co-op houses and apartment complexes located mostly in the Northside and Southside neighborhoods.

Cloyne Court is listed on the National Register of Historic Places and the State Historic Resources Inventory and is a City of Berkeley Landmark.

21. Soda Hall

Edward Larrabee Barnes Associates with Anshen and Allen, 1992–1994

Green-tiled Soda Hall, home of the Computer Science Division of the College of Engineering, forms an arcaded facade along sloping Hearst Avenue across from the central campus. A mid-block trellised walkway links the building to neo-Brutalist Etcheverry Hall (Skidmore, Owings & Merrill, 1962–64), the first building to extend the College into Northside. The

Soda Hall

terraced building was constructed over older underground laboratory extensions of Etcheverry that contained a one-megawatt nuclear reactor, which was decommissioned and removed in 1988. It doubled the space for the growing computer science program, which was previously located in Evans Hall.

Part of Chancellor Ira Michael Heyman's "Keeping the Promise" capital campaign, the $35 million building was funded by private gifts—from corporations, foundations, and individuals—topped in 1989 by a $15 million cornerstone donation from the Y & H Soda Foundation, and named in honor of Bay Area philanthropists Y. Charles and Helen C. Soda. The amount equaled that donated earlier the same year by the Haas family to fund the new business school, as the largest private donation to the Berkeley campus.

The architectural team of New York City–based Edward Larrabee Barnes and the San Francisco office of Anshen and Allen faced multiple challenges in designing the research and teaching facility. It had to be high-tech and evoke a sense of identity for the division, but also conducive to social interaction, while relating to the neighboring residential community. Their solution utilized a mid-building east-west circulation atrium between a five-story Hearst frontage that relates to the scale of Etcheverry, and a north block that, unlike Etcheverry, steps down in a series of terraces to an open space (reserved for future low-rise expansion) facing the neighborhood.

Inside, faculty offices are clustered to facilitate interaction, and the atrium-illuminated corridors include open discussion lounges for planned or impromptu student-faculty brainstorming. Windowed offices and carrels are peripherally located, with interior spaces used generally for classrooms and laboratories for research and teaching of integrated circuits and robotics. Supporting the premise that "the building is the computer," Soda Hall incorporates the latest networking and communications infrastructure, utilizing a distributed supercomputer and multimedia technology. Filled with corporation-donated hardware, the building's classrooms, offices, and laboratories—some 300 computer workstations—are interconnected with hundreds of miles of fiber-optic cables and copper wiring, in addition to the latest in wireless technology. Together all the computers link to form a cluster computer—a Network of Workstations—with increased resources and speed. Building and supercomputer have become one.

The green skin, two-story arcaded loggia, and palm trees along Hearst, give Soda Hall a distinctive Mediterranean appearance. The variegated colors of the German clay tiles were selected for their vegetation-like tones to relate to the residential neighborhood and provide a warm, non-industrial feeling. The building's base and horizontal bands of light green English slate with brown edging mark the floor levels and provide a sense of scale to the facade.

Euclid Avenue and Euclid Apartments

22. Euclid Avenue Neighborhood and "Holy Hill"

Directly across from North Gate, the low-rise shops and restaurants along narrow tree-lined Euclid Avenue are in keeping with the scale of the Northside neighborhood, which still has some of the character of its First Bay Tradition roots. Easily accessible to graduate and engineering students of the university and the advanced-degree seminary students of the nearby theological schools, Euclid's relaxed tempo is a pleasing contrast to the density of Southside and urban busyness of Westside. Euclid also serves as a southern gateway to the hillside residential neighborhoods, which were reached by an electric streetcar line in the early twentieth century.

At its south end the street is anchored by the dignified Euclid Apartments (1865 Euclid), designed by John Galen Howard and built in 1912. Standing across Hearst from Howard's shingled North Gate Hall, the symmetrical four-story building was considered by Howard's junior partner, William C. Hays, to be "[a]mong the most successful of [his] domestic buildings," where "enough color has been used in the cornice to make one wish there had been more."[16] Departing from the rustic Northside tradition of his nearby shingled Cloyne Court, Howard designed the stucco-finished Euclid building in an eclectic neoclassical style. Along with its decorative—but now monochromatic—cornice, the building's detailing includes a rusticated storefront basement, large arched entry, and balustrade-enclosed porch bays.

During the period of redevelopment of Northside following the 1923 firestorm, the Theological Seminary acquired property on a knoll with a bay view, one block west of Euclid at the intersection of Scenic Avenue,

Ridge Road, and LeConte Avenue. Later named the Pacific School of Religion, it was followed by other seminaries attracted by the proximity of the university and suitability of the Northside for conducting educational programs. Several relocated to the area in the 1960s by acquiring vacated fraternity houses for reuse. This community now includes six schools clustered within a three-block area on "Holy Hill," fronting on Scenic, Ridge, LeConte, and Euclid. They comprise part of the Graduate Theological Union (GTU), a multi-denominational theological consortium of nine seminaries, whose students benefit from interactive scholarship and shared library facilities, as well as access to university libraries and courses.

This grouping of small campuses includes a number of distinctive buildings—embracing a range of architectural styles from eclectic turn-of-the-century revivalism to modernism—that characterize the neighborhood. Among the most picturesque is Holbrook Hall at the Pacific School of Religion (1798 Scenic). Designed by Walter Ratcliff, Jr., and built in 1924, the gable-roofed rusticated-stone building is a prominent landmark in the English Academic Gothic style, with its decorative pinnacles and Gothic-arched windows. Also by Ratcliff are the chapel and hall of the Church Divinity School of the Pacific (2451 Ridge), a small brick Gothic Revival complex built in 1929. Nearby is the Dominican School of Philosophy and Theology (2401 Ridge), which includes an English Tudor Revival building built in 1923 and designed by Architecture Professor Stafford L. Jory, who, like Ratcliff, studied under and worked for John Galen Howard.

Holbrook Hall, Pacific School of Religion (1798 Scenic Avenue)

The Flora Lamson Hewlett Library of the GTU at the corner of Ridge and Scenic (2400 Ridge) was conceptualized by Louis I. Kahn and, following Kahn's death in 1974, completed by San Francisco architects Peters, Clayberg and Caulfield in association with Esherick Homsey Dodge and Davis. Built in two phases from 1981 to 1987, the modernist three-level terraced library-office building is crisply detailed with wood siding and geometrically patterned windows with metal frames and shades. A central atrium skylight illuminates the library, which contains one of the largest theological collections in the nation.

On the slope of "Holy Hill" are the former house and reception hall of Phoebe Hearst (2368 LeConte and 1816 Scenic), designed by Ernest Coxhead and completed in 1902. Next door is the former brown-shingle home of President Wheeler (1820 Scenic), designed by Edgar A. Matthews and built in 1900. Lewis Hobart remodeled the house in 1911, after the Wheeler family moved into the President's House on campus (see University House, Walk 3).

Central Campus Northwest

Replica of Lion *by Antonio Canova, University House*

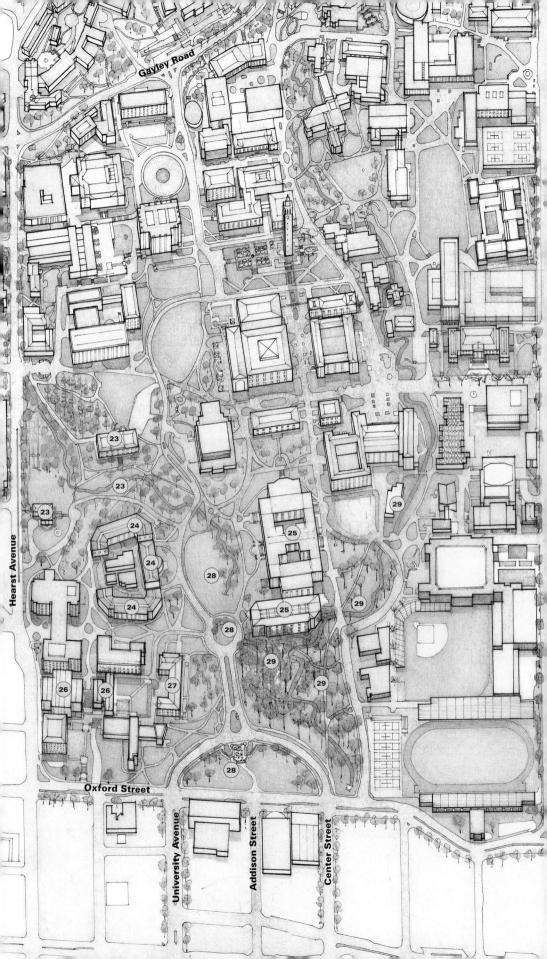

Gayley Road

Hearst Avenue

23
23
23
24
24
24
25
25
26
26
27
28
28
28
29
29
29
29

Oxford Street

University Avenue

Addison Street

Center Street

From the nineteenth-century agricultural origins of the university to genetic research at the forefront of the twenty-first, this walk through the northwest part of the central campus is rich in both campus history and scientific scholarship. It contains the only building completed under the 1900 plan of Émile Bénard, the western portion of John Galen Howard's Beaux-Arts ensemble, and an eclectic sampling of 1930s Art Deco, postwar neoclassicism and modernism, and late twentieth-century postmodernism. Within its open space is the meeting place of both forks of Strawberry Creek and two of the three designated central campus Natural Areas.

Most of the area—that west of the creeks to Oxford Street—was acquired from the College of California trustees one year after they transferred the original campus property to the university in 1868. A main entrance to the grounds was established close to the present one at Center Street and branched into a campus loop road that followed William Hammond Hall's plan of 1873. The present pathway through the Grinnell Natural Area generally follows the south branch of this loop. Use of the area also followed Hall's suggestion for "experimental and practical agriculture." By 1886 "economical gardens," grains, and orchards of pears, apples, plums, apricots, peaches, and a small grape vineyard occupied the area, with a few small hothouses and greenhouses and a stable near the north fork of the creek. The students' Cinder Track was in place, an oval constructed in 1882 and dedicated as "a monument to the untiring efforts of Colonel Edwards," the mathematics professor for whom Edwards Stadium and Fields were later named (see Walk 4).[1] Located on the present site of Life Sciences Addition, the track was protected from the Bay winds by the Eucalyptus Grove, planted in 1877 between the forks of the creek.

Class of 1905 Bench

Development of the area was first suggested in Émile Bénard's revised 1900 Plan, followed by Howard's 1908 proposal for peripheral dormitories, a concept later dropped in favor of leaving the western portion of the area open, with his monumental group of buildings to the east. Within this Walk, that group includes Haviland Hall and the Agriculture Group—Wellman, Hilgard, and Giannini (William C. Hays, architect)

Halls—which are counterbalanced across the central axis by California Hall and Valley Life Sciences Building, respectively.

With the exception of a row of headhouses and greenhouses along the Hearst Avenue edge, the area north of the present Crescent remained undeveloped until the mid-twentieth century. Called Hilgard Field or Memorial Drill Field, it was used for recreation and the drills of the Reserve Officers' Training Corps (ROTC), which was established at the advent of World War I and became part of the university curriculum in 1917. Howard's Crescent was finally completed in 1929, and for the next two decades his western "Forecourt" remained in a natural or open state.

But with the growth in enrollment following World War II, it was not possible to leave the land undeveloped, and Arthur Brown's 1944 Plan included a row of peripheral buildings sited along Hearst and Oxford. Though his plan was not exactly followed, the completion of Forestry's Mulford Hall (Miller & Warnecke, 1947–48) four years later initiated the permanent development of Hilgard Field. After Mulford came Morgan Hall (Spencer & Ambrose, 1952–53) for Home Economics and the International Style Warren Hall (Masten & Hurd, 1953–55) for Public Health. The following decade, two six-story concrete buildings, massive Tolman Hall (Gardner A. Dailey & Associates, 1959–62) for Education and Psychology, and boxy Barker Hall (Wurster, Bernardi & Emmons, 1962–64) for Biochemistry, completed a quadrangle of unrelated modernist buildings. The infill development of Koshland Hall and the Genetics and Plant Biology Teaching Building complex (Hellmuth, Obata and Kassabaum, 1986–90), linked to the rooftop landscaping of the underground Northwest Animal Facility (NBBJ, 1988–93), added density but also coherence as a focal point to the area. Across the West Circle the Life Sciences Addition (MBT Associates, 1986–88) for the Biological Sciences rose between the Valley Life Sciences Building and the Eucalyptus Grove during the same period.

The replacement of outmoded Warren is planned for the northwest corner, as part of the university's $500-million Health Sciences Initiative. An interdisciplinary center of biomedical and health sciences is proposed to accommodate new research in areas such as bioinformatics, combining computer sciences with bioengineering for work related to human genome studies.

Haviland Hall

23. Haviland Hall, Wickson Natural Area, and University House

Haviland Hall

John Galen Howard, 1923–1924;

Callister & Payne, interior alterations, 1962–1963;

Blake-Drucker/Kay, interior restoration and alterations, 1986

Wickson Natural Area *Designated 1969*

University House

Albert A. Pissis, 1900–1902;

John Galen Howard, interior finishing,

East Terrace addition, garden and landscaping, 1910–1911;

Brocchini Associates, seismic alterations, 1990;

Page & Turnbull, alterations and renovation, 1997–1998

Haviland Hall was built for the School of Education, which included the Lange Library of Education, the first of the campus branch libraries established to relieve overcrowding in Doe Memorial Library. At its dedication in 1924 Education Dean William W. Kemp praised the building as being the "capstone for the arch of the public school system of California." It now houses the School of Social Welfare and offices of the School of Public Health.

Haviland stands at the base of the west slope of Observatory Hill, atop a steep embankment overlooking the north fork of Strawberry Creek. Its rectangular shape and location conform to Howard's Plan, although a Fine Arts building was originally designated for the site. The building was aligned with California Hall to form a counterbalance across the central axis, a relationship that was obfuscated by the intermediate construction of Moffitt Undergraduate Library in 1970 (see Walk 1). Construction of the building and its approaches required the removal of the Victorian glass and steel Conservatory (Lord & Burnham Company, 1891) that stood on the site of the present adjacent parking lot.

Constructed of concrete and steel with mission-tile hipped roofs, Haviland is a symmetrical neoclassical building comprised of a four-story central block, capped with a large copper skylight and flanked by north and south three-story end wings. It is rich in detailing and exemplifies Howard's remarkable skill in achieving variety among his individual buildings, while maintaining the unity of the ensemble through the use of a family of forms and materials and the application of guiding Beaux-Arts principles.

Symbols related to the building's original use are expressed on the central attic zone, where open books within swags appear between the windows, and over the entrances, with medallions of Pegasus—regarded as the horse of the Muses—in the patinated ornamental railings. Other details—ornamented soffits, floral-patterned quoins, spiral torus moldings, volute brackets—enrich the exterior.

Arched double golden-oak doors open to the west lobby where stairways with palmette-ornamented metal railings stand beneath a suspended Art Nouveau chandelier. The namesake of the original Education Library and director of the School of Education from 1914 to 1922, Alexis F. Lange, is memorialized in this lobby. He is the subject of a monumental oil painting, custom-mounted for the space in an oak frame that is elegantly carved with the lamp of learning and seal of the university.

In 1963, when the School of Social Welfare moved into Haviland following relocation of Education to newly built Tolman Hall, interior alterations compromised Howard's second-floor library. But in 1986 the neoclassical room, designed in the style of eighteenth-century Scottish architect Robert Adam, was restored by San Francisco architects Bonnie Blake-

Drucker and Michael Kay for use as the Social Welfare Library. Deteriorated sections of its carved bas-relief plaster ceiling were recreated from molds of existing details, and Corinthian pilasters were renewed by hand-sculpting the plaster. The restored library, along with an adjacent seminar room, is among the significant remaining interiors of Howard's campus buildings.

The building and an approach road (which no longer exists but was partially subsumed by the realignment of University Drive in 1992) were named in honor of Hannah N. Haviland, whose bequest to the university provided the majority of construction funds.

Plaster details, Social Welfare Library, Haviland Hall

Haviland Hall is listed on the National Register of Historic Places and the State Historic Resources Inventory, and is a City of Berkeley Landmark. The Social Welfare Library, in 227 Haviland, is open during the academic calendar year Monday through Thursday from 9am to 7pm, and Friday and Saturday from 9am to 5pm. Hours vary during the summer and other periods.

Wickson Natural Area

One of the treasured campus riparian environments, the Wickson Natural Area embraces the north fork of Strawberry Creek, from the creek's entry near North Gate to its culvert near Giannini Hall. It is one of three designated creek habitats—along with the Grinnell and Goodspeed Natural Areas—established by Chancellor Roger W. Heyns in 1969.[2] It was named in honor of Edward J. Wickson, Dean of the College of Agriculture and Director of the Agricultural Experiment Station from 1906 to 1912 and a member of the faculty from 1879 to 1923.

The area contains the oldest stand of coast redwoods (*Sequoia sempervirens*) on campus, dating from about 1870, and a celebrated Chinese ginkgo (*Ginkgo biloba*), one of the largest on the West Coast, standing just east of Giannini. Planted in 1881, this treasured ginkgo becomes a glorious golden landmark before dropping its foliage each autumn.

In 1962 Chancellor Edward W. Strong declared that the region should remain intact as a "natural area." But as rapid postwar development threatened to encroach upon all the creek environments, faculty who valued the areas as "living laboratories" for biology and landscape architecture proposed stronger protection. In addition to bays, oaks, buckeyes, and redwoods, the creeks were recognized as active habitats for a variety of flora, including ferns, horsetails, and thimbleberry bushes, and fauna such as squirrels, fish, salamanders, birds, and insects.

Chinese gingko treet, Wickson Natral Area

In 1968 construction of Moffitt Undergraduate Library (see Walk 1) necessitated the realignment of University Drive to the north side of the central axis. The planned route would have required removal of four redwoods and construction of a new bridge over the creek. Responding to an outpour of protests from students, faculty, and staff, Chancellor Heyns had the road redesigned to bypass the grove and directed that it be used only for essential vehicles and not cross-campus traffic. "The new plan," he promised, "will retain an important natural area, and also maintain the center of the campus as a pedestrian area."[4]

In addition to its environmental qualities, the area has been the setting for several historic commemorations. The Samuel Hopkins Willey Memorial Redwood honors the acting president of the College of California, who was one of the drafters of the Organic Act that led to the creation of the university in 1868. A century later, a new redwood, the Centennial Tree, was planted and dedicated to President Emeritus Robert Gordon Sproul a few yards north of the Willey Redwood along the creek bank opposite the entrance to Giannini. Accompanying the planting, a time capsule containing documents and mementos was buried in a concrete crypt—to be opened on the bicentennial anniversary in 2068. Of many suggestions received for the capsule contents, Executive Vice Chancellor Earl F. Cheit revealed one that campus officials could "use this occasion to bury our mistakes. That would require a somewhat larger box, and in any case, might itself be mistaken in 2068 as an attempt to leave a truly profound message about campus administration."[5] In December 1995, Cheit returned to these redwoods to dedicate the Roger W. Heyns Grove, in memory of the former Chancellor and savior of the trees, who was fondly remembered as "a gift of heaven to leadership of the Berkeley campus" and "a model academic man."[6]

The Samuel Hopkins Willey Memorial Redwood is a City of Berkeley Landmark.

University House

Sited on a bluff adjacent to Hearst Avenue, the President's House—as it was originally named—was the only building constructed in conformance with

Émile Bénard's revised 1900 Plan. With a silver shovel, Regent Phoebe Apperson Hearst broke ground for the house on May 12, 1900, in a spirit of optimism for the transformation the Hearst Plan would effect at the university in the new century. The ceremony was included in the traditional pilgrimage on Class Day, when members of the senior class bade farewell to the campus, and it attracted a large group of spectators gathered around "the picturesque site in the University gardens."

"It is peculiarly fitting that the first official act of helping towards the realization of our plans for the greater University should be the laying of a foundation for a home," Regent Hearst remarked in her address read by President Wheeler. "It is our hope that, as time brings the opportunity, there may rise on these grounds noble buildings ideally adapted to the needs of the ever-broadening domain of thought, investigation and experiment, not merely for erudition, but for the preparation that will enable it and take the initiative in the intellectual and moral advance of the years to come."[7]

Beaux-Arts trained architect Albert Pissis was known for classic designs with Italian or Palladian influences, and the house, described in a 1909 article as "a villa in sunny Italy," was no exception. Topped with a red mission-tile hipped roof, the neoclassical mansion has a symmetrical front facade composed of a triple-arched, colonnaded entrance portico, flanked by east and west two-story wings with hooded rectangular windows. On the first floor, bow-shaped bays with surmounted balustrades project on the east and west facades. Inside the sandstone-faced residence, a central reception hall leads to a living room in the west wing and drawing and dining rooms in the east. These wood-paneled areas are used for special events and receptions, while the upper floors are for private use.

For the pedestals flanking the granite entrance stairs, a pair of terracotta jars was first proposed, until Regent Philip E. Bowles presented the university with Carrara marble replicas of a pair of lions that Italian sculptor Antonio Canova (1757–1822) created for the tomb of Clement XIII in the Vatican.[8] President Wheeler responded enthusiastically that the pedestals "seem to have been made for the Canova lions," recommending that "those beautiful sculptures might fittingly have their place."[9]

But the Wheeler family had to remain in their private home a block north of campus (at 1820 Scenic Avenue) for eleven years after the groundbreaking. Uncertain funding delayed the mansion's completion, and academic needs pressed the house into service as a classroom building. In 1910 John Galen Howard finished the interior, which included furnishings by J. Henry P. Atkins, of Vickery Atkins & Torrey, the distinguished San Francisco design and decorating firm that also contributed to the interiors of Durant (Boalt) Hall and Doe Memorial Library. Howard also added the East Terrace, installed the private garden, and completed the landscaping and approaches around the house.

In early 1911, President Wheeler belatedly moved into his new home, the first in a succession of resident-presidents, who included David Prescott Barrows, William Wallace Campbell, and Robert Gordon Sproul. Occupancy was interrupted following President Sproul's retirement in 1958, when President Clark Kerr chose to maintain his private residence. The mansion was then renamed University House and used for official functions, until it was reoccupied by the first resident Chancellor, Roger W. Heyns, in 1965. Succeeding Heyns as residents were Chancellors Albert H. Bowker, Ira Michael Heyman, Chang-Lin Tien, and, presently, Robert M. Berdahl.

Shortly after President Wheeler moved in, he received as house-guest his close friend and former U. S. President Theodore Roosevelt, who arrived to address the 1911 Charter Day ceremonies. He was the first of many distinguished guests and visitors, among whom were U. S. Presidents Harry S. Truman and John F. Kennedy; the kings of Morocco, Iran, Greece, and Nepal, and the queen of the Netherlands; the president of France; and prime ministers of India, Canada, Germany, and Pakistan.

University House is listed on the National Register of Historic Places, is included in the Berkeley campus designation as a California Registered Historical Landmark, is listed on the State Historic Resources Inventory, and is a City of Berkeley Landmark.

University House

Wellman Hall, with Hilgard Hall, left, *and Giannini hall,* right

24. The Agriculture Group: Wellman Hall, Hilgard Hall, and Giannini Hall

Wellman Hall

> *John Galen Howard, 1910–1912;*
> *Ratcliff, Slama and Cadwalader, interior alterations, 1966–1967*

Hilgard Hall

> *John Galen Howard, 1916–1917;*
> *Ratcliff & Ratcliff, interior alterations, 1960–1961*

Giannini Hall   *William C. Hays, 1929–1930; Ratcliff & Ratcliff, interior alterations, 1962*

"Of all the departments of the University, the well-being of the State is most closely interlocked with the college of agriculture," President Wheeler addressed the dedication ceremony of Agriculture (now Wellman) Hall in November 1912. "Training in the science and art of agriculture short courses and spreading of information through farmers' institutes are the chief aims." His comments recalled the importance of the university's largest college, which the state legislature established when it created the university in 1868.

Reflecting that significance, John Galen Howard sited the building on a knoll overlooking the central axis near the western entrance to the grounds. It was the first building and the focal point of an Agriculture Group that would form a trapezoidal courtyard with future buildings Hilgard and Giannini Halls on the west and east, respectively. Each building—though distinct in treatment and built in different periods—was designed to form part of a unified whole, a composition that Howard modeled after a Tuscan farm. A greenhouse structure was also proposed but never built to define the north side of the courtyard, which has yet to be completed as a landscaped space; it has functioned instead as a parking lot and more recently as a location for temporary buildings. Restoration of the outdoor space was proposed in the 1990 Long Range

Study of Agriculture Group, circa 1912, John Galen Howard

Development Plan. The group was to align on a cross-axis south of the central glade with a Natural Science Group that took the form of the (Valley) Life Sciences Building in 1930.

Wellman Hall is a four-story rectangular building with a distinctive semicircular apse centered on its principal or south facade. The red tile hipped roof is prominently capped by a copper-framed skylight in the theme of the greater ensemble. As the fifth academic building of the Hearst Plan, its construction generated excitement when its framework began to silhouette the curved form. "The steel for Agriculture Hall has now been erected although not yet riveted," Secretary of the Regents Victor Henderson wrote to the architect. "It is already apparent how greatly the realization of the Plan has advanced by this monument in the westward expansion of the buildings. It has a glorious situation there on its bluff."[10]

Wellman was sheathed in granite, but not the same stone from the Raymond quarry in the Sierra foothills that graced Howard's earlier buildings. That quarry was narrowly outbid by the California Granite Company in Rocklin, causing concern for architect William Otis Raiguel, in charge of the office while Howard was in Europe. "[I]t is desirable," he commented, "to have the buildings of the University on the Campus correspond with each other in the color, texture, weathering properties, etc. of the granite."[11] This issue was so important to Howard's office that Raiguel even suggested that, for future buildings, the university continue to contract with Raymond to maintain a supply of rough stone, which could then be subject to bid for cutting and construction. Before accepting the low bid, Raiguel and Geology Professor Andrew C. Lawson visited the Rocklin quarries and inspected other buildings that had used that company's stone. After evaluating tests, the contract was let, but on the condition that an inspector reside at the quarries to make sure that Howard's high standards would be met.

Howard detailed the granite facade with rustication and quoins, and used a central, projecting monumental arch that originally provided public access to a steeply tiered, semi-circular 250-seat auditorium within the apse. Surmounting the south entrances of the two end pavilions, he featured granite-arched and mullioned windows, reminiscent of those in Leon Battista Alberti's Palazzo Rucellai (c. 1450) in Florence.[12]

In addition to the auditorium, the first floor originally contained a semicircular agriculture museum within a corridor beneath the highest tier of seats, library, laboratory for horticulture and viticulture, and offices. Laboratories for entomology and plant pathology, apparatus rooms, a lecture room and studies occupied the second floor, while the basement included areas related to plant spraying and beekeeping. The skylighted attic also provided useable space.

Coincidental with the completion of the new building was the appointment of a new Dean of Agriculture, Thomas Forsyth Hunt. He promptly recruited John W. Gregg, who taught under Hunt at Penn State University, to establish in the building a new Division of Landscape Gardening and Floriculture—forerunner of today's Department of Landscape Architecture and Environmental Planning in the College of Environmental Design. An attempt to name the new division Landscape Architecture was thwarted by Howard, who felt that the discipline should be under the purview of the Supervising Architect and not the College of Agriculture. Despite this feeling, Gregg and his faculty colleagues advised Howard on planting plans for several buildings including Wellman, but Gregg would not become Consulting Landscape Architect to the campus until 1926 when Howard was no longer Supervising Architect.[13]

In the 1960s the college was restructured, leading to interior alterations of the building including conversion of Howard's tiered auditorium to a museum. In 1966 the name in the curving frieze over the apse windows was changed to honor Harry Richard Wellman, professor of agricultural economics and then vice-president of the university. The following year he was appointed acting president after President Clark Kerr was dismissed during the student protests of that period.

With the merger of the College of Agriculture and the School of Forestry and Conservation, the College of Natural Resources was established in 1974. It now encompasses four departments that reflect further reorganization of the college during the 1990s. College functions in Wellman now include the Essig Museum of Entomology, which maintains a research collection of terrestrial Arthropoda, numbering approximately 4.5 million specimens.

Hilgard Hall

The second building of the Agriculture Group, Hilgard Hall was funded by the $1.8 million state bond issue of 1914 that also enabled construction of Wheeler Hall, Gilman Hall, and the completion of Doe Memorial Library. John Galen Howard intended to continue his use of granite on all of these buildings, but rising costs brought about by World War I caused the

Regents to consider less expensive alternatives. They agreed not to compromise the Library and Wheeler and at first thought Hilgard could also be
granite. But space needs ultimately governed their decision and in March
1916 Howard was authorized to use reinforced concrete for both Gilman
and Hilgard. Howard, of course, was not happy with the change, as his former partner and faculty colleague William C. Hays recalled: "He was hired
to come out here and do monuments in granite."[14] But the use of granite
for the classical "City of Learning" had come to an end.

Construction in reinforced concrete was still relatively new,
used mostly since the 1906 San Francisco fire and earthquake, and Civil
Engineering Dean Charles Derleth, Jr., who had consulted with Howard on
the structural design of the Campanile, was brought in to engineer Hilgard.
Planned in the shape of an asymmetrical "C" to form the west side of the
courtyard, the four-story building consists of a north-south block, flanked by
lower, hipped-roof, elbowed north and south wings. The building's width
and height relate to Wellman, the centerpiece of the group. The principal
west facade is a symmetrical neoclassical composition of eleven bays
defined by an engaged Doric colonnade with paired pilasters at each end.
Establishing the theme of agricultural extension and production, a large
inscription, composed by President Wheeler, spans the long frieze above
the main entablature: "TO RESCUE FOR HUMAN SOCIETY THE NATIVE
VALUES OF RURAL LIFE."

Reflecting this credo, Hilgard is a feast for the eyes, richly decorated with agricultural icons. Within the classical entablature, garlanded
bull's heads gaze down over each column capital. These project from a decorative Tuscan-red and creamy gray colored frieze formed by the Italian

Hilgard Hall

Sgraffito frieze and decorative motifs symbolize agriculture, Hilgard Hall

Renaissance art of sgraffito, in which a shallow cameo effect is created by scratching through overlaying coats of contrasting plaster. This frieze and other sgraffiti panels and friezes on the building were the work of Paul E. Denneville, who had been Supervisor of Texture and Modeling at the 1915 Panama-Pacific International Exposition in San Francisco.

Centered in the bays between the bull's heads are vases and cornucopia overflowing with flowers and fruits. Similar images appear on the end pilasters, while each spandrel between the windows features a farm-animal medallion within a festoon of fruits and flowers. The central entrance is surmounted by a sculpted bowl of fruit with additional cornucopia, while the grillwork of the metal doors is patterned with stylized California poppies, the state flower. Additional sgraffiti decorate the end wings, where other entrances and windows are surmounted by bracketed balconies ornamented with sheaves of wheat and vegetative forms. Not to be overlooked in this botanical and zoological celebration is the cast classical detailing, exquisitely formed from base moldings to entablatures.

Housed within the building were laboratories, lecture rooms, classrooms, and offices for use by the divisions of Agronomy, Citriculture, Forestry, Genetics, Pomology, Soil Technology, and Viticulture. To celebrate the building's opening, President Wheeler presided over a Saturday morning dedication ceremony in October 1917 in the Eucalyptus Grove. A program of speakers was followed by afternoon conferences and a closing convention of the California Nurseryman's Association in the new building, where citrus and semi-tropical fruits and new plant creations were displayed during the day.

The building was named for Eugene Woldemar Hilgard, venerated professor of agriculture and agricultural chemistry (1874–1904), who established and directed the California Agricultural Experiment Station in 1888, the first such station in the United States. A bronze bust of Professor Hilgard stands atop a fluted pedestal within a niche in the first floor lobby. Sculpted by San Francisco artist Ralph Stackpole in 1912, it was originally placed at the entrance of Wellman. A gift of the college's faculty and alumni and the Agricultural Club, it was praised at the time as being "exceedingly well thought out in poise and pattern, and the treatment of the countenance is full of dexterity and knowledge." In the 1960s the interior of Hilgard was extensively remodeled, and the building now houses offices and labs of the College of Natural Resources.

Giannini Hall

For twelve years following the construction of Hilgard, the Agriculture Group remained incomplete, awkwardly unbalanced without its third building to form the east side of the courtyard. Its completion was made possible in 1928 by a $1.5-million grant from the Bancitaly Corporation in honor of its president, Amadeo Peter Giannini. Two-thirds of this amount established the Giannini Foundation of Agricultural Economics, with the remaining one-third donated for the construction of a building that would house the foundation. The new building and its specialized library would be named for Giannini, founder of the Bank of Italy in San Francisco (later to become the world's largest bank, Bank of America) and a future Regent of the university (1934–1949).

With John Galen Howard no longer Supervising Architect, the selection of his former junior partner and faculty colleague William Charles Hays to design Giannini Hall was appropriate. Hays played a role in the execution of the Hearst Plan and assisted in the design of Doe Memorial Library and Hilgard. Within the predetermined footprint and envelope of Howard's plan for the group—the third building being an opposing "C" to mirror Hilgard—Hays designed Giannini in a neoclassical mode with Moderne elements.

Like Hilgard, Giannini is four stories with a red-tile hipped roof and composed primarily of reinforced-concrete construction, though less adorned. But to orient the building to the central circulation patterns of campus, Hays placed the main entrance on the chamfered southeast wing, with sweeping stairs ascending from a brick and marble-banded entry

Giannini Hall

Lobby, Giannini Hall

court. Facing the creek, this entry facade is distinguished by a Regency style projecting bay of travertine, surmounted by a balcony. Decorative bas-relief panels with floral patterns and flowering urns flank the central recessed doorway and reflect the agricultural theme of the group.

The Moderne style wrought-iron entrance leads to a two-level lobby, which historian Gray Brechin has called one of the finest spaces of Art Deco design in the San Francisco Bay Area.[15] The concrete-beamed ceiling is decorated in polychromatic Art Deco and Indian motifs and has hanging metal Art Deco light fixtures. A multi-colored marble niche memorializes and frames a bronze bust of donor Giannini. Within the space a curving stairway with an ornamental railing leads to the main level.

The long east facade is decorated with cast-concrete toga-draped Roman figures in relief. These were the work of the architect's wife, Elah Hale Hays, an accomplished sculptor who taught the fine arts for thirty-two years at the California College of Arts and Crafts in Oakland. The west facade has a two-story loggia—a feature that could be more appreciated if the courtyard is developed in the future. Composed of nine bays formed by squared columns and with four monumental urns, the loggia is reached from the courtyard by a straight stairway leading through an elaborate ornamental metal gateway. Additional ornamental ironwork is used on balconies on the side wings of the building.

As with Wellman and Hilgard, the interior of Giannini was remodeled during the 1960s. The building is now occupied primarily by the College of Natural Resources and also houses the Electron Microscope Laboratory, an instruction and research unit of the College of Letters and Science.

Wellman, Hilgard, and Giannini Halls, comprising the Agriculture Group, are listed on the National Register of Historic Places, are included in the Berkeley campus designation as a California Registered Historical Landmark, are listed on the State Historic Resources Inventory, and are City of Berkeley Landmarks.

Valley Life Sciences Building

25. Valley Life Sciences Building and Life Sciences Addition

Valley Life Sciences Building
  George W. Kelham, 1929–1930;
  The Ratcliff Architects, alterations and renovation, 1989–1994
Life Sciences Addition *MBT Associates, 1986–1988*

Before its completion in 1930, George W. Kelham's Life Sciences Building (LSB) was proudly proclaimed as "the largest and best equipped" academic building in the world. Funded primarily by a 1926 state bond issue that was actively campaigned for by students and alumni, the five-story building created a mammoth footprint, approximately 250 feet wide and 500 feet long, and its racetrack corridors and hallways totaled well over one mile in length. Its record size prompted some architects to tag LSB as the "Life Size Building."

Thirteen departments moved into the building, many of them prominently inscribed on its corner pavilions: Botany, Zoology, Bacteriology, Physiology, Vertebrate Zoology, Anatomy, Psychology, and Biochemistry. In the process eleven old buildings scattered across the campus—most long considered wooden fire traps or otherwise inadequate—were emptied and removed from the grounds. The building's opening occurred in the inaugural year of incoming President Robert Gordon Sproul, who praised his predecessor, stating that the new building "represents a crowning achievement of President Campbell's administration."

Kelham applied Beaux-Arts principles in siting the building in alignment with the campus axis and in general conformance with Howard's Plan, by centering it on California Hall to the east, and forming a north-south cross-axis with the Agriculture Group across the glade to the north. The major difference was that Howard, never anticipating such growth, envisioned a symmetrically arranged Natural Science Group of five smaller buildings, rather than one giant block. And whereas Howard's group would have been classically designed, Kelham introduced an eclectic Moderne style to the Beaux-Arts ensemble.

The building's size was somewhat mitigated by articulation of the mass into blocks and the creation of scale through the size and pattern of fenestration and display of geometric and naturalistic figures and symbols—which comprise a three-dimensional encyclopedia of Art Deco ornamentation. To season the mix, a few neoclassical elements were tossed in as well, expressed in columns, denticulation, and egg-and-dart moldings.

Detail, Valley Life Sciences Building

Art Deco cast decorative medallion by Robert Howard

The concrete, neo- or perhaps pseudo-Babylonian building is a large rectangle with taller projecting corner pavilions marking the four original entrances, and lower wings extending out from the east and west facades. The corner pavilions feature fluted Composite columns beneath a frieze with peering, garlanded ox skulls (bucranium), and, in the attic zone, facing griffins that guard the inscribed departmental names. The entrances are flanked by Egyptian-Babylonian priest-figures agriculturally engaged in planting trees and potted plants.

The main facade—uninterrupted prior to the 1994 renovation—is rhythmically composed of narrow bays with industrial steel-sash windows, defined by pilasters with anthemion-decorated capitals. Medallions of stylized creatures—lions, rams, crabs, snails, geckos, snakes, and fish—encircle the building along the base, echoing the rhythm of the window bays. This creative menagerie is attributed to sculptor Robert

Boardman Howard (John Galen Howard's son). The east wing displays a *feroher*, or winged disc, above the entrance to the Chan Shun Auditorium (named for Hong Kong businessman and donor Chan Shun), which is flanked by a herd of more ox-heads atop fluted pilasters. At the skyline, the building's parapet has repeating, palmetted antefixae that accentuate the horizontal rhythm of the facade. Collectively, this ornamental explosion of flora and fauna heralds the study of the life sciences pursued within. Architectural critic Allan Temko was not so celebratory, characterizing the building as "an outburst of total eclectic confusion."[16]

Art Deco style of naturalistic and geometric ornament

The renovation of the building by The Ratcliff Architects some sixty years later completed the three-phase construction program for the biological sciences that was included in Chancellor Heyman's "Keeping the Promise" campaign. Funded by state appropriation, gifts and other sources, the $91 million make-over accompanied the building's renaming in 1989 in honor of Wayne and Gladys Valley, whose Foundation's contribution of $15 million matched those made for the Haas School of Business and Soda Hall as the largest gift in campus history. Valley Life Sciences Building is now home to the Department of Integrative Biology, which was reorganized from many of the former departments whose names still grace the facade.

The renovation project completely gutted old LSB and increased its space by infilling most of the interior courtyard and adding rooftop enclosures to accommodate some fifty laboratories, research centers, two auditoriums and six classrooms, a library, three research collections, offices, and service areas. To improve circulation and communication and create adequate library and collection areas, the architects, led by Crodd Chin (Class of 1966), replaced much of the long ring corridor system with a transverse lobby-corridor that connects to a dramatic, three-story atrium at the building's center. This was accomplished by introducing two new main entrances, centered on the long north and south facades. Initially proposed as projecting postmodern steel porticos, these were given more subtle entrance marquees, formed by a trio of cantilevered, dark-bronze, aluminum canopies. They are the most obvious exterior modifications to provide a clue that the large Moderne box contains state-of-the-art scientific facilities.

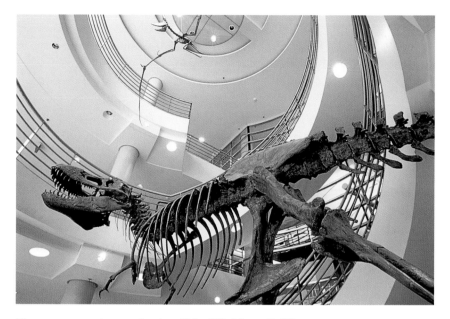

Tyrannosaurus rex in central atrium, Valley Life Sciences Building

But the focal point of the central atrium is not High-Tech, but rather Cretaceous, a freestanding skeletal mount of a full-grown *Tyrannosaurus rex*, the largest known carnivore. This dinosaur, cast from a skeleton excavated in Montana in 1990, stands imposingly on the first floor within the atrium's open-spiral stairwell. To keep him company, a pterosaur, or flying reptile, *Pteranodon ingens*, is suspended from the third-floor ceiling, soaring high above in a banked left turn.

T. rex stands between the entrances to two of the university's oldest collections. The west side of the first floor houses the Museum of Paleontology, which has approximately twenty million specimens, fourth largest collection in the nation. Established in 1874, it contains fossil and modern organisms, including protists, plants, invertebrates and vertebrates. Across the atrium is the University and Jepson Herbaria, with combined botanical collections dating from 1895 and totaling approximately 1.8 million specimens, the largest at an American public university.

On the west side of the second floor, the atrium opens to the 450,000-volume Marian Koshland Bioscience & Natural Resources Library. The open stacks extend into the building's low west wing, where two mezzanines form a three-level atrium with a steel-framed glass roof that transmits daylight and offers glimpses of Kelham's Art Deco facade. Above the library, on the third floor, is the Museum of Vertebrate Zoology (MVZ), a premier center for the research, conservation, and study of terrestrial vertebrates. Founded in 1908, its collections total approximately 625,000 specimens, among the largest in the nation, and include amphibians, reptiles, birds, and mammals.

Across from the library and MVZ, the building's central atrium opens onto a remnant of the old LSB courtyard, but one floor higher and transformed from a utilitarian light well into a colorful, postmodern, High-Tech feature. Here a shed-roofed sky-light reaches into the T-shaped space, which has pillared light fixtures and glass-block cubes that allow light into the herbaria below. The courtyard walls are painted in differing earth tones beneath a glass-gabled rooftop greenhouse that forms a stylized pediment flanked by open pairs of columns and architraves.

Courtyard, Valley Life Sciences Building

The Valley Life Sciences Building is listed on the State Historic Resources Inventory.

Life Sciences Addition

Threaded between Valley Life Sciences Building and the Eucalyptus Grove is MBT's Life Sciences Addition, a six-story laboratory facility for research in the fields of ethology; neurobiology; behavior, cell, and developmental biology; immunology; and endocrinology. Funded by state bonds, the $47 million facility was the first of the three Biological Sciences projects.

The building replaced a surface parking lot and occupies the former site of the historic oval Cinder Track. Its adjacency and connection to Valley Life Sciences Building provides occupants of both buildings shared access to shops, library resources, and animal facilities. Within the constraints of the narrow site, the architects were asked to provide forty-three state-of-the-art research labs, a 100-seat lecture hall, and separate controlled environments for housing both cold- and warm-blooded animals used in research.

Life Sciences Addition

The poured-in-place concrete structure is laid out on twenty-foot modular bays and includes three transverse shear walls and a waffle floor slab system designed to control vibrations and maximize flexibility in lab arrangements. Pre-cast concrete wall panels form the window openings, and a steel frame supports the roof. The architects related the building's form and materials to the classical vocabulary of the campus, especially the historic Agriculture Group across the glade. This is most apparent in their use of the red mission-tile hipped roof with its corner chamfers, rusticated wall panels, hierarchy of window sizes, and compatible colors. The sixth-floor circular windows—alternating with square ones—also recall the gabled windows of Hearst Memorial Mining Building. In addition to these classical influences, a postmodern touch is seen in the three-story-high stylized architrave that defines the main northeast entrance. But the siting of the 300-foot-long building, which protrudes into the central axis, resulted in an awkward eccentric relationship to the symmetrical Valley Life Sciences Building and upset the long-established cross-axial balance between that building and the Agriculture Group north of the glade.

26. Koshland Hall and Genetics and Plant Biology Teaching Building

Hellmuth, Obata and Kassabaum, 1986–1990

This two-building complex formed the second phase of the program linked to the comprehensive reorganization of the biological sciences. The complex, constructed over a parking garage, includes a five-story research building, Koshland Hall, joined by a plaza to a two-story teaching building, which opens onto a landscaped square to the south. The laboratory and classroom facilities are used for programs in biochemistry, molecular biology, plant genetics, and genetics.

Genetics and Plant Biology Teaching Building

The site was formerly a large surface parking lot, a paved quadrangle surrounded on three sides by the disparate grouping of Tolman, Morgan, Mulford, Warren, and Barker Halls. Within this framework of architectural disunity, the two buildings and their related open spaces form a focal point that ties the densely packed northwest corner together. Koshland, tightly sited between Barker and Tolman, fills-in the frontage along Hearst Avenue, while the smaller teaching building stands as a pavilion within the public open space.

Koshland Hall

By organizing the large program into two components, William Valentine of internationally renowned architects Hellmuth, Obata and Kassabaum was able to reduce the more massive scale that a single structure would have presented. The scale was also skillfully controlled by expressing the cruciform-plan of Koshland and half-cruciform of the teaching building as individual gabled wings. This massing and the style of the two buildings were influenced by the architect's understanding of the classical vocabulary of the campus. This is evident in the use of base molding to form a plinth; white striated concrete walls; formally composed windows with green-colored sash; circular attic openings under the gables and ventilation "chimneys" that are drawn from Howard's Mining Building; and red-tile gabled roofs. The Mining Building also influenced the original design, which featured stepped end gables—but those were dropped for budgetary reasons. Also deleted because of cost was a gabled glass canopy that would have sheltered the connecting plaza, which forms an east-west view corridor and gateway linked to the terraced roof of the underground Northwest Animal Facility (NBBJ, 1988–1993) to the west.

The complex was the first facility constructed under Chancellor Heyman's "Keeping the Promise" capital campaign. In 1992, the research building was named to honor Daniel E. Koshland, Jr., distinguished professor emeritus in the department of molecular and cell biology, who spearheaded the reorganization of the biological sciences and provided leadership, and a significant contribution, to the fundraising campaign. At the building's dedication, Koshland recognized the greater role of the university: "A building named in one's honor is a great experience, but it pales next to the pleasure of being a student, alumnus, and faculty member of this great university, which I hope will stand forever on the world stage as a symbol of scholarly excellence, academic freedom, and innovative social concepts."[17]

Mulford Hall

27. Mulford Hall *Miller & Warnecke, 1947–1948*

Part of the postwar building boom, Mulford Hall was constructed with
state funds for the School of Forestry and was the first permanent building
to be sited on Hilgard Field. The school was established in 1946 under its
first dean and the building's namesake, Walter Mulford, who guided the
program from its inception as a division of the College of Agriculture in
1914 and growth into a department in 1939. Mulford was also renowned for
having been the first state forester in the nation. In 1974 the school became
part of the College of Natural Resources, and it is now organized as the forest science division of the college's interdisciplinary Department of Environmental Science, Policy, and Management.

      Mulford was sited in accordance with John Galen Howard's 1914
Plan, except that it was aligned perpendicular to the west facade of Hilgard
Hall and Oxford Street, rather than parallel to the central axis. Conforming
to this shifted alignment, architects Chester H. Miller and Carl I. Warnecke
designed a four-story building on an east-west orientation, with short wings
at each end forming a shallow U-shaped plan. The steel and concrete structure is transitionally modern but with a stripped neoclassicism in its use of
horizontal moldings that divide the facade into three sections. With its symmetrical and horizontally proportioned south elevation and red-tile hipped
roof, the building forms a reserved north edge to the central axis (despite its
lack of alignment) and is a compatible companion to the earlier group of
classical buildings.

Of special interest to researchers and visitors is a permanent display of native woods that lines the corridors of Mulford. Boards mainly from the United States and Canada on the first floor were donated by lumber companies and alumni. Samples on the second floor from other parts of the world, especially Japan, Argentina, and the Philippines, were initially exhibited at the San Francisco 1915 Panama-Pacific Exposition.

28. Crescent, West Circle, and Glade
John Galen Howard, 1929

The landscaped crescent and circle that form the west vehicular entrance to campus, along with the oval creek-side glade just to the east, are elements left from the unfinished central axis envisioned by John Galen Howard. They were to link to a major sunken formal garden (now Memorial Glade), in turn linked to the Mining Circle, to form a series of open spaces—the grand Beaux-Arts allée aligned with and reaching out to the Golden Gate. They were completed in 1929 in general accordance with Howard's Hearst Plan.

Along with the creek-side vegetation, the crescent is the remaining open space of Howard's "Forecourt." A visitor entering from Center Street, he foretold, would find "a beautiful park confined within a small campus but possessing all the elements of great natural scenic beauty." To the right of the curving roadway would be seen "an idyllic grove of ancient oaks" and "a glorious bouquet of eucalyptus." The road would swing to the left and then circle around the Eucalyptus Grove "to the central line of the composition."[18]

Crescent, West Campus Entry

A major vehicle entrance during the middle years of the twentieth century, the crescent has become relatively ceremonial and less heavily used today because of the restrictions on cross-campus traffic—though it still serves some vehicles and functions as an important transit and shuttle area. To enhance the area for pedestrians, the Springer Memorial Gateway, a brick and concrete plaza at the head of the crescent and linked to the Addison entrance, was designed by landscape architect Thomas D. Church and constructed in 1964. Manufacturer Russell Severance Springer (Class of 1902) bequeathed funds for the plaza in 1953. He also contributed $3 million for research and scholarships in medicine and mechanical engineering. Like the crescent drive, the plaza is now used lightly, the major west pedestrian entry being from Center Street and through the Grinnell Natural Area.

Springer Memorial Gateway

A West Campus Entry at Center Street was completed in 2000, a forty-fifth anniversary gift of the Class of 1953. Designed by Perkins Associates, landscape architects, it draws its classical inspiration from Howard's Sather Gate. Its two granite-like pre-cast concrete pillars support a convex bronze grillwork that is decorated with acorns and California poppies and displays the name of the university. The metal work was designed by Richmond-based artisan Michael Bondi, who also crafted the bronze handrails installed at Sather Esplanade (see Walk 1). The class gift also included landscaping across the drive that includes woodland creek-side planting and sitting stones near the Fages monument, which commemorates the Spanish expedition that is believed to have stopped along Strawberry Creek while exploring the eastern shore of San Francisco Bay in the spring of 1772.

The West Circle originally linked to two roadways, Wickson Road along the north side of the glade, and University Drive along the south. The south roadway was converted to a pedestrian walkway in the late 1960s to improve the landscaping in front of Valley Life Sciences Building and Doe Memorial Library, and to make room for the construction of Moffitt Undergraduate Library (see Walk 1).

The glade was an important element of Howard's plan, symmetrically shaped and axially aligned as the centerpiece between the Agriculture Group on the north, and a Natural Sciences Group—later developed as the (Valley) Life Sciences Building—on the south. With the exception of the relationship between California and Haviland Halls, it is the only place along the central axis where the cross-axial balance that was such an important part

North Fork of Strawberry Creek, north of Valley Life Sciences Building

of the Hearst Plan was achieved. (In both cases this balance was later interrupted, with the siting of Moffitt Undergraduate Library between California and Haviland Halls, and Life Sciences Addition appended to the west end of Valley Life Sciences Building.) The glade also differed from the formalized gardens Howard planned to the east. Although geometrically shaped, it was intended as a more picturesque meadow that incorporates the winding north fork of Strawberry Creek between Wickson Bridge and the Eucalyptus Grove.

Exotic plantings along the creek date from about 1877 and include the distinctive weeping elm (*Ulmus glabra* 'camperdownii') across from the

Valley Life Sciences Building. The creek was also the original site of the two Japanese lanterns and twenty-six stepping stones installed in 1935 and relocated to the Alumni House garden forty-five years later (see Walk 4).

The Thomas Forsyth Hunt Bench was installed in 1937 along the north edge of the glade facing the Agriculture Group in honor of the dean of

Thomas Forsyth Hunt Bench

the College of Agriculture (1912–1923), director of the Agricultural Experiment Station (1912–1919), and Professor of Agriculture (1912–1927). The classical curvilinear marble bench was designed by Supervising Architect George W. Kelham and placed on axis with Wellman, opposite a central path that then led directly to the building's arched entrance.

29. Grinnell Natural Area, Eucalyptus Grove, Football Players, Class of 1905 Bench, and Dwinelle Annex

Grinnell Natural Area   *Designated 1969*
Eucalyptus Grove   *Planted 1877*
Football Players   *Douglas Tilden, sculptor, cast 1893, installed 1900*
Class of 1905 Bench   *John Galen Howard, 1911*
Dwinelle Annex   *John Galen Howard, 1920; Michael Goodman, addition, 1949*

Strawberry Creek, Grinnell Natural Area

Rich in campus tradition, the Grinnell Natural Area is the largest of the three protected central campus habitats designated by Chancellor Roger W. Heyns in 1969 (see Wickson Natural Area). It extends from the Center Street entrance on the west to the bridge aligned with Dana Street on the east and reaches northward to encompass the Eucalyptus Grove, where the north and south forks of Strawberry Creek flow together. It honors Zoology Professor Joseph Grinnell (1877–1939), the first director of the Museum of Vertebrate Zoology in 1908.

A route from the west campus entrance has been located here since the early development of the campus.

Eucalyptus Grove

The existing pathway generally follows that built by male students on Labor Day 1896, when the tradition of donating a day of labor every leap year to improve the university grounds was initiated. On that day a footpath was graded from the Center Street entrance to the footbridge over the creek, under the supervision of horticulturist John McLaren, superintendent of Golden Gate Park. The pathway continuing through the oak grove soon became known as "Lovers Lane," and today it provides a contemplative respite from academic and urban life for thousands who walk between the campus and downtown. The stairway leading to the athletic facilities and the cross-campus bicycle path were added to the area in 1998 (Eldon Beck Associates, landscape architects).

The coast live oaks (*Quercus agrifolia*) that inhabit the area have acquired a mystical significance for generations of Cal students, inspiring artwork, poetry, and pageants performed by allegorical spirits and dryads of the forest. The tradition of the Partheneia, a "Festival of Maidens," was initiated under these oaks on April 6, 1912. Suggested by Lucy Sprague, the first dean of women, the festival comprised an original outdoor masque—a symbolic expression of the passage from maidenhood to womanhood— written, produced and performed each spring by several hundred female students. In an era when cultural constraints limited women's opportunities for expression and the development of self-confidence, the dean desired "to provide a mode of utterance for the endeavor of the students which should be informed with beauty and with memorial ritual."[19] That first performance was attended by President Wheeler and featured a stone altar and proscenium arch inscribed with Greek quotations, set against the backdrop of the Eucalyptus Grove. When the oak grove became too crowded for performers and spectators, later presentations were held in Faculty Glade, until 1931 when the tradition was discontinued. The Spirits of Maidenhood, Earth, Rain, Fog, Water, Ideals, and Light, who emerged from beneath the oaks and along the creek bank in flowing gowns and capes that April afternoon, can still be imagined on a walk through this wooded area.

Near the location of that first Partheneia stands the LeConte Oak, successor to a large old oak bearing that name that was felled by strong winds in 1939. The original was dedicated by the Class of 1898 on their Class Day in honor of John LeConte, third university president (1876–1881) and his brother, Joseph LeConte, Professor of Geology, Natural History, and Botany (1869–1901). A plaque, mounted originally on the trunk of the old tree, is affixed to a granite block at the base of the present tree, which stood at the center of a semi-circular group of five oaks that was to be landscaped as a larger LeConte Memorial in 1940. Selected plantings were to have formed a background for the group, which was to have a smooth foreground linked by a flagstone pathway to Campanile Way. Although the plan was approved by President Sproul, it was never completed, perhaps because of other exigencies brought about by World War II.

From the LeConte Oak, the view eastward across the bridge to Douglas Tilden's *Football Players* standing among more oaks has remained familiar for more than a century. The concrete bridge, designed by John Galen Howard, was built in 1908 to replace a wooden bridge dating from the initial development of the campus. Drawing instructor Bernard Maybeck advised President Wheeler and Tilden on the siting of the sculpture at the convergence of the pathways under the oaks and near the old Cinder Track. Tilden's highly acclaimed piece was unveiled on May 12, 1900, as the culmination of the traditional Class Day pilgrimage that included the groundbreaking for the President's House (University House).

Tilden, a California native who became deaf at an early age, attended and later taught at the California School of the Deaf, located at the site now occupied by the university's Clark Kerr Campus (see Walk 8). He became the first professor of sculpture at the Mark Hopkins Institute of Art, then an affiliated college of the university and now the San Francisco Art

Institute. Known as "the father of sculpture on the Pacific Coast," Tilden inspired many Bay Area artists; his most successful pupils included Robert Ingersoll Aitken, who created the sculpted corbels on Hearst Memorial Mining Building, and Melvin Earl Cummings, whose campus work can be seen on Sather Gate and Doe Memorial Library. Architects Ernest Coxhead and John Bakewell, Jr., also studied under the sculptor. Among his other renowned Bay Area works are the *Mechanics* monument and fountain in San Francisco, considered his masterpiece, and two in Golden Gate Park, *Father Junipero Serra* and *Baseball Player*.

Football Players *by Douglas Tilden*

Football Players, a larger-than-life-size statue of a kneeling player bandaging a teammate's leg, was cast in bronze in 1893, one of five major works Tilden created in Paris. The following year, the plaster cast was exhibited at the Salon of the Societé des Artistes Français et Societé Nationale des Beaux Arts in Paris, Tilden's fifth piece accepted by the Salon, a tribute unmatched by any other American sculptor. When the bronze was shown in an exhibition at the Mark Hopkins Institute of Art in 1898, it was purchased by James Duval Phelan, Mayor of San Francisco (1897–1902) and a keen admirer of Tilden's work. Phelan, also a University Regent from 1898 to 1899, offered the sculpture as a permanent trophy to the team winning two out of the next three football games between California and Stanford. The Blue and Gold team responded with two shutout victories over its traditional rival, and Phelan awarded the piece to the university as "the prize of superiority in football." This wording appears on the front of the statue's pedestal, which also lists the players and, in Greek, the inscription, "Everyone that striveth for mastery is temperate in all things."

It seemed not to matter at the time that Tilden's figures represented rugby rather than American football players, but on more than one occasion in the following years unsuccessful attempts were made to remove the statue. These actions may have been related to President Wheeler's criticism that American football was too brutal a sport, and the subsequent decision to drop the game at California in favor of rugby from 1906 through 1914. Nevertheless the Associated Students maintained a general admiration for the statue and installed a four-foot-high iron-picket fence around the pedestal to discourage vandalism of the inscriptions by "local urchins."

Across the flagstone path from the statue is a small bench commemorating President Wheeler's establishment of "self-government to undergraduate students." Wheeler's belief in student self-discipline and his consultation with senior class leaders led to the establishment of the Order of the Golden Bear in 1900 (see Senior Hall, Walk 5), and the gradual transfer of certain responsibilities from the Academic Senate to the Associated Students. A gift of the Class of 1905, the neoclassical bench was designed by John Galen Howard and constructed of California marble from the Columbia quarries in Tuolumne County. Although the inscription on the bench refers to it being set in place in 1910, because of late delivery it was installed in the spring of 1911.

North of the creek, the grove of Tasmanian blue gum eucalyptus (*Eucalyptus globulus*) is a well-known Berkeley landmark, rising some 200 feet high. One of the oldest groves in California, it was planted in 1877 to form a windbreak for the Cinder Track that once occupied the site of the Life Sciences Addition. The track, with its wooden bleachers, was the first formal athletic facility on campus and the site of other university events, including President Wheeler's inauguration ceremony in 1899. It was removed in 1916, when a new Running Track was completed to the east of Barrow Lane. Approximately 100 trees remain from the 150 originally planted in the grove.

The wooden deck-bridge (Thomas D. Church, landscape architect, 1968) upstream from the Class of 1905 Bench is the site of one of the oldest campus entrances, where Dana Street originally terminated at the creek. Just to the east stands Dwinelle Annex, a two-story wood-frame building

Dwinelle Annex

sheathed in redwood board-and-batten siding. John Galen Howard designed the original east wing to house the Department of Military Science in 1920, when the cadet corps numbered about 1,500 male students. The building was one of several temporary wooden structures Howard designed on campus to meet pressing interim space needs. With informal floor plans and the use of natural materials and banded windows, they followed the vernacular style of the Bay Region. Most, except for the Annex, North Gate Hall, and Naval Architecture, were eventually removed.

When Military Science moved to the new Harmon Gymnasium in 1933, the Annex was assigned to the growing Department of Music, which added the west wing for the Music Library in 1949, compatibly designed by Architecture Professor Michael Goodman. The versatile building was reassigned again when Music moved to newly built Morrison and Hertz Halls in 1958 and is now home to the Department of Dramatic Art and the College Writing Programs.

Douglas Tilden's *Football Players* is listed on the State Historic Resources Inventory. The Eucalyptus Grove is a City of Berkeley Landmark.

Central Campus Southwest

Golden Bear *by Tom Hardy, Lower Sproul Plaza*

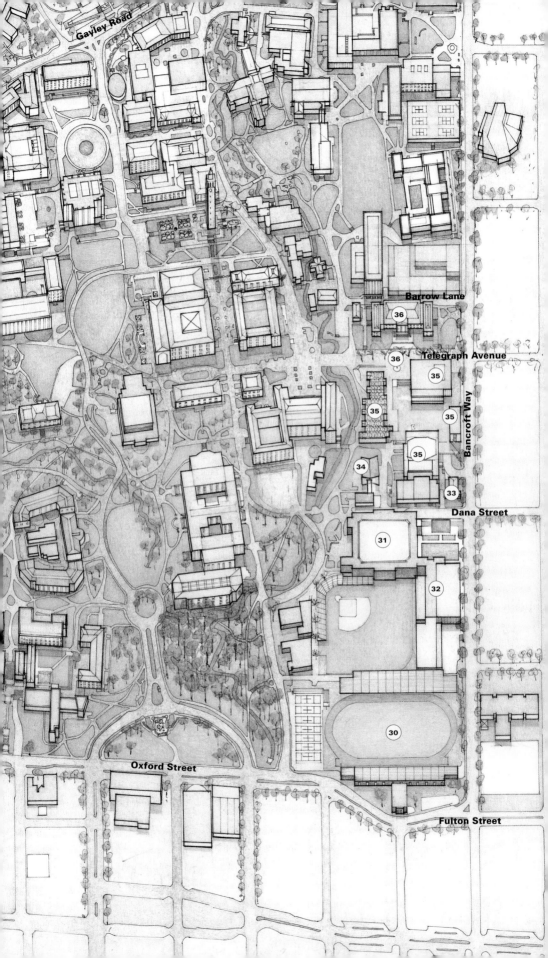

Gayley Road

Barrow Lane

36

36

Telegraph Avenue

35

35

35

35

34

33

Bancroft Way

Dana Street

31

32

30

Oxford Street

Fulton Street

The center of student services, recreation, and athletics, the southwest corner of the central campus that comprises this Walk extends from Sproul Hall to Fulton Street between the south fork of Strawberry Creek and Bancroft Way. It was developed on the site of a former residential neighborhood, assembled from properties acquired between the 1920s and the 1950s. The area was the second large increment of expansion south of the creek following the acquisition of the Hillegass Tract between Telegraph and College Avenues at the beginning of the twentieth century.

The university first considered athletics for the western half of this area when John Galen Howard proposed it as the site of California Memorial Stadium in 1921. A huge 60,000-seat double-deck coliseum, the stadium would have extended over 700 feet north to south from the creek to Bancroft, and over 500 feet east to west between Chapel and Atherton Streets (north-south streets then between Dana and Ellsworth, and Ellsworth and Fulton, respectively). But property acquisition costs and other factors led the Regents to change the site to the mouth of Strawberry Canyon, where the stadium was constructed in 1923 (see Walk 6).

Less than ten years later the same general area between Dana and Fulton was cleared for a new concrete athletics complex designed in the Moderne style: Warren C. Perry's Edwards Stadium for track and field, and George W. Kelham's Harmon Gymnasium and baseball field. With enrollment nearly doubling in the decade following World War I—from about 6,000 in 1918 to 11,000 in 1928—Old Harmon Gymnasium, a wooden structure dating from 1879, quickly became inadequate. The removal of California Field for the construction of Hearst Gymnasium in 1926 left intercollegiate baseball without a permanent home field. And the popularity of track and field as a major spectator sport required a more substantial stadium than the running track with its wood bleachers west of Hearst Gymnasium provided. The athletics complex was later expanded with the completion of the Recreational Sports Facility (ELS/Elbasani & Logan) in 1984, and the conversion of Harmon to Haas Pavilion (Ellerbe Becket Architects) in 1999.

The residential neighborhood within the four city blocks razed to construct these athletic facilities contained some notable structures. They included the former home of renowned California landscape artist William Keith (1838–1911) where such luminaries as naturalist John Muir, poet Ina Coolbrith, and writer Charles Warren Stoddard often gathered. A plaque commemorating the house is on the west wall of Edwards Stadium across from Allston. Also removed were six of the eight wooden cottages designed by David Farquharson and built in 1874 for lease to student clubs. These were located in the area now occupied by the Hellman Tennis Center (Hansen/Murakami/Eshima, 1982), Hazardous Materials Facility (Ehrlich-Rominger, 1999), and Central Heating Plant (George W. Kelham, 1930;

George Matsumoto, addition, 1987). (The other two cottages were located near the Faculty Club.)

Stiles Hall, a Romanesque Revival brick building constructed in 1893 that housed the University Young Men's Christian Association (YMCA) and Young Women's Christian Association (YWCA), occupied the corner of Allston and Dana. Named for College of California Trustee Anson Gale Stiles, the building also accommodated other student organizations and was used by the university for much-needed classrooms prior to the completion of California Hall in 1905. The building was the precursor to the present Stiles Hall at 2400 Bancroft.

The east end of this Walk is defined by Arthur Brown's neoclassical administration building, Sproul Hall, which replaced the row of Telegraph Avenue businesses between Sather Gate and Bancroft in 1941. In his 1944 General Plan, Brown proposed a Beaux-Arts arrangement of buildings on axis with Sproul to the west of Telegraph, which he envisioned as a formal campus entrance drive. Opposite Sproul at the end of an esplanade formed by two unidentified buildings, he planned an auditorium flanked by buildings for Military Science and Optometry. By the late 1930s this eastern half of the residential neighborhood had been partially cleared, with a large section used for Union Field, a recreational field located on the present site of Zellerbach Hall. The needs of the postwar student body, which had outgrown Stephens and Moses Halls for its union and activities, led to the redevelopment of the area, but not with Brown's Beaux-Arts formality. It was completed in the 1950s and 1960s with Clarence W. Mayhew's International Style Alumni House and the complex of modernist buildings by Hardison and DeMars forming the California Student Center.

Like the western half of the neighborhood, the clearance of the area removed some buildings of historic interest. At the corner of Allston and Union Street (then a north-south street between Telegraph and Dana) was "The Cottage," designed by Julia Morgan and built in 1922 for the University YWCA, which had previously shared Stiles Hall. Opposite the creek and just a few steps from Sather Gate, the building included offices, an auditorium, and meeting rooms and served "as a place of rendezvous for campus women, for meetings, rehearsals and other demands of women's activities."[1] The building was replaced in 1958 by the present University YWCA at 2600 Bancroft, designed by Joseph Esherick.

Next door to "The Cottage" on Union was "The Hangar," a rooming house operated by Mary Elizabeth "Mother" Tusch. This small white house, also called the "Shrine of the Air," was a virtual museum of aviation artifacts. During World War I, Mother Tusch opened her home to cadets training in the U.S. School of Military Aeronautics at the university, stationed just across Strawberry Creek in Old Harmon Gymnasium (located where the south wing of Dwinelle Hall now stands). Over time, the Air Cadets' signatures and photographs accumulated on the walls of the house, and propellers and other war relics were contributed by airmen returning from the front. The signatures of these early aviation pioneers included Jimmy Doolittle (Class of 1918), who described "The Hangar" as "the first USO." Other notables contributing their names included Admiral Richard Byrd, General Billy Mitchell, and flyer Amelia Earhart. In 1950, with demolition of the home a certainty, the autographed wallpaper containing over 2,000 signatures, along with scrapbooks, photographs, correspondence, and thousands of relics and souvenirs from two wars were shipped to the Smithsonian Institution, where they now comprise a collection in the National Air and Space Museum.

The development of the Student Center and Sproul Plaza, where the Free Speech Movement would begin in 1964, also required the demolition of the commercial structures and relocation of long-established merchants, whose businesses occupied the remaining west side of Telegraph. The changes transformed the area, creating the linear promenade and plaza that now form the main southern entrance to the campus. The sole survivor from the old neighborhood is Albert C. Schweinfurth's former First Unitarian Church, built in 1898 at the corner of Bancroft and Dana. The university has used the historic First Bay Region building since 1960.

30. Edwards Stadium

Warren C. Perry with Stafford L. Jory, 1931–1932;
CMX Group, engineers, field renovation, 1997–1999

Edwards Stadium is an ornamented monument to the spirit of California athletics and the ideals of amateur competition. It is the third campus facility for track and field, replacing the California Oval, a running track with wood bleachers used from 1915 to 1932 (on the site now occupied by Barrows Hall and Hearst Field Annex). That oval was preceded by the venerated Cinder Track (sited where Life Sciences Addition now stands), where formal athletics started in 1882.

A stadium exclusively for track and field was first proposed in John Galen Howard's revised 1914 Hearst Plan, adjacent to a proposed football stadium on the Hillegass Tract in the vicinity of where the California Oval was located. Typically, the sport was held within a multi-use stadium or at a designated oval running track, like those described above. But the popularity of track and field as a revenue-producing spectator event had grown since the reestablishment of the Olympic Games in Athens in 1896. The year before, a small California track team brought national attention to the university by defeating several prominent schools on a trip through the East. Success continued under legendary coach Walter M. Christie, whose teams won Pacific Coast Conference titles in 1919, 1920, and 1923, and the National Collegiate Athletic Association championship in 1922.

Edwards Stadium

Reflecting this heritage, Warren Perry's Edwards Stadium would become the nation's largest and most expensive stadium built for track and field and part of a larger athletics complex including George Kelham's men's gymnasium and baseball field to the east. At the time Perry was Director of the School of Architecture and chairman of President Sproul's Committee on Campus Development and Building Location. Assisting Perry on the stadium was fellow architecture professor Stafford L. Jory, who, like Perry, was a graduate of the school and had worked for Howard. A gifted renderer, Jory was later credited by Perry for being "largely responsible for the good features" of Edwards Stadium.[2]

Financing of the land acquisition, site development, and stadium were shared by the Regents and Associated Students (ASUC), who raised revenue from the sale of scrip at the California-Stanford football game. Construction began in June 1931 and quickly intensified, when the university was selected to host the Intercollegiate American Amateur Athletic Association (ICAAAA) national championship, scheduled for the following year as a qualifying meet for the 1932 Los Angeles Olympic Games.

The original track—named the Walter Christie Running Track for the coach of thirty-one years—consisted of a 440-yard oval surface of graded and bonded cinders. Two straight-aways long enough for running 220-yard events extended to the north, where the Hellman Tennis Center is now located. On the east and west sides of the field, Perry designed concrete bleachers with angled profiles integrated with a peripheral concrete wall on the south and west sides. The spaces beneath the high side of the stepped bleachers were used for open concourses to handle the flow of the crowds expected to fill the 22,500-seat stadium. Separate quarters for the home and visiting teams, public rest rooms, a bus garage, and other functions were housed under the stands.

Cross Campus Road (now Frank Schlessinger Way) bordering the north side of the field was considered to be a temporary road that would be removed in the future. For this reason, Perry designed the north enclosure as a wooden wall with concrete piers, and planned to extend the field to the north by seventy feet upon removal of the road. But the road was never eliminated and the "temporary" wooden wall has remained in place, now forming the north side of the tennis center.

Perry, a Beaux Arts–trained architect, treated the complex in a Moderne style, giving careful attention to the surfacing of the concrete facade and walls, and to the attainment of unity and scale through the use of cast-in-place concrete ornamentation. These decorative elements are particularly rich on the west bleachers, though they are partially obscured by the university's five-story building at 2223 Fulton. The central part of this facade consists of nineteen open bays defined by structural columns, which at the base frame alternating wood-gated entrances and decorative concrete grilles. The stadium's geometrical ornamentation, including the spherical, conical, and chevron moldings of these gateways, was integrally cast with wood forms and is attributable to Jory. The surrounding wall along Bancroft and Fulton-Oxford forms a horizontal pattern that unifies the whole, and reflects Perry's care in controlling the concrete mix to achieve the desired effect of color and texture. Both the smooth surfaces and textured, exposed-aggregate panels were created by specially prepared paper-lined forms. One panel on the south wall bears a large inscription to George Cunningham Edwards (1852–1930), for whom both the baseball and track fields and the track stadium were originally named. "Colonel" Edwards was a member of the first graduating class in 1873 and never left the university. He was professor of mathematics for fifty-seven years, commandant of the university cadets, and a "patron of sport and fine example of sportsmanship."

The two pairs of pylons along the south wall marked the termini of the east and west straightaways. Unfortunately missing from the two large pedestals on this wall and four of the west entrances are groups of figures designed by sculptor Robert Boardman Howard (John Galen Howard's son). Despite the completion of one-eighth size plaster models,

Gate, Edwards Stadium

praised by Perry as "very fine indeed, vigorous, architectural and especially harmonious with the design of the structures themselves,"[3] the sculptures were never executed because of cost restrictions.

The stadium was completed in March 1932, and was inaugurated with a meet against the University of Southern California the following month. The Olympic team trials of the ICAAAA meet followed in July and produced two University of California medalists in the Los Angeles Olympics the following month. Over the decades, the stadium has been the scene of a number of world records, among them the famous mile run by Jim Ryun of Kansas in 1966. But decline in the sport's popularity had left the stadium mostly empty in recent years.

To give Edwards Stadium new life, the field was renovated by the Phoenix-based engineering firm, CMX Group, in 1999. The transformation raised the field level, installed a polyurethane running surface, and reconfig-ured the oval to enable field events to be held at the north and south ends of the track. This enlarged the grass infield—now named Goldman Field, in honor of donors Richard and Rhoda Goldman—for use as an intercollegiate soccer field, which was dedicated in April 2000.

The upgraded stadium is still watched over by a large grizzly fea-tured in a mural inside the south wall, executed by artist Dale Bogaski in 1993. And the California Spirit is still represented at the north end of the track by the Walter M. Christie Memorial Bench, which bears the inscription: "My heart and soul for the good of California."

Edwards Stadium is listed on the State Historic Resources Inventory and is a City of Berkeley Landmark.

31. Haas Pavilion (and Harmon Gymnasium)

Ellerbe Becket Architects, with Carter, Tighe, Leeming & Kajiwara,
*   landscape architects, 1997–1999;*
George W. Kelham, Harmon Gymnasium, 1931–1933,
*   partially demolished 1997*

The metamorphosis of Harmon Gymnasium—revered by Cal students and fans and despised by visiting basketball teams for sixty-four years—created a better-equipped and larger athletic facility still within the domain of cen-tral campus student life. Harmon was one of the last of an era of noisy, cramped boxes that intimidated opponents and gave home teams an emo-tional edge. Most have been gradually replaced by larger arenas, which usually lack the intimacy and spirit of these old gyms.

Supervising Architect George W. Kelham designed Harmon (origi-nally the Gymnasium for Men and for an interim period Harmon Gymna-sium for Men) along with the adjacent Edwards Baseball Field (now Clint Evans Diamond) to complete the athletic complex begun with Warren C.

Haas Pavilion

Perry's Edwards Stadium to the west. Kelham's building replaced the original Harmon Gymnasium, a wooden octagonal building erected in 1879 and subsequently expanded for use as an auditorium and armory in addition to athletics. Its name, for donor Albion Keith Paris Harmon, was transferred to the second building in 1959, although the latter was funded primarily by a gift from the estate of Ernest V. Cowell (in addition to funds from the Associated Students and the state). The second Harmon was the most modern athletic facility on the West Coast when it was built, and, like its predecessor, doubled in use as the largest campus assembly space. The versatile building was also utilized for student registration, final exams, lectures, and concerts, until the completion of Zellerbach Hall in 1968.

In addition to the central basketball court with bleachers for approximately 6,600 spectators, the three-level building included gymnastics, fencing, boxing, and wrestling gymnasia, training rooms, and offices. Locker rooms and squash courts, as well as an armory and facilities for the Reserve Officers' Training Corps (ROTC) were housed in the basement. Two outdoor swimming pools at the south end of the gym were renovated as the Spieker Aquatics Complex (Hansen/Murakami/Eshima) in 1982.

Compatible with Perry's track stadium, Kelham designed the concrete gym in a Moderne style with a modest use of neoclassical fluting and window dentils. The principal ornamentation used was at the main east and west entrances, each composed of three double-doorway concave bays and surmounted with six Art Deco Greco-Roman athletic figures, cast in bas-relief and flanked by Mercury-like figures in winged helmets kneeling within octagonal medallions.

The basketball gymnasium rose from the center of the building, a rectangular block with chamfered corners, encircled with large clerestory windows. These windows illuminated the space and allowed it to ventilate (as well as heat-up from the afternoon sun) and enlivened the building during night games. The upper level took on the appearance of a great lantern, while the open windows allowed the brassy sounds of the Strawhat Band, the cheers of the crowd, and the buzz of the claxon-horn to penetrate the surrounding campus area.

Below the deep steel trusses that spanned between the clerestories, six decades of sports history were made on the gym's hallowed hardwood floor, named Pete Newell Court in 1987 for the coach whose 1959 team won the men's NCAA national championship. Between the first game in January 1933 (a victory over UCLA)

Sculptures, Harmon Gymnasium, Haas Pavilion

and the final men's game in March 1997 (a victory over Arizona State), generations of student-athletes—from gymnasts and boxers to basketball and volleyball players, from dedicated reserves to renowned stars—contributed to the lore and legend of Harmon. Beginning in 1973, when the women's basketball and volleyball teams moved from Hearst Gymnasium, these have included both men and women.

The decision to renovate and expand the aging gym stemmed from recommendations of a Chancellor-appointed committee on intercollegiate athletics in 1991. A commitment followed to make revenue-producing basketball highly competitive, and to have a facility suitable for hosting NCAA Division I games and tournaments at the regional and national level. The challenge was to create a larger arena, while retaining the intimate, crowd-intimidating qualities of Harmon.

To accomplish this, Ellerbe Becket transformed Harmon into Haas Pavilion by demolishing the clerestory inner-box and extending the seating upward on all sides to double the capacity to 12,300 spectators,

Pete Newell Court, Haas Pavilion

while preserving the proximity of the existing lower bleachers to the court. New concrete shear walls, constructed outside the old facade, extended the building's width by twenty-eight feet. These are interrupted on both the east and west facades by a high colonnaded portico that envelops and preserves Kelham's Art Deco entry bays. Also preserved in its entirety is the main east Harmon entrance lobby, a barrel-vaulted vestibule with custom chandeliers. This tile-floored space is oak-paneled and features university-seal medallions and a display of bronze plaques commemorating athletes and patrons. A Latin inscription in the wood frieze quotes the Roman writer and statesman, Pliny the Younger, and recalls the ideals of athletic participation: "It is wonderful how the mind is stimulated by the exercise and movement of the body."

The architects spanned the enlarged arena with ten 220-foot-long steel arched trusses, somewhat reminiscent of the old Harmon trusses, but painted blue to fit with the traditional university blue-and-gold color scheme predominant throughout the building. The gently arched roof, thirty-seven feet higher than the old gym, is an identifiable feature of the north and south elevations, though it forms a slightly faceted, rather than smooth, graceful curve.

On the west side of the building, a two-level club room opens to a balcony that overlooks the baseball field and provides a closer look at Kelham's Greco-Roman figures on the preserved facade. The building also contains press facilities, concession areas, offices for the Department of Intercollegiate Athletics and Recreational Sports, improved locker rooms and training quarters, and research and teaching facilities for the

Department of Human Biodynamics. In all, about fifty percent more space was created in the transformation of Harmon.

The new pavilion did not emerge from its Art Deco larva without some struggle. High bids, changing market conditions, and other factors escalated costs and caused delays in the schedule. The $57.5 million building was mostly gift-funded, led by an $11 million donation from the Evelyn and Walter Haas Jr. Fund, and named in honor of Walter A. Haas, Jr. (Class of 1937), a major patron of the Berkeley campus.

The renovated pedestrian forecourt to the building, Spieker Plaza (named for donors Ned and Carol Spieker) was completed in 2000 by landscape architects Carter, Tighe, Leeming & Kajiwara. It includes a grid of tulip trees and new lighting, and extends from Bancroft Way to a parking area on the north side of the building. Restored in this area is the Clinton R. "Brick" Morse Memorial, presented to the university in 1946 by the Big "C" Society and the Brick Morse Alumni Glee Club. Its four marble benches and inscribed marble slab honor Morse (1872–1942), "a devoted Californian who dedicated his life to the athletic and musical activities of the University of California." He was director of the University Glee Club and composer of *Hail to California*, one of the beloved school songs. Just north of the memorial is a C-shaped teak bench given by the Naval ROTC Class of 1942 in memory of classmates lost in World War II.

32. Recreational Sports Facility

ELS/Elbasani & Logan, 1982–1984

Supported by a referendum overwhelmingly approved by the students in 1981, the Recreational Sports Facility (RSF) was the first new athletic building constructed since the completion of Harmon Gymnasium in 1933. The $20 million building filled a growing need for a student population active in sports and fitness, but nearly three times the enrollment the old gym was designed to serve.

RSF was sited along Bancroft Way to be convenient to students and to link to shower and locker facilities in Harmon (now Haas Pavilion). Constructed over an underground parking garage that serves as a podium, the building's high-volume spaces include three exercise rooms, seven basketball courts, and six squash and seven racquetball/handball courts, in addition to administrative offices. To modulate the size of the program, Donn Logan of Berkeley architects ELS/Elbasani & Logan organized the building into three components: an entry-office wing at the east end that connects to the adjacent locker rooms; a long central wing containing the exercise rooms, ball courts, and two "Blue" and "Gold" basketball gyms; and, on the west end, a multi-use field house with three basketball courts.

Recreational Sports Facility

To link the three units, he created a central, 250-foot-long, skylit atrium. This promenade-lobby faces the glass-enclosed ball courts on its north side; on the south, it is defined by a horizontally-banded wall of balconies and stair-ways that lead to viewing windows of the exercise rooms and the upper gyms. The forty-foot-wide circulation spine extends from a windowed over-look of the Spieker Aquatics Complex on the east and terminates at the opening to the boxy field house at the west. It effectively orients the user and emphasizes the inward-looking nature of the building, whose program required windowless activity areas free from glare and sunlight.

The scale of the building and its virtual lack of fenestration required an imaginative exterior treatment by Logan. He painted the plaster-surfaced concrete and steel-frame structure with a palette of soft colors to differenti-ate the three wings and visually reduce the massing. The blue-green of the principal central-wing facade serves to recede the large block against the sky, while the terracotta tone of the field house provides a subtle reference to the tile roofs of many campus buildings. Other elements were used in lieu of windows to create voids and scale in the facade. Ventilation louvers for the required natural ventilation were used as patterned design elements, and horizontal banding and scoring on parts of the facade helped to add a sense of scale. Logan also used diagonal lines to refer to the steel cross-bracing of the upper gyms, and repeated these on the concrete field house. The symmetrical south facade of the long central wing was divided by expressing in gray its ten structural bays, which form a colonnaded loggia on the first floor—a classically proportioned composition that perhaps attempts to pay homage to the older campus buildings. To the west of this wing, a touch of whimsy was introduced by the use of two ship-like ventilators, which extend from the underground garage.

While these efforts achieved scale and interest in the facade, the inward-looking program contributed a somewhat imposing public presence on Bancroft. The high facade is a virtual wall that makes little concession to pedestrians or to historic St. Mark's Church across the street. The loggia serves little purpose and lacks activity, and, south of the field house, a courtyard forms a pleasant but little-used outdoor space. Despite these impacts, the building has been immensely popular with students to the point where overcrowding has resulted in the placement of exercise machines in the atrium lobby. But another referendum in 1999 did not gain student approval to expand the facility into the courtyard.

33. 2401 Bancroft Way

Albert C. Schweinfurth, 1898; Muller & Caulfield, restoration, 1998–1999

Albert Schweinfurth's former First Unitarian Church at the corner of Bancroft Way and Dana Street played an important role in the development of the Arts and Crafts Movement and the Berkeley way of life near the end of the nineteenth century. Simplicity of construction, use of local materials, regional references, and closeness to nature characterized the movement, which had its origins in England. It was a reaction against the mechanization of society, with a commitment to a simple, natural life. Architecturally, it coincided with rejection of the stylized Victorian period.

2401 Bancroft Way

2401 Bancroft Way

Schweinfurth, who arrived in San Francisco from the East in 1891, worked in the office of architect A. Page Brown, where he contributed, possibly with Bernard Maybeck, to the rustic design of the Swedenborgian Church in San Francisco in 1894. The following year Maybeck designed a shingled house north of the university grounds for his first private client, poet Charles Keeler. His use of rough, exposed redwood construction, shaped to the hillside terrain, created a revolutionary style that grew in popularity with the intellectual community growing around the campus. The Arts and Crafts principles were also popularized by Keeler in his leadership of the Hillside Club and his book of 1904, *The Simple Home*, which he dedicated to Maybeck, his "friend and counselor." Schweinfurth's First Unitarian Church served as the first meeting place of Keeler's Hillside Club, which was formed in 1898 to follow the ideals of the movement. Keeler and Maybeck, as well as a number of important citizens and university people, were early parishioners of the church.

The wood-shingled building exemplifies the First Bay Region style that evolved from the Movement. A shallow-pitched gabled roof covers two entrance porches at the northwest and, by extended eave, the southwest corner. Rough-barked redwood tree trunks support the porch roofs. Centered in the west facade is a twelve-feet-in-diameter amber-colored circular window that bathes the interior in golden light. The shingle work around this window is carefully detailed. Four arched amber-glazed windows grace the south facade, within bays defined by curving shingled buttresses. Trusses span the former chapel space, which has a pulpit expressed by a semi-circular apse on the east facade.

In 1960, as part of its two-block property acquisition for development of the Student Center, the university purchased the church, whose congregation relocated to a larger facility in nearby Kensington. While a parish house and auxiliary structure were demolished in 1965 for the construction of Zellerbach Hall, the church building remained in use by the university for various functions, including drawing classes, and today serves as a dance studio for the Department of Dramatic Art.

The 1999 rehabilitation by Oakland architects and alumni Rosemary Muller and Thomas Caulfield improved the seismic safety of the building, while sensitively retaining its historic appearance. In addition to other upgrades, new shear walls and a roof diaphragm were added, the trusses strengthened, and an interior steel frame constructed. The original shingled exterior was carefully replicated with new cedar shakes.

2401 Bancroft is listed on the National Register of Historic Places and the State Historic Resources Inventory, and is a City of Berkeley Landmark.

34. Alumni House

Clarence W. Mayhew, with H. Leland Vaughn, landscape architect, 1953–1954;
Ari Inouye, landscape architect, garden modifications, 1980

Alumni House

"A home on the campus." That is how the California Alumni Association proudly described its new building under construction in 1953 along the south bank of Strawberry Creek. The organization developed from an association of College of California and university alumni established in 1872, and adopted its present name in 1917.

Once closely related to the Associated Students, it acquired a home in 1923 in Stephens Union (now Stephens Hall), which benefited from the fund-raising efforts of alumni, a tradition that continues strongly today.

An "Alumni Hall," meant as a gathering place for students and alumni, was proposed on John Galen Howard's 1908 and 1914 Hearst Plans on a site along the north bank of the creek, south of where Valley Life Sciences Building is now located. A little upstream from that site, Alumni House would be built on land purchased by the university from the Pacific Unitarian School of Religion in 1938. The site occupied the northwest corner of a two-block area that would later be developed for the Student Center, a proximity that would symbolize the earlier relationship. More than 18,000 alumni contributed funds for the building, along with funds from the university for preparing the site.

Selected as designer was San Francisco architect Clarence W. Mayhew, an alumnus of the School of Architecture, Class of 1927, the last class to graduate while Howard was director of the school. Mayhew organized Alumni House into two stone-and-brick-faced wings linked by a central glass-enclosed entrance lobby, creating an L-shaped plan embracing a creek-side terrace. The Modern building includes a one-story-and-basement rectangular office wing on the west, and a larger one-story east wing for conferences and events. The conference wing features a "butterfly" roof, a reverse pitch with a valley rather than a ridge at its center. Initial design studies showed a similar style for the office wing, but this was changed to a flat roof, possibly in anticipation of a future additional floor. Steel-framed curtain walls with awning windows provide a modular pattern on the office wing, which cantilevers over its stone basement to achieve a "floating" horizontal composition in the landscape.

The massing of the building is gracefully proportioned, with the two wings asymmetrically balanced about the central lobby link. The design is an excellent example of the International Style, reflecting the European influence of Le Corbusier, Mies van der Rohe, and Walter Gropius, and akin to the Bay Area residential work of William W. Wurster and Gardner Dailey. The influence of the Bay Area Tradition is also seen in the building's indoor-outdoor relationship to the garden landscape and creek environment.

The interior conveys this naturalistic feeling through the use of walnut paneling and doors, red brick walls, and green slate floors, and the daylight illumination of the lounge-meeting and conference rooms in the east wing, which opens onto the north terrace with large sliding glass doors. These custom decorated and furnished spaces include fireplaces, an alcove, and other features bearing the names of class and individual donors and memorialized alumni. The conference room, which opens by sliding paneled doors to extend the lounge space, is named for alumnus Stephen D. Bechtel, who served as chairman of the Alumni House building committee and subsequently was the principal donor of the Bechtel Engineering Center.

Landscape architect H. Leland Vaughn, a member of the faculty for four decades and chairman of the Department of Landscape Architecture from 1925 to 1962, designed the terrace and landscaping. Gracing the terrace garden are two Japanese stone lanterns and a group of twenty-six stepping stones, which have a storied past. A gift of the Japanese Alumni Association in 1934, they were originally installed along Strawberry Creek in the glade opposite Wellman Hall (see Walk 3). They were formally dedicated in that location on Easter Sunday of 1935 following a tea for about 250 people hosted at the President's House by President and Mrs. Robert

Japanese lanterns and garden, Alumni House

Gordon Sproul. The tall lantern, a *Kasuga* type, is a reproduction of one in the Sangatsudo Todaiji monastery in Nara, Japan. The small one is a *Yukimigata* type, known as a "snow-viewing" lantern, so called because its light can be seen even in a blizzard by adjusting the stone lid. When this smaller lantern was vandalized during World War II, the pair was removed from the creek and placed in storage and forgotten until 1980. At that time they were restored and installed with the stones at Alumni House by former Campus Landscape Architect Ari Inouye, who also redesigned the garden around the lanterns.

35. California Student Center: King Student Union, Chavez Student Center, Eshleman Hall, and Zellerbach Hall

California Student Center
Hardison and DeMars, with Lawrence Halprin, landscape architect, 1959–1968
King Student Union *Hardison and DeMars, 1959–1961*
Chavez Student Center
Hardison and DeMars, 1959–1960;
John Wells of Kennedy/Jenks/Chilton Architectural Division, interior
alterations, 1989–1990
Eshleman Hall *Hardison and DeMars, 1963–1965*
Zellerbach Hall *Hardison and DeMars, 1965–1968*

An award-winning complex of urban design, the California Student Center is comprised of four major buildings that form a sunken central plaza and define the western edge of Sproul Plaza, the primary campus entryway. King Student Union anchors the southeast corner of the complex and marks the Telegraph-Bancroft campus entrance. Chavez Student Center, originally the Dining Commons and now a student services building, borders Strawberry Creek and forms the north side of the lower plaza, while the student office building, Eshleman Hall, defines the south side along Bancroft. Zellerbach Hall, a regional performance center, completes the group on the west.

The need for new student facilities followed a two-year study completed in 1948 by the California Alumni Association to replace overcrowded Stephens Union (now Stephens Hall) and old Eshleman Hall (now Moses Hall), used since 1923 and 1931, respectively (see Walk 1). The postwar study reflected an alumni initiative to have a program on campus that would "symbolize its debt to both those who lost their lives in the service and to those who served and returned." That led to a plan for a "California Memorial Center" to include a cafeteria, auditorium, memorial student activities building, and student office building, to be funded by student fees, gifts, university funds, and the sale of Stephens and old Eshleman by the

Associated Students to the university. Architecture students of Professor Vernon DeMars prepared design studies, which were displayed in Stephens to generate interest in the project. When a more detailed concept was desired for fund-raising, fellow professor Joseph Esherick and a group of students joined DeMars to prepare a model of a suggested scheme. The area between Sproul Hall and Harmon Gymnasium (now Haas Pavilion) was approved as the site, requiring acquisition of the remaining private properties north of Bancroft.

To select a designer for the Student Center, the Regents invited six firms, three each from northern and southern California, to participate in an architectural competition in 1957, for which Esherick was asked to write the program. The jury unanimously awarded the $12 million project to associated architects Vernon DeMars and Donald Hardison, a joint venture of the small Berkeley office of DeMars and Reay and the larger Richmond firm Hardison and Komatsu. DeMars and Hardison had worked together on Easter Hill Village, a 300-family public housing development in Richmond, completed in 1954. Donald Reay, DeMars' partner and a faculty colleague, brought valuable experience in the design of new towns in Britain. In the joint-venture arrangement, DeMars had overall design responsibility, with assistance by Reay through 1965, after which John Wells became a partner in the renamed firm, DeMars and Wells.

The winning design was strongly influenced by the scale and urban setting of the Piazza San Marco in Venice. The variety of the buildings—the umbrella-like hyperbolic-paraboloid roof shells of the Dining Commons, the formal colonnade of the Union, the office tower, the more massive forms of Zellerbach—and the diversity of materials and textures were inspired by the random elements that work together in that Italian Renaissance space. And while Berkeley's Campanile stands a thousand feet from Lower Sproul Plaza, unlike its counterpart within the Venetian piazza, it was consciously integrated into the scheme by keeping the roof of the Dining Commons low. This relationship is all the more appropriate, and a measure of campus continuity, considering that San Marco also inspired John Galen Howard's bell tower. To DeMars, the Commons with its roof of shells was like "a continuum of shelters and terraces filling the end of the square like the stalls and booths of a great market," while the Union "was intended to dominate the square as a 'splendid' edifice."[4]

Like the piazza of San Marco, the plaza, with its varied activities and cross-circulation, was intended to be a lively pedestrian space, though it has become less so since the removal of the cafeteria and its terrace diners from the Chavez Center. The mix of diners (now mostly at the Bear's Lair in the Union), theater-goers, people enjoying the outdoors or passing through, and occasional gatherings and rallies contributes to its urban character, described by DeMars as "a synthesis of streetscape and plazascape, great building and small, shop and pub, terrace and mall."[5] The balconies and

Detail of mural by Emmy Lou Packard, Chavez Student Center

terraces facing onto the plaza are analogous to the loggia of San Marco and serve as podiums for ceremonial events or spectator vantage points.

DeMars organized the area with several axial relationships. Linear Sproul Plaza establishes a north-south axis from Sather Gate to the Bancroft-Telegraph entrance. The symmetrical neoclassical facade of Arthur Brown's Sproul Hall is recognized with an east-west axis aligning that building's portico with a concrete stairway descending to the lower plaza. This axis originally passed beneath a bridge roofed with hyperbolic-paraboloid shells, connecting and unifying the Union with the Commons. But for seismic safety reasons the bridge was demolished in 1998, opening up the previously veiled vista. This axis becomes offset to the north as it aligns with the old Harmon Gymnasium entrance to Haas Pavilion. A secondary east-west axis establishes the centerline of Zellerbach Hall and bifurcates the plaza as the forecourt to the theatre. Additionally, DeMars established two view corridors from the Bancroft side of the plaza. The southwest entrance, between Zellerbach and Eshleman, is diagonally aligned with the Campanile, creating a dramatic view beyond the "market stalls" of Chavez Center. At the southeast corner between the Union and Eshleman, a cross-diagonal vista focuses on the tall Eucalyptus Grove, which serves as a backdrop for the *Golden Bear* sculpture sited before Zellerbach Hall.[6]

The piazza's winged lion of St. Mark's high atop a column, the symbolic embodiment of the city of Venice, inspired DeMars to include the Golden Bear, the symbol of the state and the university on the student center. Not wanting a sentimental-looking creature, he selected sculptor Tom Hardy, then teaching on campus and known for his welded-bronze abstractions of natural subjects. Donated by the Class of 1929 for their fiftieth anniversary, the bear was unveiled in 1980. The 500-pound sculpture, covered with a thin layer of gold leaf, stands upon a pedestal eighteen feet high, designed to be inaccessible.

California symbolism is also expressed on the terrace parapet of Chavez Student Center facing the plaza. Here, a five-foot-high by eighty-five-foot-long bas-relief is the work of artist Emmy Lou Packard (Class of 1936), a student and biographer of artist Diego Rivera, known for her devotion to public art. The abstract concrete mural represents the land forms of the state of California: coastlines, agricultural fields, mountain ranges, clouds, and rivers. Cast in reverse, the artist utilized various vegetables, including radishes, potatoes, onions, and puffed wheat, to create textures on a wallboard form.

King Student Union

By the time of the competition, the idea of identifying the Student Union as a World War II memorial had been dropped, and in 1985 the building was named for civil rights leader Martin Luther King, Jr. It was designed to be the prominent element of the lower plaza, a glass pavilion that also presents a public face to Sproul Plaza and the Telegraph-Bancroft intersection. Intended to convey a sense of community openness, the five-story steel-frame building was conceived by DeMars as a "student club" with a variety of both informal and formal functions. The formal encompassing colonnade provided a classical sense of shelter and unity to the building, which was sited to be framed by Sather Gate when approaching from the north. DeMars meant the trellis crown to be "in a sense a homage to the late Bernard Maybeck, first architect of the University."[7] He topped the trellis with finials

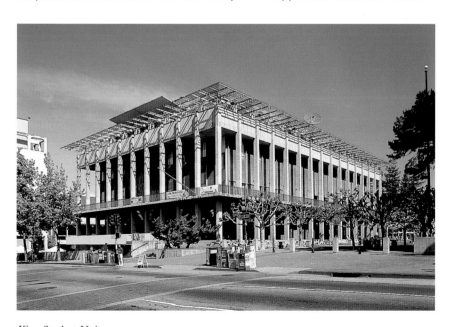

King Student Union

representing the California poppy, the state flower, much as John Galen Howard provided on the entry door of Hilgard Hall some forty years earlier.

The new Union shed itself of the segregated men's and women's clubrooms that were in Stephens. The second floor lobby, a few steps above Sproul Plaza, was designed as an open space with a central core containing an information desk, music listening booths, and offices—now occupied by a travel center. To the west of this is the Clara Hellman Heller Lounge, a gift of Regent Edward H. Heller in honor of his mother. This area has lost its original openness, having been partitioned to create a study hall and computer laboratory in response to changing student priorities. At the south end of the floor under the grand stairway are several displays describing the history of the Stanford Axe, the Golden Bear, and student life. Included are a donated stuffed bear, and an Axe display case, designed by DeMars with the same poppy finials that accentuate the roof trellis.

The third floor, finished in wood parquet flooring and paneling, contains the Henry Morse Stephens Memorial Room, named for the beloved history professor and namesake of the old Union (see Walk 1), and the two-story Barbara McHenry Pauley Ballroom, a gift of Regent Edwin W. Pauley in honor of his wife. The versatile room was designed to accommodate 800 people for meetings, banquets, formal dances, and other events, and has a north glass wall that affords a memorable view of the campus and the Campanile.

Eight meeting rooms occupy the fourth floor, each named for and featuring wood paneling from a native California tree. The rooftop Tilden Meditation Room was a gift of Mr. and Mrs. Charles Lee Tilden, Jr., as a memorial to their son, Cal student Charles Lee Tilden III. It features a window composed of forty heavy glass panels made in Munich by French sculptor Robert Pinard, who also designed the stained glass windows in Hertz Hall (see Walk 5).

The lower plaza level of the $5.7 million building contains the Cal Student Store, food services in the Bear's Lair, and, extending beneath the upper plaza, a game arcade and art studio. In the basement is a textbook and supplies store that was originally a sixteen-lane bowling center, and a warehouse space connected to the garage that extends under the plaza.

Chavez Student Center

Designed with the Union as a connecting structure, the former Dining Commons was converted to primarily student services in 1990 and renamed Golden Bear Center, until 1997 when it was renamed again in honor of United Farm Workers leader Cesar E. Chavez. The three-level reinforced-concrete structure originally contained a cafeteria with a split-level seating area for 1,800 diners. The glass curtain walls vary in size and shape under the hyperbolic-paraboloid roof shells and permit north light to illuminate the tall space, while giving diners (and current users) a pleasant view of the creek. This exposure and the informal articulation of the building relate well to the riparian landscape.

Also included in the $2.3 million building was the Golden Bear Restaurant with broiler-grill service opening onto Sproul Plaza. The lowest level provided rehearsal halls and other facilities for the California Marching Band and singing groups that were previously housed in old Eshleman

Grizzly Bear *by Raymond Puccinelli*

(Moses) Hall. The music groups have remained in the Chavez Center, and on football game days members of the band can be seen giving a traditional good-luck rub to the nose of the *Grizzly Bear* that stands just north of the building along the creek bank. This black granite bear is the work of sculptor and former art faculty member Raymond Puccinelli, who studied under Beniamino Bufano. Presented to the university in 1955 by O. J. Woodward II (Class of 1930), it was the first bear statue of appreciable size to be installed on campus.

The dining area was later subdivided into several specialty-food serving areas, and in 1989 the centralized cafeteria was discontinued and replaced by smaller satellite facilities around the campus. The vacated cafeteria space was then remodeled by Kennedy/Jenks/Chilton architect John Wells, the former partner of Vernon DeMars who contributed to the original design of the Student Center, in particular Zellerbach Hall. The space permitted the consolidation of student services, including the Student Learning Center, Disabled Students' Program, Women's Resource Center, and other activities.

Chavez Student Center

Eshleman Hall

Eshleman Hall

The second increment of the Student Center following the Union-Commons construction was the student office tower along the Bancroft edge of Lower Sproul Plaza. Its name was transferred from the former publications and activities building (renamed Moses Hall) in honor of John Morton Eshleman, Class of 1902, an ASUC President who was prominent in student publications, and who served on the Board of Regents while Lieutenant Governor of California.

The narrow tower was built to house offices, organizations, publications, a library, and the senate chamber of the ASUC. DeMars later regretted that the concrete building had to be eight stories high, casting its shadow on the Union.[8] It also shades the plaza, making some of the tree-well benches undesirable on colder days, and is of a larger scale than other Bancroft buildings. After receiving a lukewarm response from the Regents on the building's design, the architects enhanced the top floor loggia with an open metal railing and added windows and balconies on the east and west ends. Concrete sunshades with fins give the south facade some interest, while the plain north facade has acquired assorted placards placed in the office windows of student organizations. The $1.3 million building was dedicated in September 1965 with members of the Eshleman family and President-emeritus Robert Gordon Sproul participating.

Zellerbach Hall

The last increment of the center, Zellerbach Hall reflects the architect's love for the theatrical arts. As a student during the Depression years, Vernon DeMars designed stage sets and performed in a program of Plains and Southwest Indian dances in the International House auditorium. For Zellerbach, he studied the theaters of Europe and consulted with leaders in acoustical and seating design, drawing on lessons from the past and incorporating the latest in contemporary theater technology.

The concrete and steel building houses two theaters: a 2,100-seat auditorium entered from the plaza, and 500-seat multi-form playhouse for the Department of Dramatic Art opposite Alumni House on the north. The large auditorium was acoustically designed with the trained voice in mind,

Zellerbach Hall

but also for a range of performing arts, including drama, dance, and symphonies, with its large 62-foot proscenium arch suitable for major opera and ballet productions. The interior is compact and intimate, with an upper balcony and lower balcony that embraces the orchestra seating by cascading down the sides of the hall to the stage front. The side walls are composed of artistically lit and colored solids and voids that serve as sound diffusers and are a modern expression of the sculptural modeling used in Baroque opera houses and concert halls. These sculptural boxes, which were influenced by a theater DeMars visited in Sweden, are deeply modeled near the sound source and less so further back for acoustical reasons. The large ceiling panels above the audience were meant to suggest canvas awnings of an outdoor theater, with the light spilling over the sides serving to model the sculpted walls.[9]

The foyer for the large hall forms the two-level concrete-framed glass box that fronts on the plaza. Displayed within is a set of ten banners, nine depicting the history of Western theater and the tenth, Asian theater. These were designed by artist Betty DeMars, wife of the architect, a collaboration that recalls that of sculptor Elah Hale Hays and her husband, architect William Charles Hays, on Giannini Hall nearly forty years earlier (see Walk 3).

The playhouse is oriented on a north-south axis, perpendicular to that of the auditorium, and is separated from the large hall by a soundproof buffer that permits simultaneous performances. A flexible laboratory for the Department of Dramatic Art, the space can conform to a number of uses, including proscenium, Elizabethan, theatre-in-the-round, and unconventional productions. Sliding panels control the size of the proscenium opening, and the use of elevators and wagoned seats enables a variety of seating and orchestra pit arrangements.

In order to open the hall in time for the university's centennial celebrations, the incomplete auditorium was inaugurated with an invitational pre–opening night concert in May 1968. The program featured the music of composer Igor Stravinsky, who was in attendance, and the narration of actor and 1938 graduate Gregory Peck. In the plaza, theater patrons were met by a demonstration of student pickets protesting the building's name. The $7 million hall was funded primarily by student fees, along with endowment funds and a $1 million gift from the Zellerbach Family Fund. It was named in memory of Isadore Zellerbach, wildlife conservationist and former president of the Zellerbach Paper Company, and his wife, philanthropist Jennie Baruh Zellerbach. The students, feeling they should have determined the name, rejected the Regents' choice in two referendums, desiring instead to honor the recently slain Martin Luther King, Jr., who would eventually be memorialized in the naming of the Student Union. Several months later the building was officially dedicated with its public opening. The Playhouse opened to an invitational audience for a Department of Dramatic Art workshop in January 1969, followed three days later with a public production of Eugene O'Neill's trilogy, *Mourning Becomes Electra*. Ironically, the night before this public opening, fire destroyed venerated Wheeler Hall Auditorium, used for the previous five decades for Dramatic Art productions (see Walk 1).

36. Sproul Hall and Sproul Plaza

Sproul Hall

> *Arthur Brown Jr., 1940–1941; Office of Architects and Engineers, interior alterations, 1958 and 1973*

Sproul Plaza

> *Hardison and DeMars, with Lawrence Halprin, landscape architect, 1959–1961*

The scene of historic political demonstrations since the 1960s, Sproul Hall was built to house university administrative offices, so that California Hall in the heart of the campus could be freed for much-needed classroom use. It was also the first increment in "a monumental development on the axis of Telegraph Avenue" planned to form "a handsome vestibule to the Campus."[10] Originally called the Administration Building, it was renamed in 1958 to honor Robert Gordon Sproul, eleventh university president (1930–1958).

The site, on the east side of Telegraph between Bancroft and Sather Gate, was occupied by campus-oriented businesses backed by maintenance shops and storehouses of the university's Corporation Yard on Barrow Street (now Barrow Lane). Arthur Brown, Jr., chose to set back the building, envisioning that a future parkway drive—not a plaza—would

Sproul Hall

replace the commercial street. Sproul Hall would be the most prominent of the five campus buildings designed by the Beaux Arts–trained architect.

The symmetrical neoclassical building is comprised of a four-story central block above a basement with projecting three-story north and south wings. As with Brown's other campus buildings, the style and choice of materials harmonize with John Galen Howard's Beaux-Arts ensemble. But the days of using costly granite extensively were long past. To finish the concrete and steel structure in a manner appropriate to the new main campus entrance, Brown used granite for the base and entrance portico and a terracotta facing for the walls (later resurfaced with another material), in a color and finish that simulated the older granite buildings. The three red-tiled hipped roofs were also in keeping with the dominant theme established by Howard.

The facade of the main block is divided into zones that include a basement plinth, middle zone, and recessed attic, while the side wings each have two zones consisting of a basement and main section. The stripped style features plain window openings without sills or decorative details, the classical entrance portico being the central feature with its pediment supported by four monumental Ionic columns. Classical entablatures crown the walls of the main zones, and the side wings have iron balcony railings ornamented with crouching grizzly bears and California poppy rosettes, symbols of the university and state.

The main entrance leads to a spacious lobby finished in Indiana limestone, with a green- and white-streaked black marble floor. Following criticism of the lobby for its large blank wall with only a side opening to the building's central corridor, Architecture Professor Michael Goodman and Art

Professor Eugen Neuhaus were consulted about improving the space "and its rather cold aspect as people come in."[11] Suggestions for the wall included a mural, a map of the statewide university system, an inscription, and another opening to the corridor, but no changes were made, until the recent installation of a small postmodernist directory.

Facing each other across this marble court are two notable bronze busts. One of President Sproul in the north niche was presented by the Class of 1907, and created in 1959 by Emil Seletz, an accomplished sculptor as well as a renowned neurosurgeon. At the south staircase is a classically heroic likeness of John A. Britton, Regent from 1903 to 1923. It is the work of Melvin Earl Cummings, whose sculptures also adorns Sather Gate and Doe Memorial Library. The grand staircase, inspired by gilded stairways in the Chateau de Versailles, is ornamented with the script California "C" and grizzly bear, like those used on the exterior railings.

The grandeur of the lobby and staircase reflected the presence of the second floor Regents' boardroom, which was entered from a formal vestibule at the top of the staircase. This vestibule and the oak-paneled room were subsequently partitioned to create Berkeley campus offices after the Board of Regents and President's offices moved to University Hall in 1959. Also partitioned were the president's paneled suites at the north end and deans' offices at the south, each entered through an octagonal lobby illuminated by a circular skylight above a carved plaster cornice. Various administrative offices still occupy the building, including Undergraduate Admission and Relations with Schools, Financial Aid, the Registrar, Student Activities and Services, the Graduate Division, Public Information, and the Police Department.

On several occasions Sproul Hall has received notoriety during political demonstrations, the most famous being the sit-in on December 2, 1964, at the height of the Free Speech Movement (FSM) rallies. Approximately 1,000 mostly student protesters, accompanied by the singing of Joan Baez, marched in and occupied all the floors until a mass arrest—the largest in California history—took place the following day. Arthur Brown's neoclassical building had become the icon of bureaucracy and the establishment, as well as the *skene*, or backdrop, for events staged on its stepped podium and the plaza that replaced Telegraph Avenue.

Sproul Plaza

Sproul Plaza, designed by Hardison and DeMars with landscape architect Lawrence Halprin, was developed twenty years after Sproul Hall, in con-junction with King Student Union and Chavez Student Center, the first incre-ment of the California Student Center. It consists of a 550-foot-long tree-lined promenade on the former Telegraph right-of-way that widens from 75 to 100 feet to form an open brick plaza opposite the Sproul Hall entrance. The pollarded London plane trees (*Platanus X acerifolia*)—similar to those used on Sather Esplanade at the base of the Campanile—are aligned to form an axial view corridor that extends from Telegraph to Sather Gate. On any given day, the plaza is a changing landscape of student life, often lined with tables of student organizations, and visited by a variety of "Hyde Park" personalities harping religious messages, entertaining, or demonstrating personal agendas.

A central and popular gathering place on the plaza is Ludwig's Fountain. The circular pool received its name from Ludwig von Schwarenberg, a German shorthaired pointer, who commuted from his Berkeley home every day to romp in his adopted fountain, play with the students, and humbly accept a sandwich or two. Ludwig captured the hearts of the student body, and at the request of the Associated Students' Executive Committee, the Board of Regents officially named the fountain in 1961, the first time an animal was so honored on campus. Ludwig finally retired from his fountain in 1965, when his family moved back to his birthplace, the City of Alameda. But he was not soon forgotten. His official portrait was hung in the student union, and the alumni magazine proclaimed him "Friend of the famous, hero of coeds, and acknowledged power behind the University."

Ludwig may have also been exhausted from the famous events in the vicinity of his fountain that placed Sproul Hall and Sproul Plaza at the center of international attention. When Sproul Plaza was developed, the tradition of freedom of speech and assembly that had been concentrated outside Sather Gate moved south, to the new boundary along the Bancroft sidewalk, which was considered city property. But when it was believed that

Sproul Plaza and Ludwig's Fountain

the narrow strip of land belonged to the university, new rules banning social or political advocacy were announced in September 1964. At issue was a small group of students who had been soliciting funds from card tables set up on the strip. When the university took disciplinary action against the students, a small sit-in was staged inside Sproul Hall, and tables appeared—against the regulations—on the plaza. To demand a more liberal university policy for freedom of expression, students founded the Free Speech Movement (FSM), which intensified its actions on the first of October. On that day thousands of demonstrators surrounded a police car used in an attempt to arrest student Jack Weinberg. For 32 hours they blocked the plaza, while student activists spoke from atop the car—among them their emerging leader, philosophy student Mario Savio.

Noon rallies with up to 5,000 in attendance followed on the plaza and the steps of Sproul Hall, leading to the occupation of the building and to Savio's now-famous speech on December 2, 1964: "There is a time when the operation of the machine becomes so odious, makes you so sick at heart, that you can't take part; and you've got to put your bodies upon the gears and upon the wheels, upon all the apparatus, and you've got to make it stop. And you've got to indicate to the people who own it, that unless you're free, the machine will be prevented from working at all."[12]

New rules for "time, place and manner of political activity on the Berkeley campus" followed the events of the FSM. So did the complex social and political issues of the late 1960s and early 1970 s—among them, racial discrimination, labor protests, the Vietnam War, People's Park—that led to additional demonstrations, sit-ins, and eventually the violence and National Guard actions that left the Sproul Plaza area under clouds of tear gas. Subsequent movements, most notably the anti-apartheid demonstrations of the 1980s, have continued the tradition of the plaza as a place for free expression.

Mario Savio returned to the steps of Sproul Hall two more times to address plaza-filled crowds, in 1984 and 1994, on the twentieth and thirtieth anniversaries of the FSM. In a ceremony on December 3, 1997, exactly thirty-three years after the historic demonstration, those steps were named for Savio, who died the previous year. Near the steps on the plaza the FSM is also memorialized with a monument designed by San Francisco artist Mark A. Brest van Kempen and installed in 1992. The conceptual work of art was the winning design in a national competition initiated by faculty members "to commemorate the 25th anniversary of the FSM and the political activities that ensued, including the Civil Rights and anti-war activities" and "to celebrate the highest ideals of student movements of the past and to serve as an inspiration for future generations of students."[13] It consists of a six-inch diameter column of "free space," centered in a six-foot diameter granite disk inscribed: "This soil and the air space extending above it shall not be part of any nation and shall not be subject to any entity's jurisdiction." The FSM was also commemorated with the Mario Savio/Free Speech Movement Endowment, a $3.5 million gift in 1999 from alumnus Stephen Silberstein, which established the FSM Cafe in Moffit Undergraduate Library and supports the FSM Archives in the Bancroft Library.

The steps and plaza are also used for rallies of a more traditional sort, when, before every home football game, members of the California Marching Band ascend from the lower plaza and rush onto the steps to perform in front of the Sproul Hall portico. This pre-game concert, accompanied by pompon-waving song and cheer leaders, precedes the band's march through Sather Gate and up to California Memorial Stadium. The steps are also the place of the Axe Rally, a century-old tradition involving the Stanford Axe, now an annual trophy awarded to the winner of the California-Stanford Big Game.

Sproul Plaza is listed on the State Historic Resources Inventory.

Central Campus Southeast

Les Bears *by Dan Ostermiller, Haas School of Business*

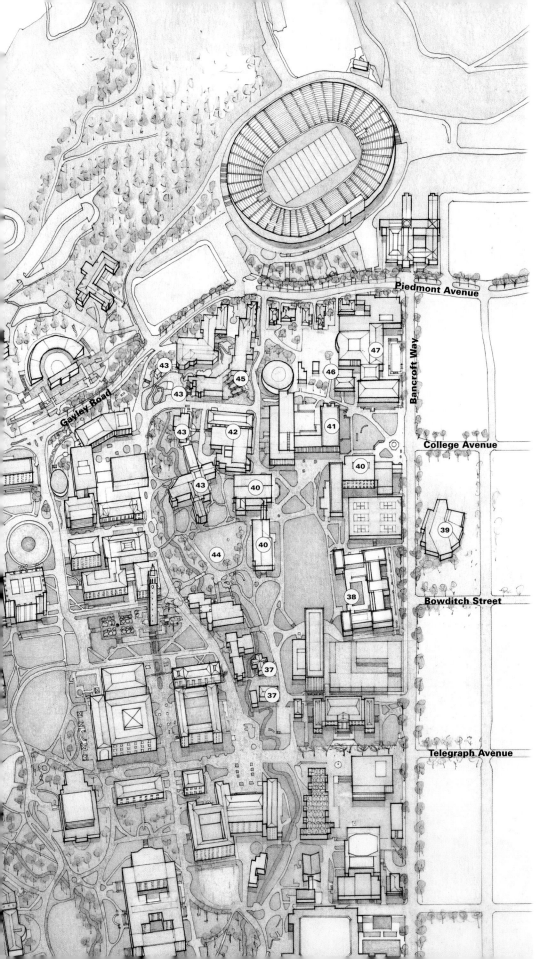

Piedmont Avenue

Bancroft Way

Gayley Road

College Avenue

Bowditch Street

Telegraph Avenue

43

43

45

46

47

43

42

41

40

43

40

39

40

44

38

37

37

This Walk from Strawberry Creek to Bancroft between Sproul Hall and Gayley-Piedmont offers diverse examples of the design and influence of several leading Bay Area architects, who span the twentieth century. It includes the creek-side Bay Tradition works of Bernard Maybeck, John Galen Howard, Julia Morgan, and Joseph Esherick, an incomplete visionary Beaux-Arts centerpiece by Maybeck and Morgan, and the last major work conceived by Charles Moore. The area is rich in academic and social history, embodied in its present buildings or recalled through knowledge of its past ones. Primarily home to the Art, Music, and Professions Precinct, its pattern of development reflects the land-use planning legacies of Howard, Maybeck, Arthur Brown, Jr., and William Wilson Wurster.

Historically, the area was developed in two segments divided by College Avenue, which until the 1960s continued northward from Bancroft to the creek. The land to the west—between the Law Building and Sproul Hall—was developed on the Hillegass Tract, a seventeen-acre wedge of property that belonged to early landholder William Hillegass and was acquired at the beginning of the twentieth century. It extended the university grounds south of the creek, where several small cottages and shop buildings were located.

The international competition for the Hearst Plan produced the first vision for using this sloping but relatively flat plateau for athletics, rendered by Émile Bénard as an extravagant Roman stadium and gymnasium. Howard, as Supervising Architect, envisioned two permanent arcaded stadiums for football and track with adjacent courts and gymnasia. In 1905 he developed California Field, enclosed by temporary wood bleachers for football and baseball, on the present site of Hearst Gymnasium and North Field, and ten years later added the Running Track, or California Oval, west of the field. Already erected east of the field on the present site of Wurster Hall was Maybeck's Gothic-arched women's gymnasium, Hearst Hall, moved from Southside in 1901 and sited with adjacent tennis and basketball courts and a swimming pool.

Between these athletic facilities and the creek assorted small structures were placed. Maybeck's Faculty Club in 1902 and Howard's Senior Hall in 1906 were constructed in the vicinity of the old cottages within Co-ed Canyon, or Faculty Glade, as it is now known. South of the glade in the vicinity of Morrison and Hertz Halls, several temporary buildings designed by Howard were built for a variety of academic uses. These included the wooden Spreckels Physiological Laboratory (renamed the Spreckels Art Building 1930–1955), one of the first campus research labs, in 1903 and, the following year, the corrugated-iron Anthropology Building called the "tin bin" that housed Phoebe Apperson Hearst's collections. West of these stood the wooden Fertilizer Control Building (renamed the Agricultural Chemistry Building 1920–1930 and the Decorative Art Building 1930–1964) and the corrugated-iron Museum of Vertebrate Zoology (renamed the Decorative Art Annex 1930–1964), both built in 1909. And between California Field and Hearst Hall, the wooden Hygiene and Pathology Laboratory was inserted in 1908. Two wooden buildings designed by Clinton Day and originally built in 1898 were also moved to this congested area in 1921: the zoology laboratory East Hall and the Botany Building from the present sites of LeConte and Stephens Halls, respectively.

A new vision for using the Hillegass Tract as a grand memorial to Phoebe Hearst emerged following the destruction of Maybeck's Hearst Hall by fire in 1922. A monumental auditorium flanked by a new women's gymnasium and museum facilities for housing the anthropological collections were proposed, but only the first increment—Hearst Gymnasium by Maybeck and Morgan—was built, aligned with Howard's axis and the Campanile.

The University Health Service began on the present site of Minor Hall, where the shingled Meyer House stood. Once the storage place of the Hearst anthropological collections, it was used to treat victims of the 1906 San Francisco earthquake before becoming the first students' infirmary in the United States in 1907, functioning in that capacity until the completion of Arthur Brown's neoclassical Cowell Memorial Hospital in 1930 (expanded by Weihe, Frick & Kruse in 1954 and E. Geoffrey Bangs in 1960). Located across College where the Haas School of Business is now sited, the hospital was designed in a style compatible with the earlier Beaux-Arts buildings of Howard, but its historic merit was more sociological than architectural. It was the original location of the Physically Disabled Students' Residence Program, begun with the admission of Edward V. Roberts, a quadriplegic, in 1962. Roberts, who earned a Ph.D., went on to co-found the renowned Center of Independent Living on Telegraph, direct California's Department of Rehabilitation, and found the World Institute on Disability. The unprecedented program was instrumental to the formation of the independence movement. It remained in Cowell until 1975, when its students moved to the Unit 2 Residence Halls in Southside, attaining a more independent and integrated educational experience. Cowell was demolished in 1993 and is commemorated by a plaque mounted on a concrete fragment of the building on the west side of the business school.

Through the late 1940s residential properties—including those in use today by the university along the old College right-of-way and Piedmont (see Walk 8)—still occupied the property south of the hospital. Along Bancroft the university's Institute of Child Welfare, housed in the former residence of legendary Professor Joseph LeConte, and the home of early campus architect Clinton Day survived until the 1960s when they were removed for construction of the Law Building addition.

Hearst Gymnasium became the dominant feature of the Hillegass Tract, surrounded by open recreation fields and tennis courts, with the exception of the Campus Cafeteria erected in 1948 on the present site of the plaza west of Wurster Hall. Compiled from four former Navy mess halls moved from Camp Parks in eastern Alameda County, it was redesigned by architects Miller and Warnecke to replace the overcrowded cafeteria in Stephens Hall and meet the needs of the student body expanded by veterans returned from World War II. The complex could accommodate about 2,000 students and was called the "[b]iggest thing to hit campus since the cyclotron." It served students for the next two decades until construction of the Student Center Dining Commons in the 1960s.

To the east of the cafeteria the former Hearst Hall swimming pool was located on the site of the Wurster tower. It transferred from women's to men's use after the construction of Hearst Gymnasium and was later enlarged to become the Hydraulic Model Basin for the College of Engineering's study of fluid mechanics. It was also utilized by the Navy for scale-model analysis of the "Operation Crossroads" atomic bomb tests conducted at Bikini Atoll in 1946.

The next comprehensive vision for the area came from Brown, whose 1944 General Plan established the use and general placement of buildings for Music, Art, Anthropology, and Law—the latter first to be implemented with the completion of Warren C. Perry's Law Building in 1951. The 1956 and 1962 Long Range Development Plans, prepared under the leadership of Wurster, refined Brown's dense low-rise plan by introducing high-rises in the 1960s to conserve open space. These included Wurster Hall (DeMars, Esherick and Olsen, 1962–64) to place Environmental Design in a related grouping with Anthropology and Art, Barrows Hall (Aleck L. Wilson & Associates, 1962–64) for Business Administration, Political Science, Economics and Sociology, and Manville (now Simon) Hall (Wurster, Bernardi & Emmons, 1965–67), a residence hall for Law students. The 1970s saw the School of Optometry expansion of Arthur Brown's Minor Hall by Mackinlay, Winnacker, McNeil and the completion of Mario J. Ciampi's art museum across Bancroft, included in this Walk because of its affinity to the art programs in Kroeber. Redevelopment of the Cowell Hospital site for the cloistered Haas School of Business by Moore Ruble Yudell and The Ratcliff Architects' expansion of the Law Building were the major changes to the area in the 1990s.

Anthony Hall with Pelican sculpture by Francis Rich

37. Anthony Hall and Old Art Gallery

Anthony Hall *Joseph Esherick, 1956–1957*
Old Art Gallery *John Galen Howard, 1904; W. P. Stephenson, alterations, 1931*

Joseph Esherick considered it his most playful building.[1] That was an apt quality for Anthony Hall, built to house the staff of the nation's top-ranked student humor magazine, *The California Pelican*, which was founded in 1903 by Earle C. Anthony and featured creative illustrations by Rube Goldberg. The "Pelly," "Old Bird," or "Dirty Bird," as it was affectionately called, drew its name from a late nineteenth-century slang description of coeds scurrying to classes. First produced in Anthony's apartment, in 1904 it was housed in North Hall, moving to Stephens Union (now Stephens Hall) in 1923 and to Eshleman Hall (now Moses Hall) in 1931, along with other student publications.

Anthony later prospered as an entrepreneur, becoming the owner of a major commercial radio station and the West Coast distributor of Packard automobiles. An admirer of Bernard Maybeck's work, he commissioned the architect in the 1920s for his Packard showrooms in San Francisco, Oakland, and Los Angeles, and to design his residence in the hills of Los Angeles. He again had Maybeck in mind when he decided to donate a building for the magazine, but when the elderly architect declined, Campus Architect Louis DeMonte suggested that Architecture Professor Joseph Esherick design the building, using Maybeck as his consultant.

Esherick, who trained at the University of Pennsylvania, came to the Bay Area in the late 1930s, where he was drawn to Maybeck's vernacular regional style, along with the work of Ernest Coxhead, Willis Polk, Albert C. Schweinfurth, and A. Page Brown. In 1952 he joined the faculty of the School of Architecture, then led by William Wurster, whose work he also admired.

Esherick consulted informally with Maybeck, discussing the design with him on the one hand, and with his client, Anthony, on the other. In Maybeck's studio he worked out ideas in the master's style, using chalk and pastels, while reporting on the building's progress to President Sproul, who hoped that Anthony might make a more significant contribution to the campus in the future.

At the creek-side site for the Pelican Building (as it was initially named), Esherick created a pavilion-like building that reflects the influences of Maybeck and the Bay Region style. The one-story post-and-beam structure, comprised of a two-room main wing with a one-room projection to the north, is exposed throughout in Esherick fashion with modular redwood trusses, posts, and wall panels. Two trellised pergolas—a Maybeck trademark—along the south entrance facade and the creek-side north terrace, provide a feeling of lightness to the structure with carved beams supporting an overhanging red-tiled gable roof. The use of rose-colored stucco on the exterior walls was inspired by Maybeck's polychromatic Oakland Packard showroom (demolished in 1974), while other Maybeck influences include the industrial steel-sash windows and redwood pilasters with cast-concrete capitals, which display thirty sculpted pelicans. Larger bas-relief medallions of pelicans with inscriptions surmount the entrance doorways.

The building was dedicated on Big Game Day 1956 with the featured speaker Anthony accompanied by a live pelican at the ceremonies. Two years later, the bronze pelican that sits in front of the building was dedicated. Sculptor Francis Rich created the bird, following Anthony's advice that "this pelican is no saint," and giving the bird its slightly mischievous grin. When the "Old Bird" retired, the building was assigned to the Graduate Assembly, which has been its occupant since 1974. It is uncertain whether the inscribed motto in the wood mantle over the brick fireplace is still followed: "Be Good—If You Can't Be Good—Be Careful."

Old Art Gallery

Powerhouse—art gallery—supply store—and proposed music hall—the small brick building at the end of Barrow Lane has given yeoman's service to the university for nearly a century. Constructed as the central heating and power plant, for almost thirty years it produced and distributed the electricity and steam needed to operate the "Athens of the West" that John Galen Howard was building north of Strawberry Creek.

Howard gave some style to the utilitarian structure. Its Romanesque influences include round-arched openings and brick corbels that crown the inset panels of the facade. The red mission-tile gabled roof, enclosed by stepped end walls, is crowned with a copper-framed skylight that harmonizes with Howard's central architectural theme. The steel trusses that support the roof are exposed in the interior.

In 1917, to meet increased demand from new bond-financed construction—which included Wheeler, Hilgard and Gilman Halls and the completion of Doe Memorial Library—a small addition to the east was constructed, along with tunnels and subways carrying steam and electrical lines to the buildings. But by the end of the 1920s the plant could not keep pace with campus growth and was replaced by a new Central Heating Plant (George W. Kelham, 1930) in the southwest part of campus.

When Art Professor Eugen Neuhaus saw that the high-ceilinged powerhouse was being vacated, he realized it could serve as a small gallery for exhibiting art on campus. He had to overcome opposition by some faculty members, who could not see the need for an art museum for other than research purposes. Philosophy Professor Stephen C. Pepper supported Neuhaus, proclaiming the benefits to be realized by students: "If the least endowed of us have our creative capacity stirred even to a little production it will unite us to a common understanding with the greatest creative artists and their achievements."[2] President Sproul agreed, approving the conversion of the building at a cost of $5,000. Financial help came from funds raised by San Francisco art patron and benefactor Albert Bender and contributions from the Class of 1933 and the Regents.

With the east addition removed along with transformers and a tall metal flue, an entrance canopy was installed and the forty-by-eighty-

Old Art Gallery

foot building cleaned, its brick interior painted white, for use as the new University Art Gallery. A collection of Asian art, donated by Bender, was hung for its dedication and opening in March 1934. Bender also donated a pair of stone Buddhist lions, which flanked the building's entrance until the 1980s, when they were moved to Durant Hall (see Walk 1). During the next thirty-five years, curators Neuhaus and Professor Winfield Scott Wellington presented diversified exhibitions that included paintings, tapestries and other objects from the Phoebe Hearst collections, artifacts from China, Egypt, and the California Indians, kinetic sculpture, and displays of student work.

The mosaic-tile murals were installed on the east facade of the building as part of the Federal Art Project of the Works Progress Administration (WPA) in 1936–37. As gallery openings were often accompanied by receptions with musicians, the fine arts depicted in the murals were apropos of the building's use. Artists Florence Alston Swift portrayed *Music and Painting* on the south mural, while Helen Bruton created *Sculpture and Dancing* on the north.

The small gallery closed when the University Art Museum (now the University of California, Berkeley Art Museum and Pacific Film Archive) opened on Bancroft Way in 1970. The university considered remodeling the building as an artistic center for visual arts shows, experimental projects, and informal theatrical productions, but it has been used since the early 1970s for office supplies and campus police and financial aid functions.

The Department of Music now proposes to rehabilitate the building as an international performance center. In addition to accommodating the department's historic Javanese gamelan orchestra and chamber, jazz, and other contemporary ensembles, it would facilitate the training of student musicians as they prepare for larger performances. The WPA mosaics of artists Swift and Bruton remain well suited to this new use of the former powerhouse.

The Old Art Gallery is listed on the State Historic Resources Inventory.

38. Hearst Gymnasium

Bernard Maybeck and Julia Morgan, 1926–1927;
Hansen/Murakami/Eshima, interior alterations, 1996

Built for the physical education and social enrichment of women students, Hearst Gymnasium is a fragmented temple, the only completed part of a grandiose complex to memorialize university Regent and patron Phoebe Apperson Hearst, who contributed to the cultural and educational benefits of women with endowed scholarships and the construction of the precursor to the gymnasium, Hearst Hall, in 1899.

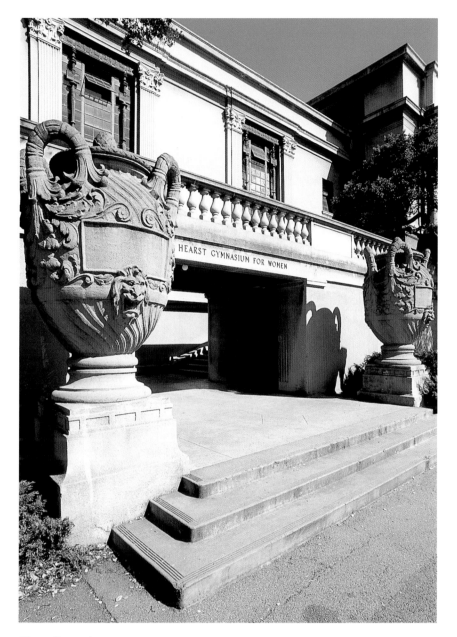

Hearst Gymnasium

The need and concept for the new gym were linked to that venerated but short-lived structure, whose initial purpose was to receive visiting
jurors and others involved in the final phase of the international competition
for the Hearst Plan. It was designed by Bernard Maybeck and constructed on
the south side of Channing Way, adjoining the Hearst residence on Piedmont
Avenue. The enormous reception hall—it could seat 500 people at banquet
tables and stage musical and dramatic productions—was also used for balls,
art exhibits, and performances that enriched university cultural life at the

turn of the century. Maybeck began design studies for the hall in 1897 while still in Paris coordinating the competition; he was assisted at the time by Julia Morgan, who was then residing in the same apartment building as the Maybecks while applying for entrance to the École des Beaux-Arts.

The wooden structure was intended to be relocated eventually to the campus grounds—Maybeck's ingenious design used laminated Gothic arches that supported movable sections—and following adoption of the Hearst Plan, it was moved and reassembled in 1901 where the south wing of Wurster Hall now stands. The hall was then converted to fill "the great need," expressed by President Wheeler, "of a strictly women's building."[3] Equipped with gymnastic apparatus, it was gradually expanded as a physical education complex with adjacent outdoor basketball and tennis courts and a swimming pool. More than a gym, the building served as "a general rendezvous for the women students,"[4] a social center as well as a place for campus events and performances.

But on the morning of June 20, 1922, a fire destroyed the hall, leaving the women suddenly without facilities and equipment. William Randolph Hearst immediately notified President David P. Barrows of his pledge to replace the building with a fireproof structure in honor of his mother, who had died in 1919. He recommended that the design commission go to Bernard Maybeck.

But Hearst had in mind more than a gymnasium to memorialize his mother—here also was the opportunity to provide the university with its long-desired auditorium and museum. Along with an art gallery, the complex could house and exhibit the vast collections of art and "antiquities"

Hearst Hall, 1901

acquired by expeditions sponsored by Phoebe Hearst around the turn of the century. These were needs envisioned for years on John Galen Howard's Hearst Plan: the Pantheon-like auditorium positioned at the head of the great central axis, and the classical museum as a counterbalance across from Doe Memorial Library. But with support for Howard weakened following his objection to the siting of California Memorial Stadium in 1922, the university proceeded to assign the grand memorial to Maybeck and construct it on the Hillegass Tract, on the site of California Field.

Maybeck—some nine years after the completion of his magnificent domed Palace of Fine Arts that formed the focal point of the 1915 Panama-Pacific International Exposition in San Francisco—went to work with colored chalk and large sheets of brown kraft paper. His visionary sketches reflected familiar Maybeckian themes: a great auditorium-rotunda similar to the Palace of Fine Arts; a barrel-vaulted museum reminiscent of his promotional illustration for the Hearst Plan competition in 1896; and a complex of polychromatic buildings with classically sculptured pools, promenades and terraces. The Beaux-Arts composition was aligned with the Hearst Plan axis, with the large rotunda centered on the Campanile and its Esplanade. To the south of the dome and also on axis, the symmetrical gymnasium was placed as a forecourt to the 600-seat auditorium. These buildings were envisioned to link to an extended complex to the east of museum buildings, colonnades, courtyards, and gardens.

The picturesque renderings gave little attention to the practical workings of the buildings, and the first drawings Maybeck submitted to the university were unacceptable. President William W. Campbell then consulted with William Randolph Hearst, and the two concluded that Julia Morgan should be commissioned to join Maybeck to plan and design functional interiors for the complex. Morgan, who had been employed by Hearst since 1919 as architect of his famous castle at San Simeon, formed the association with Maybeck in 1924. The following year the university authorized construction of the gymnasium, but before it was completed Hearst reported that a shortage of funds caused him to abandon the remainder of the complex. Left alone was the completed gymnasium, the only major building south of the creek aligned with the campus axis. Its large pool-terrace, which was intended to double as a promenade and outdoor lobby for the crowds attending performances in the great rotunda, now faces only onto the open space left from the demolition of California Field (now North Field), where the domed auditorium was to stand.

The U-shaped concrete gymnasium consists of three wings that define the upper level swimming-pool terrace. This main pool is aligned with the doorway aedicule of the central pavilion, described by the architects in a telegram to Hearst during design studies as having "columns like an old temple," behind which is "glass supported by Pompeiian bronze

Study for Hearst Memorial with proposed domed auditorium, 1924, Bernard Maybeck

iron."[5] These copper colonnettes were custom fabricated and occur with ornamental copper friezes at window and door openings around the building. Never executed was the Maybeck trademark polychromatic plasterwork—green columns and rose-tinted walls—or the sculpted female figures and other motifs proposed as an attic frieze.

Sculptural groups do flank the central pavilion facing the swimming pool. The cherub-and-urn sculptures, which are repeated at the south pools, are virtually identical to those surrounding the nymph at the Jardin de la Fontaine in Nîmes, France. And the bas-relief draped Greek female figures bearing garlands on the adjacent planter boxes resemble those by architectural sculptor Ulric H. Ellerhusen (1879–1957) on the flower urns of Maybeck's Palace of Fine Arts. The thirty-three-yard swimming pool and its deck are surfaced in green-streaked white marble tiles from a Vermont quarry, which closed long ago. When repairs were made in 1997, the deck tiles were replaced with matching ones created from the original quarry's remaining marble slabs, which were discovered at another company.

Small pavilions, containing a recreation room and offices of the Department of Human Biodynamics, form the north ends of the two side wings. Between these wings and the pool terrace are two interior courtyards that admit daylight into the first floor, which, in addition to locker rooms, now includes a weight room, scientific diving facilities, and ROTC headquarters. A long gallery, entered through arched doorways and lit with north-facing industrial-sash windows, connects the two east and west building entrances.

On the south side of the building three high-ceilinged, skylit gymnasia form larger projecting pavilions facing Bancroft. Between these are smaller gymnasia and skylit ramped passageways that lead to the first-floor locker rooms. Two exterior niches between these pavilions contain smaller swimming pools with walled gardens at ground level, where classical balustrades are interspersed by ornamental urns with sculpted lion heads. These monumental urns, which continue around the east and west facades, now consist of fiberglass replicas, cast from the original deteriorating concrete urns and installed in 1981.

Lion's head sculpture on decorative urn, Hearst Gymnasium

Julia Morgan's influence on the gymnasium was more extensive than her design of the interior spaces. The working drawings were prepared in her office, and she was responsible for on-site construction supervision. Nearly five years following the destruction of Hearst Hall, the Phoebe Apperson Hearst Gymnasium for Women was dedicated on the evening of April 8, 1927, with remarks from President Campbell and William Randolph Hearst. "Happily Mr. Hearst is making an investment," the president said, "which will yield splendid and constant dividends of high educational value to the women students of the university through decades to come."[6] The neoclassical gymnasium would also stand as a reminder of a larger unfulfilled dream and as a transitional element in the architectural vision for the campus.

Hearst Gymnasium is listed on the National Register of Historic Places, is included in the Berkeley campus designation as a California Registered Historical Landmark, is listed on the State Historic Resources Inventory, and is a City of Berkeley Landmark.

39. University of California, Berkeley Art Museum and Pacific Film Archive

Mario J. Ciampi, with Paul W. Reiter, Richard L. Jorasch, and Ronald E. Wagner, 1967–1970;

C. David Robinson with Forell/Elesser Engineers, interim structural retrofit, 2001

Apropos of its use, the segmented concrete structure that houses the university's Berkeley Art Museum and Pacific Film Archive is itself the museum's largest piece of sculpture, an object artistically set within an urban landscape. In recognizing the building for its Twenty-Five Year Award in 1996, the American Institute of Architects, California Council proclaimed it "a work of California architecture of enduring significance, one that has retained its central form and character, and with its architectural integrity intact." However, its integrity has been compromised by an interim structural retrofit, while the building faces an uncertain future because of concerns about its seismic safety.

The building was proposed as the University Arts Center in 1963 to provide a long-needed art gallery, to support the teaching activities of the Art and Humanities Departments, and to enhance the cultural life of the student body and community. Since 1934, exhibits had been limited to space in the University Art Gallery, the converted campus powerhouse constructed in 1904 (see Old Art Gallery). The project gained momentum with a gift from artist and faculty member Hans Hofmann (1880–1966) of forty-seven paintings and $250,000, on condition that a proper museum be built to house the collection. The balance of the nearly $5 million building cost would come primarily from student fees, as well as other sources. The site between Bancroft and Durant was selected for its proximity to both the academic center of campus and the concentrated student population of Southside.

Desiring a building of artistic merit, the Regents conducted a two-stage architectural competition, which produced 366 national entries. From seven finalists, the jury selected a San Francisco team led by Mario Ciampi in July 1965. The jury was impressed with the scheme's "play of natural light and the interaction of floor levels and room heights" and "the sculptural beauty of its rugged forms."[7]

The neo-Brutalist building forms a fan-like series of galleries that radiate from the Bancroft entrance lobby. Ascending ramps connect these galleries and project into a skylit atrium overlooking additional galleries below. At the bottom level, the George Gund Theater (used until recently by the Pacific Film Archive), ticket office, conference room, and cafe are organized around a lobby-gallery that opens onto a sculpture garden entered from Durant. The exterior expresses the angular galleries that step up the sloping site and cantilever over the surrounding garden.

Several sculptures are displayed within the Museum's garden and grounds, the most notable being Alexander Calder's stabile, *The Hawk for Peace*, which stands gracefully juxtaposed before the Bancroft facade. Created in 1968 in memory of the artist's brother-in-law, Kenneth Aurand Hayes (Class of 1916), the six-ton steel piece was installed in 1970. A work by the artist's father, A. Sterling Calder, can also be seen on campus in Faculty Glade, where *The Last Dryad* stands by Strawberry Creek (see Faculty Glade).

Originally named the University Art Museum, the facility was renamed in 1996 in conjunction with a $5 million anonymous donation. The museum houses a collection of more than 9,000 diverse works of art, from European masters to major twentieth-century artists, from traditional Asian objects to Abstract Expressionist paintings. Each spring, the works of graduate art students from the Department of Art Practice are also exhibited in the galleries. The Pacific Film Archive is internationally recognized for its exhibition, collection, preservation and study of film and video, and contains over 7,000 titles from around the world. Rare classic prints, independent works, and retrospectives are among the variety of films screened nearly daily at the Hearst Field Annex.

The $4 million seismic retrofit, completed in 2001, includes a series of steel braces on parts of the exterior and interior to strengthen the cantilevered galleries. The bracing enables the continued use of the building while a long-term solution is studied, including the possible relocation of the museum and film archive to the site of the UC Printing Services on Oxford Street (see 2120 Oxford Street, Walk 10).

University of California, Berkeley Art Museum and Pacific Film Archive; The Hawk for Peace, *right by Alexander Calder*

Kroeber Hall

40. Kroeber Hall and Morrison and Hertz Halls

Kroeber Hall   *Gardner Dailey, with Douglas Baylis, landscape architect, 1957–1959*
Morrison and Hertz Halls

Gardner Dailey, with Douglas Baylis, landscape architect, 1956–1958

A modernist utilitarian building, Kroeber Hall defines the south side of the arts square opposite Morrison and Hertz Halls and the west side of the land-scaped quadrangle at the College Avenue entrance. It was designed for and still houses the Departments of Art Practice and Anthropology and the Phoebe Apperson Hearst Museum of Anthropology. The building honors Alfred Louis Kroeber, the distinguished scholar of Native American tribes, who was the first full-time anthropology faculty member at Berkeley, founder of the museum, and department chairman for fourteen years.

Gardner Dailey organized the building into three wings. The north-facing studio wing forms a three-story L-shaped box with the east wing, which houses the 70,000-volume George and Mary Foster Anthropology Library and has industrial-style sawtoothed skylights to bring north light into interior offices. This wing also contains the Worth Allen Ryder Art Gallery, which is used primarily for student exhibitions; it was named for Art Professor Worth Allen Ryder, who served on the faculty from 1927 to 1955 and was instrumental in establishing the curriculum of the depart-ment. An open stairway at the junction of these two wings is the building's most interesting feature. Topped with gilded concave pyramidal panels, the vertical space tonally resonates with each footstep.

The adjoining two-story south wing along Bancroft houses the renowned museum, which contains approximately 3.8 million ethnographic and archaeological objects from around the world, with an emphasis on California. It is named for the university patron and Regent, who established the Department of Anthropology and the museum in 1901, with her support of university archaeological expeditions around the beginning of the twentieth century.

For more than a half-century the growing collection followed a nomadic path, housed in San Francisco and dispersed in several campus buildings. The completion of Kroeber in 1959 enabled the consolidation of the scattered department and establishment of proper exhibition space in the new museum. When it opened, the museum was named in honor of Professor Robert H. Lowie, pioneering faculty member since 1917, chairman of the department from 1934 to 1950, and recognized authority on the Crow Indians. In 1992, amidst some faculty opposition, it was renamed for Phoebe Hearst, while Lowie's name was transferred to the exhibition hall.

The Phoebe Apperson Hearst Museum of Anthropology in Kroeber Hall is open Wednesday through Sunday from 10am to 4:30pm (Thursday until 9pm) during the academic year, except for national and university holidays. The Worth Allen Ryder Art Gallery in Room 116 is open Tuesday through Friday during the academic year. Phone 510-642-2582.

Morrison and Hertz Halls

Gardner Dailey's two adjoining buildings for the Department of Music form the south side of Faculty Glade and the north side of the arts square opposite Dailey's Kroeber Hall. The L-shaped complex includes Morrison Hall, the department's instructional facility, and Hertz Hall, considered one of the finest small concert halls in California. A

Morrison Hall

colonnaded, covered passageway connects the two buildings and forms a southeast entry portal to the glade.

The buildings provided the first permanent home for the department, one of the nation's oldest, which for the previous twenty-five years occupied Dwinelle Annex, one of John Galen Howard's temporary wooden structures (see Walk 3). Constructed of concrete, Morrison and Hertz are surfaced in siena-colored stucco and have shallow-pitched gabled roofs of red clay tile. With overhanging eaves and the tile-roofed passageway, the complex evokes elements of the California Mission style. The modernist exteriors are undistinguished, but form a compatible background of nearly residential scale for Faculty Glade.

A two-story east-west rectangular block, Morrison contains class-rooms, practice rooms, offices, and a distinguished Music Library, which includes a book and printed music collection of some 160,000 volumes, as well as recordings, rare manuscripts, and historic musical instruments. The building is named in honor of May Treat Morrison (Class of 1878), one of the first women to graduate from the university and the building's major donor.

Oriented at a right angle to Morrison, Hertz has canopied doorways opening to a south courtyard facing the square. Above the doors are three central bays of stained glass windows by French artist Robert Pinard, who also designed the glass panels in the Tilden Meditation Room of King Student Union (see Walk 4). The 700-seat concert hall contains the O'Neill Memorial Organ, bequeathed by and named for former Chemistry Professor and Dean Edmond O'Neill and his wife Edith Vernon O'Neill. In addition to scheduled performances, the hall features popular noontime concerts for the campus community. The building was named for Alfred Hertz, former musical director of the San Francisco Symphony Orchestra and conductor of the New York Metropolitan Opera Orchestra. His bequeathed funds combined with a state appropriation to construct the building.

The two buildings were dedicated in 1958 with a five-week May T. Morrison Music Festival, described by music critic Alfred Frankenstein in the *California Monthly* as "the most ambitious . . . ever attempted in the Bay Region," with seventeen performances, which included new pieces commissioned for the occasion. Plans to expand the department's facilities include the renovation of Morrison, the construction of a new Music Library south of Morrison, and the conversion of Howard's former Power House (see Old Art Gallery) for a performance center.

Hertz Hall

Wurster Hall

41. Wurster Hall

> *DeMars, Esherick and Olsen, with Isadore Thompson, structural engineer,*
> *and Thomas D. Church, landscape architect, 1962–1964;*
> *cafe alterations, Fernau and Hartman, 1984;*
> *seismic alterations, Esherick, Homsey, Dodge, and Davis (EHDD), 2000–2002*

Probably no other campus building has evoked a love-hate response as profound as Wurster Hall, home of the College of Environmental Design. The high-rises built during the 1960s—most notably Barrows and Evans Halls, which were jeered while still coming out of the ground—were seen by many as dehumanizing symbols of an expanding bureaucracy. Wurster is one of those towers, large and like Evans constructed of concrete. But, while it continues to generate strong reaction—critic Allan Temko, called it "a cold [G]oliath of a building, heavily festooned with technocratic para-phernalia"[8]—it also has supporters sympathetic to the philosophy of its architects, a process-driven functional and sculptural aesthetic that makes Wurster a very sophisticated "Goliath."

The College was created in 1959 under Dean William Wilson Wurster to administratively link Architecture, which had outgrown the Ark (North Gate Hall, see Walk 2), Landscape Architecture (today named Landscape Architecture and Environmental Planning), which was still part of the College of Agriculture, and City and Regional Planning.

Much as his predecessor Architecture Dean Warren C. Perry had assembled a faculty team to design the Law Building, Dean Wurster called upon four members of his Architecture faculty—Vernon DeMars, Joseph

Esherick, Donald Olsen, and Donald Hardison—to design the state-funded Environmental Design building. DeMars had associated with Hardison to win the competition for the Student Center in 1957. Like Wurster, he was an Ark graduate (1931), who taught briefly at M. I. T. before joining the Berkeley faculty. DeMars was one of the founders of Telesis, the San Francisco group of architects, landscape architects and city planners who proposed new social and collaborative directions for the design professions, away from the stylistic thinking of the Beaux-Arts movement. He later assisted City and Regional Planning Professor T. J. Kent (a fellow Telesis founder) in obtaining Academic Senate approval of the new college, a concept that can be linked to the young Telesis reformers and that is now embodied in Wurster Hall. Esherick, a University of Pennsylvania graduate, joined the Berkeley faculty in 1952. Influenced by the Bay Regionalism of the early residential work of Wurster and Gardner Dailey (for whom he worked), he also became a disciple of architect Bernard Maybeck. Olsen trained at the University of Minnesota and Harvard, and worked for a time for Wurster's San Francisco firm, Wurster, Bernardi & Emmons. Hardison, the fourth member, left the group early, leaving DeMars, Esherick and Olsen to develop the synergy needed for the team design process.

The three modernists brought different views to the table. DeMars was Beaux-Arts trained but developed as a modernist designer, seeing himself as combining the picturesque with functionalism. Olsen, influenced by the teachings of Gropius, contributed a purist approach to modern functionalism. Esherick was viewed as something in between his two partners, more of an aesthetician and principally responsible for the sculptural form of the building. Initially, the team met in the Berkeley office of DeMars, whose partner Donald Reay participated in early studies. But in time Esherick took the lead role, developing the drawings in his office and conferring weekly with DeMars and Olsen.

Prominently oriented to the west, Wurster Hall has a U-shaped plan, organized in three wings that form a large east courtyard. The principal north wing includes a three-story base—containing an auditorium, exhibition rooms, the Environmental Design Library, and offices, studios and classrooms—forming a podium for the tower that houses six floors of studios and rises to a tenth-floor seminar room with its signature penthouse balcony. The architects reasoned that stacking the design studios, which are occupied for long blocks of time, would require infrequent elevator trips and avoid the type of congestion that often results when classrooms with hourly changes are housed in a high-rise structure. The drawback proved to be the difficulty in creating opportunity for the kind of serendipitous interaction among class levels that more naturally occurred in the smaller Ark.

The central three-story wing contains lobbies, a cafe, exhibition spaces, and offices, and functions as a link between the north and south wings. Additional offices, workshops, and classrooms occupy the four-story south wing, along with ceramics and sculpture studios for the Department of Art Practice, which is home-based in adjacent Kroeber Hall.

Trying to instill the qualities of the Ark, Wurster and the design team envisioned that the building should be able to accommodate the rough treatment associated with the creative training of architects and artists. "The Ark," the Dean romanticized, "is a ripe building; it has been lived in, it's been used, it's been beaten up and everything else. It's arrived. Our building will take twenty years to arrive."[9]

Concrete was selected as an economical structural material early in the process, when it was determined that steel would not be necessary for any long spans. The material also lent itself to bold sculptural expression, an influence of the Brutalism movement of the time. For the end walls, floors, roof, and shaft enclosures, the architects used poured-in-place concrete, to which pre-cast elements were attached. These included units of column-and-spandrel sections that comprise the main exterior walls, and the ubiquitous slabs that shade and texture the building's sunny sides. The wall units were designed with the columns on the exterior, in order to maximize the flexibility and use of the interior spaces. The systematic assembly of these numerous parts distinguished the building as the largest then constructed with pre-cast elements.

The interior of Wurster was left unfinished to expose students to what DeMars described as "the bones and nerves and circulatory systems that make a building work"[10]—the overlapping layers of mechanical ductwork, water and waste pipes, and electrical conduits, that are usually concealed within walls or ceilings. Here they are suspended from the concrete waffle-slab ceilings, but spatially organized to not diminish the height of the spaces and to maximize accessibility for maintenance and teaching. On the interior walls, replaceable plywood panels allow student work and other material to be stapled or pinned up for exhibition or review. According to DeMars, the architects also "felt the background for training young students of design should ideally be anonymous and utilitarian so it won't influence their own self-expression."[11] Esherick saw it as being "non-tendentious; that is, it should not be either an example or a display of *formal* ideas, as Crown Hall at Illinois Institute of Technology, or of *personal* ideas, as the Art and Architecture Building at Yale."[12] For Dean Wurster, the building achieved the kind of honest functionalism that attracts many architects to work in old loft buildings: "I wanted it to look like a ruin.... It's absolutely unfinished, rough, uncouth, and brilliantly strong. This is the way architecture is best done."[13]

For landscape architect Thomas Church, there would be limited opportunity to soften the dominating building. The east courtyard, inspired by the smaller brick courtyard of the Ark, was meant to be a place suitable for graduations and outdoor classes. But the use of brick paving was rejected by the architects in favor of plain asphalt—punctuated by a few olive trees—considered to be more in keeping with the building's stark character. The west side of the building was treated a little more generously. Concrete bench-tree wells provide some relief to the area, which was enlivened and softened with the addition of the small umbrella-furnished cafe terrace by Fernau and Hartman in 1984. Church was able to contribute greenery to the south quadrangle that serves as the College Avenue entrance and includes a fountain contributed by the Class of 1914.

The phased seismic retrofit of the building begun in 2000 by Esherick's descendant firm Esherick, Homsey, Dodge, and Davis included the addition of a nine-story-high tube-structure, which also provides new space at the east end of the tower. Wurster Hall was named in 1964 in honor of Dean Wurster and his wife, Catherine Bauer Wurster, a member of the City and Regional Planning faculty and known for her social research related to housing and town planning.

42. Minor Hall and Minor Hall Addition

Minor Hall

>*Arthur Brown Jr., 1941; Mackinlay, Winnacker, McNeil, alterations, 1977–1978; Fong & Chan, addition, 1991–1992*

Minor Hall Addition   *Mackinlay, Winnacker, McNeill, 1977–1978*

Designed by Supervising Architect Arthur Brown, Jr., at the brink of the United States' entry into World War II, Minor Hall was built as the Emergency Classroom Building to house government-funded defense courses, as well as mathematics and journalism classes. The then two-story

Minor Hall

neoclassical concrete building was compatible with Brown's Cowell Memorial Hospital (1929–1930), which was located across old College Avenue, where the Haas School of Business now stands. Like Brown's other campus buildings, it quietly harmonized with the Beaux-Arts monuments of John Galen Howard. A long rectangular block, it was adorned only with rustication at the corners and at the recessed entrances, where flat arches are crowned by classical balustrades. In 1942 the building was named Durant Hall, in honor of Henry Durant, first president of the university (1870–1872).

As the war progressed, and development of the atomic bomb became a national priority, the Radiation Laboratory took over the classroom building. In 1946 it was reoccupied again for courses in mathematics and journalism, as well as naval sciences and optometry. In response to postwar enrollment growth, it was assigned to the School of Optometry, previously housed in LeConte Hall, and renamed the Optometry Building in 1952 (following transfer of the Durant Hall name to the former Boalt Hall of Law). It was again renamed in 1970 to honor Ralph S. Minor, Dean Emeritus of the school.

Increases in enrollment and outpatient use of the school's teaching clinic in the 1970s led to the need for the five-story Minor Hall Addition, funded by a health sciences bond and private contributions. Designed by Oakland architects Mackinlay, Winnacker, McNeil, the $5 million building resulted in a tripling of the school's facilities—with new space for training clinics, offices, research labs, classrooms, and the Optometry library. It also consolidated school functions that were scattered around the campus.

The modernist concrete structure is characterized by horizontally proportioned window bays and deep wood beams, which provide warmth to the facade. The main second floor Eye Center and clinics—arranged in specialty modules—form a terrace for the upper three-story block of offices and labs that connects by a bridge to

Minor Hall Addition

the older building. Unanticipated in the university's 1962 Long Range Development Plan, the expansion utilized the site to the maximum, squeezing next to the nine-story Wurster Hall tower to the south and the high blank wall of Hertz Hall to the west. Despite these constraints, the building achieved an openness through the use of windowed areas facing onto exterior courts.

In 1992 San Francisco architects Fong & Chan created two additional floors in Brown's building by developing the former attic space and raising the roof by one story. Funded by gifts and Chancellor's funds, the gained space provided research and teaching labs and offices that replaced some facilities housed in Cowell. The use of dormers on the east and west sides of the roof extend the upper level labs, while the window treatment and use of the red tile hipped roof are sympathetic to Brown's original Beaux-Arts design.

43. The Faculty Club, Senior Hall, Women's Faculty Club, and Girton Hall

The Faculty Club
> *Bernard Maybeck, Great Hall, 1902 and west wing addition, 1903;*
> *John Galen Howard, south addition, 1903–1904;*
> *Warren C. Perry, north wing, southeast, and Great Hall additions, 1914;*
> *and north wing addition, 1925;*
> *Winfield Scott Wellington, alterations, ca. 1925;*
> *Downs and Lagorio, east and south addition and west wing alterations, 1958–1959;*
> *Michael Goodman, alterations, 1974–1975;*
> *Christopherson & Kositsky, seismic alterations, 1976;*
> *Sam Davis, alterations, 1992*

Senior Hall
> *John Galen Howard, 1905–1906 and addition, 1914;*
> *The Ratcliff Architects, alterations, 1985*

Women's Faculty Club
> *John Galen Howard, 1923; Ratcliff and Ratcliff, addition and alterations, 1956;*
> *Kolbeck and Christopherson, addition and alterations, 1975;*
> *Bennett Christopherson, alterations, 1976–1977*

Girton Hall *Julia Morgan, 1911*

Though expanded incrementally from a single-room clubhouse, Bernard Maybeck's Faculty Club has proven to be remarkably adaptable while maintaining its original identity. Its growth has been compatibly accomplished by a succession of architects sensitive to the master's style and intent.

Situated at the east edge of Faculty Glade and along the south bank of Strawberry Creek, the club developed from the university's dining association, which occupied one of two cottages at the site built in 1874 to house women students. The shortage of reputable dining facilities in the community led in 1893 to the formation of the association to provide meal service to both students and faculty. By 1898, as private homes, clubs and fraternities developed near campus to provide room and board for students, the association switched to serving just faculty, who also found the cottage a convenient place to socialize after meals.

When members desired a better place to congregate, they decided to form the "Faculty Club of the University of California" and construct a clubhouse to the west of the dining cottage for "general gatherings, entertainments, lectures, concerts, etc.," as well as "smoking, billiards, reading, [and] shower baths."[14] Drawing instructor Maybeck, architect of Hearst Hall (1898) and the coordinating genius behind the successful Hearst Plan competition, donated his services to design the new building.

Maybeck designed a rectangular Great Hall, with the long axis oriented approximately east-west, affording a view towards the creek from a porch on the north side, and sunny exposure on the south. Inside, he created a steep-gabled Gothic hall of rough-sawn, dark-stained redwood, with a monumental stone fireplace as the focal point at the west end. Paired near the ends of the hall, on either side of glass-paneled wood doors centered on the north and south sides, he

placed heavy-timber trusses, supported by freestanding, built-up wooden piers. A reflection of his youthful apprenticeship to his woodcarver father, Maybeck topped each pier with paired hammer beams, carved as dragon heads projecting into the medieval hall to gaze upon the diners beneath them.

Dragonhead beams, Great Hall, The Faculty Club

Great Hall, The Faculty Club

While the facility in the early part of the twentieth century had all the hallmarks of an exclusive men's club, members early on voted Phoebe Apperson Hearst, who contributed decorations, as a life member. Still, for many years the building served as a retreat for cigar-smoking, bearded faculty colleagues. Adding to the lodge atmosphere, were elk antlers, animal-head trophies, and artifacts from the Spanish American War, including "caribou horns, Filipino arms, Moro flags and other mementos." For collegial ambience, stained-glass university shields were installed above the glass-paneled doors to represent the associations of early faculty members. These include on the north side, the U. S. Military Academy, Brown, California, Cornell, and Oxford; and on the south, Stanford, Columbia, Harvard, Yale, and Princeton. At its east end, the club connected to the old dining association cottage, which was kept in service as a kitchen.

Maybeck did not express the high-gabled hall on the exterior, but instead provided a lower-pitched gable, roofed in red mission tile. At the porch he extended the paired hammer-head beams through the stucco skin of the building, but without the dragon heads, to support a wooden trellis. The one-room clubhouse was completed in September 1902, and that month members gathered in front of the stone fireplace for a ceremonial "first lighting of the fire."

But before the initial construction was completed, some bachelor members proposed that a two-story wing be added to the west of the Great Hall to provide club rooms on the first floor and apartments above. Their offer to pay for the cost of the addition in exchange for ten years of rent-free residency was approved, and Maybeck proceeded with the building's first addition, adopting the style of the California Missions with plaster walls and red-tile roof.

The Faculty Club

The first floor of the new wing, containing the present-day bar, included billiard and reading rooms with large arched windows on the north and south, while bracketed windows were cantilevered at the second floor. A smaller arched opening was provided at the doorway of a three-story tower placed at the junction of the Great Hall and new wing.

The following year, with club membership grown to 150, another two-story addition to the south was completed—designed by John Galen Howard, who was then established as both the university's Supervising Architect and the first professor of the Department of Architecture. This addition provided a first-floor lounge and larger billiard room (in the present lounge named in Howard's honor), with living quarters above for two professors, including the beloved Henry Morse Stephens. Howard aligned the double fireplace of his addition with the center of the Great Hall's south-facing glass doors, which were converted from exterior to interior use. Between the old and new sections, he placed a glass skylight, a respectful linkage to the Great Hall and a subtle reminder that the doors with their stained glass transoms were once a part of the club's exterior facade.

In 1914, a second issue of bonds combined with a Regents' appropriation and personal notes from the club's directors financed the next addition by architect Warren C. Perry. The club was growing organically, much like the venerable oaks dotting nearby Faculty Glade. The most assertive of the additions, this phase extended Maybeck's Great Hall to the east and built a new north wing toward the creek to create an L-shaped footprint with the west wing. This two-story wing added another dining room with a west-facing deck and a modernized kitchen to the east, with additional rental living quarters above.

A southeast wing was also built, providing a still larger room for billiards, in the present Heyns Dining Room. A legacy of this activity remains in the form of two allegorical murals, painted by art instructor Perham Nahl, whose gowned nymphs amongst the billiard balls seem to pay reverence to the springtime Partheneia pageants performed for years by female students in Faculty Glade (notches in Nahl's murals were completed by Professor of Art Practice Emeritus Karl Kasten in 2000). Above the entrance to the billiard room read a Greek inscription, one presumed to have also marked Plato's door: "Let no one enter who is rusty in geometry." Placed on the second floor of this southeast addition was the old dining association cottage, no longer needed as a kitchen but venerated in its roles as one of the original student cottages, the one-time residence of Professor Joseph Le Conte, a classroom, and the dining quarters from which the Faculty Club itself sprouted.

The 1959 addition by architects George A. Downs and Henry J. Lagorio extended the building's footprint to nearly its present configuration. Funded by donations and a loan from the Regents, it expanded dining, kitchen, and residential space, and provided additional private meeting and dining rooms, raising the total to fifteen. The second floor of Maybeck's west wing was also remodeled by removing the four residential rooms and the north-facing windowseat gallery to create one large library space.

Following the cancellation of a plan to expand to the east in 1973 (see Senior Hall), the Faculty Club was limited to minor expansion and interior alterations. Architect Michael Goodman's alterations in 1975 extended the skylit east dining area (now the buffet room), added the lower dining terrace on the west side, provided a new south entrance and lobby, and remodeled the Howard Room and west wing.

The most recent alteration, by Sam Davis in 1992, converted the second-floor library space in the west wing into the Seaborg Room, named in honor of Nobel Laureate and former Chancellor Glenn T. Seaborg. The room includes a fireplace panel honoring all campus Nobel Laureates. Though no longer subdivided into rooms off a north gallery, the renovation exemplifies the sensitivity applied by Maybeck's succeeding architects—who, like him, were also members of the faculty—to be compatible with the spirit of the original building.

The Faculty Club is listed on the National Register of Historic Places, is included in the Berkeley campus designation as a California Registered Historical Landmark, is listed on the State Historic Resources Inventory, and is a City of Berkeley Landmark.

Senior Hall

Few places on campus evoke the legacy of the California Spirit as does the rustic log cabin that stands between the two faculty clubs along the south bank of Strawberry Creek. The idea for the cabin came from a meeting of the Order of the Golden Bear in May 1903. Established in April 1900 as a senior men's honor society, the Order was often consulted on campus problems by President Wheeler, who was committed to the concept of student self-government.

Senior Hall, while owned by the university, was managed by the Order, which had the exclusive use of its back room. A second larger room would be dedicated to the men of the senior class, but open to alumni and men of the faculty, for such uses as meetings, smokers, and singing—"the home and fireside of the class, to become associated with its best traditions."[15] Since its beginnings the hall was established as "a center for the moulding of public opinion through free discussion." It remains so today as the traditional meeting place of the student-led Order, whose lifetime members (now male and female)—students, faculty, administrators, staff, and alumni—discuss campus issues within a framework of frankness, tolerance, and confidentiality.

By September 1903 about $2,000 had been subscribed for the construction, half a gift from Regent Phoebe Apperson Hearst and half from individual pledges. Supervising Architect John Galen Howard, who prepared preliminary plans near the end of 1904, waived his architectural fees. Though short of the total amount of funds needed, the Order decided to proceed with construction, and by spring 1905 the foundation was in place. The following October the hearth stone was laid in a ceremony attended by President Wheeler.

The redwood logs for the "Golden Bear Lodge," as it was sometimes called, were obtained with some difficulty from the Russian River lumber town of Guerneville. The lumber company manager reported to the building committee chairman, "There is so much water running in the gulches now, we may have some trouble to find the right sizes where we can get at them," but he added, with the cooperative spirit that typified the construction efforts: "However will get them in some way."[16] The railways also did their part. The California Northwestern Railway Company hauled the logs at no cost from Guerneville to the Sonoma County town of Shellville. From there they were delivered by Southern Pacific at a special reduced rate to Berkeley, where they arrived on campus in December 1905. Their presence was a tangible boost for members of the Order, who were still soliciting needed funds from alumni.

Log construction was familiar to Howard, who studied its use in the mountains of California, and to the contractor, Kidder and McCullough, who had experience building cabins in Alaska and Idaho. The logs were used in their natural state, with the bark in place, for virtually the entire structure, as well as for the chairs, benches, tables, and shelves that furnished the cabin.

Howard initially designed the hall in five modular bays that formed two spaces, a front room of four bays forming a space approximately thirty

Senior Hall

by sixty feet, and a small one-bay private rear room reserved for meetings of the Order. When this meeting room proved to be too small, he added an additional bay in 1914, bringing the building to its present size. The two spaces are separated by a log partition with a double-sided arched fireplace of clinker bricks. A "secret" jib door—originally concealed with a hanging bearskin—leads to the inner chamber. Notched king-post trusses support the pitched roof and rest on log pilasters between the window bays. The west facade of the gable-roof structure has a single jib door reached by a stairway, which was originally bifurcated. An early scheme by Howard featured a straight stairway that was approached through a colonnaded arbor extending westward from the building. Bands of windows, similar to Howard's other wooden campus buildings, extend under the eaves within each side bay, and are also used at the gable ends.

Dedication ceremonies—originally planned for May 1906 but postponed because of the San Francisco earthquake in April—were held the following September, with President Wheeler presenting the building to the men of the senior class. The Regents extended appreciation to Howard "for the toil and thought, the imagination and affection, that you have wrought into the building."[17]

Use of Senior Hall for issues concerning student government diminished once Stephens Memorial Union (Stephens Hall) was completed in 1923. But the Order continued to meet in the cabin until 1973, when it was declared seismically unsafe and was utilized only for storage by both faculty clubs. The dispossessed structure was then targeted to be dismantled and removed from its site to make room for a proposed dining room addition to the Faculty Club. But the planned removal caused an uproar from historic preservationists, as well as alumni, students, faculty, and staff. An ad hoc group, "Friends of the Campus for Senior Hall"—which included notable professors, a former Regent, and city and preservation leaders—exerted pressure on the university administration. The support was effective, and just one day before the scheduled dismantling in August 1973, the university stopped the project. The following year the hall was placed on the National Register of Historic Places, cited as "a prime example of a type of lumber construction at one time common and now almost extinct."

Minimal alterations, which included a ramped entrance to the rear room, by The Ratcliff Architects in 1985 permitted the Order to resume its traditional use of Senior Hall, while planning for a more extensive future restoration.

Senior Hall is listed on the National Register of Historic Places and the State Historic Resources Inventory, and is a City of Berkeley Landmark.

Women's Faculty Club

Women's Faculty Club

The Women's Faculty Club, the last of John Galen Howard's wooden campus buildings, is a four-story structure sheathed in brown shingles above a stucco basement, and covered with a shingled hipped roof. Together with the Faculty Club and Senior Hall to the west, it completes a small enclave of rustic, residential-scaled buildings along the south bank of Strawberry Creek.

A group of faculty women and administrators organized the club in 1919 to provide a meeting place and accommodations for women on the faculty and those who were in professional positions or university donors. Early meetings were held in Hearst Hall and a small building that was used by forestry students. After Hearst Hall burned in 1922, the Regents' granted the club permission to construct the building, which was funded by bond sales to members.

Howard's preliminary studies for the club included a Mediterranean Revival–style design, probably stucco-faced and tile roofed, with round-arched windows and projecting loggias. The final wood-shingled design, in the vocabulary of the First Bay Region style, forms an east-west rectangular block with a projecting wing facing the creek to the north. The south facade is divided into three parts of three bays each, with a white wooden entrance portico that distinguishes the slightly projecting central part. This has a simple entablature, surmounted by a classical balustrade and supported by a pair of Tuscan columns, which were built-up from glued sections. Double-hung windows are used throughout, generally either paired or single, depending on interior uses. A seismic safety investigation of the building in 1973 revealed that Howard utilized steel beams faced with wood to span some of the first floor spaces in the otherwise wood-frame building.

The club was opened in October 1923, but its first occupants were refugees from the catastrophic fire that destroyed the community north of campus the previous month. Some of those made homeless remained in the building for several years and, in appreciation of the club's hospitality, gave their salvaged furniture and works of art to help furnish the building.

In addition to its twenty-five guestrooms on the upper two floors, the club provides luncheon service for members and their guests and facilities for meetings and special events. The first floor contains the Lucy Stebbins Lounge, named for the dean of women who assisted in the creation of the club in 1919. A library and dining facilities with a creek-side garden deck, added in 1976, are also on this floor.

The club is listed on the State Historic Resources Inventory.

Girton Hall

Completed five years after Senior Men's Hall (now Senior Hall), Girton Hall initially served as a meeting and informal gathering place for women of the senior classes. "If the men have one," President Wheeler reasoned in 1911, "the women, who are assuming also responsibility concerning order and government, feel that they should have one too. I am inclined to think they would make as much use of it as the men do of their hall."[18]

Girton Hall

When their Senior Women's Singings and other activities could no longer be accommodated in Hearst Hall, the Associated Women Students began raising funds for the building. It would be named for historic Girton College, the first residential college for women, established in 1869 at Cambridge University. For building plans they turned to Julia Morgan, well admired for her many residential designs in the area and for her work at Mills College in Oakland, as well as for her involvement with the Hearst Greek Theatre and Hearst Memorial Mining Building while employed by John Galen Howard. Just as Howard had contributed his services to design a log cabin for the senior men, Morgan, an 1894 College of Engineering graduate, donated her work on Girton. This was of great help to the Classes of 1910 and 1911, whose fundraising was also augmented by a donation from Lucy Sprague, the Dean of Women.

The women petitioned and received approval to site the building on a wooded knoll south of the Greek Theatre and along the north bank of Strawberry Creek. This original site was near the mouth of Strawberry Canyon, about 160 feet east of the building's present location. Morgan's design for the one-story building—which would also be known as Senior Women's Hall—combined the axial organization of her Beaux-Arts training and the rustic qualities of the First Bay Region style. It consisted of a central block with two lower set-back side wings, one containing an entry vestibule and small kitchen, the other a covered open porch (later enclosed). In the center she provided a meeting room with exposed redwood roof trusses and wall framing, and a large brick fireplace with a round-arched opening. Opposite this, overlooking the creek, was a windowseat bay with doors leading to a brick terrace. The exterior, sheathed in redwood clapboards and shingles with banded windows under the hipped-roof eaves, fit nicely into the creek-side environment. "[A]n inoffensive bungalow," President Wheeler called it, "a wooden building of such humble dimensions and quality."[19]

The building was opened in November 1911, equipped with donated tableware from the wives of faculty members and draperies from the Class of 1913.[20] The following March the Associated Women Students presented it as a gift to the Regents, who accepted it with an expression of appreciation to Morgan for contributing her services. In time its original exclusive use by senior women was expanded to include meetings of other women's groups. Its natural setting also changed following construction of California Memorial Stadium in 1923, when most of the creek that flowed by the building was rerouted to an underground culvert extending west to Faculty Glade.

When the women proposed the building they agreed to move the hall if the site were to be needed for dormitories in the future. A different need arose when the construction of Lewis Hall for the College of Chemistry in 1946 required the rebuilding of Gayley Road from its alignment with College Avenue to one further east with Piedmont Avenue. To make room for this development, Girton was moved westward to its present site, which at the time was still natural in character and well north of Cowell Memorial Hospital. The building was reoriented on its new site, with its window bay facing southwest rather than south, and its brick terrace was replaced by a wooden deck. As the hospital expanded and was later replaced by the Haas School of Business, the small building remained huddled under the remaining trees without the open vistas it once had.

Since 1969 Girton Hall has adapted well as a childcare center, one of eight campus child care facilities that serve over 200 university families. Although the creek is no longer a surface feature, Girton occupies the easternmost position of the four wooden riparian buildings that include Senior Hall and the two faculty clubs to the west.

Girton Hall is listed on the National Register of Historic Places and the State Historic Resources Inventory, and is a City of Berkeley Landmark.

44. Faculty Glade, Goodspeed Natural Area, The Last Dryad, and Class of 1910 Bridge

Goodspeed Natural Area *Designated 1969*
The Last Dryad *Alexander Sterling Calder, sculptor, 1921, cast ca. 1926, installed 1968*
Class of 1910 Bridge *Bakewell and Brown, 1911*

The most historic and picturesque open space on campus, Faculty Glade evokes a spiritual presence linked to decades of campus tradition. Once a camping ground of the Ohlone people, this sloping greensward along the south fork of Strawberry Creek is dotted with coast live oaks (*Quercus agrifolia*) and bordered with coast redwoods (*Sequoia sempervirens*) that provide framed views of the nearby Campanile. A popular setting for special gatherings as well as passive recreation and study, it also serves as an important pedestrian connection between the north and south areas of campus.

The bowl-shaped glade is cloistered by the creek and its vegetation on the north, the Faculty Club on the east, Stephens Hall on the west, and the Department of Music's Hertz and Morrison Halls at the top of the slope on the south. It is embraced along its north and west edges by the Goodspeed Natural Area, winding along the creek from the Faculty Club to Stephens Hall. Named in honor of Botany Professor and Botanical Garden curator Thomas Harper Goodspeed, it is one of three central campus habitats established in 1969 to be maintained in a semi-natural state as "living laboratories" for academic study (see Wickson Natural Area, Walk 3).

While the ambiance of the Faculty Club recalls the trappings of its male-dominated beginnings, when cigar smoke filled the billiards room and fumigated the mounted animal heads, Faculty Glade is imbued with the tra-

Faculty Glade

ditions of university women. In 1874 a group of twelve women students occupied the cottage east of the present glade that was later used as the kitchen and eventually part of the second floor of the Faculty Club. They founded the Young Ladies Club, the university's first women's service organization, and before long the area previously referred to as the lower extension of "Strawberry Cañon" became known as "Co-ed Canyon" along the banks of the "Illissus." From this group, the Rediviva Society was formed in 1904. Its name stemming from the Latin meaning "renewed life," this women's group, based on "character and scholarship," influenced the establishment of other honor societies. In 1955, some eighty years after the predecessor club's founding, a group of Rediviva alumnae gathered in the northwest corner of the glade to dedicate the mosaic-tiled drinking fountain near Stephens Hall, donated to the university to commemorate the Young Ladies Club. A more subtle reminder of this pioneering organization is nearby Morrison Hall, named for its contributing donor, May Treat Morrison, Class of 1878 and one of the club's founders who resided in the old cottage. In 1993 nine Rediviva alumnae from the classes of 1926–35 gathered to rededicate the fountain and remember those women founders, whose history remains inseparable from the glade.

"Co-ed Canyon" was also the setting for many of the Partheneia annual pageants, written, directed, and performed by women students (see Grinnell Natural Area, Walk 3). When the pageants needed greater spectator space than that provided under the oaks near the Eucalyptus Grove, they were moved to Faculty Glade. Every spring until 1931, creek-side maidens, dryads, and natural spirits danced in flowing gowns and capes, through

The Last Dryad *by Alexander Sterling Calder*

such dramatizations *as The Dream of Derdra, The Vision of Marpessa*, or *The Druid's Weed*.

Though the nymphs and maidens no longer dance beneath the oaks, they are forever recalled by *The Last Dryad*, the graceful bronze figure standing among the azaleas and rhododendrons by the creek. Sculpted by

Alexander Sterling Calder (1870–1945), the piece was cast about 1926 but remained in the artist's New York studio for the next twenty years. In 1948, it was presented to the university by his widow and daughter, Margaret Calder Hayes (Class of 1917). Administrators considered it too risqué to be viewed by innocent undergraduate males, however, and the nude nymph was first placed in an inner courtyard of the Hearst Gymnasium for Women. After the donor inquired about the sculpture in 1968, it was relocated to its more public and appropriate habitat by the creek. The artist, who was chief of sculpture for the 1915 Panama-Pacific International Exposition in San Francisco, was the son of Alexander Milne Calder, famous for his statue of William Penn atop Philadelphia City Hall, and father of Alexander Calder, the renowned mobile and kinetic sculptor, whose stabile, *The Hawk for Peace*, graces the Bancroft facade of the University's Berkeley Art Museum and Pacific Film Archive.

Facing Calder's dryad across the glade is the kneeling *"Pappy" Waldorf*, the legendary Cal football coach (1947–1956), whose teams appeared in three consecutive Rose Bowls. Aside from his success on the gridiron, he was known for emphasizing academics and building character among his devoted players. Sited at the west edge of the glade, not far from the coach's former Stephens Hall office, the bronze statue was sculpted by Douglas Van Howd, who also created the ferocious Grizzly Bear near California Memorial Stadium. Funded by donations raised by the coach's former players, "Pappy's Boys," the statue was unveiled in 1994. Inscribed on the tablet in Pappy's hands are his Big Game scores against Stanford University.

At the rim of the glade near Hertz and Morrison is sculptor and Art Professor Richard O'Hanlon's 1961 bronze abstract, *Voyage*. The piece was donated in the name of Helen Salz and her late husband, Ansley K. Salz, who also donated artist Ralph Stackpole's *Interior Force*, located across from Wheeler Hall. Their other gifts to the campus included a rare violin collection—which perhaps exerted some influence in locating *Voyage* near the Department of Music. The sculpture was purchased after being seen in a one-man O'Hanlon exhibition at the San Francisco Museum of Art.

Voyage *by Richard O'Hanlon*

Not far from this sculpture, near the center of the sloping lawn is a boulder bearing a plaque marking the location of the Henry Morse Stephens Oak, a once living memorial that stood between the Faculty Club residence of the beloved history professor and the former student union building that bears his name. It overlooks the glade where Stephens bid farewell to each graduating class at their traditional commencement luncheon. The professor died suddenly while returning from the funeral of Phoebe Apperson Hearst in San Francisco on April 16, 1919. Two days later, with the chimes of the Campanile playing, a procession from the tower moved through the arch of the Class of 1910 Bridge to beneath the oaks, where services were conducted between 10am and 11am, the exact hour of Stephens' most popular class. The oak was reputed to be the largest on campus and was the last of the 200- to 300-year-old trees that once stood on the glade's northern slope.

Class of 1910 Bridge

The stepped bridge crossed by the Stephens procession gracefully spans Strawberry Creek to form a classical northeast portal to the glade. It was designed by Beaux-Arts architects John Bakewell, Jr. (Class of 1893), and Arthur Brown, Jr. (Class of 1896), to replace a wooden crossing between East Hall and the Faculty Club. Its Roman arch bears the inscription (in Latin): "The class going forth in 1910 gave this bridge lest the memory of them be lost among generations. Phoebe Apperson Hearst rendered aid." With the important Regent and benefactress contributing, the bridge received much attention. But the completed inscription composed by Latin Professor William A. Merrill became controversial when a student pointed out that the Latin *Hanc pontem* ("This bridge") should have been spelled *Hunc pontem*.[21] In 1912, the year following the bridge construction, Professor Merrill reluctantly authorized the change, though claiming that there was classical authority for the grammar he first used.[22] Careful examination can reveal the correction made to the inscription. Bakewell and Brown hoped to embellish the arched entry with cement ornamentation by renowned animal sculptor Arthur Putnam, but the artist's failing health at the time probably prevented his contribution. Upon its completion, the descent through the archway was described in a news release as leading into "a region filled with oaks, laurels, and buckeyes, and picturesquely diversified in slope." While many of the ancient oaks have fallen, an old California buckeye (*Aesculus californica*) stands resolutely near the south end of the bridge, a familiar landmark since 1882.

Downstream, another crossing donated by alumni is the Class of 1923 Bridge, an element in John Galen Howard's design of Stephens Hall. For some forty years this bridge served as a primary pedestrian route, linked to the Stephens stairway and vaulted passageway that opens opposite the Campanile. Its use decreased once the student union moved from

Class of 1923 Bridge

"Pappy" Waldorf *by Douglas Van Howd*

the building, and the concrete crossing to the east of the building was added by landscape architect Thomas D. Church in the 1960s.

South of the Class of 1923 Bridge are two commemorative groves. The Arleigh and Ruthie Williams Grove on the creek's north bank was dedicated in the 1990s "to those two sturdy Golden Bears." It honors dean of students Arleigh Taber Williams (Class of 1935) and his wife Ruth Willett Williams (Class of 1934). Across the creek to the south, the Brutus K. Hamilton Grove of redwoods honors the famous track and field coach (1933–43 and 1946–65), who also served as assistant dean of students (1945–47) and director of athletics (1947–55). The latter position was held during the Pappy Waldorf era, making the grove a fitting backdrop for Pappy's nearby statue.

The natural amphitheater of the glade has made it suitable for a range of performances and events in addition to the Partheneia, from the Pelican Fashion Show to the Baccalaureate Sermon. The most famous was a 1934 Max Reinhardt production of *A Midsummer Night's Dream*, starring Mickey Rooney, Sterling Holloway, and Olivia de Haviland. The play was mounted in Faculty Glade and proceeded to the Hearst Greek Theatre for the final act under torchlight.

Faculty Glade is included in the Berkeley campus designation as a California Registered Historical Landmark. The Class of 1910 Bridge is listed on the State Historic Resources Inventory. The California buckeye tree near the bridge is a City of Berkeley Landmark.

Haas School of Business

45. Haas School of Business
Moore Ruble Yudell with VBN Corporation, 1992–1995

The last major building with the imprint of architect Charles Moore, the Haas School of Business occupies a prominent site along the Gayley-Piedmont edge of the central campus. Moore and partners John Ruble and Buzz Yudell responded well to Dean Raymond Miles' challenge to "design a school as a place that creates community and serves as a gateway to the campus and a bridge to the business community."[23]

The Santa Monica architects, in association with Oakland-based VBN, created a high-profile identity for the School, which had occupied three anonymous floors in inflexible and overcrowded Barrows Hall since 1964. Moore, who died in 1993 before completion of the building, was no stranger to the campus. He chaired the Department of Architecture from 1963 to 1965 during the transition of the College of Environmental Design from the cherished Ark (North Gate Hall) to Wurster Hall, and his familiarity with the campus and its historic context influenced the character of the new business school.

Funding for the $55 million complex was also tied to historical campus roots. A cornerstone contribution of $15 million, made in 1989 by the trustees of the Walter and Elise Haas Fund—alumni Walter A. Haas, Jr., Peter Haas, and Rhoda Haas Goldman—was, at the time, the largest gift ever made to the Berkeley campus. The donation was made in memory of the trustees' father, Walter A. Haas, Sr., for whom the building is named, a 1910 graduate of the school's predecessor College of Commerce and president of Levi Strauss & Co. from 1928 to 1955. In 1992 the contribution was increased to $23.75 million with additional funds from several Haas family foundations. The donation continued the extraordinary tradition of Haas family support for the campus, a legacy that dates from scholarship endowments contributed in 1897 by Levi Strauss, the family patriarch who produced the first riveted canvas "waist overall" during the time of the California Gold Rush.

To achieve desired collegiality and reduce the apparent massiveness of the large building program, Charles Moore and his associates organized the school into three distinct building wings, connected by two bridges and arranged around a central landscaped courtyard. Double arches at the bridges form monumental gateways to the concrete complex, which cascades in variegated hipped-roof forms down the forty-five-foot slope from Gayley on the east to old College Avenue on the west. The courtyard begins as a ramped garden—a "dry creek" symbolically recalling once-exposed Strawberry Creek, which now flows nearby by culvert from the foothill into Faculty Glade. At the low end of the L-shaped courtyard, the planted garden angles northward in the direction of the actual creek. This informal courtyard is shaped by the undulating bays and recesses of the three building wings. A flowing stairway from the eastern gateway leads the user on a deliberate pathway through the changing space, which is accentuated by two works of art.

On the overlook near the upper gateway is the whimsical *Les Bears*, a bronze work created in 1991 by Wyoming native Dan Ostermiller, one of the nation's leading wildlife sculptors. It was a gift of William and Janet Cronk, for whom the gateway is named. In the garden opposite the

Cheit Hall and Courtyard, Haas School of Business

western gateway (named for donors Donald and Doris Fisher) stands *Folded Circle Trio*, by Napa sculptor Fletcher C. Benton, known for his kinetic and delicately balanced geometric compositions. The corrosion-resistant steel work was a gift of the Haas School Advisory Board and other supporters. It was dedicated in 1997 to the memory of donors Rhoda Haas Goldman, Walter A. Haas, Jr., and Eugene E. Trefethen, Jr., whose "vision and leadership helped build this home for the Haas School of Business."

As in the courtyard, spatial experiences were carefully considered throughout the interior of the building. Stairways and corridors are not mere utilitarian exercises, but rather movements through architecture. These features of the building, along with the strategic placement of benches—at lobbies, corridors, stair landings, and windows—facilitate inter-actions of students, faculty, researchers, and staff, and strengthen the feeling of community.

The clustering of the 125 offices at corridor nodes in the north Faculty Wing also foster meetings and collaboration. The five-level wing contains the focal point of the complex, the terraced BankAmerica Forum, whose entrance is situated at the elbow of the courtyard, directly across from the western gateway. The two-story-high space overlooks the court-yard through tall windows and has the openness of a tent-like pavilion. It links to a cafe, main auditorium, and conference room on the courtyard level, and steps up to an informal student activity mezzanine. The offices along with research institutes and centers occupy the upper three stories of the wing, which is linked by the open bridge to the south Student Services Wing.

BankAmerica Forum, Haas School of Business

The eastern ends of these wings are partially tucked below ground and articulated to create a compatible residential scale with the adjacent row of Piedmont houses. Most of the four-story Student Services Wing and about one-quarter of the school is occupied by the Thomas J. Long Business and Economics Library. Named for the alumnus co-founder of Longs Drug Stores, the two-level library contains about 120,000 works in all management disciplines and features a worldwide business information center. The stairway connecting the two levels descends in landings along windows oriented to the courtyard, a feature inspired by John Galen Howard's Ark with its glazed corridor. A computer center adjoins the library at the second level, while student services and the Dean's suite occupy the third and fourth levels, respectively.

An interior bridge at the western gateway connects to the smallest of the three wings, Earl F. Cheit Hall, named in honor of the school's ninth Dean (1976–1982) who led the early planning and development for the complex. The four-level wing contains three floors of classrooms, some designed with semi-circular tiered seating to facilitate interaction between students and instructor. On the top floor is the Wells Fargo Room, a conference and banquet space, which, with its pitched ceiling and side balconies, recalls Bernard Maybeck's Great Hall in the Faculty Club. Here, the custom-designed lighting sconces that are ubiquitously placed throughout the building are echoed in copper chandeliers composed of four clustered fixtures.

Although somewhat contrived, the exterior of the complex calls up more historical references with forms and detailing that contribute a sense of scale to the three wings. The concrete walls are formed in three zones, distinct in patterns and earth-tone colors. The light tan base is striated in simulated rustication, a feature common to campus Beaux-Arts and neoclassical buildings. The tall middle zone, dark brown in color and impressed with horizontal form-boards, and the lighter upper zone of simulated board-and-batten siding, are reminiscent of the vernacular features of Bay Region wooden buildings, such as the Faculty Club and, just to the north, Julia Morgan's Girton Hall. Similar references are present in the architects' use of corbels, dormers, and roof ventilation cupolas. The forest-green window sashes recall those used on Howard's classical buildings, while the gateways call up his frequent use of Roman-arched window and door openings.

46. 2241, 2243, and 2251 College Avenue

2241 College *circa 1885*
2243 College *Carl Ericsson, 1902*
2251 College *Charles Peter Weeks, 1911*

The two late Victorian-era houses and the brick building standing behind Wurster Hall are the remaining structures of a residential neighborhood that fronted on College Avenue, when it continued northward from Bancroft Way to a bridge crossing at Strawberry Creek. When the site for Wurster was cleared in 1962, the avenue between Bancroft and Minor Hall was removed, leaving only the remaining section that now runs from Minor to the creek.

Now used for offices, the two-story house at 2241 College was built in about 1885 by Warren Cheney, not long after his graduation from the university. He pursued a journalistic career, which included writing for

2241 College Avenue

Sunset Magazine, and also became an established Berkeley realtor. His wife May Lucretia Cheney, an 1883 graduate, was the first Teacher Appointments Secretary of the university, and for forty years facilitated the placement of university-trained teachers at schools nationwide. In 1960 Cheney Hall, one of the towers comprising the Unit 1 Residence Halls (see Walk 9), was named in her honor.

With Eastlake-style characteristics, the wood-framed house features an overhanging gabled pediment at its west entrance. This is supported by wood brackets at the entry porch, which is flanked by bay windows that originally opened to a parlor on the north and drawing room on the south. The wood facade of the house is highly decorative, combining scalloped shingles, horizontal and angular board siding, and, within the pediment, diagonal latticework that forms a pattern of circles within diamonds. The informal interior has been modified, although the central hall has retained its original wood paneling and stairway with a carved banister and newel post.

In 1902 Cheney built a second smaller house, the cottage at 2243 College, as income property. Designed by Carl Ericsson, it shows influences of both Stick and Chalet styles, with its bracketed overhanging clipped-gable roof, projecting bays, and expressed framing with horizontal board siding. The interior has been modified for offices. An early resident of the cottage was Greek Professor James Turney Allen, who directed the student production of Aristophanes' *The Birds* at the opening of the Hearst Greek Theatre in 1903 (see Walk 6).

2243 College Avenue

South of the two Cheney houses and nestled by the Law Building, 2251 College is the former home of Zeta Psi, the oldest fraternity at the university. The fraternity was also the first to build a house west of the Mississippi in 1876, a three-story, mansard-roofed, Second Empire structure that stood on the same site. Artifacts from this original house— teacups with the fraternity's insignia, various bottles, and tableware dating from around the start of the twentieth century—were discovered during construction of the north addition to the

2251 College Avenue

Law Building in 1995. Ironically, the dig was conducted by archaeologists from the Department of Anthropology's Archaeological Research Facility, which presently occupies the building.

Designed by architect Charles Peter Weeks and constructed in 1911, 2251 College reflects the architect's Beaux-Arts training. It is a symmetrical classical building with a U-shaped plan and red-tile hipped roof. A vaulted entry portico, recalling a Renaissance palazzo, has triple round arches in cast cement with volute keystones. Cement medallions bearing the fraternity's insignia flank the central arch. Tall round-arched windows in cement frames continue around the first floor at the dining and living room wings, with rectangular windows above each arch in the second floor zone. The brick facing on the wood-framed structure forms decorative panels between the openings.

The pedimented wood entry door opens to a barrel-vaulted hall that extends between the side wings and leads to a central stairway with wood wainscot paneling. The former dining and living rooms, now used for seminars, are also paneled and feature coffer ceilings and fireplaces with classical oak detailing. An arch opposite the entrance leads to an atrium that was originally an exterior central courtyard open to the east. This space was enclosed and roofed over with skylights when the building was used for primate studies, prior to its use by Anthropology. After Anthropology moved in, the east wall of this atrium was decorated by artist Robert Peterson with a reproduction of the Paleolithic paintings in the Altamira caves of Spain.

2241 and 2243 College are listed on the State Historic Resources Inventory and are City of Berkeley Landmarks. 2251 College is listed on the State Historic Resources Inventory.

47. Law Building and Simon Hall

> *Warren C. Perry, with Raymond W. Jeans and Stafford L. Jory, 1950–1951;*
> *Warren C. Perry, and Anderson, Simonds, Dusel and Campani, library addition*
> *and renovation, 1958–1959;*
> *Wurster, Bernardi & Emmons, addition, renovations and Simon Hall, 1965–1967;*
> *The Ratcliff Architects, north addition, renovations, and Simon Hall renovations,*
> *1995–1996*

The first increment of the School of Law complex was built to relieve overcrowding in old Boalt Hall (now Durant Hall, see Walk 1) and to accommodate a significant postwar enrollment increase. With the move, the then-School of Jurisprudence was renamed the School of Law to represent more accurately its curriculum.

The first phase of the building exemplifies Warren C. Perry's transition as a classically trained architect into the modern movement. By his own credo, Perry regretted the "fuss made over so-called 'modern architecture,'" arguing that "good architecture has always been modern, and that

Law Building

wholesome qualities in contemporary work would have asserted themselves anyway."[24] His use of newer materials and lack of ornamentation
shows flexibility in adapting to modernist influences, while at the same time
the building's floor plan and organization reflect the clarity of his Beaux-Arts
background. Perry, then Dean of the School of Architecture, associated with
faculty colleagues Raymond W. Jeans and Stafford L. Jory (who had
assisted Perry on Edwards Stadium nearly twenty years earlier), after con-
vincing President Sproul that a team from the faculty could successfully
provide architectural services to the university.

Responding to the need to distinguish the contributions of two
principal donors, Perry organized the building in two wings with a connecting linkage to form an L-shaped footprint with a south-facing courtyard
along Bancroft. The west classroom wing, Boalt Hall, inherited the name of
the original law building as a continuing memorial to Judge John H. Boalt
and was designed to house three large lecture halls and offices. The east
library wing was named the Garret E. McEnerney Law Library, a memorial
to a long-time university Regent and San Francisco attorney, who
bequeathed funds for the library. At the linkage between the two wings
Perry placed the Luke Kavanagh Moot Court Room, named for a popular
San Francisco court reporter.

The three-story building is of steel-frame construction, except for
the reinforced concrete library stacks, which were designed to accommodate the four additional stack levels that Perry added in 1959. The building
was topped with red-tile hipped roofs, and finished on the exterior with
cement plaster with unadorned window openings, to relate to the general
vocabulary of form and color of the older neoclassical campus buildings,
while still being modern in appearance. The use of aluminum for exterior
window and door frames, special remote-controlled louvers along the
south-facing windows of the library reading room, railings, and lettering—in
lieu of more decorative elements common before the war—was considered
by Perry to be essential "to relieve the otherwise extremely plain stucco
areas" and "to achieve a reasonably modern character" for the building.[25]

The west facade along College presented Perry with a further challenge, as his early studies featuring a pleasant pattern of fenestration on the
long classroom wing were rejected by school administrators, who insisted
that the lecture halls be windowless. To add interest to the facade, Perry provided two monumental tablets of Swedish granite with raised aluminum-
lettered quotations, which faculty of the school selected from the words of
U. S. Supreme Court Justices Oliver Wendell Holmes and Benjamin N.
Cardozo. When Perry asked how they should be placed, Law Dean William L.
Prosser responded: "Better put Cardozo on the left. I have no better reason
for it than the rather perverse one which I think you may have in mind your-
self—that politically Cardozo was a left-winger, and Holmes was essentially
a conservative."[26] The large inscriptions, which President Sproul labeled the

"blackboards," were designed to be seen from a distance, but are now partially obscured by the stand of trees along the west facade.

The interior features the West African wood Limba (*Terminalia superba*), used especially for built-in benches, paneling, and trim in the lobby of the west wing lecture halls. Also of interest is a terracotta bear by San Francisco sculptor Beniamino B. Bufano, installed in 1955 and donated by the Class of 1948 in memory of classmate Martin Bordon. The bear stands atop a green terrazzo pedestal at the east end of the first-floor corridor, a location chosen by Perry after an outdoor installation was considered inappropriate.

The renovations and additions by Wurster, Bernardi & Emmons in the 1960s resulted in more convoluted interior circulation and changed the scale of the complex with Manville Hall (now Simon Hall), a seven-story concrete frame tower, which provided housing for over 100 law students as well as guest accommodations. Faced with exposed aggregate wall panels, the tower was originally named in memory of the former president of Johns-Manville Corporation, Hiram Edward Manville, and in recognition of a donation from the Manville Trusts. As was typical of the campus high-rises built during the period, the tower did not relate well to its neighbors. Sited at the northwest corner of Bancroft and Piedmont, it interrupted the residential scale of Piedmont and visually crowded George Kelham's domed International House across the street. The project also included the Earl Warren Legal Center, named for the Class of 1912 graduate who served as California Governor and Chief Justice of the United States, and a four-story addition to Perry's building to increase office, library, and classroom facilities.

Simon Hall

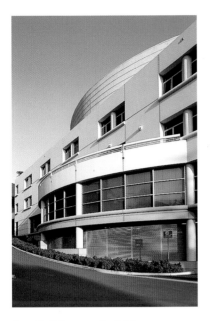

Law Building, north addition

Library, Law Building north addition

A three-part project by The Ratcliff Architects in 1995–1996 increased school space by about one-third. It converted the tower—renamed for William G. Simon, a prominent Boalt Hall alumnus and legal professional—to offices for faculty and student organizations. (The Manville name was transferred to the university's replacement housing, the Manville Apartments, in downtown Berkeley at 2100 Channing Way.) The project also renovated nearly half of the Law Building and expanded it to the north to enlarge the library and provide additional offices. The architects, led by Crodd Chin (Class of 1966), were selected with Charles Pankow Builders, as part of the winning team of a design-build competition.

Their four-story north addition, distinguished by its bowed facade, features a two-story, skylit atrium, which serves as a reading room and organizes the library in relation to the older building. Linked by a bridge to the old library, the new space includes study carrels and, within the bowed bay, a reading room for the 500,000-volume Robbins Collection, one of the world's renowned collections of religious and civil law; it was formed in 1952 from the library of San Francisco lawyer Lloyd McCullough Robbins and named in memory of the donor's parents, Reuel Drinkwater and Saditha McCullough Robbins. The top two floors of the addition contain faculty offices and a faculty lounge opening onto a balcony within the bay. While currently overlooking a parking lot to the north, the building was planned with the anticipation of a future landscaped open space in this area, as envisioned by The ROMA Design Group in the university's 1990 Long Range Development Plan.

The Foothills

Sculpture by Douglas Van Howd, near California Memorial Stadium

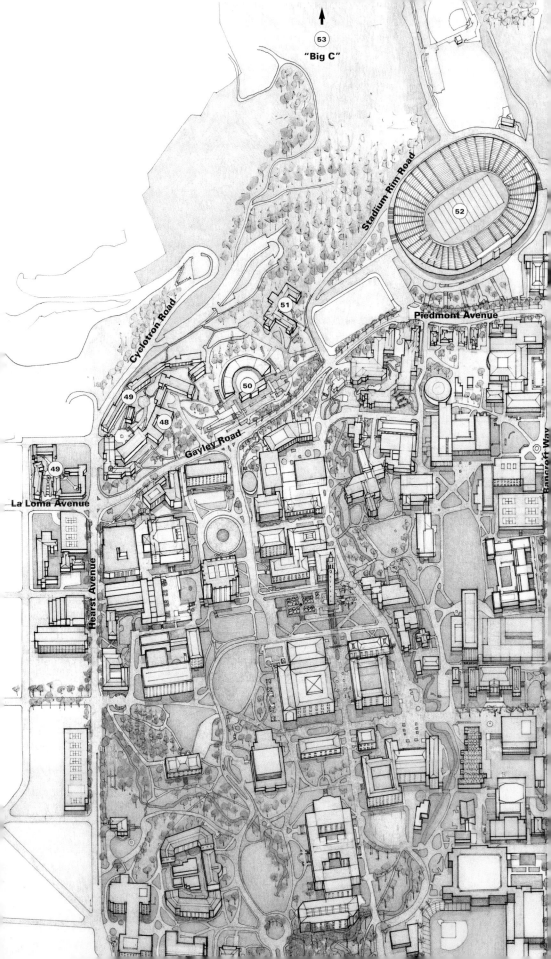

↑
(53)
"Big C"

Stadium Rim Road

(52)

Piedmont Avenue

(51)

Cyclotron Road

(50)

(49)

(48)

Gayley Road

(49)

La Loma Avenue

Hearst Avenue

Bancroft Way

Extending along the base of Charter Hill with its century-old Big C, this Walk includes a row of structures on the east side of Gayley Road and Piedmont Avenue used primarily for student housing and athletics.

The first structure constructed in the foothill, the Hearst Greek Theatre was also the first completed by Supervising Architect John Galen Howard in 1903. Built on the site of "Ben Weed's Amphitheatre," it took its Greek form following the recommendation of President Wheeler, as a suitable beginning for the new classical ensemble.

Mammoth Roman-arched California Memorial Stadium followed in 1923, sited at the mouth of Strawberry Canyon, not in accordance with Howard's Plan or with his blessings, but through a succession of administrative decisions that placed Howard as chairman of a Stadium Commission responsible for the architectural plans. At the compromise of transportation and neighborhood impacts, the result produced one of the most spectacular settings for viewing athletic events.

Six years later Howard's successor, Supervising Architect George W. Kelham completed Bowles Hall, the university's first residence hall, to the northeast of the Greek Theatre. Though not in strict accordance with the still governing Howard Plan, the Collegiate Gothic–style building was consistent with earlier proposals of both Emile Bénard and Howard for siting student housing on the hillside.

A second men's dormitory was proposed to be built behind Bowles but was abandoned because of soil conditions. Instead, the university's first women's dormitory, Stern Hall, initially completed in 1942, was constructed near the corner of Gayley and Hearst. The modernist Bay Tradition building by William Wurster was carefully sited along the contours of the foothill and later expanded in 1959 and 1981.

During the busy period of postwar growth, the area was reconfigured between 1946 and 1951 to relocate Gayley Road to the east and align it with Piedmont Avenue in order to make room for the construction of Chemistry's Lewis Hall (see Walk 2). The road was named in honor of Charles Mills Gayley, professor of English language and literature (1889–1923) who developed the English Department into a preeminent program and served as Dean of the Academic Faculties (1918–19). With Professors Henry Morse Stephens and William Carey Jones, Gayley was also a member of the Administrative Board that served as the chief administrator of the university to relieve President Wheeler, who was in ill health during the final year of his term in 1918–19. But Gayley is perhaps best remembered for his lyrics to the school song "The Golden Bear," which was inspired by the gold-embroidered banners of the California track team that triumphed during an Eastern tour in 1895. The California name and the state grizzly bear depicted on the banners established the Golden Bear as the university's spirited guardian.

The reconfiguration of the area required the relocation of Julia Morgan's meeting place for women students, Girton Hall, which was constructed in 1911 at what is now the intersection of Gayley and Stadium Rimway. The small house was moved westward to its present site north of the Haas School of Business in 1946 (see Walk 5).

The realignment also created space between Bowles and the Stadium for the insertion of Kleeberger Field in 1951. Designed for intramural sports by Walter T. Steilberg, it was built to meet the demand for recreational facilities that followed World War II and continues to be used intensively today. The field was named for Frank L. Kleeberger (Class of 1908), a physical education professor who was instrumental in establishing the intramural sports program at the university.

William Turnbull's Bay Tradition–inspired Foothill Student Housing completed the foothill development in 1991. The shingled and wood-sided complex extends across two sites that flank Hearst Avenue. The northern La Loma Housing occupies most of the block designated in the 1962 Long Range Development Plan for a high-rise residence hall complex, but with far greater sensitivity to the Northside neighborhood. South of Hearst, the Hillside Housing hugs the contours and wraps around Stern on the east, creating a dense but articulated residential village.

48. Stern Hall

Corbett & MacMurray and William W. Wurster, with John W. Gregg
and Isabella Worn, landscape design, 1941–1942;
Wurster, Bernardi & Emmons, addition, 1959;
Marquis and Associates, addition, 1980–1981

The first university-owned dormitory for women, Stern Hall was initiated with funds donated by Rosalie Meyer Stern, widow of San Francisco businessman and benefactor Sigmund Stern (Class of 1879), in whose memory the building is named. It was the first of several major campus buildings associated with the descendants of pioneer businessman Levi Strauss, whose scholarship endowments in 1897 established the family's tradition as patrons of the university.

Mrs. Stern's original intention in 1938 was to provide a men's dormitory on the hillside behind Bowles Hall. However, when soil conditions at the site were found to be unstable, she turned her attention to an alternate site between the Hearst Greek Theatre and Hearst Avenue. When informed that this site was reserved for an Alumni Dorm to house women students, she changed her project to a women's dormitory. Geological studies using the Lawson Adit (see Walk 2) extending under the site, cleared the way for the project, which the Regents approved in August 1940.

Stern Hall

Two alumni—modernist William W. Wurster (Class of 1919) of San Francisco and Beaux Arts–trained Harvey Wiley Corbett (Class of 1895 and L.L.D., 1930) of New York–based Corbett & MacMurray—teamed up for the project. The architects had to redo their plans to conform to the new site and accommodate the needs of women rather than men.

Their design for ninety female students stretched 300 feet across the new site, fitted to its sloping topography. The building reflects Wurster's strength in modern and Bay Tradition residential design, through its indoor-outdoor relationships and use of materials and color. It was organized into three functional areas. The north-south wing at the north end of the complex included a one-story service area and a three-story entrance wing with drawing and parlor rooms, dining room, library, and the resident director's living quarters and offices. This wing linked by a glass-enclosed staircase to two east-west four-story dormitory wings. The fire escapes at the west ends of these bedroom wings were designed as verandas to take advantage of the bay view, while the shady east side was used for corridors. The wood-textured concrete facade still retains its ochre and terracotta colors, with blue mullions at the glassed stairways and other colors applied to the trim, tile work, and metal trellises.

The interior of Stern also used bold colors. Black, red, chartreuse, yellow, and blue were applied profusely by Carmel decorator Frances A. Elkins, who had consulted with Wurster on his design for the Yerba Buena Club at the 1939 Golden Gate International Exposition on Treasure Island. Modern furnishings integrated with the architectural design included exotic elements—cowhide tables and chairs, black and white Holstein hide rugs, and hand-formed silver lamps and mirrors. The building also contains, at the foot of a circular stairway within the dining room foyer, a Diego Rivera fresco, *Still Life and Blossoming Almond Trees*, that was painted at the Stern home in 1931 and depicts the family children. The comfortable furnishings and colorful interiors combined with the building's graceful attention to large social spaces, glazed stairways, and view-oriented windows to provide the supportive environment that was intended for the women by the donor and university.

Wurster, Bernardi & Emmons added the second increment to Stern in 1959, while Wurster was also serving as dean of the College of

Architecture and consulting campus architect. A four-story concrete-frame wing extended to the south, it was funded by university sources and a gift from Walter A. Haas (Class of 1910), chairman of the board of Levi Strauss and Company and son-in-law of the donor of the original building. The harmonious addition provided forty-six beds to increase the hall's capacity to 136 residents.

The final increment, funded by housing bonds and revenue, included a third projecting east-west residential wing at the south end of the building and an expansion of the original dining room. The four-story 110-bed wing was designed by Cathy Simon of Marquis and Associates to be "a responsive and respectful addition with the characteristics of the building enhanced, but not copied."[1] Instead of concrete, the new wing utilized wood-frame construction with stucco finish. Rooms were arranged in groups with small common spaces, reflecting the changing trends in student living.

Stern now houses approximately 250 women students and forms the western edge of the linear series of courtyards created by the development of the Foothill Student Housing complex in 1991. It is listed on the State Historic Resources Inventory.

49. Foothill Student Housing

*William Turnbull Associates and The Ratcliff Architects, with MPA Design,
landscape architects, 1989–1991*

A shingled hillside village, Foothill Student Housing reflects the legacy of the Bay Region tradition with forms and materials rooted in the century-old Arts and Crafts movement. Design architect William Turnbull of San Francisco teamed with East Bay–based The Ratcliff Architects to create the 800-bed $50 million complex that stretches from the Greek Theatre on the south to Ridge Road in the Northside neighborhood.

Two unified but also distinct housing communities comprise the complex. Linear Hillside Housing informally hugs the topographic contours to the east of William Wurster's Stern Hall, forming a series of angled

Foothill Student Housing

La Loma Housing

courtyards and an interesting juxtaposition with that Modern women's dormitory. It terminates in a Commons rotunda near the southeast corner of Hearst and Gayley. Across Hearst, La Loma Housing takes on a more urbanized form, stepping down from Highland Place to La Loma Avenue with a cloistered diagonal configuration of courtyards. Turnbull planned to link the two communities with a covered footbridge over Hearst that would also serve as a gateway for the Lawrence Berkeley National Laboratory located higher up the hill. But the air rights to span the avenue were denied by the City of Berkeley, leaving only the piers in place on either side of Hearst, should the connection be approved at some future time.

Originally planned to provide over 1,500 beds, the project was scaled back and redesigned on a narrow strip of buildable hillside following community opposition and litigation over concerns that the buildings were being planned too close to the active trace of the Hayward Fault. The controversy resulted in a one-year construction delay and required extensive geological studies involving thousands of feet of trenching. In response to the fault presence, the buildings were designed with special concrete mat foundations enabling them to float over any potential ground fissures.

Sheathed in panelized shingles and plywood resembling board-and-batten siding, the complex relates well to the Northside residential tradition and incorporates a number of forms that recall the styles created by Albert C. Schweinfurth, Bernard Maybeck, Ernest Coxhead, and other Bay Area masters. Dormers punctuate the long gabled-roofs at the residential entrances. These are framed at the ground by balcony-supporting redwood-log columns—with the bark left on—like those used at Schweinfurth's for-mer First Unitarian Church at 2401 Bancroft Way (see Walk 4). Trellised colonnades link parts of the complex, which uses bracketed balconies and grouped small-pane windows to provide residential variety and adapt to the hillside setting. More decorative balconies at the prominent corner facade of La Loma Housing create a chalet-like image.

The cupola-topped rotunda of the Commons building serves as a focal point and identifying element for the complex and contains a soaring dining center, assembly rooms, lounge, and mail service. A smaller octago-nal turret is skillfully used as a circulation hub and a hinge between the complex and the north end of Stern Hall.

50. Hearst Greek Theatre

John Galen Howard assisted by Julia Morgan, 1902–1903;
Ernest Born, alterations, 1957

On a summer day in 1894, a line of figures dressed in "brown gowns and cowls, and chanting a dirge, wound slowly through the trees"[2] on the foothill overlooking the campus and assembled around a smoking altar created from a large eucalyptus stump. This was not a secret medieval court but a dramatization performed by costumed members of the grad-uating Class of 1894 who wanted to do something different for Class Day—a farewell traditionally observed with recitations and satirical skits.

This exercise occurred in "Ben Weed's Amphitheatre," named for the senior who founded it as a more suitable setting for the class drama than "Co-ed Canyon" (as Faculty Glade was then called), where the celebration was usually held. The new site was larger, had better acoustics and sight-lines, and required only the university's permission to fell the large eucalyp-tus in the center of the hollow to create the court altar, as well as a dais fashioned from its trunk and branches. Use of the natural amphitheatre con-tinued for the next several years for annual senior class "Extravaganzas" presented in the form of original dramas and farcical sketches.

President Wheeler, a Greek scholar, conceived of turning the popu-lar spot into something more permanent. Upon visiting the sloping site he saw its potential as a Greek Theatre, a fitting monument for the "Athens of the West." There was a growing need for a large place of assembly, and while old wooden Harmon Gymnasium provided shelter for meetings, it lacked in acoustic qualities and was used for other competing activities. For some occasions, the president observed, the university had "trusted itself to the open California sky, and not having been deceived has learned that the Greeks of the West must follow the Greeks of the East."[3] Stepping forward with the financial support needed to turn vision into reality was William

Randolph Hearst, following the suggestion of his mother, Regent and sponsor of the international competition for the Hearst Plan.

Though not included in the original program for the plan, the theatre would become the first structure completed under newly appointed Supervising Architect John Galen Howard. As a model he chose the well-preserved and acoustically perfect theatre at Epidauros, Greece. Built about 350 B.C. and attributed to sculptor-architect Polykleitos the Younger, it nestles into a natural hillside much like that at Berkeley. Howard adopted its traditional form: the circular *orchestra* (originally a dance floor for the chorus); the *theatron*, or auditorium, of semicircular seating; the *skene*, or stage building, with its raised stage, or *logeion*; and on each side of the orchestra, a *parodos*, or ramped gangway, used originally for the chorus and actors to make their entrance. Unlike Epidauros, which has two sections of tiered stone seating for about 12,000 spectators, Howard encircled the orchestra with eleven shallow-pitched deep tiers for moveable chairs, creating a first section that rises to the *diazoma*, the semicircular aisle set at the level of the stage. Here, an incomplete row of marble commemorative chairs forms the top of the first section, while above the wall a second section of tiered concrete seating rises steeply into the hillside behind. This upper section contains nineteen rows of seats divided by radiating stairways into ten wedge-shaped segments, or *kerkides*, which rise to the height of the stage building. The grassy slope above accommodates additional informal seating.

The marble chairs, donated over the years by classes and individuals, now number thirty-one and are inscribed in honor of beloved faculty, administrators, alumni, and Regents. "It would be a fine idea," President Wheeler suggested, "if every class would present one such seat, an action that would form an attractive and useful remembrance."[4] The straight-backed chairs were initially modeled after the seats of honor installed in the Theatre of Dionysus at the Acropolis in Athens between the third and first centuries B.C. They were designed by Melvin Earl Cummings (1876–1936), instructor in modeling in the architecture department who also contributed to Howard's Sather Gate and Doe Memorial Library. Cummings had to make a second model after his original and two completed marble chairs were destroyed in the workshop of the Columbia Marble Company, which was consumed by the fire that followed the San Francisco earthquake of 1906. However, the first chair installed was imported from Italy by Regent Frederick W. Dohrmann and dedicated in 1909 to Phoebe Apperson Hearst. Subsequent chairs were made of both Italian and California marble.

The west side of the theater is formed by the concrete stage building that rises over forty feet high with side wings that enclose the 135-foot-long stage. It is classically ornamented with a row of attached Doric columns and entablature. The stage walls are penetrated by five openings.

Study of Hearst Greek Theatre, circa 1901–1902, John Galen Howard

A central monumental "royal door" of the ancients is flanked by two minor doorways, while two large entrances in the side wings are doorways to the "strangers' house."

Howard's vision for a more fully enclosed theatre, "which in majesty and beauty shall in the fullness of time rival the temples of old Greece,"[5] was never realized. A second zone above the entablature with sculpted caryatids crowning the Doric columns was to have given the stage building greater prominence; the upper rim of the seating area was to be encircled with a roofed double-colonnaded peristyle that would meet side walls extending from the stage building. Finishing the exterior surfaces in costly marble also could not be done.

Before the stage building was complete, the theatre was put to use, so that U.S. President Theodore Roosevelt, a close friend of Wheeler, could address commencement exercises on May 14, 1903. Architect Julia Morgan, on Howard's staff as project manager, rushed to decorate the unfinished *skene*, which had only its freshly-poured columns in place. These she draped in canvas and linked together with garlands to form a makeshift backdrop for a speakers' canopy set up before the stage. Morgan, who, like Ben Weed, was a Class of 1894 graduate, would return to the theatre twenty-six years later to be awarded an honorary LL.D. in recognition of her distinguished architectural career.[6]

Four months after President Roosevelt's address, the completed theatre was dedicated on September 24 with ceremonies that drew 8,000 spectators. Following comments by President Wheeler, Ben Weed, and

Hearst Greek Theatre

Howard—interspersed with rousing student cheers—Aristophanes' Greek comedy *The Birds* was performed by a student cast in original Greek. The Hearst-owned *San Francisco Examiner* glowingly described the setting as "the noblest theatre the world has seen since the days when Greeks were Greeks."

Two days later, the first of many professional productions was staged with *Twelfth Night* performed by the English Shakespearean company, the Ben Greet Players. But it was actress Sarah Bernhardt who boosted publicity, when one month after the 1906 earthquake and fire had destroyed all the playhouses in San Francisco, she performed in Racine's tragedy, *Phèdre*, to an audience that included many refugees of the disaster. "Divine Sarah" would repeat the performance five years later and, along with other notable performers, such as Margaret Anglin and Maude Adams, help establish an international reputation for the outdoor theatre.

In its storied history, a variety of other uses have kept the theatre "booked": choral recitals, bands, operas, lectures, meetings, observances, and bonfire rallies—when the cries of "More wood, freshmen!" would arouse even the Greek gods. And like Teddy Roosevelt's appearance in 1903, nearly a century of commencement exercises, Charter Day ceremonies, and other occasions has brought many notables to the rostrum: President William Howard Taft in 1909; Roosevelt again in 1911; poet Robert Frost in 1958; Senator Robert F. Kennedy in 1966; Senator Edward M. Kennedy in 1975; and Philippines President Corazon C. Aquino in 1986. There would be other poignant and momentous events. At a war rally in

1943, nearly 300 male students in the Armed Forces were remembered in silence as the old North Hall Bell was repeatedly tolled. On December 7, 1964, in the midst of the Free Speech Movement (FSM), a spillover crowd of nearly 12,000 witnessed the removal of FSM leader Mario Savio from the microphone during a special meeting called by President Clark Kerr to find a peaceful resolution to the dispute. From Cal mascot Oski's first appearance to Luciano Pavarotti to the Grateful Dead, "the noblest theatre" has kept alive some of that mystical and dramatic spirit that inaugurated Ben Weed's Amphitheatre in 1894.

The Hearst Greek Theatre is listed on the National Register of Historic Places, is included in the Berkeley campus designation as a California Registered Historical Landmark, is listed on the State Historic Resources Inventory, and is a City of Berkeley Landmark.

51. Bowles Hall

George W. Kelham, 1928–1929;
W. P. Stephenson, alterations, 1938; Michael Goodman, alterations, 1977–1978

A Gothic manor at the base of Charter Hill, Bowles Hall was the first university-owned residence hall. It was dedicated in January 1929 by donor Mary McNear Bowles in memory of her husband, Regent Philip Ernest Bowles, to further the ideals of "Education through Fellowship." That became the motto of the men's hall, which has been closely tied to university traditions and produced notable "Bowlesmen" alumni ever since.

Bowles Hall

Among them have been English Professor James D. Hart, who also served as vice chancellor and director of the Bancroft Library, and Supreme Court Justice Wakefield Taylor. Taylor, a former student body president, helped establish the tradition with Stanford University of awarding the Axe as an annual trophy to the winner of the Big Game.

Supervising Architect George W. Kelham visited dormitories at Eastern colleges, finding the Collegiate-Gothic or Tudor style predominant, especially at Princeton University. It was a style used by Kelham's predecessor, John Galen Howard, for Stephens Hall in 1923, and would lend itself well to the desired image of home-and-hearth and to the hillside terrain of the site. The site was a fitting place to remember Regent Bowles, who was devoted to beautifying the campus and funded the planting of many of the trees on the hill above the building.

Kelham organized the reinforced-concrete building in three wings with steep-pitched gabled tile roofs. The central four-story block is comprised of five bays above Tudor arches that form an entrance loggia at its base. Two projecting side wings embrace the front court, a steep-sloping greensward ascended by concrete steps and flagstone walkways lined with Italian cypress. The flexibility of the Tudor style is exemplified by the westerly wing that steps down this embankment. A castle-like crenellated tower, topped by a flagpole, marks the intersection of this wing with the central block. Befitting the manor style, the entry hallway is finished in stained oak paneling with a carved oak staircase. A two-story-high three-bay lounge is similarly finished and has decorative pilasters, ornamental chandeliers, molded beams and cornices, and an arched marble fireplace.

Bowles originally accommodated 104 students, housed mostly in suites containing two bedrooms with a common study. During World War II, the students were temporarily moved to empty fraternity houses, and the hall was taken over by approximately 300 Army Air Forces enlisted men training in meteorology and Chinese language programs. Since the war, Bowles has doubled-up the original capacity to accommodate approximately 200 male students, but arranged to encourage interaction between freshmen and upperclassmen and foster the fellowship and shared educational experiences aspired to in the Bowles credo. Reinforcing this tradition is the students' self-government of the hall, rooted in the student leadership principles promoted by President Wheeler at the beginning of the twentieth century.

Bowles Hall is listed on the National Register of Historic Places and the State Historic Resources Inventory, and is a City of Berkeley Landmark.

California Memorial Stadium

52. California Memorial Stadium

John Galen Howard and the California Memorial Stadium Commission, 1923;
Ratcliff Slama Cadwalader, press box addition, 1969;
Hansen/Murakami/Eshima, interior alterations, 1981–1990;
CMX Group, field renovation, 1995

It was called "The House Andy Built." The picturesque home of Golden
Bear football, beginning with the "Wonder Teams" of Andy Smith who
coached from 1916 to 1925, California Memorial Stadium is nestled at the
mouth of Strawberry Canyon. It is a hybrid structure—part earthen bowl,
part Roman coliseum—an oval concrete ring, 760 feet long by 570 feet
wide, that rises to the height of a five-story building at its west facade.
Heroic in its proportions, the stadium was also heroically constructed—
initiated in July 1923 following excavation and completed in time for
73,000 fans to see a 9-0 Cal victory over Stanford in the Big Game on
November 24 that same year.[7]

A major athletic stadium had been a university objective since
the competition for the Hearst Architectural Plan in 1897. John Galen
Howard initially proposed construction of "the Grand Stadium" on the former Hillegass Tract, where California Field was developed in 1904 and
where Hearst Gymnasium now stands. It was not until the 1920 Big Game,
when nearly 28,000 spectators strained the bleachers of the old field, that
a new 60,000-seat stadium was proposed by the Executive Committee
of the Associated Students (ASUC) who then had the responsibility for

intercollegiate athletics. Funded by more than $1 million in subscriptions raised within one month in a statewide campaign, the stadium would be dedicated to the memory of Californians lost in World War I. And it would be built with the understanding that Stanford would also construct a stadium of similar size to continue the mutual benefits to both schools of hosting alternate Big Games.

The story of how the stadium site and design were determined is one filled with as many feints, blocks, and lateral passes as were later performed on the gridiron in "The Play," California's famous game-ending kickoff-return victory over Stanford in the 1982 Big Game. Howard researched stadium types and studied suitable sites, which in addition to California Field, included the northwest part of campus, used then for recreation and military drills, and an area southwest of campus (now occupied by Edwards Stadium, Evans Baseball Diamond, and the Recreational Sports Facility). The Regents decided to keep the existing field and northwest grounds as reserves for future growth and rejected other remote sites because they lacked the proximity desired to maintain student spirit and involvement and encourage alumni to return to campus. They also initially rejected the present site at the mouth of Strawberry Canyon, then the location of the university's nursery grounds, which was considered too small for the stadium and a potential site for student housing.

In December 1921 Howard was directed to proceed with plans for the southwest area, where he envisioned building an arched double-deck oval coliseum. But the following month he was told to stop work on

California Memorial Stadium

his plans, while the Regents reconsidered the mouth of the canyon. They were influenced by reports about Stanford Stadium, an earth-fill type bowl completed in time for the 1921 Big Game. Edward E. Carpenter, a partner in the San Francisco engineering firm of Baker and Carpenter who supervised construction of that stadium, suggested that an earthen bowl would be more economical than Howard's proposed structure, and that a seating capacity greater than 60,000 would be possible at the canyon site. Another proposal came from engineer George F. Buckingham, a consultant to the Great Western Power Company, whose president was Regent Guy Chaffee Earl. Buckingham convinced the Regents that the best solution for the site would be a combination of the earth bowl and coliseum types—a blending of the Carpenter and Howard proposals.[8] In August 1922 the Regents adopted the Buckingham scheme and appointed a stadium commission—composed of Howard as chairman and engineers Buckingham and Carpenter, with University Comptroller and Secretary of the Regents Robert Gordon Sproul, as secretary—to prepare the plans.

The plan was adopted with considerable controversy. Howard himself had earlier opposed the Strawberry Canyon site, possibly in part out of self interest, because his contract with the Regents permitted a speci-fied percentage for all work done on campus *west* of Piedmont Avenue. His agreement to serve with Buckingham and Carpenter on the commission was an indication of his diminishing influence as supervising architect since 1919, following the death of Regent Phoebe Hearst and retirement of President Wheeler, his two strong supporters. He was appointed chairman of the commission despite the feelings of some Regents that he should not be put in charge of the project.

In addition, a community-based Campus Protective Association was formed to oppose the project at the canyon site. Supporters of the Association included alumni architects William G. Corlett, Henry H. Gutterson, Walter T. Steilberg, Walter H. Ratcliff, landscape architect Bruce Porter, and the director of the California Academy of Sciences. Their con-cerns included defacement of the canyon, transportation and accessibility, architectural constraints, lack of future expansion room for athletics, and loss of the site as a natural biological laboratory. Objection also came from property owners, whose homes would have to be removed or views com-promised by the stadium.

Despite this opposition the Regents proceeded with the project. Seven properties were acquired, and excavation began in January 1923. Horse-drawn wagons and steam-powered shovels moved tons of earth loosened by blasting and hydraulic force to cut into the southern slope of Charter Hill and reshape the natural terrain. A four-foot diameter concrete culvert, 1,450 feet long, was constructed to divert Strawberry Creek under the stadium, then northward past Girton Hall and to Faculty Glade.

Because of the presence of the Hayward Fault the elliptical bowl was constructed as two halves with expansion joints at the north and south ends to permit movement of the structure in a major earthquake. On the neoclassical exterior Howard retained his Roman arches, alternating single ones with groups of three at entrances leading to seating sections and the concourse level within the west structure. This level was renovated in the 1980s by Michael Murakami (Class of 1966) of Oakland architects Hansen/Murakami/Eshima for athletics offices, training and locker facilities, and the California Athletic Hall of Fame, where Cal sports memorabilia are displayed.

The north tunnel leading onto the field is the traditional entrance for the dramatic arrival of the home team and the California Marching Band. At the tunnel entrance are two historic plaques. One memorializing those lost in World War I was a traditional location for the placing of a wreath each Memorial Day. The other honors President John F. Kennedy, who spoke in the stadium at the 94th annual Charter Day ceremonies on March 23, 1962, to an audience of 90,000, the largest gathering in the university's history. Fourteen years earlier, 50,000 people saw President Harry S Truman address the 1948 graduating class in the stadium, the first U.S. President to address a Berkeley commencement since Theodore Roosevelt did so in the Hearst Greek Theatre in 1903.

Inside the stadium along the east fifty-yard line in front of the Cal rooting section, the spirit of Coach Andy Smith is kept alive by a granite team bench named in his memory. Its inscription recalls the principles he established in his "House" for his successful teams to follow: "We Do Not Want Men Who Will Lie Down Bravely to Die. Winning is Not Everything. And it is Far Better To Play The Game Squarely And Lose Than To Win At The Sacrifice Of An Ideal."

California Memorial Stadium is listed on the State Historic Resources Inventory. The Hall of Fame is open to the public the first Thursday of every month, from 10am to 3pm.

53. Charter Hill and the Big C

Big C *Classes of 1907 and 1908, 1905*

With the golden Big C anchored to its west-facing slope, Charter Hill displays one of the most historic icons of the California Spirit. Rising 400 feet behind the Greek Theatre and Bowles Hall, the hill acquired its name from nineteenth-century traditions associated with Charter Day, the anniversary of the creation of the university on March 23, 1868.

In the late nineteenth century, on the eve of Charter Day, freshmen would attempt to mark their class numerals into the slope of the hill, only to be rushed by members of the sophomore class, who would try to prevent

Charter Hill and the Big C

them from doing so. This "class rush" inevitably led to brawls that were despised by the faculty, who then controlled student affairs, and upperclassmen, who were trying to persuade the faculty to transfer that responsibility to the students themselves. The inter-class violence also conflicted with the principles of President Wheeler, who believed that students should become responsible leaders in self-government, and after 1903 the Charter Day Class Rush was discontinued.

Seeking to establish a more civilized alternative, a small group of male students, who met regularly in the spring of 1905, discussed resurrecting an idea of the Classes of 1882 and 1888 of planting trees on Charter Hill in the form of a large "C." These sophomores from the Class of 1907 called themselves the "Hillside Luncheon Gang," because they shared their noon meal on a slope near North Hall overlooking the central Botanical Garden, present site of Memorial Glade. One of the group, engineering student Herbert B. Foster—who would later become University Engineer— proposed a more permanent "C." He suggested it be built of masonry, coated with yellow ochre, and traditionally maintained and re-painted by successive classes.

After obtaining the approval of campus administrators, Foster enlisted the help of William C. Hays, then John Galen Howard's junior partner, to survey the hill and determine the best site for the emblem. The position chosen on the slope was calculated to be visible from North Hall (then the center of student activities), California Field, the Berkeley business district, and even the Key System commuter train mole at the Oakland waterfront. (Charter Hill was relatively unforested at this time, but the hill tree-planting program during the following decade left the Big C less visible from some vantage points.) It would emulate the block football "C" that was officially adopted by the Associated Students (ASUC). Foster drew up plans for a reinforced-concrete "C" sixty-feet long by twenty-six-feet wide, dimensioned so as not to appear foreshortened, with deep pier footings penetrating the hillside.[9]

Other campus and community individuals offered support as well. Civil Engineering Dean Frank Soulé, one of Foster's professors, consulted on the design and concrete mix, which was tested in the College's materials testing laboratory. The contractor for California Hall, then under construction, provided reinforcing steel and broken roof tiles to be used in drainage ditches, while other local contractors, Southern Pacific, and the Key System contributed hand tools. But when the project was publicized, not all were content. Some members of the faculty and community objected to the yellow "C," fearing it would blight the Berkeley hills and eventually slide down the steep slope in a crashing heap.

Nevertheless, on Saturday, March 18, 1905, a holiday was declared to enable men of the freshman and sophomore classes of 1907 and 1908 to construct the "C." On that rainy morning the lowerclassmen worked together, forming a long human chain to pass sacks of cement, sand, stone aggregate, and other materials up the hill from the Dairy Barn in Strawberry Canyon, where they were stockpiled.

Five days later on Charter Day, as keynote speaker Princeton University Professor Henry Van Dyke was about to address the audience assembled in the Greek Theatre, a rousing cheer of "Oski-wow-wow!" came down from the hill proclaiming completion of the Big C. A bronze plaque anchored to the concrete emblem symbolized the new spirit of cooperation between the classes: "In Memory of the Rush, Buried by the Classes 1907 and 1908, March 23, 1905. Requiescat In Pace."

But class rivalry would not completely vanish. Freshmen would surreptitiously attempt to paint the "C" green, so that the sophomores, who were responsible for its custody, would have to re-apply several gallons of new yellow enamel. Occasional raids from across the Bay also succeeded, and during more than one Big Game Week, the "C" has suddenly appeared an embarrassing Stanford red. Like the rings of a tree, the numerous paintings told a story. A thorough cleaning in 1938 uncovered seventy-nine coats, twenty of them Stanford red, while 120 subsequent layers were scraped off in 1976.

On the morning of February 29, 1916, the traditional Leap Year Labor Day, approximately 2,500 male students joined to construct the Big C Trail, winding some 2,000 feet up the steep slope of Charter Hill from the

Greek Theatre to the Big C. Working with picks and shovels to the tunes of school songs, they "cut a monument carved by the hands of Californians," with each of the ten colleges or schools building a portion of the path.

Soon after the inaugural football game in California Memorial Stadium in 1923, the southern slope of Charter Hill acquired the nickname "Tightwad Hill," because of the free view it affords of the games. It is here where the Victory Cannon, also called the Golden Cannon, is fired whenever Cal scores. A gift of the Class of 1964, the 750-pound cannon has a golden barrel supported by a wooden chassis, sporting forty-inch-diameter blue wheels with gold rims. It made its thunderous debut at the 1964 Big Game.

Charter Hill is listed on the State Historic Resources Inventory.

WALK SEVEN

Strawberry Canyon and Hill Area

Bear, Witter Rugby Field

Centennial Drive

Cyclotron Road

Stadium Rim Road

57

56

58

55

54

54

The rugged west-facing scarp above the central campus is the geological signature of the mid-Pleistocene epoch, when the Berkeley-Oakland hills were formed hundreds of thousands of years ago. Extending from the foothill to Grizzly Peak Boulevard and rising from about 400 to 1,700 feet above sea level, the area includes about 850 acres of Berkeley campus property, which wraps around the 200-acre site of the university's Lawrence Berkeley National Laboratory (the Lab). Its most dramatic feature is Strawberry Canyon, comprising about one square mile of watershed of the south fork of Strawberry Creek, extending from the ridge of the hills westward to California Memorial Stadium.

Lower and upper hill areas divide the terrain and are roughly demarcated by the Berkeley-Oakland boundary. The lower hill is dominated by the Lab, which is scattered on buildable knolls and plateaus between Blackberry and Strawberry Canyons. Within the canyon are the Strawberry Canyon Recreation Area just above California Memorial Stadium and further east the thirty-four-acre Botanical Garden nestled into the hillside. The upper hill contains the Lawrence Hall of Science and its terraced parking and, on the ridge above, the clustered research complex of the Silver Space Sciences Laboratory and Mathematical Sciences Research Institute.

This watershed ultimately persuaded the College of California Trustees to select the former ranchland between the forks of the creek for their new campus. The Trustees had organized a water works to develop springs and dam the creeks to supply both their college and its adjacent new town. But when the Regents acquired the property in 1868 they considered the commercial venture to be inappropriate for a state university and sold the water rights to private concerns.

At that time the hills were not forested as they appear today but were open grasslands. It was not until speculators in the following decade planted eucalyptus trees that the hills began to acquire a new look. They hoped that the "wonder gum tree" imported from Australia would serve as a substitute for other hardwoods that had become depleted nationwide, but the trees proved to be impractical for commercial use and remained rooted in the hills. Nearly a century later in December 1972 freezing temperatures devastated the well-established eucalyptus, and an estimated three million of the trees died within a fifteen mile strip of the East Bay hills. By the following spring the dead trees had become potential ground fuel for the dry fire season and had to be removed from hundreds of acres of university hill land.

By 1908 water again became an issue for the growing university. The campus had two sources, drinking water supplied from the People's Water Company and water for other uses from a creek-fed university reservoir near the Dairy Barn, in the vicinity of the present Strawberry Canyon Recreation Area. But costs were high and supplies inadequate, often resulting in low pressure and leading to concerns about fire safety and irrigation of the campus grounds. The need for a larger and more reliable water supply led the Regents in 1909 to expand eastward into the City of Oakland and acquire an additional contiguous 257 acres of hill watershed to increase the reservoir supply. It was reasoned that the additional land might also create opportunities for developing new dormitories as Supervising Architect John Galen Howard envisioned, as well as residences, laboratories, and athletic fields. Other potential uses included pasture land for university herds, large-scale forestry experimentation, and agricultural research, while the water system could do double-duty as an instructional facility for the College of Civil Engineering. The Regents were anxious to make the acquisition, knowing that delay would mean a lost opportunity as developers were considering the land for subdivision as residential building lots.

About the same time there was also a growing desire to beautify the campus grounds and "to make the planting of Charter Hill and the rest of the University property immediately back of it, as comprehensive and lasting as our building scheme now is."[1] With the help of donations from Regent Philip E. Bowles, by 1913 an ambitious planting program of the Strawberry Creek watershed had been accomplished. Nearly 19,000 trees were planted that year, utilizing seedlings of varieties of deciduous and coniferous trees shipped from Tennessee and France, as well as eucalyptus, redwood, cypress, and pine trees.[2] A campus nursery was established and, under the care of propagator Knud Nyeland, thousands of additional trees were planted the following years.

Nyeland's nursery would soon be displaced by the first major development to impact the canyon, the construction of California Memorial Stadium at the canyon mouth in 1923. The large bowl required extensive reshaping of the natural terrain and diversion of Strawberry Creek into an underground culvert (see Walk 6).

At a higher elevation the first large research facility was constructed in 1940 to accommodate the 184-inch cyclotron used for the nuclear research led by physics professor Ernest Orlando Lawrence. Supervising Architect Arthur Brown, Jr., sited the large domed building on Howard's axis, evoking something of the image of a domed observatory that Howard proposed but was never built. This move of the Radiation Laboratory from the central campus to "The Hill" was followed by additional wartime structures rapidly constructed around the Cyclotron and in 1946 acquisition of the 98-acre Wilson Tract for Lab expansion. The complex evolved into the present campus of the Lawrence Berkeley National Laboratory. An additional acquisition of 286 Oakland acres from the East Bay Municipal Utility District in 1951 expanded the upper hill property to the northeast.

The introduced plantations, as well as native trees such as the madrone, enriched the hillside with a variety of flora and fauna, making it a useful outdoor laboratory for botany, forestry, entomology, and zoology, and leading in the 1930s to the designation of a thirty-eight-acre "primitive area" in the upper reaches for study. Research use was further recognized as an "invaluable asset" to the campus by a faculty advisory committee in 1958 who recommended that "[t]he guiding principle in the development of Strawberry Canyon and the hill area should be that of achieving maximum use consistent with conservation of native values."[3] Evolving from this recommendation, two protected Ecological Study Areas totaling some 300 acres in the canyon were established by Chancellor Roger W. Heyns in 1969, along with the designation of the Wickson, Grinnell, and Goodspeed Natural Areas on the central campus (see Walk 3).

Extending uphill from the Botanical Garden, Centennial Drive was completed in the 1960s along with the development of the upper hill with the Lawrence Hall of Science at "Fog Bluff" overlooking the Lab and, on the ridge above, the Silver Space Sciences Laboratory. This ridge plateau was expanded with the Mathematical Sciences Research Institute in the 1980s and Space Sciences Annex in the 1990s.

54. Strawberry Canyon Recreation Area and Haas Clubhouse

Haas Clubhouse, Stern Pool, and East Pool
Wurster, Bernardi & Emmons, with Lawrence Halprin & Associates, landscape architect, 1959; and East Pool, 1966–1967

Witter Rugby Field and Levine-Fricke Softball Field
Singer & Hodges, landscape architects, 1993–1994

Located at the mouth of the canyon on the wedge-shaped plane between Charter and Panoramic Hills, the Strawberry Canyon Recreation Area includes recreational swimming facilities and playing fields for intercollegiate softball and rugby.

A former dairy farm, the area contained a livestock barn and wood structures for veterinary science (John Galen Howard, 1924). In addition to supplying reservoirs, Strawberry Creek was used to fill the forerunner of the present swimming pools at the east end of the site. Constructed in 1911 as the Men's Swimming Pool, it was designed by Sanitary Engineering Professor Charles Gilman Hyde, who later served as Dean of Men. The concrete kidney-shaped pool, which had a small adjacent bathhouse, became known as the Canyon Pool when it was opened to women in 1943, but was abandoned eight years later because of maintenance problems. At the west end of the site, six wooden shop buildings and

Haas Clubhouse

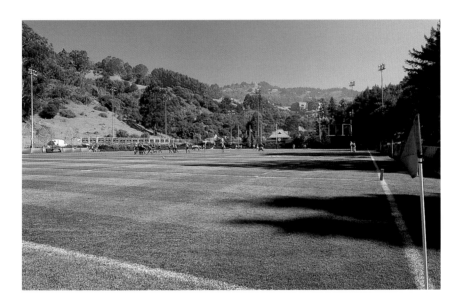

Witter Rugby Field

storehouses were constructed in 1940 (Arthur Brown, Jr.) for the relocation of the university's Corporation Yard from the site of Sproul Hall.

These facilities were removed by 1959 to make room for the recreational center, which was funded by gifts from Elise and Walter A. Haas (Class of 1910) and the estate of Lucie Stern, the aunt of Elise Haas and sister of Sigmund Stern, for whom Stern Hall was named (see Walk 6). Designed by San Francisco architects Wurster, Bernardi & Emmons with landscape architect Lawrence Halprin, it included the Haas Clubhouse and Stern Pool, along with tennis courts and a turf athletic field. The East Pool was added to relieve overcrowding in 1967.

The two-story wood-frame Haas Clubhouse reflects the Bay Region tradition and also evokes elements of early California rancho buildings, with its gable roof, deep overhangs, and broad verandah, designed for both sunning and group entertaining. The pavilion-like structure fits naturally in its canyon setting and has an open plan to accommodate a variety of activities. Lockers and shower rooms occupy the first floor, while the second floor has a kitchen and Club Room that is used for events or meetings for up to 250 people. In 1993 the tennis courts were removed and the athletic field and parking area reconfigured by landscape architects Singer & Hodges to create the present athletic fields.

55. Botanical Garden

John W. Gregg, landscape architect, with Thomas Harper Goodspeed, ca. 1920–1926

Uniquely situated on the sloping terrain of Strawberry Canyon overlooking San Francisco Bay, the thirty-four-acre University of California Botanical Garden is renowned as one of the largest and most diverse collections in the nation. Ranging in elevation from approximately 600 to 900 feet, the garden experiences a variety of climatic exposures and moderating seasonal changes created by marine air funneled eastward through the Golden Gate. These conditions, former garden director Thomas Harper Goodspeed observed, "permit an association of plants, birds, and mammals not duplicated elsewhere in middle western California."[4]

Goodspeed moved the garden to the canyon from its central campus location in the 1920s, with help from Landscape Design Professor John W. Gregg, who prepared a plan for the site. The original garden was established in 1890 by Botany Professor Edward L. Greene, who initiated a collection of native California trees and plants, which he planned to expand with other Pacific Coast plants. It was laid out in the central swale of the campus grounds, in the region now occupied by Moffitt Undergraduate Library, and later expanded eastward where Memorial Glade is now located. The following year a glass and steel Conservatory was erected on the north side of the swale, at the base of Observatory Hill. Designed by New York greenhouse manufacturers Lord & Burnham, it remained a popular campus landmark until 1924, when it was removed for site work related to the construction of Haviland Hall (see Walk 3). In 1920, the canyon site was first utilized for the experimental cultivation of the tobacco related *Nicotiana* species, and was soon expanded for the full garden, as development of the central campus intensified.

Japanese Pool in the Botanical Garden

Unlike the central campus garden, which was arranged in the customary manner by botanical taxonomy, Goodspeed organized the canyon plantings by geographic origins in surroundings similar to native habitats. Plants collected on international expeditions during the next three decades expanded and diversified the garden, and included rhododendrons from China, succulents and cacti from South America, and succulents from southern Africa. Today the collections include over 13,000 species and varieties of plants from around the world, organized in African Hill, Asian, Australasian, New World Desert, European/Mediterranean, South American, Mesoamerican, North American, and Californian sections, the latter occupying about one-third of the total garden area. Incorporated in the garden layout is Strawberry Creek, which flows from north to south across the site.

Within these settings, the garden contains several special areas of interest, including Chinese medicinal herbs, a Japanese pool, a garden of economic plants, an area of palms and cycads, and a garden of old roses with cultivars from the nineteenth and early twentieth centuries. Across Centennial Drive, the garden includes the Mather Redwood Grove, which was dedicated in 1976 in honor of Stephen Tyng Mather, Class of 1887, founding director of the National Park Service and co-founder of the Save-the-Redwoods League. The five-acre grove of Coast redwoods was planted in 1936 with associated flora and is an extension of the garden's Californian section. It forms a Miocene Sequoia Forest Area of descendants of plants that grew with ancient redwoods. Within the grove are an amphitheater and several glades memorializing notable alumni and faculty, including Newton Bishop Drury (Class of 1912), former Director of the National Park Service, and Knowles Augustus Ryerson (Class of 1916), former dean of the College of Agriculture.

The Botanical Garden is listed on the State Historic Resources Inventory. It is open daily from 9am to 4:45pm, and from Memorial Day through Labor Day from 9am to 7pm.

56. Lawrence Hall of Science   *Anshen and Allen, 1965–1968*

Conceptualized at a time of intense scientific competition between the United States and the Soviet Union, the Lawrence Hall of Science was first proposed as a combined museum and educational facility "to educate the public of all ages in the nuclear sciences."[5] It developed from Chancellor Glenn T. Seaborg's desire to create a living memorial to the inventor of the cyclotron and fellow Nobel Laureate Ernest Orlando Lawrence, who died in 1958. As the project progressed, it expanded in concept and today is a national center of science education, curriculum development, and science–teacher training.

The site selected for the building, a hillside perch with a panoramic view of San Francisco Bay, afforded a prominence for the hall while maintaining a desired proximity to the teaching and research activities of the

Lawrence Hall of Science

campus. It was known informally as "Fog Bluff" and officially as "Vista del Cerro," and its position some 300 feet above the Lawrence Radiation Laboratory (now the Lawrence Berkeley National Laboratory) also provided a symbolic linkage to the facility that evolved from Lawrence's development of the cyclotron.

An overall funding goal of $12 million was initially established, proposed as a combination of fees from the Atomic Energy Commission for the university's management of nuclear laboratories, private gifts, and National Science Foundation grants. The building was envisioned to include a planetary dome, exhibit spaces, educational facilities, and a large auditorium. To select an architect for the prestigious project, the Regents conducted an invited competition, in which three Bay Area and two East Coast firms participated in 1962: Anshen and Allen, San Francisco; DeMars and Reay, Berkeley; Skidmore, Owings & Merrill, San Francisco; Louis I. Kahn, Philadelphia; and Eero Saarinen and Associates, Hamden, Connecticut. Since only a portion of the funding was in place, the competition was based on designing an expanding program that could be built in stages.

The unanimous choice of the jury was a reinforced-concrete design by Anshen and Allen that featured a 200-foot Planetary Space Hall with a circular convoluted roof, surrounded by eight smaller exhibit halls forming points of a star. It included a large entry plaza above a three-story science education center—octagonally shaped to represent eight physical and life sciences—a science information center and Lawrence Memorial Hall at the main entrance, a 600-seat auditorium, and a tiered parking lot connected by a footbridge to the plaza.

But only two of four planned phases were constructed. Left for the future but never built were the large auditorium at the north end, and the circular Planetary Space Hall with six of its eight radiating star points—the hull-like exhibit-hall pods that were to project dramatically from the southern promontory of the site.

The dedication of the hall in May 1968 was an important event during the university's centennial celebration. Seaborg returned from Washington, D.C., where he was serving as chairman of the Atomic Energy Commission, to deliver the principal address. He later recalled that "it was one of the happiest and most rewarding moments in my life to see such a goal achieved."[6] Beginning in 1984 he resumed his involvement as chairman of the hall.

Today over 300,000 people annually visit the hall and its three centers. The Public Science Center includes changing events and exhibits ranging from animatronic insects to dinosaurs, interactive programs in the intimate Holt Planetarium, a Biology Discovery Laboratory with live animals, as well as computer education, outreach programs, and science and mathematics workshops. The Center for School Change provides curriculum development and support for K-12 schools, while the Center for Curriculum Innovation offers programs for the development of instructional materials.

Displayed inside the hall is the first cyclotron that demonstrated the acceleration of protons on January 2, 1931, built by Lawrence and M. Stanley Livingston. Outside, at the hall's driveway, stands the electromagnet for Lawrence's thirty-seven-inch cyclotron, now recognized as being "a major stepping-stone in the history of science." The eighty-five-ton instrument was used in world-leading nuclear research from 1932 to 1939 and during World War II for the separation of uranium-235.

The entry plaza, with its aggregate concrete Children's Fountain at the center, features two large educational sculptures. The sixty-foot-long plastic and stainless steel double helix is an 800-million-to-one scale model of a DNA (deoxyribonucleic acid) molecule, designed by Michael E. Jantzen and installed in 1992. Further west is "Pheena," a fiberglass and steel life-size replica of a young fin whale. The fifty-foot-long, 3,000-pound sculpture was designed by Ken Norris and installed in 1975.

The Lawrence Hall of Science is open daily from 10am to 5pm except for some holidays. Phone 510-642-5132.

57. Silver Space Sciences Laboratory, Space Sciences Annex, and Mathematical Sciences Research Institute

Silver Space Sciences Laboratory

Anshen and Allen, with Theodore Osmundson, landscape architect, 1964–1966; Fisher Friedman Associates with Forell/Elesser Engineers, seismic alterations, 2000–2001

Space Sciences Annex

MBT Associates, with Patricia O'Brien, landscape architect, 1996–1998

Mathematical Sciences Research Institute   *Shen/Glass Architects, 1983–1985*

Perched atop the hill near Little Grizzly Peak at an elevation of 1300 feet, the Silver Space Sciences Laboratory commands a panoramic Bay view, shared only by its next-door neighbor, the Mathematical Sciences Research Institute. The laboratory was established in 1959, when the new technology of rockets and satellites was expanding the opportunities for multi-disciplinary research of space exploration. It began operating the following year in the old Leuschner Observatory (see Walk 2) under its first Director and Professor of Engineering Science, Samuel Silver, for whom the laboratory is named. Overcrowding and dispersal of research projects at remote facilities led to

Silver Space Sciences Laboratory

the need for the present building, which was made possible by a $2 million grant from the National Aeronautics and Space Administration in 1962.

San Francisco architects Anshen and Allen designed the laboratory to be harmonious with their Lawrence Hall of Science, constructed concurrently on the bluff 200 feet below. The four-level concrete structure features deep pre-cast "eyebrows" that form horizontal bands along the facade. Viewed from the campus and community, its facade relates to Lawrence Hall's horizontally layered education center. The interior included specialized spectroscopic laboratories with copper shielding to filter extraneous electromagnetic radiation.

As research needs expanded, activities of the laboratory spilled over into temporary facilities, including a small adjunct structure on the west and assorted trailers on the east, affectionately and symbolically named "Mars," "Jupiter," and other planetary bodies. Removal of the trailers and improvement of the grounds were made possible in 1998 by the construction of the $14 million Space Sciences Annex to the east of the laboratory.

The L-shaped Annex, approximately equal in size to the laboratory, is composed of three main elements. A high-bay laboratory in the long north wing provides the volume needed for the assembly and testing of high-altitude and space payload packages. The shorter south wing functions as an entrance lobby and a centralized commons serving both the annex and original laboratory. The lounge, library, and conference room in this wing open onto a deck that affords a panoramic view to the southwest.

Architects Michael Hearn and Paul Harnery of San Francisco–based MBT Associates designed the Annex in a style suggestive of the high-tech functions housed within, striving for an impression of lightness with clean, taut forms. The rectilinear forms of the building are punctuated by the sculptural profiles of the high-bay tower, ventilation equipment, and staircases.

Space Sciences Annex

Lighter attached elements, such as the metal colonnaded entry portico and south deck canopy, contribute to a sense of human scale. The mass of the building is also skillfully manipulated by the use of different colors and articulation of the scored-stucco boxes.

Mathematical Sciences Research Institute

Unlike Silver Laboratory's gleaming white concrete facade, the redwood-sided Mathematical Sciences Research Institute blends more naturally into the wooded hillside. The rustic but sleek design evokes elements of the Bay Tradition, with its wood skin, banded windows, projecting bays, balconies, and trellised sunshades. In addition, a shed-roof profile is formed by four east-facing skylights that illuminate an interior gallery. The building is a think-tank for international scholars—a place for "mental mountain climbing,"[7] as one scholar described his research—modeled after the Princeton Institute for Advanced Study, but dependent on federal rather than private funding.

East Bay architects William Glass and Carol Shen teamed with S. J. Amoroso Construction Company and were selected for the $2.5 million project, following a design/build competition with four other teams. Their interior design of the building responds to the Institute's objective to provide both a haven for individual contemplation and an environment for intellectual synergism. It was to be "a place to be alone, to sit down and work on very hard detailed problems," as Mathematics Professor Calvin Moore described it, as well as to provide "the stimulation of others."[8] To achieve

Mathematical Sciences Research Institute

these goals, the architects arranged fifty-three private offices, many with Bay views, along a three-story atrium with second and third floor galleries. Chalk boards are generously placed for spontaneous brainstorming, and the skylit white atrium with its oak-railed balconies and stairways provides an atmosphere conducive to impromptu meetings or British-influenced tea breaks scheduled to bring the scholars together.

58. Lawrence Berkeley National Laboratory

Arthur Brown, Jr., Cyclotron Building, 1940

The Lawrence Berkeley National Laboratory is founded upon a legacy of break-through research in nuclear physics and biophysics, historic contributions to the Manhattan Project during World War II, and high-energy physics research. Originally administered by the Berkeley campus, the non-classified multidisciplinary research facility is an independent academic unit of the University of California system and is operated by the university for the U.S. Department of Energy (DOE). The DOE owns most of the Lab's approximately eighty buildings, which were constructed on university land leased on a long-term basis to the federal government.

Extending from the foothill to the Lawrence Hall of Science and Botanical Garden, the 200-acre Lab is sited on the steep slopes of Blackberry Canyon and the edge of Strawberry Canyon to the south. Research is also conducted in about twenty Berkeley campus buildings, especially Donner and Calvin Laboratories, and in various leased facilities in the community.

Building 6, Advanced Light Source (former Cyclotron) Lawrence Berkeley National Laboratory

It is the oldest of the national laboratories, established on the Berkeley campus in 1931 as the Radiation Laboratory by Physics Professor Ernest Orlando Lawrence, the founding director, inventor of the cyclotron, and Nobel Laureate for whom the Lab is named. When the need for higher-energy accelerators required the construction of a much larger facility than could be conveniently sited on the central campus, the lab moved to "The Hill," where its landmark dome was built to house the 184-inch cyclotron in 1940. Designed by Arthur Brown. Jr., then supervising architect for the Berkeley campus, the circular building was sited just above Charter Hill in alignment with John Galen Howard's central axis oriented to the Golden Gate. The steel-frame dome was built around the cyclotron's horseshoe-shaped magnet yoke, which was anchored to a concrete pad in the center of the site. At first the steel necessary for the magnet was difficult to obtain, but manufacturing progressed in the face of national defense needs, when the magnet was "rated as a mechanism of warfare."[9]

Rapid growth during the war years crowded the hill with temporary wooden buildings, which were replaced with permanent structures in subsequent years.

The oil crisis during the 1970s led to new directions in research related to the nation's energy supply and to multi-program research and development in basic energy sciences involving materials science, chemistry, biology, physics, and the environmental sciences, in addition to high-energy and nuclear physics.

In 1993 the historic dome was remodeled to house the Advanced Light Source, a national user facility that generates the world's brightest soft x-rays and ultraviolet light used for scientific and technological research in many fields. Other national user facilities at the lab include the National Center for Electron Microscopy, where atomic-level research is conducted; National Energy Research Scientific Computing Center, one of the world's leading centers for supercomputing; and the 88-Inch Cyclotron, used for programs in basic nuclear science.

These facilities and others are used by more than 2,000 guest researchers who visit the Lab each year. Its 3,500 staff includes about 1,300 scientists and engineers, of which some 250 are also members of the Berkeley faculty, as well as 800 students employed at the Lab. Approximately 3,000 guests on school and public tours visit each year, in addition to science education programs offered to college students and teachers.

The Lawrence Berkeley National Laboratory offers public tours usually limited to fifteen participants, on Fridays, with advanced reservation. Special group tours can also be arranged. Tour information is available by phone at 510-486-5183.

Piedmont Avenue and Clark Kerr Campus

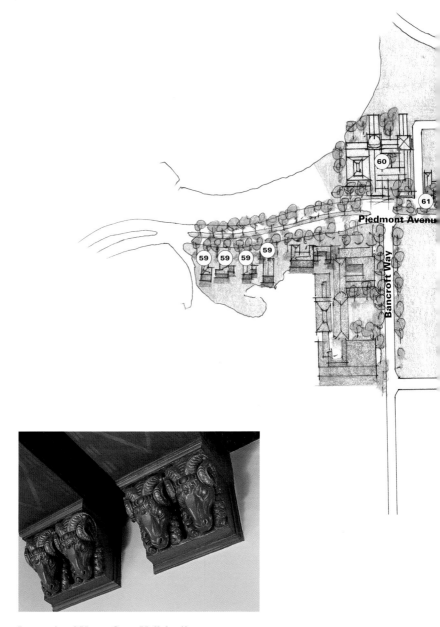

International House, Great Hall detail

Warring Street

Piedmont Crescent

Parker Street

Warring Street

Channing Way

Dwight Way

61

62

Frederick Law Olmstead's Piedmont Way Neighborhood

This Walk centers along Piedmont Avenue, a gently curving 100-foot-wide parkway originally named Piedmont Way that was conceived by landscape architect Frederick Law Olmsted as part of his 1865 plan for the College of California. It was intended to connect the campus with the grounds of the State Asylum for the Deaf, Dumb and Blind, which opened in 1869 on the site now occupied by the university's Clark Kerr Campus. Along the parkway he planned a residential subdivision, the "Berkeley Property," situated east of College Avenue (then Audubon Street), and extending from Piedmont's present juncture with Gayley Road on the north to approximately Dwight Way on the south.

Envisioned as a roadway following the natural topography and lined with overhanging trees, the parkway was the first street design undertaken by Olmsted. Although Olmsted's plan for the College of California was abandoned, his concept for the Piedmont Way neighborhood was generally followed. The roadway was deeded to the City of Berkeley when it incorporated in 1878 and in 1900 was renamed Piedmont Avenue and paved for the first time.

Within a decade, as the city grew around the university, Olmsted's neighborhood developed into elegant landscaped homes along the curving parkway. Many of the large residences were built by prominent businessmen, who commissioned the leading architects of the period. By the 1920s this fashionable community began to change as university development pushed eastward and displaced many residences. Along with the construction of California Memorial Stadium in 1923 and International House in 1930, came a community transition from single family homes to fraternities and sororities. This change Olmsted may not have foreseen, but it resulted in a form of student housing remarkably similar to his own views. When planning the campus, he advised against the construction of dormitories, suggesting instead that students might rent accommodations within the planned College Homestead subdivision. But if necessary, he recommended that student residences have "the general appearance of large domestic houses, and containing a respectably furnished drawing-room and dining-room for the common use of the students, together with a sufficient number of private rooms to accompany from twenty to forty lodgers."[1] It was a concept he later realized with the student houses developed from his plan for Lawrenceville School, New Jersey, in 1886.

Today virtually all of the nearly fifty fraternities and sororities provide housing for approximately 1500 students in a Greek-letter community extending along Piedmont, concentrated between Prospect Street on the east and College on the west. Also accommodating hundreds of additional students within the area are privately-owned cooperatives, residence clubs, and boarding houses, as well as the university's ten-acre Smyth Fernwald student family complex (Walter Ratcliff, Jr., 1946–1948), north of the fifty-acre Clark Kerr Campus, which was acquired in 1982.

Piedmont Avenue (Way) is a State of California Registered Historic Landmark.

59. Piedmont Houses: (2222, 2224, 2232, 2234, and 2240 Piedmont Avenue)

2222 Piedmont Avenue *Fred D. Voorhees, 1908*
2224 Piedmont Avenue *William A. Knowles, 1909*
2232 Piedmont Avenue *Julia Morgan, 1909*
2234 Piedmont Avenue *William C. Hays, 1909*
2240 Piedmont Avenue *Gwynn Officer, 1923*

The five houses fronting on the west side of Piedmont Avenue between the Haas School of Business and the Law Building provide a representative glimpse of the character of the residential neighborhood that formed near the university in the early twentieth century along Frederick Law Olmsted's parkway. A sixth house at the north end of the row at 2220 Piedmont, originally the Kappa Sigma fraternity house (William C. Hays, 1922), was used by the university for research centers and offices from 1959 until its demolition in 1992 to make room for the business school. While most of these houses have been altered, they retain elements of their original spaces and architectural detailing.

Adjacent to the business school, 2222 Piedmont was originally the home of Charles Bancroft, the brother of Hubert Howe Bancroft, the San Francisco publisher, book dealer, and historian whose book collection on western America formed the nucleus of the university's distinguished Bancroft Library, established in 1905. The oldest house on the row, it was designed by architect Fred D. Voorhees in 1908 in an English Tudor style, with wood shingles at the first floor and stucco with half-timbering above. Although the interior has been subdivided for offices, it retains the original inlaid oak flooring, paneling, and moldings, including a built-in glass china cabinet with carved Ionic columns.

2222 Piedmont Avenue

2224 Piedmont Avenue

Built the following year, 2224 Piedmont was designed by William A. Knowles for Professor Charles A. Noble, who was among a small group of distinguished faculty in the Mathematics Department during its growth years. The house is used today by the Departments of Anthropology and Demography. A two-story flat-roofed stuccoed house designed in a simplified Mission Revival style, it presents a symmetrical street elevation with two projecting first-story wings, which originally contained the living and dining rooms, flanking a recessed entrance. Tuscan columns with wood brackets support the entry porch, which opens to a central hall with original wood molding and stairway. The north wood-paneled dining room, now a seminar room, was occasionally used by Professor Noble to serve dinner to some of the Kappa Sigmas from up the street.

Also built in 1909, 2232 Piedmont was designed by Julia Morgan for Walter Y. Kellogg, manager of the California Door Company. It was later occupied by Kellogg's father-in-law, judge and community leader William Olney. The plans were prepared during the period when Morgan had a junior partner, Ira Wilson Hoover, with whom she had worked in John Galen Howard's office before forming the partnership in 1904. Along with Girton Hall (see Walk 5), the house is one of only two campus buildings that was done entirely by Morgan's office. It is occupied by the Department of Demography.

Partially hidden by trees, the two-story English Tudor–style house is finished in stucco with half-timbered framing. Wood brackets, lead-paned windows, ornamental iron railings, and a trellised rear deck distinguish the exterior. The side entry—a feature often favored by Morgan to enable placement of a full-width living room facing the street—has a segmental arch and carved wooden pediment supported by Tudor columns. The interior is finished in blue-gum woodwork, with sliding pocket doors leading from the central entry hall to the living room, which has oak flooring and a fireplace with a bracketed wood surround. A west-facing billiard room is wood-paneled with a window niche, a common Morgan feature.[2]

Constructed the same year, 2234 Piedmont was the home of Dr. B. P. Wall and was moved in 1929 from its original site across Piedmont to make room for the construction of International House. It is currently used for the Berkeley Roundtable on the International Economy and other university offices. The two-story house, designed by William C. Hays, professor of architecture and junior partner of John Galen Howard from 1904 to 1908, features distinctive wood-shingle siding in alternating horizontal broad and narrow courses.

2232 Piedmont Avenue

Programs of the School of Law occupy 2240 Piedmont, adjacent to the school at the south end of the row. Designed by Gwynn Officer for Sigma Phi fraternity, the house was built in 1923 on a site around the corner on Bancroft. The university acquired the house after the fraternity relocated to the historic Thorsen

2234 Piedmont Avenue

House at 2307 Piedmont in 1943. It was later moved to its present location to make room for construction of the Law Building in 1949.

The three-story neo-Tudor house is U-shaped in plan with two bay-windowed side wings flanking the arched entrance. The exterior is stuccoed with half-timber framing, and the steeply pitched gabled roof houses a large attic space that served as a meeting hall. The building is the best preserved of the houses on the row, and the interior is generally unaltered. Entered

2240 Piedmont Avenue

from the long entry hall, the south wing contains the original living room, now used for seminars. This space features a large cast-cement fireplace featuring the fraternity's coat of arms, decorative Gothic-arched detailing, and a Tudor-arched opening.

2222, 2224, 2232, 2234, and 2240 Piedmont Avenue are listed on the State Historic Resources Inventory.

60. International House

George W. Kelham, 1928–1930; Gardner Dailey, alterations, 1946–1947;
William Gillis, alterations, 1977–1978;
John G. Wells and HCO Architects, interior restoration 1981–1982

A prominent domed landmark at the head of Bancroft, International House is the second of thirteen worldwide centers dedicated to "the day-to-day practice of international fellowship among men and women." It is part of a movement founded by YMCA official Harry E. Edmonds, who obtained the support of John D. Rockefeller, Jr., to establish the first International House at Columbia University in New York in 1924. With the success of that East Coast center, they decided to create a West Coast counterpart in Berkeley, because of the significant number of foreign students already present and the importance of the Bay Area as the gateway to Asia.

The first Berkeley executive director, Allen C. Blaisdell, appointed in 1928, had to overcome resistance from many in the community, where attitudes were not initially receptive to racial integration, foreign residents, and the concept of a coeducational residence hall. President William W. Campbell first suggested a location on Northside, where many properties remained vacant following the fire of 1923, by for the new center, but Edmonds favored a place more central to university life. He chose the top of Bancroft, where several private homes were located, because it looked out symbolically through the Golden Gate and afforded the prospect of changing the prejudicial sentiments that were then common in the nearby fraternities and sororities.

Funded by a $1.8 million gift to the university from Rockefeller, the new center was placed under the trusteeship of the Regents but governed by an independent board. Edmonds consulted with Supervising Architect George W. Kelham on the design, which both felt should not emulate the New York building but should rather reflect the heritage of California—leading Kelham to choose a Mission and Spanish Colonial theme. Certain ideas from New York, however, such as the separation of men and women, were initially adopted, and Kelham benefited from helpful communication with the New York center's architect, Louis Jallade, an old friend. The two had studied together at the École des Beaux-Arts in Paris and began their careers in New York.

Edmonds responded favorably to Kelham's drawings for the concrete structure, reporting to President Campbell that "on the whole his conception is delightfully beautiful and charming."[3] Kelham concentrated the public spaces—the Great Hall, Auditorium, meeting rooms, soda fountain (later called Ye Olde Coffee Shop, now the International Café), and offices—along Piedmont. Flanking a central sunken patio, the dining room, and residential wings were stepped up the hill in tile-roofed gabled wings

two to six stories high, with the signature nine-story-high domed tower placed on axis with Bancroft. The original triple-arched entrance loggia, which opened to the western vista and reflected the Spanish theme of the building, was unfortunately converted to a modernist glazed corridor in a later alteration.

The Spanish-Moorish interiors of the Great Hall, auditorium, and other public spaces were originally decorated by W & J Sloane of San Francisco and restored at a later time. In 1943, residents were relocated to five vacant fraternity houses, so that

International House

Great Hall, International House

the building could be occupied by up to 900 Navy and Marine trainees. For the next three years, the building was temporarily renamed Callaghan Hall, in honor of Admiral Daniel J. Callaghan, who died on the bridge of the USS *San Francisco* during the Battle of the Solomon Islands (Admiral Callaghan's name was transferred in 1947 to a wooden Naval ROTC building and to a subsequent replacement building, which both stood on the present site of the university's Hazardous Materials Facility near the Evans Baseball Diamond). But the Great Hall's ornamental plaster beams and hand-painted ceilings were painted white during this World War II period

Great Hall beams, International House

and covered and partially destroyed in a postwar remodeling. Four decades later, the decorative ceiling was structurally rebuilt and restored by architect John Wells and HCO Architects of San Francisco. Artist Edward Bates studied historic photographs and created new templates of floral patterns, which were finished with gold-leafing and grained to resemble wood. This ceiling, along with ornamental woodcarving, metal work, and stone mantles, was originally modeled by artist Paul E. Denneville, who also had worked with Kelham on buildings of the 1915 Panama-Pacific International Exposition in San Francisco.

I-House (as it is often called) opened in August 1930 with facilities for 338 men and 115 women, with "splendidly furnished" rooms priced at

$14 to $25 per month. The week before, the building was appropriately inaugurated with an eight-day conference of the sixth Institute of International Relations, attended by government leaders, economists, and international affairs experts from around the world.

California Governors Edmund "Jerry" Brown, Jr., and Pete Wilson, California Supreme Court Chief Justice Rose Elizabeth Bird, five Nobel Laureates, ambassadors from several countries—these are among the prominent individuals of the 50,000 Berkeley I-House alumni, who have represented over 100 countries and thirty states. Today approximately 600 students, half from foreign nations and half from the United States, live in I-House with the cross-cultural spirit established by Harry Edmonds in the 1920s and expressed on the building's engraved dedication plaque: "the Promotion of Understanding and Fellowship among the Peoples of all Nations."

International House is listed on the State Historic Resources Inventory.

61. Thorsen House (2307 Piedmont Avenue) and 2395 Piedmont Avenue

Thorsen House *Charles Sumner Greene and Henry Mather Greene, 1908–1909*
2395 Piedmont Avenue *Frederick Reimers, 1928*

One of the most distinctive houses in the Piedmont neighborhood is the former Thorsen House at 2307 Piedmont, the only East Bay work of brothers Charles Sumner Greene and Henry Mather Greene. The home was completed in 1909 for lumberman William R. Thorsen, whose wife was inspired

Thorsen House, 2307 Piedmont Avenue

by a house the Greene brothers designed for her sister in Pasadena, where many of their buildings were concentrated. The architects' expression of the Arts and Crafts Movement was harmonious with Bay Regionalists but elevated to a fine degree of detail. Like a habitable piece of furniture, the house exhibits the mortise-and-tenon joinery and handcrafted woodwork that are hallmarks of their work. Set on a clinker-brick foundation integrally designed with exterior stair and garden walls, the gabled brown-shingle house also shows the brothers' admiration for Japanese motifs, evident in framing and balcony detailing. The elegance is carried throughout the interior, with crafted wood detailing and custom light fixtures of Tiffany glass. Sigma Phi fraternity has occupied the house since 1943.

A later contributor to the elegance of the Piedmont parkway is the Phi Gamma Delta fraternity house at 2395 Piedmont (originally the home of Sigma Pi fraternity and for a time leased to Sigma Phi Epsilon fraternity), completed in 1928. Prominently sited at the northeast corner of the Channing Circle intersection, the brick-veneer house was designed by architect and 1915 graduate Frederick Reimers. The L-shaped two-story Italian Renaissance Revival building has a red-tile hipped roof and is oriented to the circle with a graceful double stairway flanked by a classical balustrade at the front terrace. The prominent entrance at the elbow of the two wings is framed by a wide rusticated archway and surmounted by a triple-arched window at the second floor.

The Thorsen House, 2307 Piedmont, is listed on the National Register of Historic Places and is a City of Berkeley Landmark. 2395 Piedmont is a City of Berkeley Landmark.

2395 Piedmont Avenue

Gingko Court, Clark Kerr Campus

62. Clark Kerr Campus (2601 Warring Street)

Office of the State Architect (primarily Alfred Eichler), Charles F. B. Roeth, and Langhorst/Kirby/Mulvin, 1922–1962;

E. Paul Kelly, Hunt and Company, Hansen Associates, George Matsumoto, Wong and Brocchini, Hansen/Murakami/Eshima, The Ratcliff Architects, restoration and interior alterations for University of California, 1982–1984

Located approximately six blocks southeast of the central campus, the Clark Kerr Campus is a twenty-five-building coed residential complex that houses 825 students. In addition to its eleven residential buildings, the fifty-acre campus includes dining, recreation, child-care and conference centers, two faculty apartment buildings, and three storage buildings. It is named in honor of the first Berkeley Chancellor (1952–1957) and twelfth president of the university (1958–1967).

Prior to its use by the university, the site was an established landmark, occupied for nearly 115 years by the California Schools for the Deaf and Blind and its two predecessor institutions. Partly because of its proximity to the new university campus, it was originally developed as the home of the State Asylum for the Deaf, Dumb and Blind, which opened in 1869. In 1905 the asylum became the California Institution of the Deaf and Dumb, and Blind, until 1921 when it changed to two institutions as the California Schools for the Deaf and Blind. The university acquired the site in 1982, two years after the schools relocated to Fremont in southern Alameda County.

Situated on Warring Street between Dwight Way and Derby Street, the institution formed the southern anchor to Frederick Law Olmsted's Piedmont parkway that linked to the university grounds. Built on former farmland, it was housed originally in a large west-facing Gothic-spired building (1867–1869) designed by San Francisco architects John Wright and George H. Sanders, the same firm that prepared but withdrew a plan for the university in 1869. When that edifice burned in 1875, Wright and Sanders prepared a new plan and designed a complex of separate Romanesque Revival buildings constructed during the 1880s and 1890s, dominated by a central Education Building at the head of an entrance driveway from Warring. When the two schools were separated in 1921, the site was roughly demarcated with the northern two-thirds for the School for the Deaf and southern one-third the School for the Blind.[4]

In 1929 the Office of the State Architect recommended that the older buildings were no longer functional for the needs of the two schools and should be removed and replaced with a new complex of buildings. A new campus plan was prepared, possibly by architect Alfred Eichler and slightly modified in 1933 by Oakland architect Charles F. B. Roeth. The new plan provided a more compact arrangement of buildings than the more scattered layout of Wright and Sanders, in order to facilitate student super-vision and have covered connections between buildings. The linked build-ings were arranged around courtyards with loggias and designed, generally by Eichler and Roeth, in a Spanish Colonial Revival style, with some Moderne influences. The architects used exposed concrete construction, patterned by wooden forms and painted white, with red-tile roofs to convey the desired image. The use of towers, balconies, star and circular grilled windows, and other elements provided detail in the Spanish theme.

Among the most important of these buildings are three designed by Roeth and constructed in 1931. The Great Hall Dining Room (Building 9) is a two-story-high concrete-arched space with decorative metal chandeliers and high circular windows at the end gables. Wood-paneled wainscot lines the peripheral walls, and French doors open to an enclosed southern court-yard. The north loggia was planned with the original design but not con-structed until 1950. The space and its adjoining food service area were restored and renovated by John G. Wells of San Francisco architects Hunt and Company in 1983.

The two most prominent buildings seen from Warring are adjoining Buildings 11 and 14, which together define the south side of the main entrance driveway and forecourt. Building 11, a wing of residential suites, conveys the Spanish theme with its use of tile, grilled windows, and other detailing. Building 14 contains the Clark Kerr Campus Center, which includes the Joseph Wood Krutch Theatre (originally the D'Estrella Assembly Hall) and four classroom-conference rooms. The theatre, which can seat up to 375

Great Hall Dining Room, Clark Kerr Campus

people, features an arched simulated wood ceiling, wood-paneled wainscot, and hardwood floor. Its Art Deco redwood sculpted panels, commissioned by the Federal Arts Project, were created by sculptor Sargent Johnson and installed in 1937. San Francisco architect George Matsumoto restored and renovated this theatre and conference center in 1983.

Additional buildings were constructed following World War II, designed primarily by Eichler, who also abandoned the rectilinear cloistered theme in favor of obliquely sited buildings in the northwest part of the site (Buildings 2 and 4). The change in plan altered the definition of the entrance forecourt, without the enclosing north wing intended by Roeth to balance the wing on the south.

Additional historic restoration and alterations by several architects were completed in the early 1980s for the university's reuse of the complex. The $14 million project was financed by funds from the university's housing and parking operations.

The Clark Kerr Campus is listed on the National Register of Historic Places and the State Historic Resources Inventory, and is a City of Berkeley Landmark.

Southside

Columns, First Church of Christ, Scientist

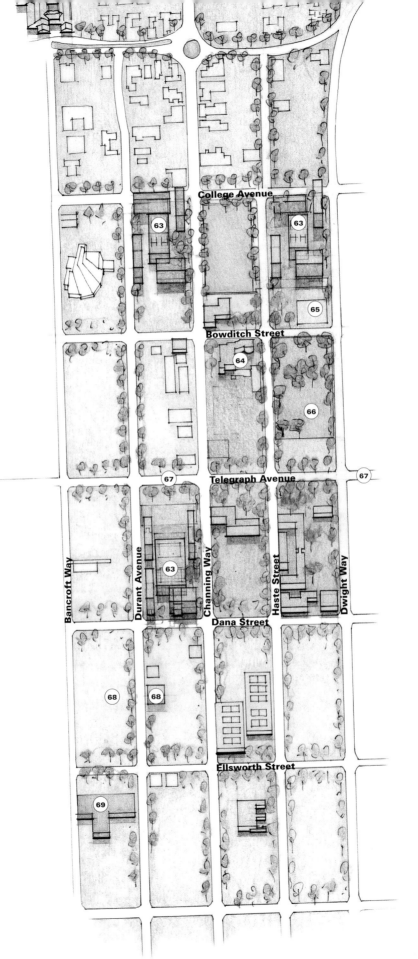

College Avenue

63

63

65

Bowditch Street

64

66

Bancroft Way

Durant Avenue

Channing Way

Haste Street

Dwight Way

67

Telegraph Avenue

67

63

Dana Street

68

68

Ellsworth Street

69

Southside is a vibrant, eclectic, and densely populated center of student life, social activism, and commerce admixed with the traditions embodied in the historic homes, churches, clubs, and other buildings that have dignified the neighborhood for more than a century. It is an area of intellectual energy and but also conflict that often tests the durability of town-gown relations.

Extending from the Bancroft edge of campus to Dwight Way between College Avenue and Fulton Street, this Walk encompasses the College Homestead Association Tract that was subdivided and recorded by the trustees of the College of California in 1866. The trustees intended to establish a respectable college town and use the profits from lot sales in the tract to help finance the development of new college buildings on their land between the forks of Strawberry Creek. Arranged in a standard grid pattern, the one-acre home lots were approximately 150 feet wide by 300 feet deep, large enough to accommodate stables and other auxiliary buildings that would be needed in the sparsely populated rural area. Durant Avenue and Haste Street were not then delineated, so that the blocks were twice the width of those today.

The street names, adopted by the trustees before selecting a town name, still reflect the idealism of their academic mission and desire to dignify the subdivision they hoped would attract buyers of intellect and refinement. They chose thirteen names each of American men of science for north-south streets and men of letters for east-west ways arranged in alphabetical order. Of these only twelve were actually used within the limits of the tract boundaries. Audubon, Bowditch, Choate, Dana, Ellsworth, Fulton, Guyot, and Henry formed the north-south streets, while the east-west ways were named Allston, Bancroft, Channing, and Dwight. College and Telegraph Avenues replaced Audubon and Choate in 1890, in order to match the names of those streets extending into Oakland, while pioneer businessman and civic leader Francis K. Shattuck was later honored for the main downtown street instead of the naturalist Guyot.[1]

The Southside began to develop shortly after the university opened in 1873. The Telegraph commercial area grew from a small rooming house, hotel, restaurant, and grocery store that catered to student and faculty needs at the corner of Bancroft and Choate, along the route of a horse-drawn streetcar that connected the campus to Oakland. As the university gained in reputation and enrollment, the area became more populated and characterized by fine residences, such as the Colonial-Revival McCreary-Greer House at 2318 Durant. Elementary schools and college preparatory institutions, such as the shingled Anna Head School (Soule Edgar Fisher, 1892), at Channing and Bowditch, were also attracted to the neighborhood.

Additionally, a number of churches were drawn to the area, which was subject to a law prohibiting saloons and alcohol sales within a mile of the university. The university—which was imbued with the moral principles the Protestant founders of the College of California advocated, and whose faculty were often active parishioners—received the congregations warmly. The church presence still strongly characterizes Southside. The First Congregational Church of Berkeley, founded in 1874, was the first to take root. Its Colonial Revival brick church (Horace Simpson, 1924) on Dana between Durant and Channing replaced one designed by Clinton Day in 1884. Anchoring Durant across the street is the Gothic Revival tower of Trinity United Methodist Church (George Rushforth, 1928). And nearby, at the southeast corner of Dana and

St. Mark's Episcopal Church

Channing, is the modernist sunken First Presbyterian Church (William Duquette, 1973), which replaced a Romanesque Revival edifice (Charles W. Dickey, 1907) that was a landmark for seven decades. Another familiar bell tower still standing at the northeast corner of Bancroft and Ellsworth belongs to domed Saint Mark's Episcopal Church (William Curlett, 1902), founded in 1877. One of the earliest Mission Revival–style buildings in Berkeley, it features Tiffany stained-glass windows in its nave. The most distinguished feature of Southside is Bernard Maybeck's masterpiece and National Landmark, the First Church of Christ, Scientist (1910–1912, addition with Henry H. Gutterson, 1927–1929) at the northeast corner of Dwight and Bowditch.

Another Maybeck building, the shingled Town and Gown Club (1899) at Dwight and Dana, designed in the mode of the Bay Tradition, was one of a number of women's clubs that first developed around the turn of the century and contributed to the cultural development of the Southside community. The most prominent of these is Julia Morgan's Berkeley City Club (originally Berkeley Women's City Club), a Gothic-Romanesque tower at 2315 Durant that opened in 1930. The same period produced the College Women's Club, now the twenty-two-room Bancroft Hotel, at 2680 Bancroft. Completed in 1928, the Mediterranean-style building was designed by Walter T. Steilberg, a former associate of Morgan, and—like Morgan's club—it is listed on the National Register of Historic Places. It stands a short distance east of Mario J. Ciampi's innovative modernist concrete structure (1970) that houses the university's Berkeley Art Museum and Pacific Film Archive (see Walk 5).

Also offering Southside accommodations, the 140-room Hotel Durant has been a fixture at Durant and Bowditch since 1928. The six-story hotel is the largest in Berkeley and was designed by San Francisco architect William H. Weeks in reinforced concrete with Mediterranean Revival–style detailing. Further west is the Beau Sky Hotel at 2520 Durant (Shea & Lofquist), a wood-frame building with modest classical detailing on its front porch and facade. Originally one of the early rooming houses for university students, it opened for women residents in 1911 as The Brasfield and later housed men students as Stratford Hall. Such rooming houses served students who would have otherwise commuted from San Francisco and other areas, and contributed to the conversion of Southside from a family-based to student neighborhood.

University expansion following World War II profoundly reshaped the neighborhood. A policy established by the Regents to provide university housing for twenty-five percent of the student body led to an ambitious property-acquisition program that included the purchase of over thirty acres in the Southside—land that ironically was once part of the original College Homestead Association Tract. Private land owners insecure about university plans neglected the upkeep of their properties, and the university drew criticism as a "slum landlord" for not maintaining properties it had already acquired and sublet while assembling parcels.[2] Blocks of homes were eventually cleared to build the three high-rise residence hall complexes (Warnecke & Warnecke, and John Carl Warnecke and Associates) in the early 1960s, as well as parking structures and recreational facilities. But when financial conditions prevented completion of the development program, already cleared land blighted the community and led to the establishment of People's Park and the associated aftermath of events and social problems that still impact the area today (see People's Park and Telegraph Avenue).

The transformation of Southside to a student neighborhood—approximately 9,000 of the area's 11,000 residents, including the Greek-letter community along Piedmont, are students—has resulted in a transient and less stable population than the families who originally settled the area. The number of student residents is projected to increase with additional infill housing and dining facilities, planned to enhance the social and physical environment of the area.

Residence Halls, Unit 1

63. Residence Halls, Units 1, 2, and 3

Unit 1 (2650 Durant Avenue)

> *Warnecke & Warnecke, with Lawrence Halprin, landscape architect, 1958–1959;*
> *Sandy & Babcock, alterations, 1993–1994*

Unit 2 (2650 Haste Street)

> *Warnecke & Warnecke, with Lawrence Halprin, landscape architect, 1958–1960;*
> *Sandy & Babcock, alterations, 1995–1996*

Unit 3 (2400 Durant Avenue)

> *John Carl Warnecke and Associates, with Lawrence Halprin, landscape architect,*
> *1961–1964;*
> *Gordon H. Chong & Associates, alterations, 1986–1988*

The three complexes of high-rise residence halls in the Southside provide housing for up to 3,100 undergraduates. They were developed in response to the enrollment growth that followed World War II and a Regents' policy established in 1945 to provide university-operated housing for twenty-five percent of the student body. To meet the need the university undertook an ambitious land acquisition program, especially in the Southside, where the university planned to develop six residence hall complexes to accommodate 4,800 students.

Only three complexes—financed by federal loans, university housing revenues, a state grant, and a private donation—would eventually be constructed, beginning with Units 1 and 2 just west of College; Unit 3 financing included a state grant and a $550,000 gift bequeathed by Sally McKee Spens-Black, daughter of Regent Samuel Bell McKee (1868–1883) and for whom one of the Unit 3 towers was named. To select an architect and design scheme, five Bay Area and two southern California architectural firms were invited to participate in a competition in 1956, the first conducted for Berkeley since the international competition for the Hearst Plan in 1897. The competitors were asked to design a complex of four self-contained buildings to house 800 students on College between Durant and Channing, the Unit 1 site. Centralized facilities, including a recreation room, administrative and support functions, and a kitchen with four dining rooms arranged in two pairs, were also to be provided.

The winning firm of San Francisco and Oakland architects Carl I. Warnecke and John Carl Warnecke sought to attain three goals: "a sense of enclosed free space within the building group, a plan that would not hamper the future campus development, and a sense of variety and spatial movement while still achieving the required identical units."[3] Their plan reflected the influence of Walter Gropius and other modernists in the use of high-rise structures to conserve open space. The complex—repeated at Unit 2—featured four nine-story concrete-frame towers placed at the corners of the site, with a central two-story commons building linked to the towers by covered-trellis walkways and landscaped courtyards. Pagoda-style parabolic roofs were used to distinguish the dining rooms, whose relationship to the courtyards was intended to emphasize an indoor-outdoor lifestyle. This feature, along with the Asian influence of the roof forms and the use of trellises, reflected the architects' intent "to retain the character of the Bay Area tradition of architecture, which had its origin in the City of Berkeley, and of which there are still outstanding examples, in the work of Bernard Maybeck."[4]

Completion of the first two units, along with an addition to Stern Hall (see Walk 6), increased the number of students housed in university residence halls to about 12.5% of the enrollment. With the housing shortage still critical Unit 3 was rushed ahead. Although another architectural firm had been appointed, the need to accelerate the housing program and take advantage of federal financing caused the Regents to recommend re-use of the Warnecke & Warnecke plans for Unit 3, and appoint John Carl Warnecke and Associates (the successor firm) as architect. However, the reused plans were modified to take advantage of suggestions from the residents of Units 1 and 2 and make other cost-related design changes. Small random windows were used at the bathroom areas instead of the decorative screens used in the older units. And to reduce the glare and heat build-up experienced in the first towers, the window openings were reduced, with concrete-finish spandrels used instead of colored metal panels. In the central commons building, the distinctive pagoda roof of the dining commons was replaced with a flat roof with ornamental copper facing.

Renovations in the 1980s and 1990s included the addition of concrete bases and steel X-braces to strengthen the towers in Units 1 and 2. Planned changes to Units 1 and 2 include construction of additional peripheral housing between the towers and replacement of the central commons buildings with courtyards, following the construction of a new central dining facility at Channing and Bowditch.

Residence Halls Units 1 and 2 are City of Berkeley Landmarks.

64. Anna Head Complex (2536–2538 Channing Way)

Soule Edgar Fisher, 1892; Walter H. Ratcliff, Jr., 1911–1927

The former Anna Head School is a notable example of the American Arts and Crafts Movement and of the preparatory schools that developed near the university in the late nineteenth century. It was established as Miss Head's School for Girls in 1887 by Anna Head, whose mother had operated a French and English school. First located at Channing and Dana, the school moved to its present site in 1892.

In 1909 Anna Head sold the school to the head of its English Department, Mary Elizabeth Wilson, who ten years later changed the name to Anna Head School. When the complex was purchased by the university in 1964, the school moved to Oakland,

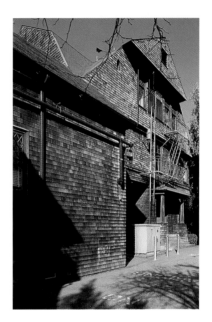

Anna Head Complex

where it merged with a boys school and continues to operate today as a co-ed college preparatory institution, the Head-Royce School.

The first building, Channing Hall (2438 Channing), designed by Anna Head's cousin, architect Soule Edgar Fisher, is believed to be the first brown-shingle structure in Berkeley. Designed in the genre of the emerging Arts and Crafts period, it is sometimes compared to the East Coast shingled work of McKim, Mead and White. The gambrel-roofed hall, with its prominent dormers, eyebrow sunshades, projecting bays, and stone-pillared porch, evoked the response that it seemed less like a school building and "rather a quaint old English country house or private mansion," as one newspaper termed it. That perception was appropriate, as the school was set in a cultivated garden with tree-sheltered glades, flowerbeds, a bird fountain, and ornamental hedges and palms.

The immaculate interior of the hall featured decorative rugs on wood floors, and dark-stained wood wainscoting and staircase, and cornices that complemented plaster walls and ceilings. Described as "the center of home life of the school," the building contained a parlor where lectures and concerts were given, as well as library, dining room, sleeping porches, infirmary, and classrooms.

Following Fisher's death, buildings added between 1895 and 1901 may have been constructed by John B. Sprague, the contractor of Fisher's Channing Hall. Subsequent buildings and additions were completed between 1911 and 1927 by architect Walter H. Ratcliff, Jr., who was among the first students taught by John Galen Howard at the university and who worked for both Howard and Bernard Maybeck before opening his own office in 1908.

By 1927 the school consisted of six principal buildings, as well as smaller structures and additions. Channing Hall was connected by a large second-floor sleeping porch to a building along Bowditch called The Gables, which also contained offices, a bookstore, and classrooms. This building opened onto the Quadrangle defined on its west by one of the Ratcliff-designed buildings, which included classrooms, an art studio, and study hall. The gabled rectangular building included a shed-roofed Tuscan-colonnaded cloister that continued along the other buildings to enclose the open yard. Originally used for class assemblies and recreation, this space now functions as a parking and service yard. The adjacent Ratcliff-designed Alumnae Hall along Haste Street included an auditorium, supported by decorated trusses, with a fully equipped stage and capacity for seating 600 students. The complex also included "The Cottage," containing a chemistry laboratory and music room; an indoor swimming pool; and a large fireplace-appointed room used for eurhythmics classes, singing rehearsals, and club meetings.

In its long Berkeley history, the Anna Head School upheld a standard for "earnest, honest work, and all that tends towards cultured, upright womanhood," and produced a number of notable graduates. Among them were tennis champions Helen Wills Moody and Helen Jacobs, artist and conservationist Margaret Wentworth Owings, art critic Miriam Dungan Gross, educator Mary Woods Bennet, war correspondent Marguerite Higgins, photojournalist Margaret Jennings, and the daughter of naturalist John Muir.[5]

The ambience the complex once displayed as a "cheerful, homelike school with outdoor life the year 'round," has deteriorated over the past forty years, with parking lots and temporary trailers displacing the lush gardens. The buildings, once considered by the university as expendables, presently house research centers, a child-care center, and offices.

The former Anna Head School complex is listed on the National Register of Historic Places and the State Historic Resources Inventory, and is a City of Berkeley Landmark.

First Church of Christ, Scientist

65. First Church of Christ, Scientist (2619 Dwight Way)

Bernard Maybeck, 1910–1912; addition with Henry H. Gutterson, 1927–1929

The acknowledged masterpiece of Bernard Maybeck, the First Church of Christ, Scientist is the only National Landmark in the City of Berkeley. It is a remarkable harmonious composition of proportioned space, light, and structure sculpted in an imaginative combination of natural and industrial materials. Incorporating eclectic influences—Byzantine, Romanesque, Gothic, and Japanese—Maybeck selected his palette of materials to create an honest building reflecting his client's sincerity and express a feeling of religious permanence.[6]

The building consists of two parts, a 700-seat church, completed in 1912, connected to a Sunday School on the east, added seventeen years later. The square cross-axial church hall is spanned diagonally by four six-foot-deep wooden trusses that are paired to form a Greek cross and are supported by four hollow reinforced-concrete piers, which also serve as ventilation ducts. The exposed roof structure enriches the space with its carved bracketing and Gothic tracery and use of color and stenciled ornamentation. The periphery of the main space is of post-and-beam construction and is illuminated with windows of industrial steel sash with imported translucent Belgian glass. The custom-designed interior includes steeled-brass chandeliers, red-cushioned oak pews, cast-concrete readers' desks, and modeled and carved detailing. The adjacent school, an expansion of the original school wing, was designed by Maybeck in association with Henry

H. Gutterson, who earlier in his career worked for John Galen Howard and was a member of the congregation.

The exterior of the building expresses the cross axes with shallow-pitched gabled roofs overhanging windows of Gothic tracery. Entrance porches and redwood-trellised pergolas are supported by square fluted concrete columns with capitals modeled with hooded medieval figures. A hanging lantern at the entrance porch was fashioned of hammered iron, as if it had just been forged by some medieval artisan. But for the walls Maybeck turned to the Industrial Age, using gray cement-asbestos board (Transite) panels secured through red diamond-shaped pieces of the same material. His imaginative and unorthodox use of this material and the industrial-sash windows required some negotiation with the manufacturers, who were unaccustomed to their use for a church building.[7]

The wisteria vines that drape the windows each spring with purple blossoms are part of the original landscaping planned by Maybeck and an example of the dominant presence of nature he often incorporated into his designs. The building was originally roofed with standing-seam tin-clad sheet iron, rather than the red mission tiles presently used.

Maybeck's artful mastery of these elements created a building that engages the visitor in a unique spatial experience and leaves a lasting impression of awe and admiration. "His church," observed Maybeck historian Kenneth H. Cardwell, "makes man its measure and reflects the humanistic qualities of the religion it shelters."[8]

The First Church of Christ, Scientist is a National Landmark and a City of Berkeley Landmark. The church conducts free public tours on the first Sunday of every month beginning at 12:15pm. Phone 510-845-7199.

66. People's Park *1969*

Long a symbol of anarchy to the university and social revolution to park activists, the 2.8-acre plot of green bordered by Haste, Bowditch, and Dwight bears the legacy of the most violent confrontation in the history of the university and the City of Berkeley.

The former residential tract was included in the university's forty-five-acre postwar acquisition program that the Regents adopted in 1956. Planned as the site of the Unit 4 Residence Halls, one of six proposed high-rise complexes in the Southside (of which only Units 1, 2 and 3 were built), the land was purchased in 1967–1968 and cleared of its homes and apartment buildings. But the university postponed construction of the 850-bed complex for financial reasons related to changing market conditions and a reduced demand for student housing.

While the university sought funds to develop the land for interim recreational use until viable student housing could be built, the blighted property was informally utilized as an unmanaged parking lot. But in April 1969 it was claimed as a "People's Park" and occupied by a group described in the *California Monthly* at the time as "local hippies, radicals, and students." They were urged on by an advertisement in an underground newspaper calling for the conversion of the property into "a cultural, political freak-out and rap center for the Western world." In an attempt to resolve the situation, Chancellor Roger Heyns met with representatives of a park committee, the Associated Students, and the College of Environmental Design, and discussed a park plan proposed by Architecture Professor Sim Van der Ryn. But it was a period of high social tension. Anti–Vietnam War protests were common, and only two months earlier a strike led by the Third World Liberation Front resulted in Governor Ronald Reagan declaring a state of extreme emergency and ordering National Guard troops to intervene and tear gas to be dropped on Sproul Plaza.

Still operating under those emergency conditions, in the predawn hours of May 15—a date that would become known as "Bloody Thursday"—the university erected a chain-link fence around the property. At noon a rally held on Sproul Plaza led to a march by thousands of people to the fenced site. When police barricades were confronted, the situation quickly turned hostile, and the Southside erupted into riotous street battles. That night, at the city's request, Governor Reagan called in National Guard troops and three battalions of the 49th Infantry Brigade. Curfew was established and public assembly banned. Berkeley became an occupied city. The violence and martial law continued during the next two weeks; rallies and marches were broken up, assemblies of people tear-gassed by police and National Guard helicopters, and masses arrested. In the end, one person was killed, 128 injured, and hundreds more arrested.

People's Park

Near the end of the conflict, the Academic Senate overwhelmingly passed a resolution demanding that the fence be taken down and the police and military troops removed. About the same time, in the university's largest student referendum, approximately 13,000 of 15,000 students voted in favor of maintaining a park on the site. Recreation courts and a small parking lot were built, but the fence remained in place until May 1972, when—following an announcement by President Richard Nixon that Haiphong Harbor had been mined—a crowd of some 300 people rioted on Telegraph and tore down the fence.

In the early 1970s the university considered several options for the site, the most serious being the development of married student housing, which proved not to be economically viable. Some community gardening was permitted on the property, but it also became a haven for homeless people and the scene of drug dealing and other crimes, activities that continue to be problems to the present day.

A residence hall and dining facility were proposed on a portion of the site in April 1989, when the university was drafting its 1990 Long Range Development Plan, but following community resistance, the site was designated for recreation use in the final plan. In 1991 the Board of Regents and Berkeley City Council approved an accord linked to the 1990 Plan that was signed by Chancellor Ira Michael Heyman and Mayor Loni Hancock to establish shared control of the park for a five-year period. The university leased the east and west portions to the city and maintained control over the central portion for some recreational uses. But when the university proceeded to construct sand volleyball courts and a basketball court, twelve days of conflict followed with some 600 demonstrators rioting and looting Telegraph, resulting in over 200 arrests. Five and one-half years later the volleyball courts, subjected to vandalism and underutilized, were removed by the university.

In April 2000 another student referendum resulted in a narrow majority favoring continued use of the site as a park. The user-developed park has a native-plant garden on the east portion, vegetable and flower gardens on the west, and a central area of lawn and recreation courts.

People's Park is a City of Berkeley Landmark.

67. Telegraph Avenue

Bisecting the former College Homestead Association Tract, the northern end of Telegraph, between Bancroft and Dwight, is a lively concentration of diverse businesses that form the primary commercial district of the university. Surrounded by the densest residential community in the city, the four-block area, including businesses along Bancroft and other adjoining streets, generates the second highest sales in the city.

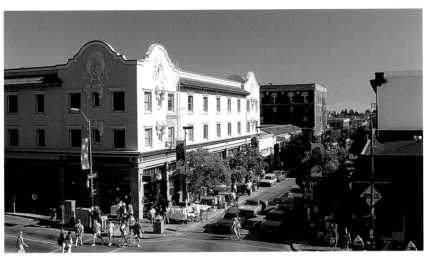

Granada Building (left) and Cambridge Building (right), east side of Telegraph Avenue

Sequoia Palazzo, and Medico-Dental Buildings (left to right), west side of Telegraph between Haste and Channing

Many of Telegraph's buildings date from the early twentieth century, when the avenue developed as a commercial street. Their facades provide a view of "Main Street" that is still to be appreciated despite later modernization. The Granada Building (1905; Robert Walker, restoration, 1995) anchors the Bancroft corner across from Sproul Hall, its Mission Revival–style curvilinear gables forming a distinctive gateway to the avenue. Across the street is the clinker brick–faced Hotel Carleton (Meyers & Ward, 1906; Charles Kahn, restoration, 1998), and at the southeast corner of Durant, The Cambridge, designed by Walter Ratcliff, Jr. (1914). The west

Telegraph Avenue, site of Sproul Hall, looking north to Sather Gate, 1938

side of the next block between Channing and Haste is well preserved with three four-to-five-story buildings, beginning with the Medico-Dental Building (O'Brien Brothers, 1923) at the corner of Channing. The Palazzo (Clay N. Burrell, 1920), with its bracketed cornice, stands at mid-block, next to The Sequoia (Richardson & Beverell, 1916) at Haste, distinguished by its polychromatic brick facade and ornamented cornice.

The Granada Building did not always mark the entrance to Telegraph, which extended one block north to Sather Gate until King Student Union and Chavez Student Center were constructed along with Sproul Plaza in 1959–1961 (Hardison and DeMars, with Lawrence Halprin, landscape architect, see Walk 4). The businesses on the east side of that block had been removed nearly twenty years earlier for the construction of Arthur Brown's Sproul Hall in 1940–1941 (see Walk 4).

The avenue had two-way traffic and streetcar tracks before then, when its shops reflected their close ties to the university. Opposite Sather Gate was the Students Inn, an eatery that declared itself "First in Sight, First in Excellence." Lank's Lunchery was "where the California Bear ties on the feed bag," while the Varsity Candy Shop served as both confectionery and restaurant. The Golden Bear lunch counter was next door to the Co-ed Shoppe, which provided "marcel and water waving, shampooing, facial and scalp treatments, and manicuring." The Cosy Cafeteria promised "Strictly Home Cooking," while Dad's was the place to go "for milkshakes, candies, smokes, billiards, [and] pool."

Marcel waving has now given way to body piercing and tattooing. Internationally renowned Cody's Books and Moe's Books and some eight other booksellers have continued the legacy of the Sather Gate Book Shop, once a Telegraph landmark. And the "luncheries" of old have been replaced by Blake's Bar Restaurant & Night Club, Café Mediterraneum, and sixty other multicultural restaurants, cafes, coffee houses, and food outlets that now serve the community. They are joined by some eight popular music stores, thirty clothing and accessories shops, fifteen hair stylists, and another seventy businesses offering art supplies, cards, electronics, flowers, eyeglasses, baked goods, gifts, and a variety of other goods and services.

While the Telegraph of the 1930s was characterized by Bohemian student hangouts, with the 1960s came a new activism and counterculture presence. Militants, hippies, and transients moved into the Southside, and their anger was often vented along Telegraph. Anti-establishment protests led to the riots over People's Park and other issues, which left broken store windows an all too familiar sight. Some of this revolutionary history is depicted in mural art near the corner of Haste and Telegraph. Many merchants reacted to the riots by building new facades or installing shutters that gave their storefronts a bunker-like appearance that is still in evidence today. Their defensive efforts were not in vain, as recurring rioting and looting have continued to occasionally plague the avenue, often as the result of wanton civil disobedience.

Crime and drug problems, panhandling, and the plight of people who are homeless, distressed, or mentally ill have often made the Telegraph experience a challenge and adventure. But efforts by the university and the city to improve the area have helped to clean up the avenue, provide assistance to those in need, and discourage anti-social behavior. On most days the sidewalks are lined with the stands of street vendors and artists that transform the avenue into a lively bazaar of handmade pottery, jewelry, clothing, candles, and other crafts. This outdoor market expands for two weeks each December for the annual Holiday Christmas Fair. And for special events, such as the World Music Festival, streets are closed off and the avenue converted to a pedestrian mall. Such events, as well as the unique array of merchandise and food offered throughout the year, have made Telegraph—despite its lingering social problems—a regional attraction and commercial success.

68. Berkeley City Club (2315 Durant Avenue) and McCreary-Greer House (2318 Durant Avenue)

Berkeley City Club (2315 Durant Avenue) *Julia Morgan, 1929–1930*
McCreary-Greer House (2318 Durant Avenue) *1901*

Berkeley City Club

Designed during Julia Morgan's long tenure as architect for William Randolph Hearst's hilltop castle at San Simeon, the Berkeley Women's City Club—as it was initially called—was often nicknamed Morgan's "little castle." Though smaller and far less opulent than Hearst's edifice, the reference is understandable, as the club's medieval style and massing give it an imposing bearing in the Southside. The freedom of Morgan's creative expression at San Simeon may also have influenced her design for the club, especially in its exciting public spaces and the quality of its decorative details by some of the same skilled craftsmen who worked on the castle.[9]

When commissioned by the club in 1929, Morgan also had an established reputation as the designer of several independent women's clubs, as well as YWCA facilities, and gymnasia, including her collaboration with Bernard Maybeck on Hearst Gymnasium, completed just two years earlier (see Walk 5). Morgan, who was a club member, extended her creativity beyond the architecture, designing the light fixtures, furnishings, linens, and even club china using motifs borrowed from a member's Spanish rug.

The six-story reinforced-concrete building consists of a residential tower atop a two-story base that forms flanking east and west wings. Two planted interior courtyards serve as outdoor lounges and bring natural light into the public spaces, which are linked by vaulted lobbies, lounges, and corridors. The two public floors are connected by a main staircase flanked by carved shield-bearing crouching lions, which resemble ones used at San Simeon. Quatrefoil motifs, tracery, and diamond-paned windows contribute to the medieval atmosphere of the Gothic-Romanesque building, which received close attention from Morgan in every area. The seventy-five-foot-long swimming pool, for example, was placed under great spanning Tudor arches that form bays with triple-arched windows providing a garden outlook. This turquoise-tiled "plunge" was meant to be central to club activities and includes a spectator gallery and adjacent dressing room. On the second floor above the pool and sheltered from the west wind by the tower is an awning-covered garden terrace intended as "a favorite place for tea or chat" and now used for open-air meetings. Adjacent to the terrace are the members lounge and the auditorium, which includes a full stage.

The ornamented main entry has a multifoil arch flanked by fluted pilasters, while ornamental quatrefoils and double- and triple-arched windows are featured throughout the building's asymmetrical facade. The tower, which is defined by corner buttresses and features corbeled arches at the top floor, contains forty residential rooms and suites with dramatic views of the Bay, campus, or hills.

The Berkeley City Club is a California Registered Historical Landmark and a City of Berkeley Landmark. Accommodations are provided to club members as well as visitors, and club facilities are used for meetings and special events. Phone 510-848-7800.

McCreary-Greer House (2318 Durant Avenue)

McCreary-Greer House

Across the street from Julia Morgan's "little castle" is the McCreary-Greer House, which contains the office of the Berkeley Architectural Heritage Association (BAHA), a 1,500-member non-profit preservation organization founded in 1974. The Colonial Revival house was completed in 1901 and purchased in 1907 by oilman J. Edward McCreary. It was occupied by his family and descendants until 1961, when it was sold to Ruth Alice Greer, a resident of the neighborhood and a member of the staff of the university's Education Department. In the interest of preservation, she donated the house to BAHA in 1986.[10]

The wood-frame, hipped-roof house has a distinctive concave-shaped front porch supported by carved Ionic columns. Additional classical detailing, including balustrades, pedimented attic dormers, an oval bull's-eye window, corner Ionic pilasters, and entablature, provide a sense of dignity to the house, which is sheathed in horizontal shiplap siding.

The main public rooms on the first floor of the house are used by BAHA, whose office is entered by a small porch at the rear of the building, in order to minimize disturbance to occupants of the house's three apartments. An original carriage house-barn, topped with a louvered cupola, stands in the rear yard.

The McCreary-Greer House is a City of Berkeley Landmark. The Berkeley Architectural Heritage Association office is open Wednesday and Thursday from 2pm to 5pm. Phone 510-841-2242.

69. Tang Center (2222 Bancroft Way)

Anshen and Allen; Aviva Litman-Cleper, Founders Building restoration; Meacham O'Brien, landscape architect, 1991–1992

Located across Bancroft from Edwards Stadium, the Tang Center is the third building in the century-spanning history of one of the nation's first student health programs. It replaced outmoded Cowell Memorial Hospital, which succeeded the Meyer House in 1930 and was removed in 1993 to make room for the Haas School of Business (see Walk 5). Operated by the University Health Services, the Tang Center provides primary outpatient, specialty, and urgent care for the student body, as well as a variety of services for faculty and staff. The $18 million facility was funded by campus sources and a $5 million donation from the San Francisco–based Tang Foundation, led by Hong Kong businessman Jack C. Tang. It is the first campus building to be given a name of Asian descent.

Linked by a central atrium, the three-story T-shaped building includes a modular clinic wing extending between Bancroft and Durant, and a smaller conference and administrative wing adjacent to a campus parking lot on the west. Project designer and alumnus Bill Weber of San Francisco architects Anshen and Allen utilized traditional Bay Region elements in the building, recalling those introduced by Bernard Maybeck and developed by Joseph Esherick, William Wurster, and Vernon DeMars.[11] The glazed circular atrium, which functions as entrance lobby and communal hub, opens to landscaped courtyards on the north and south, forming an indoor-outdoor relationship characteristic of Bay Area design. The concrete and steel structure is surfaced in terracotta colored stucco, which is contrasted by blue curtain walls and detailing, a bold use of colors that can be compared with Esherick's Anthony Hall (see Walk 5) and Wurster's Stern Hall (see Walk 6). Other elements, including the use of trellises, bracket-like rain leaders, and balconies, also recall this heritage.

Weber situated the north and south courtyards to reduce the massing along Bancroft and Durant and to better relate to possible future development of the parking lot. Designed by landscape architect Patricia O'Brien of Meacham O'Brien, they define the entries and provide pleasant sitting areas with trellises and plantings to buffer the nearby traffic and parking.

The north courtyard incorporates the Founders Building, which houses the Center's Career and Educational Guidance Library. The small

Tang Center

Mediterranean-style building was constructed in 1942 to house an insurance agency office and was acquired by the university in 1953 and used as a custodial services office prior to its present use. The mission-tile hipped-roof building was reconstructed by San Francisco architect Aviva Litman-Cleper. Within its arched entry are the original building-name plaque from Cowell Memorial Hospital, and a plaque dedicating the Founders Building to the S. H. Cowell Foundation in recognition for its support for student health care at Berkeley as well as other northern California colleges and universities.

Westside and Downtown

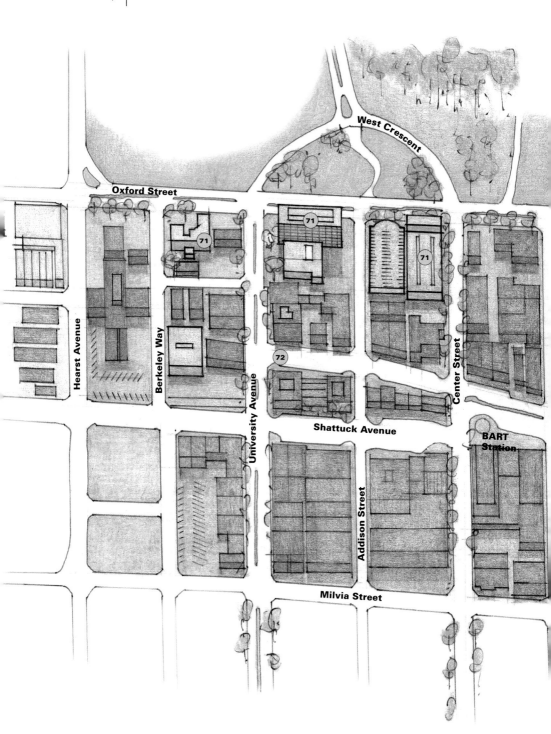

Mason McDuffie Company Building, detail

Bancroft Way

Durant Avenue

Channing Way

Haste Street

Shattuck Avenue

72

70

This Walk encompasses the historic core of Berkeley's central business and arts district. It includes a scattering of university properties, mostly acquired in the early twentieth century and concentrated along Oxford across from the greensward of the Crescent. Further south at Channing and Shattuck is the Manville Apartments student housing, developed near the end of the century.

The main street of downtown Berkeley bears the name of pioneer landholder, civic leader, and legislator Francis Kittredge Shattuck, who built his mansion on the site of the present Shattuck Hotel. Through his leadership the street developed as a commercial corridor and major transportation route with the establishment of a Southern Pacific steam-railroad terminal on a northern branch line from Oakland in 1876.

Along with the opening of the university three years earlier, the railroad signified a shift of the center of gravity of the community from the shoreline to the town building up around the new campus. It ran along the east side of Shattuck to Stanford Place, named for ex-Governor and Southern Pacific stakeholder Leland Stanford, who in the following decade would found the great university across the Bay. Here Berkeley Station was located, on the site of present Berkeley Square, the wedge-shaped block on Shattuck between Addison and Center. Shattuck became a principal point of arrival and departure for commuting university students and staff and visitors and Center the main pedestrian route to campus.

Postcard view of Shattuck Avenue, circa 1925

The wide Shattuck right-of-way became laced with tracks and occupied by a railroad freight yard. A real estate boom followed the railroad, and soon a business community of late Victorian and frontier wooden buildings—hotels, drug stores, newspaper offices, a Wells Fargo Express office, livery stables, bakeries, and hardware stores—grew up in the vicinity of the station. Round turrets and faceted towers topped with witches' caps and fancy cupolas marked the street corners. By the turn of the century paved streets began to replace the dirt roads, and concrete sidewalks the wood-planked walkways. In the early 1900s the downtown expanded as population surged in Berkeley, brought about at first by a rapid growth in university enrollment, which rose from about 400 students in 1890 to 2,000 at the turn of the century and 3,500 by 1910. Contributing to the growth was the introduction of the electric trans-bay trains of the Key System and an influx of new residents following the 1906 San Francisco earthquake and fire.

By 1908 the downtown had fully developed into a transportation hub bustling with streetcars, inter-urban electric trains, and steam engines that left a sooty residue on pedestrians and residents not quick enough to close their windows. A brick and concrete station had replaced the old wooden one at Berkeley Square, and a number of multi-story period revival masonry buildings had risen among the remaining frontier facades.

University Supervising Architect John Galen Howard first opened a downtown office in the Eastman Building at the southwest corner of Center and Oxford, where he also conducted an atelier for the first students enrolled in the department of architecture he founded in 1903. He moved to a building of his own design, the five-story brick First National Bank Building (1904), on the site of the present "PowerBar Building" at the southwest corner of Shattuck and Center. He continued instruction there until North Gate Hall was completed on campus three years later (see Walk 2). He later rented the top-floor suite of another Howard building, the six-story Berkeley Bank Building (1908), located diagonally across the intersection at the northeast corner of Shattuck and Center.[1] That brick-faced neoclassical building stood until 1971, when the site was developed for the present Bank of America building. In the 1920s and 1930s, additional period revival and Art Deco buildings were constructed, making downtown the remarkable early twentieth-century main street museum that it is today.

As a business district the downtown nearly equals the sales revenues of Southside's Telegraph Avenue district (see Walk 9) but with a more cosmopolitan mix of goods and services that include over ninety retail stores and 100 diverse restaurants, pubs, and cafes. Major contributors to the downtown economy and culture of the city are its arts and entertainment resources, which are centered in the Addison Arts District between

Detail, United Artists Theater

Shattuck and Milvia and anchored by the Tony-award winning Berkeley Repertory Theatre (2045 Addison). The Berkeley Rep stages performances in two adjacent theatres, a 400-seat thrust stage opened in 1980 (Gene Angell), and 600-seat proscenium theatre opened in 2001 (ELS/Elbasani & Logan). Other small theatres and performing arts cafes make up the district, as well as six downtown movie theatres, including the modified Art Deco showcases, United Artists Cinema Seven at 2274 Shattuck (C. A. Balch, 1932) and California Cinemas at 2113 Kittredge (1914; Balch & Stanberry, alterations, 1930).

70. Manville Apartments (2100 Channing Way)

David Baker and Associates, and Topher Delaney, landscape architect,
associated with Crosby Helmich, architects, and Gates and Associates,
landscape architects, 1993–1995

The Manville Apartments at the southeast corner of Shattuck and Channing provides housing for 132 law and graduate students in single-occupancy studio apartments. It replaced the former Manville Hall housing, a high-rise converted to offices and other uses for the School of Law and renamed Simon Hall in 1995–1996 (see Walk 5). The original name was transferred to the building and honors Hiram Edward Manville, president of the Johns-Manville Corporation. Constructed on the former site of a service station, the $12 million building is the only university student housing in the downtown and with its ground-floor retail frontage contributes to the vitality and scale of the south Shattuck corridor.

San Francisco architect and alumnus David Baker designed the four-story, wood-frame, stucco building in two blocks, with varying colors and idiosyncratic details to reduce the apparent scale and mass of the structure. The variations in the facades also relate to the community context. The north facade, with its main entrance oriented towards the campus along residential Channing has projecting bays topped by awnings. The two west facades on Shattuck are distinctly different and quirky. The peach-colored north block forms six bays with eccentrically angled metal score lines, an extended parapet, and colonnaded and canopied storefronts. The dark-green south block is topped with a bracketed awning, has an irregular fen-

Manville Apartments, 2100 Channing Way

estration pattern, and rises above an orange-colored storefront base with angled columns.

A gated walkway separates the two sections along Shattuck and leads to a central courtyard. This interior second-story courtyard-light well is enclosed by the top three floors, which are situated above the shops and a parking garage. Here landscape architect Topher Delaney and sculptor Buddy Rhodes treated the forty-by-eighty-foot outdoor space with playful concrete spheres, cubes, and inverted cones, and five lilac-stone boulders quarried in southern California.

71. 1952 Oxford Street, University Hall, and 2120 Oxford Street

1952 Oxford Street *Walter H. Ratcliff, Jr., 1930*
University Hall
> *Welton Becket & Associates, 1957–1959;*
> *Hansen/Murakami/Eshima, architect, with H. J. Degenkolb Associates,*
> *structural engineers, seismic alterations, 1990–1991*

2120 Oxford Street *Masten & Hurd, 1940*

Originally a service station built for the Richfield Oil Company in 1930, the building at 1952 Oxford was one of the later works of architect Walter Ratcliff, Jr., who designed many prominent Berkeley buildings in the early twentieth century. It reflects an era when roadside stations for automobiles were designed to fit into the community, sometimes utilizing Mission Revival or other architectural styles.

1952 Oxford Street

The stylized Moorish-Mediterranean brick building consists of an L-shaped garage with an attached office and shed-roof canopy of mission tiles extending over the former gas-pump island. The garage has arched openings on Oxford and Berkeley Way and another on a chamfer at the elbow of the two wings. The facade has unusual concave cornice lines between brick piers that are topped with pyramidal caps. Industrial steel sash is used in the arched windows. The garage interior is spanned by steel trusses supporting wood rafters and decking and is illuminated by skylights. The supporting side walls have brick corbels near the top.

Formerly called the University Garage, the building is now used by the Department of Parking and Transportation Services for university buses and shuttles.

1952 Oxford Street is listed on the State Historic Resources Inventory and is a City of Berkeley Landmark.

University Hall

University Hall was completed in 1959 to provide new statewide offices for the president and Regents of the university. Its construction freed space in Sproul Hall for campus administrative units that had been housed in various academic buildings.

The selection of Los Angeles–based Welton Becket & Associates to design the building reflected the desire of the Regents to assign projects more evenly between northern and southern California architects—and, in this case, to a firm with extensive experience in office buildings. William Wurster, who was then Berkeley Consulting Architect and dean of the College of Architecture, later regretted the decision, calling the building "a tragic mistake" and a place that its first residing president, Clark Kerr, detested.[2]

University Hall

The architects produced a reinforced-concrete building comprised of an eight-story rectangular office tower and a two-story west wing to house the Regents' suite and boardroom. The repetitively modular tower afforded splendid views of the Bay and hills, but created a symbol of institutional bureaucracy common to the period and a broadside obstruction to the vista related to the central campus axis that John Galen Howard established in the Hearst Plan.

Following President Kerr, the building was home to Presidents Harry R. Wellman (acting), Charles J. Hitch, David S. Saxon, and David P. Gardner. Its association with both the President's Office and the Regents occasionally attracted political demonstrations at the building during the 1960s, '70s, and '80s. When President Gardner and the Regents moved their offices to Oakland in 1989, the building became available for campus administrative offices. Chancellors Ira Michael Heyman and Chang-Lin Tien occupied the building in the early 1990s, while California Hall was undergoing seismic strengthening.

The appearance of University Hall was modified in 1991 following the addition of steel-braced frames (X braces), concrete spandrels, and column stiffeners by architects Hansen/Murakami/Eshima and structural engineers H. J. Degenkolb Associates.

2120 Oxford Street

A bronze plaque on the front of this Moderne building at the northwest corner of Oxford and Center commemorates the historic role of the building's occupant, the University of California Printing Services, on June 26, 1945. For four days preceding that date, university printers rushed to complete the signatory copies of the Charter of the United Nations and Statute of the International Court of Justice for delegates convened in the War Memorial Veterans Building in San Francisco.

That production, printed in five languages, was one of many distinguished works by the department, which dates back to the first years of the university, when it was established as the University Printing Office to print bulletins, forms, and other quotidian jobs. It resided in several campus buildings and in 1917 moved into its own building, a concrete structure designed by John Galen Howard that stood at the corner of Bancroft Way and Barrow Lane. In 1940, the department moved into its new quarters at 2120 Oxford, along with the editorial University Press, which was combined with the department from 1932 to 1949. The press moved to another location in 1962, and the department, now called UC Printing Services, was transferred from the Office of the President to the Berkeley campus in 1995.

Funded in part by the Work Projects Administration, 2120 Oxford is a concrete structure comprised of a three-story office block on Oxford and a one-story west wing that houses the printing plant operations. San Francisco architects Masten & Hurd were noted for their Streamline Moderne style buildings, such as the Redding Fire House in northern California and the former Gompers High School (later Mission Community College Center) in San Francisco, both completed in 1939, one year before 2120 Oxford. For the printing plant they utilized simple Moderne detailing, expressed with fluted spandrels and stepped pilasters, which provide a vertical rhythm to the facade. These form seven bays of translucent glass-block windows along Center that illuminate the plant, which also receives light from north-facing sawtooth skylights. The entrance is also expressed with a concrete canopy and flanking Art Deco light fixtures. The architects

2120 Oxford Street

enhanced the otherwise utilitarian interior in the entrance lobby, which contains an aluminum-railed spiral staircase that ascends from a black-and-white checkered terrazzo floor to the second-story offices. UC Printing Services now shares the building with the Office of Public Affairs, which occupies the third floor.

2120 Oxford Street is listed on the State Historic Resources Inventory.

72. Shattuck Avenue and Downtown

Including the Civic Center just to the west, about forty percent of the nearly 190 buildings in downtown Berkeley are listed on the State Historic Resources Inventory, with twenty-seven designated as City of Berkeley Landmarks. Eight of these, briefly described below, are also listed on the National Register of Historic Places.

At the northeast corner of Shattuck and Addison (2037 Shattuck) stands the five-story Studio Building (1905), distinguished by its mansard roof and curved metal bay windows. The top floor contained artist studios and a gallery and was the first home of the California College of Arts and Crafts, now a major Bay Area art and design school located in Oakland. The restored building was also once used as a hotel.

Across Addison at 2101 Shattuck is the Mason–McDuffie Company Building (1928) designed by Berkeley architect Walter H. Ratcliff, Jr., in a Mediterranean Revival style. It originally housed the pioneering real estate company that developed many of Berkeley's fine residential neighborhoods. Now occupied by a furniture store, the building features an interior embellished with a stenciled wood coffer ceiling, while the exterior pilasters have unique capitals with sculpted bears.

A little west of Shattuck at 2071 Addison within the Arts District is the Golden Sheaf Bakery (1905) by architect Clinton Day, who designed many late nineteenth-century university buildings, including the old Chemistry Building (see Walk 2). The two-story neoclassical brick and terra cotta building was recently renovated as part of the Berkeley Repertory Theatre complex. It stands adjacent to

Golden Sheaf Bakery Building, 2071 Addison Street

an original S. H. Kress variety store (Edward F. Sibbert, 1932), whose brick walls are decorated with polychromatic terracotta detailed in a zigzag Moderne style.

One block south at the northwest corner of Shattuck and Center (2140–2144 Shattuck) stands the eleven-story brick and terracotta Chamber of Commerce Building (1925–1927), also by Ratcliff. The Chamber's offices were originally on the top floor, and the building was later named for Wells Fargo Bank, for whom Ratcliff redesigned the ground floor with monumental classical arches. Deep ceiling coffers decorate the entrance lobby.

Two blocks south the five-story Shattuck Hotel building (Benjamin G. McDougall, 1909, addition 1913) occupies the entire block between Allston and Kittredge, site of the old Shattuck estate. The original wing of the Mediterranean Renaissance Revival building was constructed at the Shattuck-Allston corner and was later expanded to Kittredge.

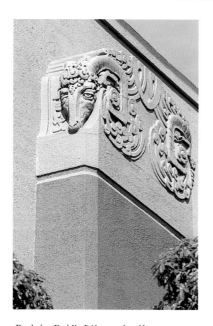

Berkeley Public Library detail

Opposite the hotel building at Shattuck and Kittredge (2090 Kittredge) is James W. Plachek's Berkeley Public Library (1930). The Art Deco building replaced an earlier main library designed by John Galen Howard in 1903. The concrete facade features decorative sgraffito panels that depict Egyptian figures in the process of producing books. The library was recently renovated and expanded by Ripley/BOORA Associated Architects.

Across the street from the library at 2271–75 Shattuck is the piper-crowned Tupper & Reed Building (1925), designed by William Raymond Yelland, known for his playful storybook designs. Now used for a restaurant and second-floor office, it originally housed a music store with the Sign of the Piper Restaurant above. At the corner of the same block (2105 Bancroft) is the four-story Classical Revival Masonic Temple Building (William H. Wharff, 1905–1907), now the Berkeley Conference Center. The entrance was originally enriched with a classical entablature with granite columns, which were considered a sidewalk encroachment and removed.

Also by Plachek, on the west side of Shattuck between Bancroft and Durant (2300 Shattuck) is the Corder Building (1921, addition 1925), later known as the Hotel Whitecotton Apartments and now the Shattuck Apartment Building. Like the Shattuck Hotel building, this four-story block forms a continuous street facade that strongly defines the scale and character of the downtown.

One block west of the Shattuck Hotel at the southeast corner of Allston and Milvia (2000 Allston) is the United States Post Office (Oscar Wenderoth, 1914). The arcaded Second Renaissance Revival building is finished in oak and marble in the lobby, which displays a mural depicting early scenes in Berkeley's history.

The last of the downtown buildings listed on the National Register of Historic Places is one block west of the confines of this Walk. Old City Hall (1908–1909) at 2134 Martin Luther King Jr. Way (at Allston) was designed by Beaux Arts–trained architects John Bakewell, Jr., and Arthur Brown, Jr. The classical building is the focal point of the Civic Center and forms the west side of Civic Center Park, part of a composition that exemplifies the principles of the City Beautiful Movement. Facing the park on the north at 1931 Center is the Veterans Memorial Building (Henry H. Meyers, 1928), a classic Moderne building that contains the museum and archives of The Berkeley Historical Society, a non-profit organization founded in 1978.

Linking the downtown to San Francisco and other Bay Area communities is the underground Bay Area Rapid Transit (BART) Berkeley Station (Maher & Martens, with Royston, Hanamoto, Beck & Abey, landscape architects, 1970). Its drum-like pavilion on the plaza was designed to harmonize with the thirteen-story "PowerBar Building," originally the Great Western Building (David E. Termohlen, 1969), at the southwest corner of Shattuck and Center. When the rapid transit system was being planned in the early 1960s, Chancellor Glenn T. Seaborg asked BART to locate the station closer to campus to better serve the thousands of campus commuters.

Shattuck Avenue, west side looking south from Center Street

But the city's requirement to place the tracks underground and cost restrictions resulted in the route under Shattuck and siting of the station at Center, close to where the old steam trains stopped at Berkeley Station in the early twentieth century.[3]

As was done at the time of the steam trains, commuters walking between BART and the campus use Center, which links to the west campus entrance and the pathway through the oaks of the Grinnell Natural Area (see Walk 3). The view up Center of the Eucalyptus Grove and Strawberry Creek vegetation has appeared similar for more than a century. An enhancement of this established pedestrian corridor was studied by the ROMA Design Group as part of their work on the campus 1990 Long Range Development Plan. Architect and Professor Donlyn Lyndon designed the widened south sidewalk as a restaurant- and shop-lined promenade with new street furnishings and trees; the project was completed using federal funds in 1997.

The Berkeley Historical Society in the Veterans Memorial Building at 1931 Center Street is open Thursday through Saturday from 1pm to 4pm. Phone 510-848-0181.

Notes to Introduction

1.   John Galen Howard, "The Architectural Plans for the Greater University of California," *University Chronicle* 5, no. 4 (January 1903): 281.

2.   Samuel Willey to Benjamin Ide Wheeler, January 16, 1901, quoted in "The Selection of the Site of the University and Its Name," *University Chronicle* 4, no. 1 (February 1901): 58.

3.   The site, which became the first location of the University of California in 1868, is a Registered California Historical Landmark. Coincidentally, a new headquarters building for the Regents and President of the University was completed across the street from this site in 1998.

4.   Witold Rybczynski, *A Clearing in the Distance: Frederick Law Olmsted and America in the Nineteenth Century* (New York: Scribner, 1999), p. 245.

5.   Verne A. Stadtman, ed., *The Centennial Record of the University of California* (Berkeley: University of California, 1967), pp. 378–382.

6.   Minutes of the Board of Regents, July 2, 1868, Secretary of the Regents, University of California.

7.   Carroll Brentano, "The First Campus Plan for the University of California" (Center for Studies in Higher Education, University of California, Berkeley, 1991), pp. 9–12.

8.   Anne Bloomfield, "David Farquharson: Pioneer California Architect," *California History* 59 (Spring 1980): 19–25.

9.   Minutes of the Board of Regents, March 4, 1873.

10.   Minutes of the Board of Regents, September 6, 1873.

11.   Kent Emanuel Watson, "A Forgotten Chapter in the History of Landscape Architecture: William Hammond Hall and the 1873 University of California, Berkeley Plan" (master's thesis, University of California, Berkeley, 1989), pp. 20–25, 34–58.

12.   In 1895–96 approximately 400 additional students were enrolled in the university's affiliated colleges in San Francisco, including the Schools of Dentistry, Medicine and Pharmacy, and the San Francisco Art Institute.

13.   Kenneth Cardwell and William C. Hays, "Fifty Years From Now," *California Monthly* 64, no. 8 (April 1954): 20.

14.   "The Phebe Hearst Architectural Plan," *University Chronicle* 1, no. 1 (February 1898): 61–63.

15.   William Carey Jones, *Illustrated History of the University of California* (Berkeley: Students Cooperative Society, 1901), pp. 234–235.

16.   Jones, *Illustrated History*, p. 262.

17.   In the final stage of the competition British architect John Belcher replaced juror Richard Norman Shaw, who had become ill.

18.   Jones, *Illustrated History*, pp. 426–430.

19.   Robert Judson Clark, curator, and Gray Brechin, exhibition *Roma/Pacifica: The Phoebe Hearst International Architectural Competition and the Berkeley Campus, 1896–1930*, University of California, Berkeley Art Museum, December 15,1999–April 23, 2000.

20.   Joan Elaine Draper, "John Galen Howard and the Beaux-Arts Movement in the United States" (master's thesis, University of California, Berkeley, 1972), pp. 29–52.

21.   John Galen Howard, "The Architectural Plans," p. 280.

22. *Biennial Report of the President of the University on behalf of the Regents to His Excellency the Governor of the State, 1900–1902*, supplement to *University Chronicle* 5 (Berkeley: The University Press, December 1902), p. 15.

23. William Carey Jones, *Illustrated History*, p. 259.

24. John Galen Howard, "The Architectural Plans," p. 286–287.

25. Albert H. Allen, "The Hearst Plan," *University Chronicle* 11, no. 1 (January 1909): 87.

26. Loren W. Partridge, *John Galen Howard and the Berkeley Campus: Beaux-Arts Architecture in the "Athens of the West"* (Berkeley: Berkeley Architectural Heritage Association, 1988), pp. 32–34.

27. George W. Kelham, "The University of California," *The Architect* 14, no. 2 (August 1917): 84.

28. Robert G. Sproul to Warren C. Perry, 6 February 1931, in Warren Perry Papers (82/97c, Box 7), The Bancroft Library, University of California, Berkeley.

29. The three-member committee also included University Comptroller Luther A. Nichols and Engineering Professor Baldwin M. Woods.

30. Warren C. Perry, et al., "A Re-Study of the Central Area of the Campus, University of California, Berkeley, California" (October 1, 1933), p. 1–8, in Warren Perry Papers (82/97c, Box 7), The Bancroft Library, University of California, Berkeley.

31. "Concerning Expansion of the University Library at Berkeley," attachment to William C. Hays to President Robert G. Sproul, January 11, 1944, in President's Records (CU-5, Series 2, Box 623, 1944: 110–B), The Bancroft Library, University of California,.Berkeley.

32. Office of Architects and Engineers, *Planning the Physical Development of the Berkeley Campus* (Berkeley, December 1951), p. 3.

33. William Wilson Wurster, "College of Environmental Design, University of California, Campus Planning, and Architectural Practice," typescript of an oral history conducted 1963 by Suzanne B. Riess, Regional Oral History Office, The Bancroft Library, University of California, Berkeley, 1964, p. 221.

34. Donald H. McLaughlin, "Careers in Mining Geology and Management, University Governance and Teaching," typescript of an oral history conducted 1970–1971 by Harriet Nathan, Regional Oral History Office, The Bancroft Library, University of California, Berkeley, 1975, p. 42.

35. Vernon Armand DeMars, "A Life in Architecture: Indian Dancing, Migrant Housing, Telesis, Design for Urban Living, Theater, Teaching," typescript of an oral history conducted by Suzanne B. Riess in 1988–1989, Regional Oral History Office, The Bancroft Library, University of California, Berkeley, 1992, pp. 538–539.

36. Donald H McLaughlin, "Careers in Mining," p. 43.

37. "Living within: Bowker defines Berkeley's predicament/challenge," *California Monthly* 84, no. 2 (November 1973): 1–2, 7.

38. Ira Michael Heyman, "Chanellor's Annual Report 1988–89," *California Monthly* 100, no. 2 (November 1989): 17–20.

39. John Galen Howard, "The Architectural Plans," p. 277.

40. Howard, "The Architectural Plans," p. 281.

Notes to Walk 1

1. Loren W. Partridge, *John Galen Howard*, p. 27–29.

2. John Galen Howard to Victor Henderson, 8 March 1909, in Regents Records (CU-1, 57:3), The Bancroft Library, University of California, Berkeley.

3.   Victor Henderson to John Galen Howard, 10 July 1909, in Regents Records (CU-1, 57:7), The Bancroft Library, University of California, Berkeley.

4.   Victor Henderson to John Galen Howard, 20 August 1909, in Regents Records (CU-1, 57:8), The Bancroft Library, University of California, Berkeley.

5.   John A. Britton to Benjamin Ide Wheeler, 23 August 1909, in Regents Records (CU-1, 66:10), The Bancroft Library, University of California, Berkeley.

6.   Benjamin Ide Wheeler to F. W. Dohrmann, 24 March 1910, in Regents Records (CU-1, 66:13), The Bancroft Library, University of California, Berkeley.

7.   J. R. K. Kantor, "Cora, Jane, & Phoebe: Fin-De-Siècle Philanthropy," *Chronicle of the University of California* 1, no. 2 (Fall 1998): 3–4.

8.   John Galen Howard to Victor H. Henderson, 9 February 1910, in Regents Records (CU-1, 57:22), The Bancroft Library, University of California, Berkeley.

9.   Victor H. Henderson to John Galen Howard, 25 August 1910, in Regents Records (CU-1, 57:13a), The Bancroft Library, University of California, Berkeley.

10. J. R. K. Kantor and A. L. Pierovich, "The University in Pictures," *California Monthly* 78, no. 6 (April-May 1968): 49.

11. Jane K. Sather to Benjamin Ide Wheeler, 10 February 1911, in Regents Records (CU-1, 78:13), The Bancroft Library, University of California, Berkeley. Although the name "Jane K. Sather Campanile" was officially adopted by the Regents in 1911, following the donor's written request, the formal names "Sather Tower" and "Sather Esplanade" have been used by the University since shortly after construction, while "Campanile" has continued as an informal, more common, name.

12. *The Abundant Life: Benjamin Ide Wheeler*, ed. Monroe E. Deutsch (Berkeley: University of California Press, 1926), p. 27–28.

13. John Galen Howard, quoted in Victor H. Henderson, "Notes," ca. 3 March 1917, in Regents Records (CU-1, 83:21), The Bancroft Library, University of California, Berkeley.

14. In addition to Derleth, San Francisco Civil Engineer Erle L. Cope worked on the structural design of the tower.

15. Margaret E. Murdock to Monroe E. Deutsch, 16 April 1943, in President's Records (CU-5, Series 2, 1943:115), The Bancroft Library, University of California, Berkeley.

16. John Galen Howard to Victor H. Henderson, 23 December 1907, in Regents Records (CU-1, 59:5), The Bancroft Library, University of California, Berkeley.

17. John Galen Howard to Victor H. Henderson, 7 April 1910, in Regents Records (CU-1, 57:18), The Bancroft Library, University of California, Berkeley.

18. William Charles Hays, "Order, Taste and Grace in Architecture," typescript of an oral history conducted 1959 by Edna Tartaul Daniel, Regional Oral History Office, The Bancroft Library, University of California, Berkeley, 1968, p. 167.

19. Loren W. Partridge, *John Galen Howard*, p. 27.

20. William Charles Hays, "Order, Taste and Grace in Architecture," p. 145.

21. John Galen Howard to Victor H. Henderson, 22 November 1911, in Regents Records (CU-1, 81:23), The Bancroft Library, University of California, Berkeley.

22. John Galen Howard to Victor H. Henderson, 28 September 1911, in Regents Records (CU-1, 81:23), The Bancroft Library, University of California, Berkeley.

23. Victor H. Henderson to John Galen Howard, 25 August 1910, in Regents Records (CU-1, 57:13a), The Bancroft Library, University of California, Berkeley.

24. Dick Heggie, quoted in William Rodarmor, "Memorial Glade: War and Remembrance," *California Monthly* 107, no. 4 (February 1997): 34.

25. Richard Haag, "Mission Statement for The Memorial Glade," 26 July 1994.

26. Don McNary, quoted in William Rodarmor, "Memorial Glade: War and Remembrance," p. 36.

27. John Galen Howard to President Benjamin Ide Wheeler, 26 August 1911, in Regents Records (CU-1, 81:16), The Bancroft Library, University of California, Berkeley.

28. "California Hall," *The University Chronicle* 8, no. 1 (September 1905): 44.

29. Victor H. Henderson to John Galen Howard, 22 August 1906, in Regents Records (CU-1, 56:15), The Bancroft Library, University of California, Berkeley.

30. Victor H. Henderson to John Galen Howard, 21 September 1906, in Regents Records (CU-1, 56:15), The Bancroft Library, University of California, Berkeley.

31. Victor H. Henderson to John Galen Howard, 24 December 1906, in Regents Records (CU-1, 56:15), The Bancroft Library, University of California, Berkeley.

32. William Rodarmor, "Raise high the roof beams," *California Monthly* 107, no. 4 (February 1997): 12.

33. *The Abundant Life: Benjamin Ide Wheeler*, p. 318–319.

34. Ira B. Cross, letter to editor, "Thanks for the eulogy," *California Monthly* 79, no. 7 (June-July 1969): 5.

Notes to Walk 2

1. Allan Temko, "The Campus Environment," *California Monthly* 76, no. 2 (November 1965): 7.

2. Susan Stern Cerny, *Gown Meets Town: Along the Northern Edge of the University of California Campus* (Berkeley: The Berkeley Architectural Heritage Association, 1991), n.p.

3. John Galen Howard, "Memorandum," 2 April 1915, in Regents Records (CU-1, 81:18), The Bancroft Library, University of California, Berkeley.

4. Victor H. Henderson to John Galen Howard, 22 August 1906, in Regents Records (CU-1, 56:15), The Bancroft Library, University of California, Berkeley.

5. John Galen Howard to Victor H. Henderson, 24 August 1906, in Regents Records (CU-1, 56:15), The Bancroft Library, University of California, Berkeley.

6. Chang-Lin Tien, quoted in Marie Felde, "New Life for Hearst Mining," *Berkeleyan* (January 15–21, 1997): 1.

7. Victor H. Henderson to J. B. Rice, 11 August 1916, in Regents Records (CU-1, 86:18), The Bancroft Library, University of California, Berkeley.

8. Steven Finacom, "Draft for Outdoor Art Brochure," 10 July 2000.

9. Joan Elaine Draper, "John Galen Howard and the Beaux-Arts Movement," 123.

10. Benjamin Ide Wheeler to John A. Britton, 23 May 1905, in Regents Records (CU-1, 66:10), The Bancroft Library, University of California, Berkeley.

11. Warren C. Perry, "The School of Architecture at Berkeley Has Completed Its Twenty-Second Year," *Southwest Builder and Contractor* (9 August 1935): 19–20.

12. Henry Gutterson, quoted in Kenneth Cardwell and William C. Hays, "Fifty Years From Now," 20–26.

13. Sally B. Woodbridge, *En Charette/On Deadline* (Berkeley: Graduate School of Journalism, University of California, 1993), 23–24.

14. Warren C. Perry to Robert Gordon Sproul, 18 January 1940, in President's Records (CU-5, Series 2, 1940:77), The Bancroft Library, University of California, Berkeley.

15.   Robin W. Winks, *Frederick Billings: A Life* (Berkeley: University of California Press, 1991), 92. Winks points out that the second line in the stanza has often been misquoted as "The first four acts already past," leaving some question as to whether Billings himself may have misquoted the bishop in his recitation at the rock.

16.   William C. Hays, "Some Architectural Works of John Galen Howard," *The Architect and Engineer* 40, no. 1 (January 1915): 80–81.

Notes to Walk 3

1.   William Warren Ferrier, *Origins and Development of the University of California* (Berkeley: The Sather Gate Book Shop, 1930), p. 624.

2.   In addition to the three central campus Natural Areas, two Ecological Study Areas were established in Strawberry Canyon.

3.   Frank T. Lindgren and Kenneth M. Sanderson, "The Future of the Campus Environment," *California Monthly* 79, no. 4 (January-February 1969): 38.

4.   "Voices in the wilderness preserve campus trees," *California Monthly* 79, no. 4 (January-February 1969): 9.

5.   Paul Thayer, "Celebrating The Centennial," *California Monthly* 78, no. 7 (June-July 1968): 35.

6.   "Heyns Grove Dedicated," *Berkeleyan* (6 December 1995–1 January 1996).

7.   "California's Boys and Girls Make a University Pilgrimage," *San Francisco Examiner* 70, no. 133 (13 May 1900): 15.

8.   Victor H. Henderson to Philip E. Bowles, 15 August 1912, in Regents Records (CU-1, 91:12), The Bancroft Library, University of California, Berkeley.

9.   Benjamin Ide Wheeler to Philip E. Bowles, 28 December 1911, in Regents Records (CU-1, 66:9), The Bancroft Library, University of California, Berkeley.

10.   Victor H. Henderson to John Galen Howard, 9 March 1911, in Regents Records (CU-1, 81:16), The Bancroft Library, University of California, Berkeley.

11.   William O. Raiguel for John Galen Howard to Victor H. Henderson, 1 September 1910, in Regents Records (CU-1, 57:13a), The Bancroft Library, University of California, Berkeley.

12.   Campus Planning Study Group, *Campus Historic Resources Survey* (Berkeley: University of California, 1978), 155.

13.   Michael Laurie with David C. Streatfield, *75 Years of Landscape Architecture at Berkeley* (Berkeley: Department of Landscape Architecture, University of California, Berkeley, 1988), 1:7.

14.   William Charles Hays, "Order, Taste and Grace in Architecture," 180.

15.   Gray Brechin, "Camera Obscura: Fiat Lux," *California Monthly* 88, no. 6 (June-July 1978): 12–13.

16.   Allan Temko, "The Campus Environment," 6.

17.   Daniel E. Koshland Jr., "My edifice complex," *California Monthly* 103, no. 3 (December 1992): 8.

18.   John Galen Howard, "The Architectural Plans," 281.

19.   Anna Rearden, "The Parthenia: A Masque of Maidenhood," *The University Chronicle* 14, no. 2 (April 1912): 144.

Notes to Walk 4

1.   *1923 Blue and Gold* (Berkeley: The Junior Class of the University of California, 1922), p. 155.

2. Warren C. Perry to Robert Gordon Sproul, 5 August 1944, in Warren Perry Papers (82/97c, Box 10), The Bancroft Library, University of California, Berkeley.

3. Warren C. Perry to Robert Gordon Sproul, 22 June 1932, in Warren Perry Papers (82/97c, Box 11), The Bancroft Library, University of California, Berkeley.

4. Vernon DeMars, quoted in Allan Temko, "'Planned Chaos' on the Piazza," *Architectural Forum* 115, no. 4 (October 1961): 192.

5. Ibid.

6. Roger Montgomery, "Center of Action," *Architectural Forum* 132, no. 3 (April 1970): 66, 68.

7. Vernon DeMars, quoted in "California Student Center," *California Monthly* 68, no. 5 (January 1958): 18.

8. Vernon Armand DeMars, "A Life in Architecture," 539.

9. DeMars, "A Life in Architecture," 496–500.

10. Minutes of the Committee on Campus Development and Building Location, 19 August 1938, in President's Records (CU-5, 1938:513), The Bancroft Library, University of California, Berkeley.

11. W. J. Norton to Michael Goodman, 17 December 1943, in President's Records (CU-5, 1943:111), The Bancroft Library, University of California, Berkeley.

12. Mario Savio, quoted in Russell Schoch, "Mario Savio 1943–1996," *California Monthly* 107, no. 3 (December 1966): 47.

13. "Berkeley Art Project Competition Announcement," supplementary material to Vernon Armand DeMars, "A Life in Architecture."

Notes to Walk 5

1. Joseph Esherick, *An Architectural Practice in the San Francisco Bay Area, 1938–1996*, typescript of an oral history conducted 1994–1996 by Suzanne B. Riess, Regional Oral History Office, The Bancroft Library, University of California, Berkeley, 1996, 270.

2. Stephen C. Pepper, quoted in Lillian B. Davies, "The little university building that led three lives," *The Independent and Gazette* (November 18, 1979): 6.

3. Roberta J. Park, "A Gym of Their Own," *Chronicle of the University of California* 1, no. 2 (Fall 1998): 26.

4. L. M. Turner, ed., "University of California," in *The Inter-Collegian* (San Francisco: The Inter-Collegian Publishing Co., 1903), 11.

5. Bernard Maybeck and Julia Morgan to William Randolph Hearst, 10 April 1924, telegram in Department of Human Biodynamics, University of California, Berkeley.

6. William Warren Ferrier, *Origin and Development of the University of California*, 536.

7. "University Arts Center," *Arts & Architecture* 82, no. 10 (October 1965): 26.

8. Allan Temko, "The Campus Environment," 8.

9. William Wilson Wurster, "College of Environmental Design," 179.

10. Paul Thayer, "That is Wurster Hall," *California Monthly* 76, no. 2 (November 1965): 27.

11. Thayer, "That is Wurster Hall," 27.

12. Joseph Esherick, "A Building For People," *California Monthly* 76, no. 2 (November 1965): 30.

13. William Wilson Wurster, "College of Environmental Design," 175.

14. Harold A. Small, "The Life and Times of the Faculty Club," *California Monthly* 76, no.6 (March 1966): 13.

15. Albert H. Allen, "The Senior Hall," *The University Chronicle* 8, no. 4 (June 1906): 414.

16. D. L. Westover to Eugene R. Hallett, 7 April 1906, in Regents Records (CU-1, 60:5), The Bancroft Library, University of California, Berkeley.

17. Victor H. Henderson to John Galen Howard, 3 September 1906, in Regents Records (CU-1, 69:7), The Bancroft Library, University of California, Berkeley.

18. Benjamin Ide Wheeler to Members of the Grounds and Buildings Committee of the Board of Regents, 17 January 1911, in Regents Records (CU-1, 89:3), The Bancroft Library, University of California, Berkeley.

19. Ibid.

20. Margaretta J. Darnall, "Girton Hall: The Gift of Julia Morgan," *Chronicle of the University of California* 1, no. 2 (Fall 1998): 60.

21. James Gilbert Paltridge, *A History of The Faculty Club at Berkeley* (Berkeley: The Faculty Club, University of California, Berkeley, 1990), 19.

22. Victor H. Henderson to Ralph P. Merritt, 4 May 1912, in Regents Records (CU-1, 74:10), The Bancroft Library, University of California, Berkeley.

23. Andy Bouman and Ute S. Frey, ed., *Haas School of Business: A Brief Centennial History 1898–1998* (Berkeley: Haas School of Business, 1998), 27.

24. Warren Charles Perry, Resume, 29 March 1941, in Warren Perry Papers (82/97c, carton 9), The Bancroft Library, University of California, Berkeley.

25. Warren C. Perry to Louis A. DeMonte, 30 January 1951, in Warren Perry Papers (82/97c, carton 11), The Bancroft Library, University of California, Berkeley.

26. William L. Prosser to Warren C. Perry, 26 January 1950, in Warren Perry Papers (82/97c, carton 11), The Bancroft Library, University of California, Berkeley.

Notes to Walk 6

1. Cathy Simon, quoted in Sally Lehrman, "Regents to Explain Stern Hall Addition," *The Daily Californian* (28 November 1979): 3, 6.

2. Ben Weed, quoted in Ashton Stevens, "University Dedicated Noblest of Theatres, Gift of William R. Hearst: 8,000 People at Ceremonies on College Campus," *The San Francisco Examiner* 89, no. 87 (25 September 1903): 8–9.

3. William Warren Ferrier, *Origin and Development of the University of California*, 485.

4. Ashton Stevens, "University Dedicated Noblest of Theatres, Gift of William R. Hearst: 8,000 People at Ceremonies on College Campus," *The San Francisco Examiner* 89, no. 87 (25 September 1903): 8–9.

5. Stevens, "University Dedicated Noblest of Theatres," 8–9.

6. Sara Holmes Boutelle, *Julia Morgan Architect* (New York: Abbeville Press, 1988), 41, 49, 52.

7. A. Huber Jr., "The University of California Memorial Stadium," *The Architect and Engineer* 75, no. 1 (October 1923): 93. Although the general contract was signed in May 1923, problems with excavation, under a separate contract, caused a delay of actual construction until July 1, 1923.

8. Herbert Bismark Foster, "The Story of the Development of the Athletic Facilities at Berkeley," 1960, 15–93, Appendix B in Herbert Bismark Foster, "The Role of the Engineer's Office in the Development of the University of California Campuses," typescript of an oral history conducted 1960 by Amelia

Roberts Fry, Regional Oral History Office, The Bancroft Library, University of California, Berkeley, 1960.

9. Herbert B. Foster, "The History of the Big 'C' at Berkeley," 1960: 1–14, Appendix A to Herbert Bismark Foster, "The Role of the Engineer's Office in the Development of the University of California Campuses."

Notes to Walk 7

1. E. A. Hugill to Victor H. Henderson, August 11, 1908; Regents Records (CU-1, 59:16), The Bancroft Library, University of California, Berkeley.
2. Philip E. Bowles to Benjamin Ide Wheeler, April 5, 1913; Regents Records (CU-1, 92:2), The Bancroft Library, University of California, Berkeley.
3. Subcommittee on Physical Development Planning of the Committee on Buildings and Campus Development, *Study of the Long Term Use Potential of Strawberry Canyon and the Undeveloped Hill Lands* (Berkeley, January 1958), pp. 3, 7.
4. T. Harper Goodspeed, quoted in Lincoln Constance, "The Garden Moves to Strawberry Canyon," *University of California Botanical Garden Newsletter* 15, no. 1 (Spring 1990): 4.
5. Glenn T. Seaborg with Ray Colvig, *Chancellor at Berkeley* (Berkeley: Institute of Governmental Studies Press, 1994): 31.
6. Glenn T. Seaborg with Ray Colvig, *Chancellor at Berkeley*, 41.
7. Robert Edwards, quoted in Lucille Day, "The Higher Math," *California Monthly* 95, no. 6 (June–July 1985): 17.
8. Calvin Moore, quoted in Lucille Day, "The Higher Math," 15.
9. J. L. Heilbron, Robert W. Seidel, and Bruce R. Wheaton, "Lawrence and his Laboratory: Nuclear Science at Berkeley," *LBL News Magazine* 6, no. 3 (Fall 1981): 32.

Notes to Walk 8

1. Witold Rybczynski, *A Clearing in the Distance: Frederick Law Olmsted and America in the Nineteenth Century* (New York: Scribner, 1999), 349.
2. Sara Holmes Boutelle, Historic Resources Inventory, 19 May 1978, in Department of Demography files.
3. Harry Edmonds, "The Founding of the International House Movement," typescript of an oral history conducted by Edith Mezirow in 1969, Regional Oral History Office, The Bancroft Library, University of California, Berkeley, 1971, 142b.
4. David Gebhard, *The Architectural/Historical Aspects of the California Schools For The Blind and Deaf, Berkeley (1867–1979)* (Santa Barbara: University of California, 1979), 67–75.

Notes to Walk 9

1. Writers' Program of the Work Projects Administration in Northern California, *Berkeley: The First Seventy-five Years* (Berkeley: The Gillick Press, 1941), 30.
2. Minutes of the Committee on Grounds and Buildings, University of California Board of Regents, 15 September 1966.
3. "Competition for a University Residence Hall," *Arts and Architecture* 73, no. 10 (October 1956): 20.

4.   "Competition Award for Design of Student Residence Hall Group," *Architect and Engineer* 206, no. 3 (September 1956): 15.

5.   Susan Dinkelspiel Cerny, *Berkeley Landmarks* (Berkeley: Berkeley Architectural Heritage Association, 1994), 174.

6. ·   Kenneth H. Cardwell, *Bernard Maybeck: Artisan, Architect, Artist* (Salt Lake City: Peregrine Smith Books, 1977), 123–124.

7.   Cardwell, *Bernard Maybeck*, 126.

8.   Cardwell, *Bernard Maybeck*, 129.

9.   Sara Holmes Boutelle, *Julia Morgan Architect* (New York: Abbeville Press, 1988), 124.

10.   Susan Dinkelspiel Cerny, *Berkeley Landmarks*, 183.

11.   Carol Shen, "University of California, Berkeley Tang Center, Anshen + Allen: San Francisco, Honor Award," *Architecture California* 19, no. 1 (Summer 1997): 33.

Notes to Walk 10

1.   Sally B. Woodbridge, *En Charette/On Deadline*, 6.

2.   William Wilson Wurster, "College of Environmental Design," 239.

3.   Glenn T. Seaborg with Ray Colvig, *Chancellor at Berkeley*, 305–306.

Bibliography

Collections

Berkeley Architectural Heritage Association

Department of Capital Projects, University of California, Berkeley, Building Plans and
    Records

Doe Memorial Library, University of California, Berkeley

Environmental Design Library, University of California, Berkeley

Moffitt Undergraduate Library, University of California, Berkeley

Office of the President, University of California, Planning & Design Records

Office of the Secretary of the Regents, University of California, Minutes of the Board of
    Regents

The Bancroft Library, University of California, Berkeley:

Master Building Files, University Archives (CU-13.4)

President's Files, University Archives (CU-5, Series 2, Boxes 392, 471, 482, 506, 535, 568,
    596, 622–623) and (CU-5, Series 6, CJH, Boxes c-366 and c-367)

Regents' Files, University Archives (CU-1, Boxes 42, 46, 56–61, 63, 65–69, 74, 78, 81,
    83–84, 86, 88–89, 91–92, 96–97)

Regional Oral History Office

University Archives Picture Collection

Warren Perry Papers (82/97c, Boxes 7–11)

Periodicals

AIA Journal, 1983

Archetype, 1980

Architectural Forum, 1918–1970

Architectural Record, 1908–2000

Architecture, 1986–1995

Architecture California, 1985–1997

Architecture Plus, 1973

Arts and Architecture, 1956–1965

Berkeley Engineering Forefront, 2000

CalBusiness, 1998

California History, 1980

California Monthly, 1928–2000

Chronicle of the University of California, 1998–2000

Indoors and Out, 1906

LBL News Magazine, 1981

News Journal of the College of Chemistry, 1997

Overland Monthly, 1898

Places, 1984

Progressive Architecture, 1956–1990

Southwest Builder and Contractor, 1935

Sunset, 1902

The Architect, 1917

The Architect and Engineer, 1905–1956

The Architectural Review, 1900

The Journal of the Association for Preservation Technology, 1987

The New City, 1993
The University Chronicle, 1898–1933
Western Architect and Engineer, 1959–1960

Newspapers

Berkeley Daily Planet, 1999–2000
Berkeley Reporter, 1908
Bulletin, 1899
Daily Californian, 1973–2000
Express, 1979–1999
Hills Publications, 1993–1998
Independent and Gazette, 1952–1983
New York Times, 1985
Oakland Tribune, 1973–2000
San Francisco Call, 1899–1912
San Francisco Chronicle, 1977–2000
San Francisco Examiner, 1900–2000

Newsletters & Other Publications

BDA Update, Berkeley Design Advocates, 1995–2000
Bene Legere, Newsletter of the Library Associates, University of California Library,
      1993–2000
Berkeleyan, Office of Public Affairs, University of California, Berkeley, 1985–2000
CalReport, Office of Public Affairs, University of California, Berkeley, 1991–1992
CED News, College of Environmental Design, University of California, Berkeley,
      1984–1991
CED Views, College of Environmental Design, University of California, Berkeley,
      1998–2000
Museum News, University of California, Berkeley Art Museum and Pacific Film Archive,
      1995–1999
The BAHA Newsletter and publications, Berkeley Architectural Heritage Association,
      1987–2000
University of California Botanical Garden Newsletter, 1990

Books and Articles

Allen, Albert H. University Record. *The University Chronicle* 7–14 (May 1905–January
      1912).
Bach, Richard F. "Hilgard Hall, University of California: John Galen Howard, Architect."
      The Architectural Record 46, no. 3 (September 1919): 203–210.
Barry, John D. *The City of Domes*. San Francisco: John J. Newbegin, 1915.
Belcher, John. "A Great International Competition: The University of California." *The
      Architectural Review* 7 (January-June 1900): 109–118.
Bender, Richard. "Building on the past." *California Monthly* 91, no. 2 (December 1980):
      15–17.
Bernhardi, Robert. *Buildings of Berkeley: Phase Two*. Oakland: Forest Hills Press,
      1991.
———. *The Buildings of Berkeley*. Berkeley: Lederer, Street & Zeus Co., 1971.

Bloomfield, Anne. "David Farquharson: Pioneer California Architect." *California History* 59 (Spring 1980): 16–33.

Blue and Gold. Berkeley: University of California, 1899–1966.

Boutelle, Sara Holmes. *Julia Morgan Architect*. New York: Abbeville Press, 1988.

Brechin, Gray. "Attic treasures: nature, art, and freedom." *California Monthly* 89, no. 2 (December 1978): 12–13.

———. "Camera Obscura: Fiat Lux." *California Monthly* 88, no. 6 (June-July 1978): 12–13.

———. "Classical dreams, concrete realities." *California Monthly* 88, no. 4 (March 1978): 12–15.

———. "The way we (almost) were: The rise and fall of Hearst Memorial." *California Monthly* 104, no. 2 (November 1993): 12–15.

Cahill, B. J. S. "A Criticism of Some of the Work Shown at the Annual Exhibition of San Francisco Architectural Club." *The Architect and Engineer of California* 32, no. 3 (April 1913): 47–81.

California Alumni Association. *Students at Berkeley*. Berkeley: California Alumni Association, 1948.

"California Hall." *The University Chronicle* 8, no. 1 (September 1905): 44–48.

"California Student Center." *California Monthly* 68, no. 5 (January 1958): 15–29.

Campus Planning Committee and Office of Architects and Engineers. *Long Range Development Plan*. Berkeley: University of California, 1962.

Campus Planning Study Group. *Campus Historic Resources Survey*. Berkeley: University of California, 1978.

Canty, Donald. "Lodged on a Precarious Site." *Progressive Architecture* 74, no. 9 (September 1993): 70–75, 109.

Cardwell, Kenneth H. *Bernard Maybeck: Artisan, Architect, Artist*. Salt Lake City: Peregrine Smith Books, 1977.

Cardwell, Kenneth, and William C. Hays. "Fifty Years From Now." *California Monthly* 64, no. 8 (April 1954): 20–26.

"Ceremonies at the Laying of the Cornerstone of Benjamin Ide Wheeler Hall, University of California, March 23, 1916, 3 p.m." *The University Chronicle* 18, no. 3 (July 1916): 299–308.

Cerny, Susan Dinkelspiel. *Berkeley Landmarks*. Berkeley: Berkeley Architectural Heritage Association, 1994.

Coburn, William P. "A Northern California Modernist Architect." *Archetype* (Fall 1980): 32–35.

Committee on Campus Planning. *Long Range Development Plan for the Berkeley Campus, University of California*. Berkeley: University of California, 1956.

"Competition Award for Design of Student Residence Hall Group." *Architect and Engineer* 206, no. 3 (September 1956): 15.

"Competition for a University Residence Hall." *Arts and Architecture* 73, no. 10 (October 1956): 20.

"Competition for a University Residence Hall." *Arts and Architecture* 73, no. 11 (November 1956): 28–29.

Copeland, Alan, ed. *People's Park*. Ballantine Books, 1969.

Croly, Herbert. "The New University of California." *The Architectural Record* 23, no. 4 (April 1908): 269–293.

Crosbie, Michael J. "Texture, Color Animate A Set of 'Shoe Boxes': Sports facility, University of California, Berkeley: ELS/Elbasani & Logan." *Architecture* 75, no. 5 (May 1986): 140–145, 272.

Darnall, Margaretta J. "Girton Hall: The Gift of Julia Morgan." *Chronicle of the University of California* 1, no. 2 (Fall 1998): 57–64.

Dean, Andrea Oppenheimer. "Lively Campus Center Atop a Buried Library." *AIA Journal* 72, no. 1 (January 1983): 56–57.

"Dedication of the Doe Library Building." *The University Chronicle* 14, no. 3 (July 1912): 351–356.

"Dedication of the Hearst Memorial Mining Building." *The University Chronicle* 9, no. 4 (October 1907): 313–325.

"Dedication of the New Greek Theatre." *The University Chronicle* 6, no. 3 (November 1903): 196–201.

Derleth, Charles, Jr. "The Sather Campanile." *The University Chronicle* 16, no. 3 (July 1914): 306–310.

"Do You Know Your Inscriptions?" *California Monthly* 56, no. 1 (February 1946): 14–15, 35–36.

Dundes, Alan. "One Hundred Years of California Traditions." *California Monthly* 78, no. 5 (March 1968): 19–32.

Esherick, Joseph. "A Building For People." *California Monthly* 76, no. 2 (November 1965): 28–30.

Ferrier, William Warren. *Origin and Development of the University of California*. Berkeley: The Sather Gate Book Shop, 1930.

Frankenstein, Alfred. "New Focus on Music." *California Monthly* 68, no. 7 (March 1958): 22–27.

Freudenheim, Leslie Mandelson, and Elisabeth Sacks Sussman. *Building with Nature: Roots of the San Francisco Bay Region Tradition*. Santa Barbara: Peregrine Smith, 1974.

Gebhard, David. *Architecture in California 1868–1968: an exhibition organized by David Gebhard and Harriette Von Breton to celebrate the Centennial of the University of California; The Art Galleries, University of California, Santa Barbara, April 16 to May 12, 1968*. Santa Barbara: University of California, 1968.

———. *The Architectural/Historical Aspects of the California School For The Blind and Deaf, Berkeley (1867–1979)*. Santa Barbara: University of California, 1979.

Gregory, Daniel. "Open For Business: The New Haas School: Venture Capitalism At Its Best." *California Monthly* 106, no. 1 (September 1995): 14–18.

Hailey, Gene, ed. *California Art Research*. Vols. 6 and 14 of First Series of Abstract from W.P.A. Project 2874. San Francisco: W.P.A., 1937.

"Hard Work For Fun." *Architectural Record* 173, no. 10 (September 1985): 90–95.

Hays, William C. "Some Architectural Works of John Galen Howard." *The Architect and Engineer* 40, no. 1 (January 1915): 47–82.

———. "Some Interesting Buildings at the University of California: The Work of Bernard Maybeck, Architect." *Indoors and Out* 2, no. 2 (May 1906): 70–75.

Heilbron, J. L. and Robert W. Seidel. *Lawrence and His Laboratory*. Berkeley: University of California Press, 1989.

Heilbron, J. L., Robert W. Seidel, and Bruce R. Wheaton. "Lawrence and his Laboratory: Nuclear Science at Berkeley." *LBL News Magazine* 6, no. 3 (Fall 1981): 2–106.

Henderson, Victor H. "The University of California." *Sunset* 9, no. 6 (October 1902): 364–372.

———. University Record. *The University Chronicle* 5–19 (October 1902–July 1917).

Howard, John Galen. "Address of John Galen Howard" in "Dedication of New Greek Theatre." *The University Chronicle* 6, no. 3 (November 1903): 199–201.

———. "The Architectural Plans for the Greater University of California." *The University Chronicle* 5, no. 4 (January 1903): 273–291.

———. "The Library." *The University Chronicle* 14, no. 3 (July 1912): 332–340.

"Howard's End." *California Monthly* 97, no. 4 (February 1987): 6–7.

Huber, A., Jr. "The University of California Memorial Stadium." *The Architect and Engineer* 75, no. 1 (October 1923): 93–98.

Jolly, William L. "Rising Above the Rat House: 125 Tears of History at the College of Chemistry." *News Journal of the College of Chemistry* 5, no. 1 (Spring 1997): 6–10.

Jones, William Carey. "Biographical Sketch of Emile Benard." *The University Chronicle* 2, no. 4 (October 1899): 292–295.

———. *Illustrated History of the University of California.* Rev. ed. Berkeley: Students' Cooperative Society, 1901.

Kalmann, Herbert, ed. *Optometry: The First 75 Years, 1925–1998.* Berkeley: School of Optometry, 1998.

Kantor, J. R. K. "Cora, Jane, & Phoebe: Fin-De-Siècle Philanthropy." *Chronicle of the University of California* 1, no. 2 (Fall 1998): 1–8.

Kantor, J. R. K., and A. L. Pierovich. "The University in Pictures." *California Monthly* 78, no. 6 (April-May 1968): 48–59.

Keeler, Charles. *The Simple Home.* 1904. Reprint, with an introduction by Dimitri Shipounoff, Santa Barbara: Peregrine Smith, 1979.

Kelham, George W. "The University of California." *The Architect* 14, no. 2 (August 1917): 81–120.

Kerr, Clark. "A second look . . . at the Berkeley campus and its students." *California Monthly* 68, no. 9 (May 1958): 9–14.

———. "Just Ahead . . . Berkeley's Greatest Permanent Growth." *California Monthly* 66, no. 1 (September 1955): 14–18.

———. "Research at Berkeley." *California Monthly* 67, no. 3 (November 1956): 16–21.

———. "The Berkeley Campus and Its Students Now and in 1965." *California Monthly* 65, no. 5 (January 1955): 8–14, 26–27.

———. "The Berkeley Campus Plan." *California Monthly* 67, no. 2 (October 1956): 22–28.

Knight, Emerson. "Outdoor Theatres and Stadiums in the West." *The Architect and Engineer* 78, no. 2 (August 1924): 52–91.

Laurie, Michael with David C. Streatfield. *75 Years of Landscape Architecture at Berkeley, Part I: The First 50 Years.* Berkeley: Department of Landscape Architecture, University of California, Berkeley, 1988.

———. *75 Years of Landscape Architecture at Berkeley, Part II: Recent Years.* Berkeley: Department of Landscape Architecture, University of California, Berkeley, 1992.

"Laying of the Corner-Stone of the Doe Memorial Library." *The University Chronicle* 11, no. 1 (January 1909): 45–50.

"Laying of the Corner-Stone of the Hearst Memorial Mining Building." *The University Chronicle* 5, no. 4 (January 1903): 292–300.

Lindgren, Frank T., and Kenneth M. Sanderson. "The Future of the Campus Environment." *California Monthly* 79, no. 4 (January-February 1969): 36–41.

London, Jack. "Simple Impressive Rite at Corner-Stone Emplacement of Hearst Memorial Mining Building." *San Francisco Examiner* 77, no. 142 (19 November 1902): 8–9.

Longstreth, Richard. 1986. Reprint. *Julia Morgan, Architect*. Berkeley: Berkeley
    Architectural Heritage Association, 1977.
———. *On the Edge of the World: four architects in San Francisco at the turn of the century*.
    New York: The Architectural History Foundation, 1983.
Lyndon, Donlyn. "Big Happening in Berkeley." *The Architectural Forum* 124, no. 1
    (January-February 1966): 56–63.
Metcalf, Woodbridge and Dale Carneggie. *Trees of the Berkeley Campus*. Berkeley:
    University of California, 1969.
Mitchell, W. Garden. "The 1915 San Francisco Architectural Club Exhibit." *The Architect
    and Engineer* 41, no. 3 (June 1915): 51–67.
Montgomery, Roger. "Center of Action." *Architectural Forum* 132, no. 3 (April 1970): 66, 68.
Morrow, Irving F. "Recent Work at the University of California." *The Architect and
    Engineer of California* 50, no. 1 (July 1917): 38–49.
———. "The Oakland Architectural Exhibition." *The Architect and Engineer* 47, no. 1
    (October 1916): 39–70.
Moss, Stacey. *The Howards: First Family of Bay Area Modernism*. Oakland: The Oakland
    Museum, 1988.
Neuhaus, Eugen. *The Art of Treasure Island*. Berkeley: University of California Press, 1939.
"New Design for the California Memorial Stadium." *The Architect and Engineer* 72, no. 2
    (February 1923): 75–77.
Newbergh, Carolyn. "An Architectural Gem Gets Ready for the Big One." *Berkeley
    Engineering Forefront* (2000): 10–15.
Nisbet, Robert. *Teachers & Scholars: A Memoir of Berkeley in Depression and War*. New
    Brunswick: Transaction Publishers, 1992.
Paltridge, James Gilbert. *A History of The Faculty Club at Berkeley*. Berkeley: The Faculty
    Club, University of California, Berkeley, 1990.
Park, Roberta J. "A Gym of Their Own." *Chronicle of the University of California* 1, no. 2
    (Fall 1998): 21–47.
Partridge, Loren W. *John Galen Howard and the Berkeley Campus: Beaux-Arts Architecture
    in the "Athens of the West."* Berkeley: Berkeley Architectural Heritage
    Association, 1988.
Perry, Warren C. "The School of Architecture at Berkeley Has Completed Its Twenty-
    Second Year." *Southwest Builder and Contractor* (9 August 1935): 19–20.
Peterson, Kenneth G. *The University of California Library at Berkeley: 1900–1945*. Berkeley:
    University of California Press, 1970.
Pettitt, George A. *A History of Berkeley*. Berkeley: The Alameda County Historical
    Society, [1976?].
———. *Berkeley: the town and gown of it*. Berkeley: Howell-North Books, 1973.
Phoebe Hearst Architectural Plan for the University of California. *The International
    Competition for the Phoebe Hearst Architectural Plan for the University of
    California*. San Francisco: Trustees of the Phoebe A. Hearst Architectural Plan
    for the University of California, [1899?].
Physical and Environmental Planning Group and ROMA Design Group. *University of
    California at Berkeley Long Range Development Plan 1990–2005*. Berkeley:
    University of California, 1990.
Pickerell, Albert G. and May Dornin. *The University of California: A Pictorial History*.
    Berkeley: University of California Press, 1968.
Rorabaugh, W. J. *Berkeley At War: The 1960s*. New York: Oxford University Press, 1989.
Rybczynski, Witold. *A Clearing in the Distance: Frederick Law Olmsted and America in the
    Nineteenth Century*. New York: Scribner, 1999.

Seaborg, Glenn T. with Ray Colvig. *Chancellor at Berkeley*. Berkeley: Institute of
    Governmental Studies Press, University of California, Berkeley, 1994.

Shay, James, A.I.A. *New Architecture San Francisco*. San Francisco: Chronicle Books,
    1989.

Sibley, Robert, ed. *The Golden Book of California*. Berkeley: The California Alumni
    Association, 1937.

———, ed. *The Romance of the University of California*. San Francisco: H. S. Crocker,
    1928.

Sibley, Robert, and Carol Sibley. *University of California Pilgrimage*. Berkeley: Robert and
    Carol Sibley, 1952.

Small, Harold A. "The Life and Times of the Faculty Club." *California Monthly* 76, no.6
    (March 1966): 12–17.

Smith, Neill. "Wurster Hall—The Campus Rebel." *Progressive Architecture* 47, no. 1 (June
    1966): 163–167.

Snipper, Martin. *A Survey of Art Work in the City and County of San Francisco*. San
    Francisco: Art Commission, City and County of San Francisco, 1953.

"Split Level Dining Commons." *California Monthly* 71, no. 2 (November 1960): 8–14.

Stadtman, Verne A., ed. *The Centennial Record of the University of California*. Berkeley:
    University of California, 1967.

———. *The University of California 1868–1968*. New York: McGraw-Hill, 1970.

Steele, James. *Faculty Club*. London: Academy Editions, 1995.

Talarico, Wendy. "Seismic Systems that Stand Up to Nature." *Architectural Record* 189, no.
    2 (February 2000): 127–134.

Temko, Allan. *No Way to Build a Ballpark and Other Irreverent Essays on Architecture*. San
    Francisco: Chronicle Books, 1993.

———. "'Planned Chaos' on the Piazza." *Architectural Forum* 115, no. 4 (October 1961):
    112–17, 192.

———. "The Campus Environment," *California Monthly* 76, no. 2 (November 1965):
    4–9.

Thayer, Paul. "A Theater Takes Shape." *California Monthly* 76, no. 4 (January 1966):
    14–16.

———. "Celebrating The Centennial," *California Monthly* 78, no. 7 (June-July 1968):
    30–39.

———. "That is Wurster Hall." *California Monthly* 76, no. 2 (November 1965):
    26–27.

The Anna Head School: forty-second year. Berkeley: The Anna Head School, 1929.

"The Phebe Hearst Architectural Plan." *The University Chronicle* 1, no. 1 (February 1898):
    61–69.

"The Phebe Hearst Architectural Plan." *The University Chronicle* 1, no. 5 (October 1898):
    469–472.

"The Plan's the Thing: How the sale of city lots made possible one of the world's finest
    campuses." *California Monthly* 58, no. 3 (November 1947): 18–19, 40.

"The Selection of the Site of the University and Its Name." *The University Chronicle* 4,
    no. 1 (February 1901): 57–58.

"The Visit of the Jurors in the Hearst Architectural Competition." *The University
    Chronicle* 2, no. 4 (October 1899): 277–291.

"The Work of Albert Pissis, Architect." *The Architect and Engineer of California, Pacific
    Coast States* 17, no. 3 (July 1909): 34–69.

Tobriner, Stephen. "South Hall and Seismic Safety at the University of California in
    1870." *Chronicle of the University of California* 1, no. 1 (Spring 1998): 13–23.

Turner, Paul Venable. *Campus: An American Planning Tradition*. Cambridge: The MIT Press, 1985.

"University Arts Center." *Arts & Architecture* 82, no. 10 (October 1965): 26.

University of California. *Gifts for Lands and Buildings*. Berkeley: University of California, [1957].

———. *University of California: An Introduction to the Berkeley Campus*. Berkeley: University of California, 1936.

Warshaw, Steven. *The Trouble in Berkeley*. Berkeley: Diablo Press, 1965.

Wheeler, Benjamin Ide. "Biennial Report of the President of the University on behalf of the Regents to His Excellency the Governor of the State, 1900–1902." *The University Chronicle* 5, no. 4, Supplement (January 1903): 13–16.

———. "Biennial Report of the President of the University on behalf of the Regents to His Excellency the Governor of the State, 1902–1904." *The University Chronicle* 7, no. 1, Extra Number (December 1904): 22–48.

———. "Outlook of the University." *Sunset* 9, no. 6 (October 1902): 358–364.

———. *The Abundant Life: Benjamin Ide Wheeler*. Edited by Monroe E. Deutsch. Berkeley: University of California Press, 1926.

———. "The Condition and Needs of the University." *The University Chronicle* 8, no. 3 (March 1906): 238–245.

Willey, Samuel H. "Founders of the University." *The University Chronicle* 6, no. 1 (April 1903): 18–23.

Wilson, Mark A. *A Living Legacy: Historic Architecture of the East Bay*. Berkeley: Lexikos Press, 1987.

———. *East Bay Heritage*. San Francisco: California Living Books, 1979.

Winks, Robin W. *Frederick Billings: A Life*. Berkeley: University of California Press, 1991.

Woodbridge, John Marshall, and Sally Byrne Woodbridge. *Buildings of the Bay Area*. New York: Grove Press, 1960.

Woodbridge, Sally B., ed. *Bay Area Houses: New Edition*. Layton, Utah: Gibbs-Smith, 1988.

———. *Bernard Maybeck: Visionary Architect*. New York: Abbeville Press, 1992.

———. *Details: The Architect's Art*. San Francisco: Chronicle Books, 1991.

———. *En Charette/On Deadline*. Berkeley: Graduate School of Journalism, University of California, 1993.

———. "Reflections on the Founding: Wurster Hall and The College of Environmental Design," *Places* 1, no.4. (1984 Summer): 47–58, 63–65.

Woodbridge, Sally B., and John M. Woodbridge. *San Francisco Architecture*. San Francisco: Chronicle Books, 1992.

Writers' Program of the Work Projects Administration in Northern California. *Berkeley: The First Seventy-five Years*. Berkeley: The Gillick Press, 1941.

Wurster, William Wilson. "California Architecture For Living." *California Monthly* 64, no. 8 (April 1954): 14–19.

———."The Passing of the 'Ark.'" *Progressive Architecture* 45, no. 7 (July 1964): 166–171.

Oral Histories

The following oral histories were published by the Regional Oral History Office, The Bancroft Library, University of California, Berkeley, except as noted.

Church, Elizabeth Roberts. *A Life by the Side of Thomas Church: Family, Friends, Clients, Associates, Travels, Memories*. Typescript of an oral history conducted 1976 by Suzanne B. Riess, in *Thomas D. Church, Landscape Architect, Volume II*. 1978.

Coblentz, Dorothy Wormser. *Julia Morgan's Office*. Typescript of an oral history conducted 1974–1975 by Suzanne B. Riess, in *The Julia Morgan Architectural History Project, Volume II, Julia Morgan, Her Office, and a House*. 1976.

DeMars, Vernon Armand. *A Life in Architecture: Indian Dancing, Migrant Housing, Telesis, Design for Urban Living, Theater, Teaching*. Typescript of an oral history conducted by Suzanne B. Riess in 1988–1989. 1992.

DeMonte, Louis. *A University Architect Summarizes Berkeley Planning, 1940–1973 and Church's Contribution*. Typescript of an oral history conducted 1976 by Suzanne B. Riess, in *Thomas D. Church, Landscape Architect, Volume I*. 1978.

Eckbo, Garrett. *Landscape Architecture: The Profession in California, 1935–1940, and Telesis*. Typescript of an oral history conducted 1991 by Suzanne B. Riess. 1993.

Edmonds, Harry. *The Founding of the International House Movement*. Typescript of an oral history conducted by Edith Mezirow in 1969. 1971.

Esherick, Joseph. *An Architectural Practice in the San Franicsco Bay Area, 1938–1996*. Typescript of an oral history conducted 1994–1996 by Suzanne B. Riess. 1996.

Foster, Herbert Bismark. *The Role of the Engineer's Office in the Development of the University of California Campuses*. Typescript of an oral history conducted 1960 by Amelia Roberts Fry. 1960.

Gregg, John William. *A Half-Century of Landscape Architecture*. Typescript of an oral history conducted c. 1963 by Suzanne B. Riess. 1965.

Hays, William Charles. *Order, Taste and Grace in Architecture*. Typescript of an oral history conducted 1959 by Edna Tartaul Daniel. 1968.

Jensen, Norman, Edward Hussey, George Hodges, and Jack Wagstaff. *Remembering Walter Steilberg*. Typescript of an oral history conducted 1974–1975 by Suzanne B. Riess, in *The Julia Morgan Architectural History Project, Volume I, The Work of Walter Steilberg and Julia Morgan*. 1976.

Lawton, Helena Steilberg. *Walter Steilberg, Architect: The Man, His Times, His Work*. Typescript of an oral history conducted 1975 by Suzanne B. Riess, in *The Julia Morgan Architectural History Project, Volume I, The Work of Walter Steilberg and Julia Morgan*. 1976.

McLaughlin, Donald H. *Careers in Mining Geology and Management, University Governance and Teaching*. Typescript of an oral history conducted 1970–1971 by Harriet Nathan. 1975.

———. *Donald McLaughlin Interviews on April 7, 1960*. Typescript of an oral history conducted 1960 by Henry C. Carlisle, in *Engineering Project, 1962*. Columbia Oral History Research Office, Butler Library, Columbia University, New York, 1962.

Mellquist, Proctor. *A Sunset Editor Considers Church's Broad Architectural Understanding*. Typescript of an oral history conducted 1976 by Suzanne B. Riess, in *Thomas D. Church, Landscape Architect, Volume II*. 1978.

Merritt, Ralph Palmer. *After Me Cometh a Builder: The Recollections of Ralph Palmer Merritt*. Typescript of an oral history conducted 1956 by Corrine S. Gilb. 1962.

Morgan, Elmo R. *Physical Planning and Mangement: Los Alamos, University of Utah, University of California, and AID, 1942–1976*. Typescript of an oral history conducted 1991 by Germaine LaBerge. 1992.

Neuhaus, Eugen. *Reminiscences: Bay Area Art and the University of California Art Department*. Typescript of an oral history conducted by Suzanne B. Riess in 1961. 1961.

North, Morgan and Flora North. *Three Conversations with Morgan and Flora North About Julia Morgan*. Typescript of an oral history conducted 1974–1975 by Suzanne

B. Riess, in *The Julia Morgan Architectural History Project, Volume II, Julia Morgan, Her Office, and a House.* 1976.

O'Hanlon, Richard. *An Interview with Richard O'Hanlon.* Typescript of an oral history conducted by Suzanne B. Riess in 1973. 1988.

Pepper, Stephen C. *Art and Philosophy at the University of California, 1919 to 1962.* Typescript of an oral history conducted by Suzanne B. Riess in 1961–1962. 1963.

Perry, Warren C. *Reminiscences of the Department of Architecture, University of California, Berkeley, 1904 to 1954.* Typescript of an oral history conducted 1975 by Suzanne B. Riess, in *The Julia Morgan Architectural History Project, Volume I, The Work of Walter Steilberg and Julia Morgan.* 1976.

Ratcliff, Robert and Evelyn Paine Ratcliff. *Walter Steilberg, Friend and Neighbor.* Typescript of an oral history conducted 1974–1975 by Suzanne B. Riess, in *The Julia Morgan Architectural History Project, Volume I, The Work of Walter Steilberg and Julia Morgan.* 1976.

Steilberg, Walter T. *Miscellaneous Interviews with Walter Steilberg.* Typescript of an oral history conducted 1971–1972 by Leslie Freudenheim and Elizabeth Sussman, Harold B. Lyman, and Sally Woodbridge. 1976.

———. *Reminiscences of Walter Steilberg.* Typescript of an oral history conducted 1974–1975 by Sally Woodbridge, in *The Julia Morgan Architectural History Project, Volume I, The Work of Walter Steilberg and Julia Morgan.* 1976.

Underhill, Robert M. *University of California Lands, Finances, and Investments.* Typescript of an oral history conducted 1966–1967 by Verne A. Stadtman. 1967.

Wallace, Janette Howard. *Reminiscences of Janette Howard Wallace; daughter of John Galen Howard and Mary Robertson Bradbury Howard.* Typescript of an oral history conducted by Galen Howard Hilgard in 1987. 1987.

Wurster, William Wilson. *College of Environmental Design, University of California, Campus Planning, and Architectural Practice.* Typescript of an oral history conducted 1963 by Suzanne B. Riess. 1964.

Unpublished Documents

Brown, Arthur, Jr. *Report on Status of the "General Plan," Berkeley Campus, University of California.* Berkeley, 1 August 1944.

Church, Thomas D. *Landscape Master Plan.* Berkeley, 1961.

Draper, Joan Elaine. "John Galen Howard and the Beaux-Arts Movement in the United States." Master's thesis, University of California, Berkeley, 1972.

Office of Architects and Engineers. *Planning the Physical Development of the Berkeley Campus.* Berkeley, December 1951.

———. *Study of the Long Term Use Potential of Strawberry Canyon and the Undeveloped Hill Lands.* Report of the Subcommittee on Physical Development Planning of the Committee on Buildings and Campus Development, University of California, Berkeley campus. Berkeley, January 1958.

Perry, Warren C. and the President's Committee on Campus Development and Building Location. *A Re-Study of the Central Area of the Campus,* University of California, Berkeley, California. Berkeley, 1 October 1933.

Siegel & Strain, Architects. *Historic Structure Report, University of California Berkeley, California Memorial Stadium.* Berkeley, 23 September 1999.

Stebbins, Robert C. *Ecological Study Areas for Teaching and Research of the University of California Campus, Berkeley.* A Report of the Landscape Architecture Advisory Subcommittee. Berkeley, 21 February 1966.

Steilberg, Walter T. *Sather Tower—University of California, Summary of Report to U.C. Office of Architects and Engineers.* Berkeley, 16 November 1955.

Subcommittee on Physical Development Planning of the Committee on Buildings and Campus Development. *Study of the Long Term Use Potential of Strawberry Canyon and the Undeveloped Hill Lands.* Berkeley, January 1958.

Watson, Kent Emanuel. "A Forgotten Chapter in the History of Landscape Architecture: William Hammond Hall and the 1873 University of California, Berkeley Plan." Master's thesis, University of California, Berkeley, 1989.

Illustration Credits

The archival source, *University Archives, Bancroft Library, University of California, Berkeley*, is noted as *UA, BL*.

Page 3: *UA, BL*, 15A:11; Page 5: *UA, BL*, G, 4364, B5:2U5, 1866, O7P, Case XB; Page 7: *UA, BL*, 308gv 1870; Page 8: *UA, BL*, 308gv 1870; Page 9: *UA, BL*, 3:174; Page 11: *San Francisco Examiner*, April 30, 1896; Page 13: William Carey Jones, *Illustrated History of the University of California*, rev. ed. (Berkeley: Students' Cooperative Society, 1901); Page 14: William Carey Jones, *Illustrated History of the University of California*; Page 18: *Long Range Development Plan for the Berkeley Campus, University of* California (Berkeley: University of California, 1956); page 19: *UA, BL*, 3:175; Page 22: *UA, BL*, 300:60, Norris H. Richardson, photographer; Page 23: *UA, BL*, 3:88; Page 27: Ed Kirwan Graphic Arts, Negative No. E 4-7-109-K; Page 46: *UA, BL*, 8:7a; Page 50: *UA, BL*, 3:291; Page 90: *UA, BL*, 10M:4; Page 106: *UA, BL*, 22H:1; Page 141: *UA, BL*, 1000F:2; Page 206: *UA, BL*, 10A:1b; Page 208: *UA, BL*, 3:52, from *San Francisco Chronicle* Rotogravure Pictorial, July 20, 1924; Page 255: *UA, BL*, 100:9a; Page 310: *UA, BL*, 3:607; Page 318: Author's collection

Acknowledgments

I am indebted to a number of individuals—University staff and retirees, Old Blues, and members of the community—who contributed information and leads and opened doors to facilitate my research and photography. I am especially grateful to University Archivist William Roberts of the marvelous Bancroft Library, who shared his extensive knowledge, guided me through a treasure-trove of documents and images, and took extra steps to accommodate my numerous requests. Assistant Chancellor John Cummins also provided essential support in enabling my access to staff and facilities and offering guidance. I extend special thanks to University History Coordinator Carroll Brentano of the Center for Studies in Higher Education for recommending me to Princeton Architectural Press as well as providing helpful advice and information. Steve Finacom of the Physical and Environmental Planning Office frequently contributed facts and spirited anecdotes drawn from his comprehensive knowledge and extraordinary appreciation of campus history and lore. Eric Ellison of the Department of Physical Plant—Campus Services was enthusiastically supportive, briefing me on campus projects and suggesting and providing access to photographic viewpoints. Anthony Bruce and Lesley Emmington Jones graciously provided assistance and access to the valuable resources of the Berkeley Architectural Heritage Association. Leigh Trivette, Secretary of the Regents, and Anne Shaw, Assistant Secretary of the Regents, made possible my perusal of minutes of meetings of the Board of Regents. And in the Office of the President, John E. Zimmermann, Director of Planning & Design, provided records pertinent to many subjects.

Vice Chancellor Edward Denton, Project Management Director Jeffrey Gee, and Physical and Environmental Planning Director Tom Lollini facilitated my research in the Department of Capital Projects, where many of my former planning and design colleagues and others were most helpful. Paul Hanchock in particular guided me to important records and publications and contributed insightful historical perspective and valued personal support. Others to whom I am appreciative include Florence Baldwin, Jacqueline Bernier, Judy Chess, David Duncan, Percy Fordyce, Rob Gayle, Jim Horner, Harue Lampert, Antonio Leony, Stan Mar, Joyce Martin, Kerry O'Banion, Nicolas Sanchez, and Christine Shaff. In Physical Plant—Campus Services, I also thank Fred Karampour, who provided mapping information, and Phil Cody and Greg Harrington of Grounds, who helped prepare sites to be photographed.

I am grateful to my former colleagues in Space Management and Capital Programs, Assistant Vice Chancellor Tom Koster, who clarified many issues, and Steve Lesky, who helped with mapping information. Elizabeth Byrne and Susan Koskinen aided my research in the collections of the Environmental Design Library. Bob Jacobs and Iola Fay Harris of Housing, Dining & Child Care Services arranged access to facilities. Additional assistance was contributed by: Professor Emeritus Robert C. Stebbins of Integrative Biology; Professor Ken W. Wachter of the Department of Demography; Professor Joe R. McBride of the Division of Forest Science; Barney Quinn of University House; Thomas H. Reynolds and Ginny Irving of the School of Law; Mary Breunig, Nancy Johnson, Karen Holtermann, and Judy Roberts of the College of Engineering; Brian Quigley of the Kresge Engineering Library; Bethann Johnson of International House; Anna Mae Morrish of the Survey Research Center; Marian L. Gade of the Center for Studies in Higher Education; Sheila Dickie of the College of Environmental Design; Fritz Stern of the School of Information Management and Systems; Steve Lustig of the University Health Services; Luis Cutolo of the Faculty Club; Thomas Baker and Nathaniel Allen of the ASUC; Bud Travers and Maria Rubinshteyn of Resource Development; and Brian Donohue of Materiel Management.

Dan Cheatham offered constant encouragement and contributed useful documents, leads, and stories, all seasoned with his incomparable California Spirit. Valuable help also came from Nonna Cheatham, Ray Colvig, Roger Samuelsen, Phyllis Brooks Schafer, Scott Sherman, Robert Witter, and Sally Woodbridge.

Ron Kolb and Pam Patterson provided helpful orientation and access to the Lawrence Berkeley National Laboratory. Of several architectural and engineering firms, I thank David Lindemulder of MBT Architecture, Susan Millhouse of Anshen + Allen, Robert Albachten of Ellerbe Becket, Brendan Kelly of NBBJ, and Douglas R. Robertson of Rutherford & Chekene, Consulting Engineers. In addition, Jake Skaer of J. P. Systems Construction Management & Design and Ely Gilliam of Marinship Construction generously made arrangements to accommodate my photography. Valuable information also came from Carrie Ridgeway, Marketing Director of the Downtown Berkeley Association, Lucinda Glenn Rand of the Graduate Theological Union, Nicholas Sayotovich of Triangle Fraternity in Plainfield, Indiana, and Chris Ann Philips of the American Association of Neurological Surgeons in Rolling Meadows, Illinois.

To those at Princeton Architectural Press, especially Jan Cigliano, who edited the text and skillfully guided the process with encouraging words, Heather Ewing, and Jane Garvie, whose maps grace these pages, I am most grateful. Finally, I reserve special appreciation for my personal rooting section, Lana Buffington, whose support was an irreplaceable inspiration to my efforts. And last, but not least, was the assistance of my two feline advisers, Bustopher and Natasha, who insisted that I include this proper California greeting: Go Bears!